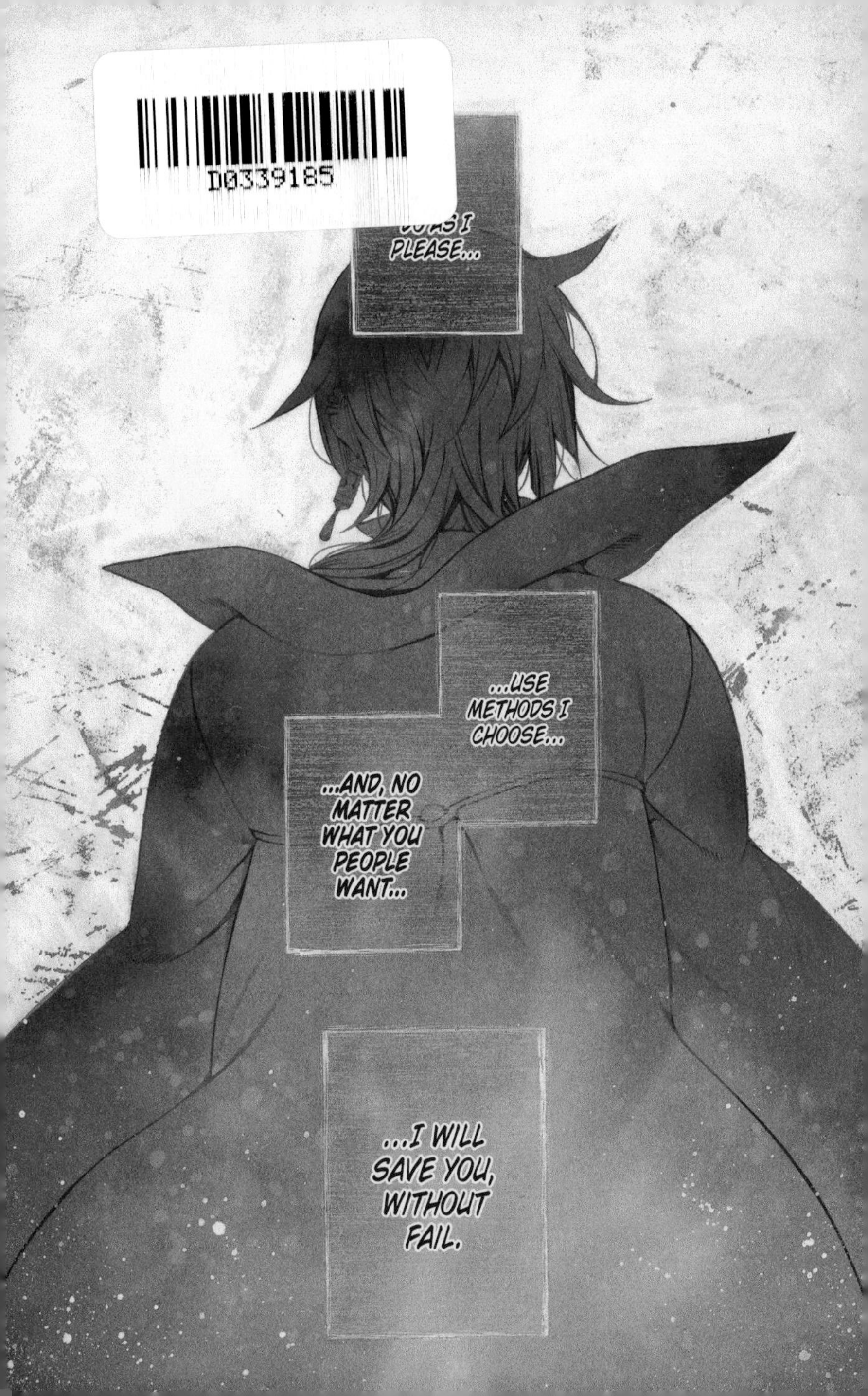
AS I PLEASE...
...USE METHODS I CHOOSE...
...AND, NO MATTER WHAT YOU PEOPLE WANT...
...I WILL SAVE YOU, WITHOUT FAIL.

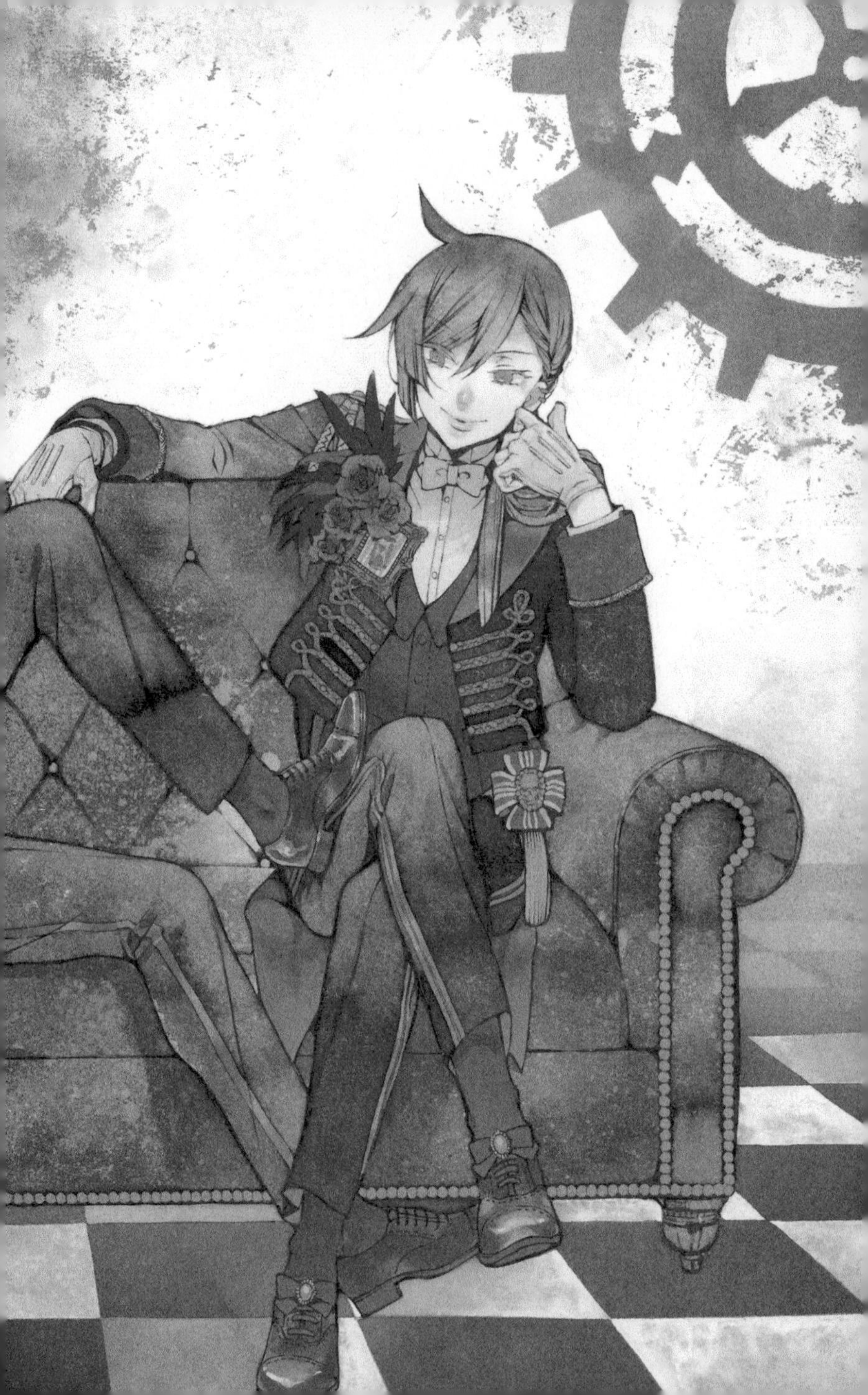

MÉMOIRE II

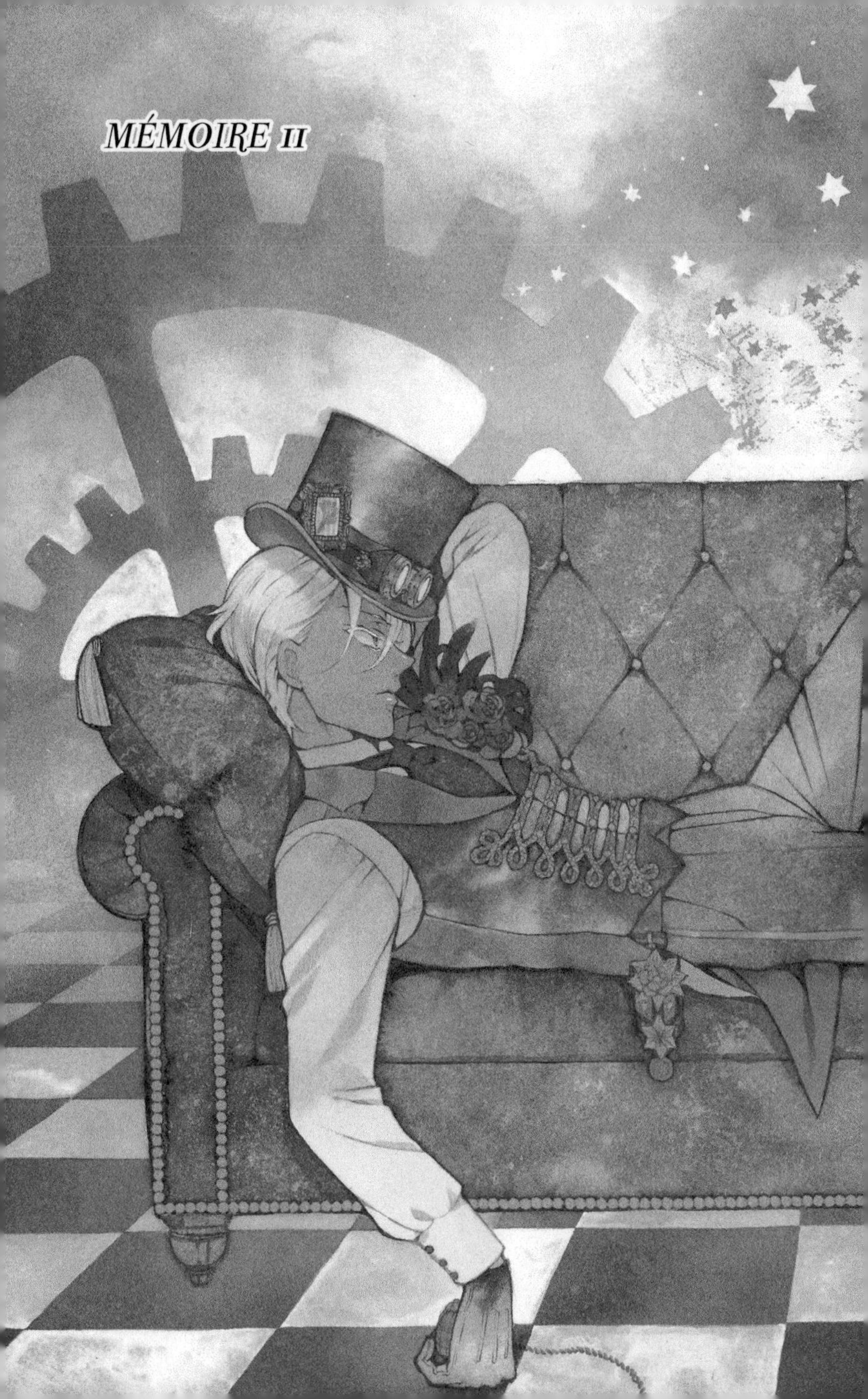

Les Mémoires de Vanitas

THE CASE STUDY OF VANITAS

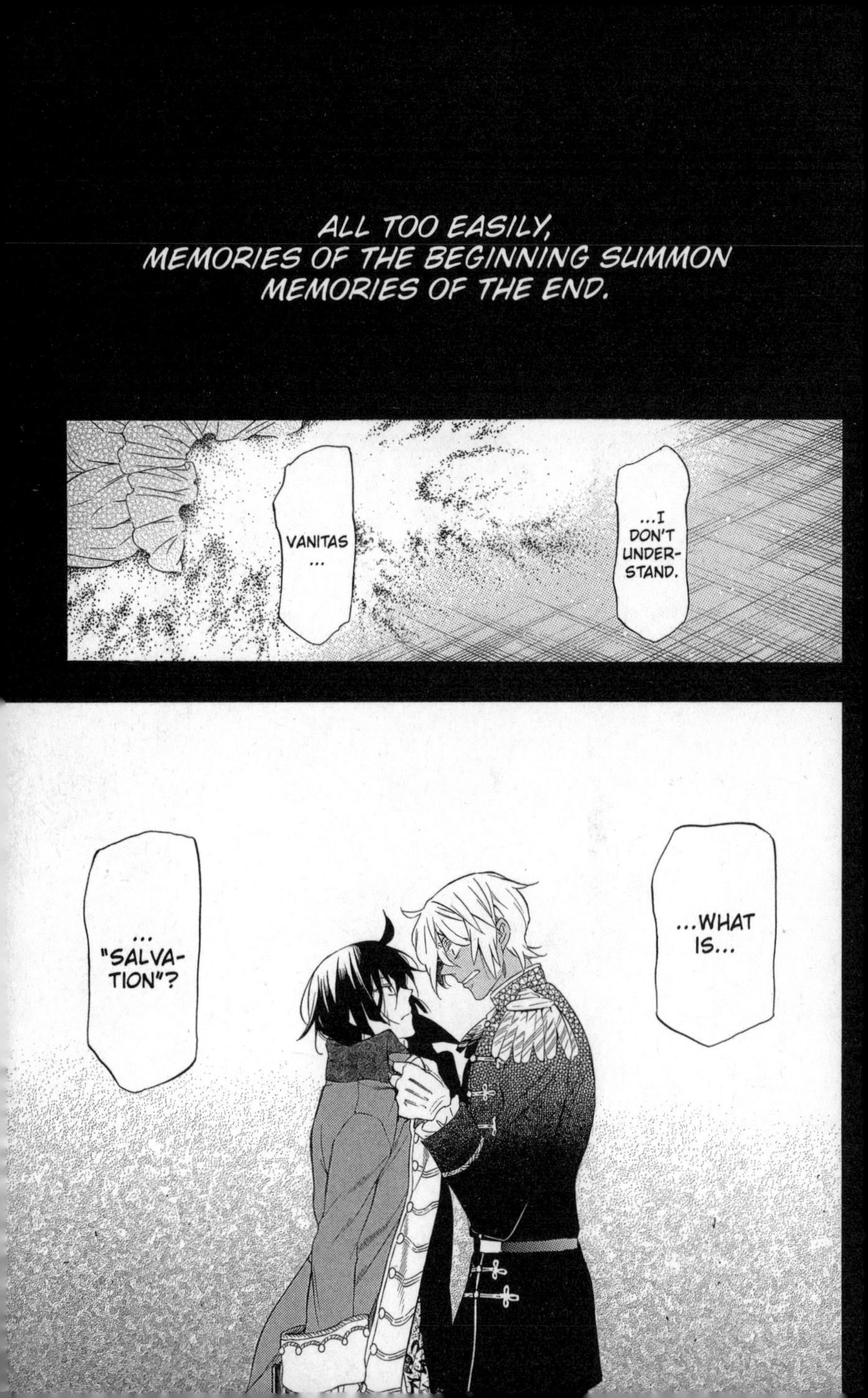
ALL TOO EASILY,
MEMORIES OF THE BEGINNING SUMMON MEMORIES OF THE END.
...I DON'T UNDER-STAND.
VANITAS...
...WHAT IS...
...“SALVA-TION”?

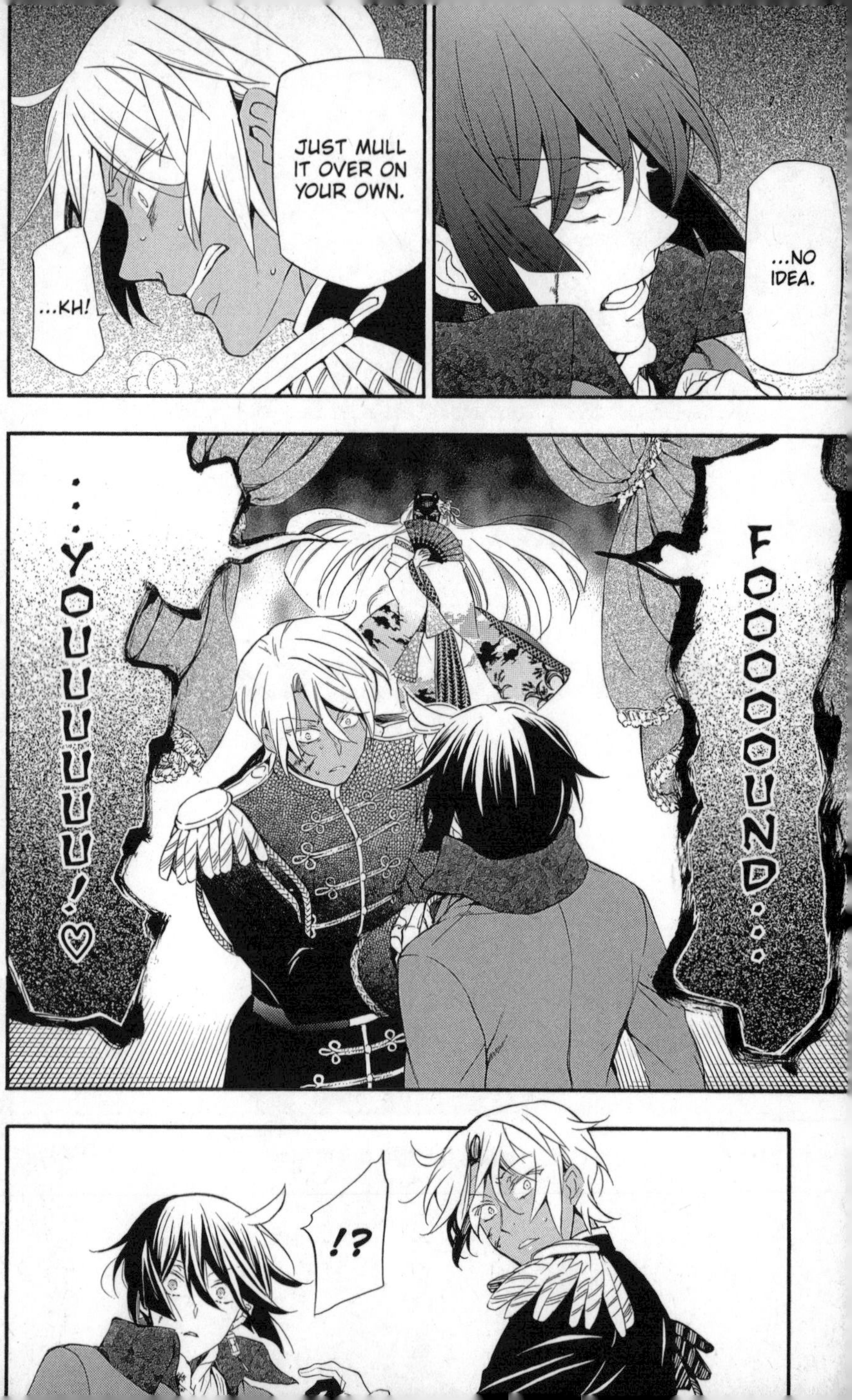
...NO IDEA.
JUST MULL IT OVER ON YOUR OWN.
...KH!
FOOOOOOUND...
...YOUUUUUUU!♡
!?

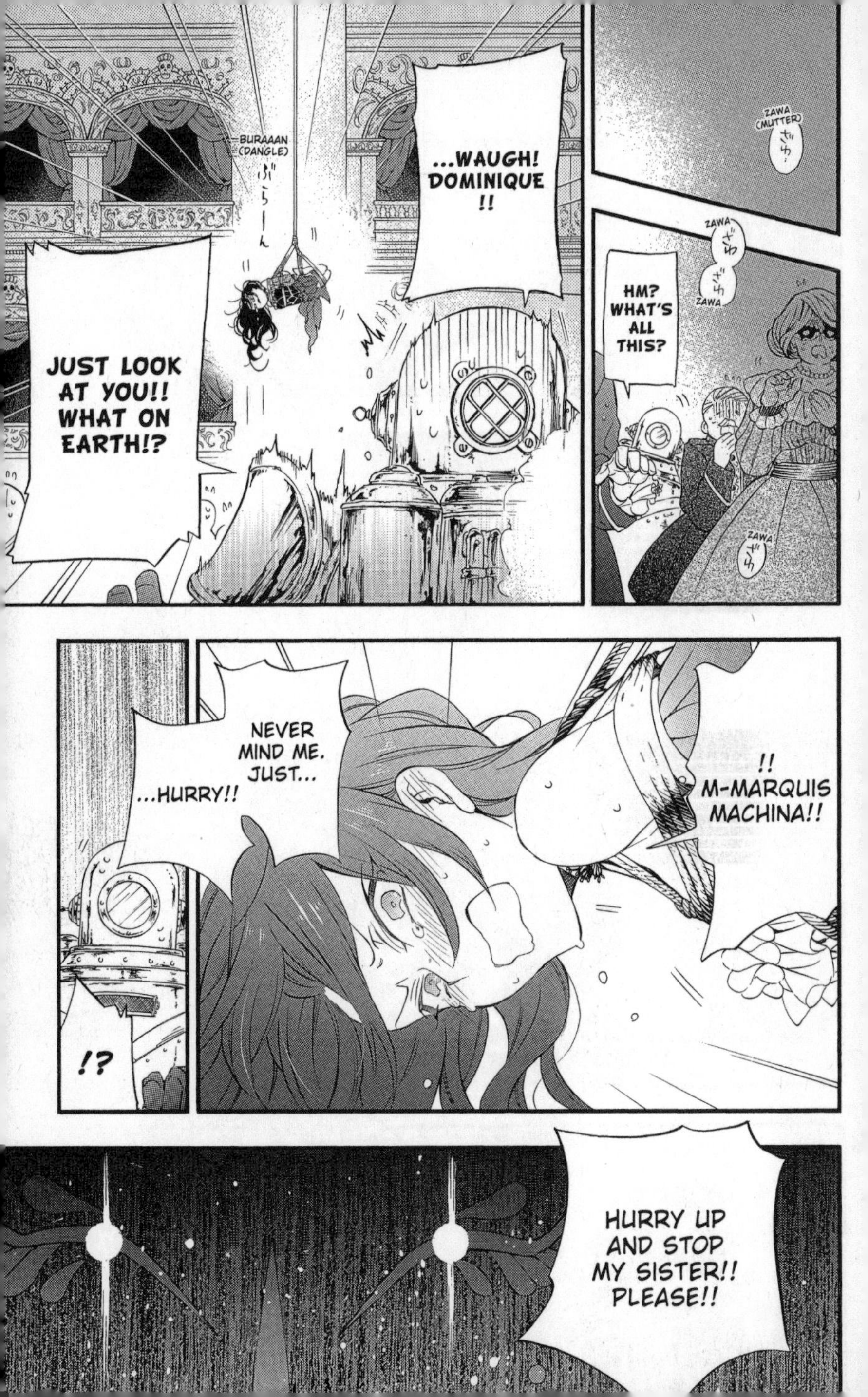

ZAWA (MUTTER)
ZAWA
ZAWA
HM? WHAT'S ALL THIS?
ZAWA
...WAUGH! DOMINIQUE!!
BURAAAN (DANGLE)
ぶらーん
JUST LOOK AT YOU!! WHAT ON EARTH!?
!! M-MARQUIS MACHINA!!
NEVER MIND ME. JUST...
...HURRY!!
!?
HURRY UP AND STOP MY SISTER!! PLEASE!!

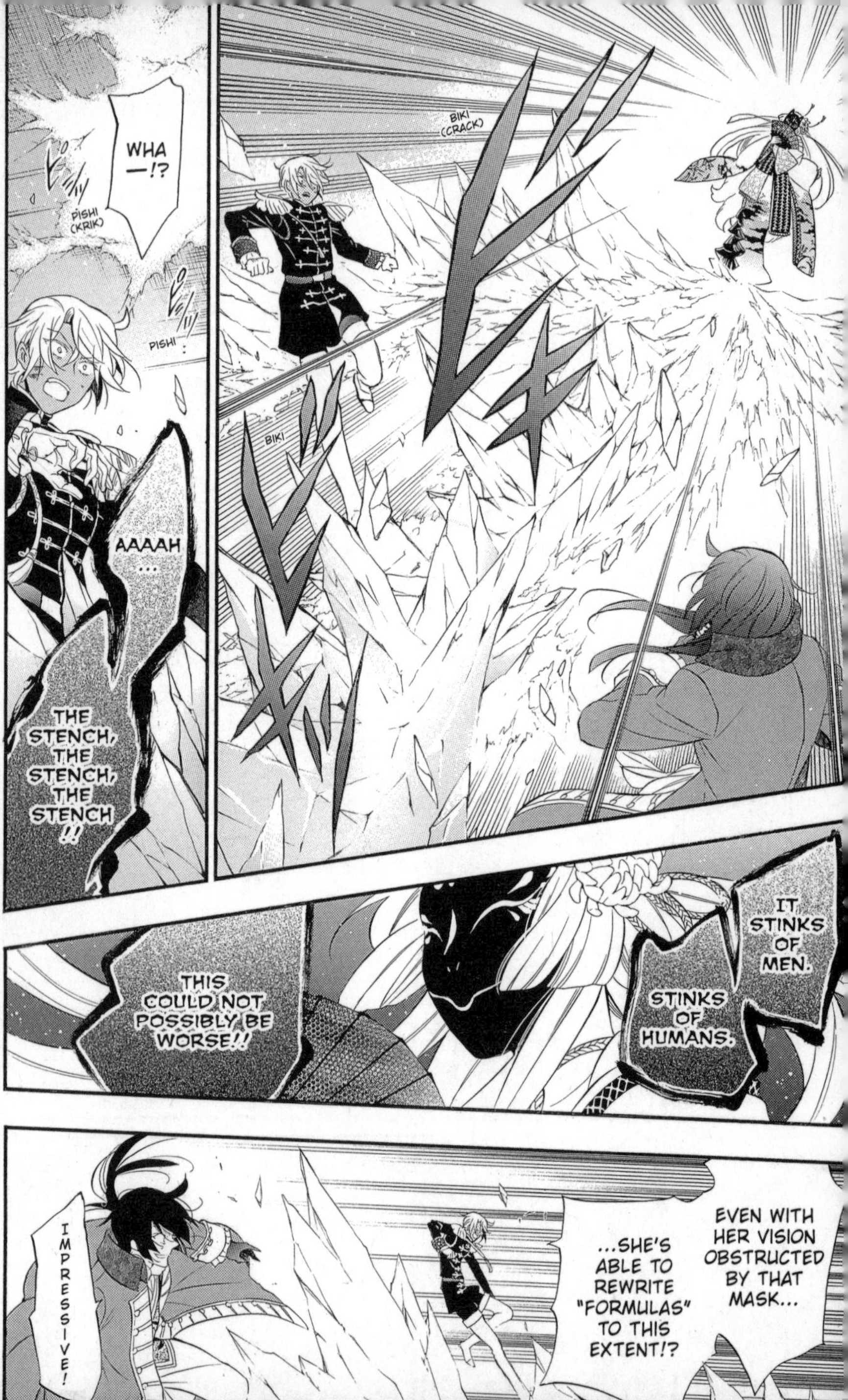
BIKI (CRACK)
BIKI
WHA—!?
PISHI (KRIK)
PISHI
AAAAH...
THE STENCH, THE STENCH, THE STENCH!!
IT STINKS OF MEN.
STINKS OF HUMANS.
THIS COULD NOT POSSIBLY BE WORSE!!
EVEN WITH HER VISION OBSTRUCTED BY THAT MASK...
...SHE'S ABLE TO REWRITE "FORMULAS" TO THIS EXTENT!?
IMPRESSIVE!

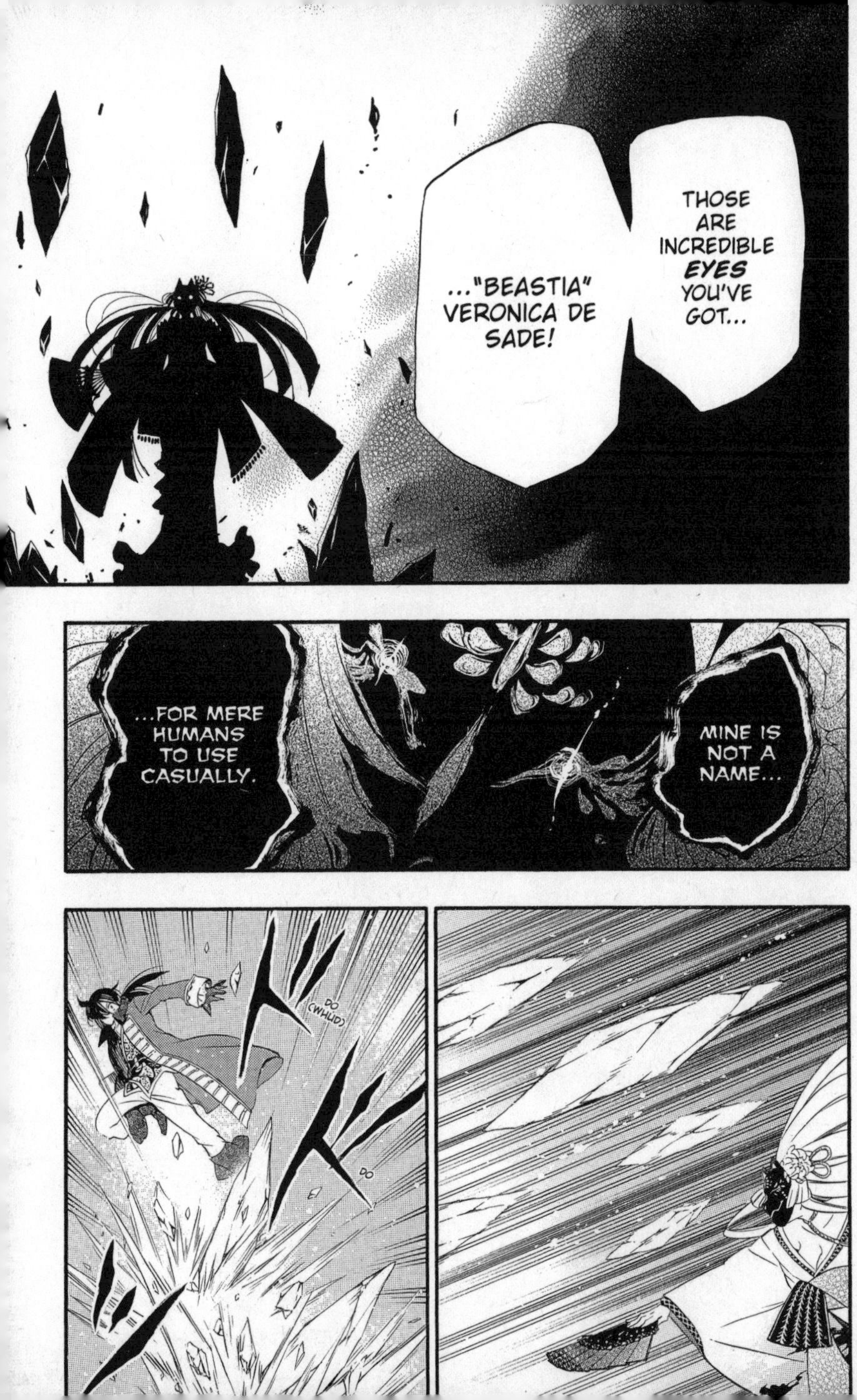
THOSE ARE INCREDIBLE EYES YOU'VE GOT...
..."BEASTIA" VERONICA DE SADE!
MINE IS NOT A NAME...
...FOR MERE HUMANS TO USE CASUALLY.
DO (WHUD)
DO

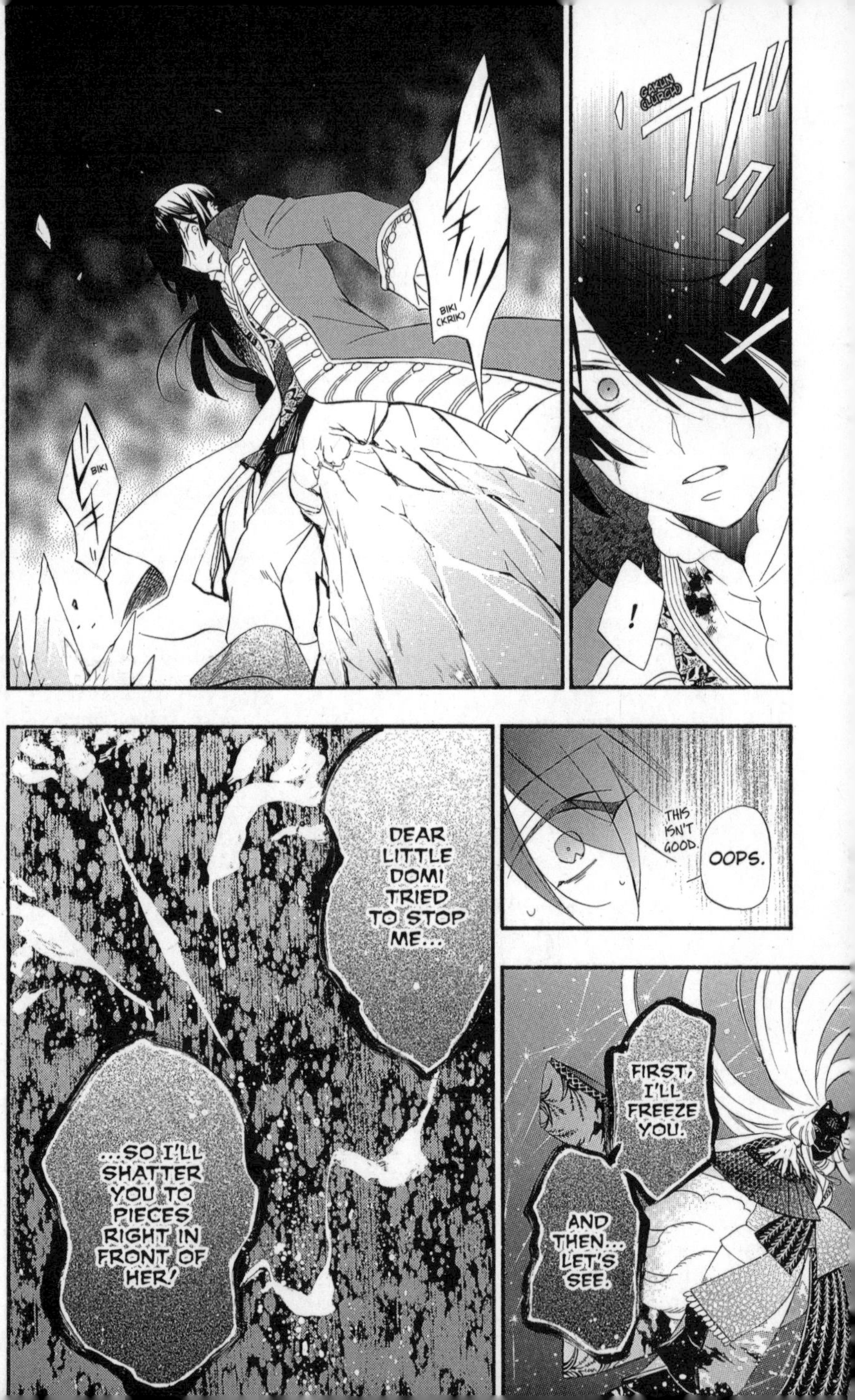
GAKUN (LURCH)
!
BIKI (KRIK)
BIKI
THIS ISN'T GOOD.
OOPS.
FIRST, I'LL FREEZE YOU.
AND THEN... LET'S SEE.
DEAR LITTLE DOMI TRIED TO STOP ME...
...SO I'LL SHATTER YOU TO PIECES RIGHT IN FRONT OF HER!

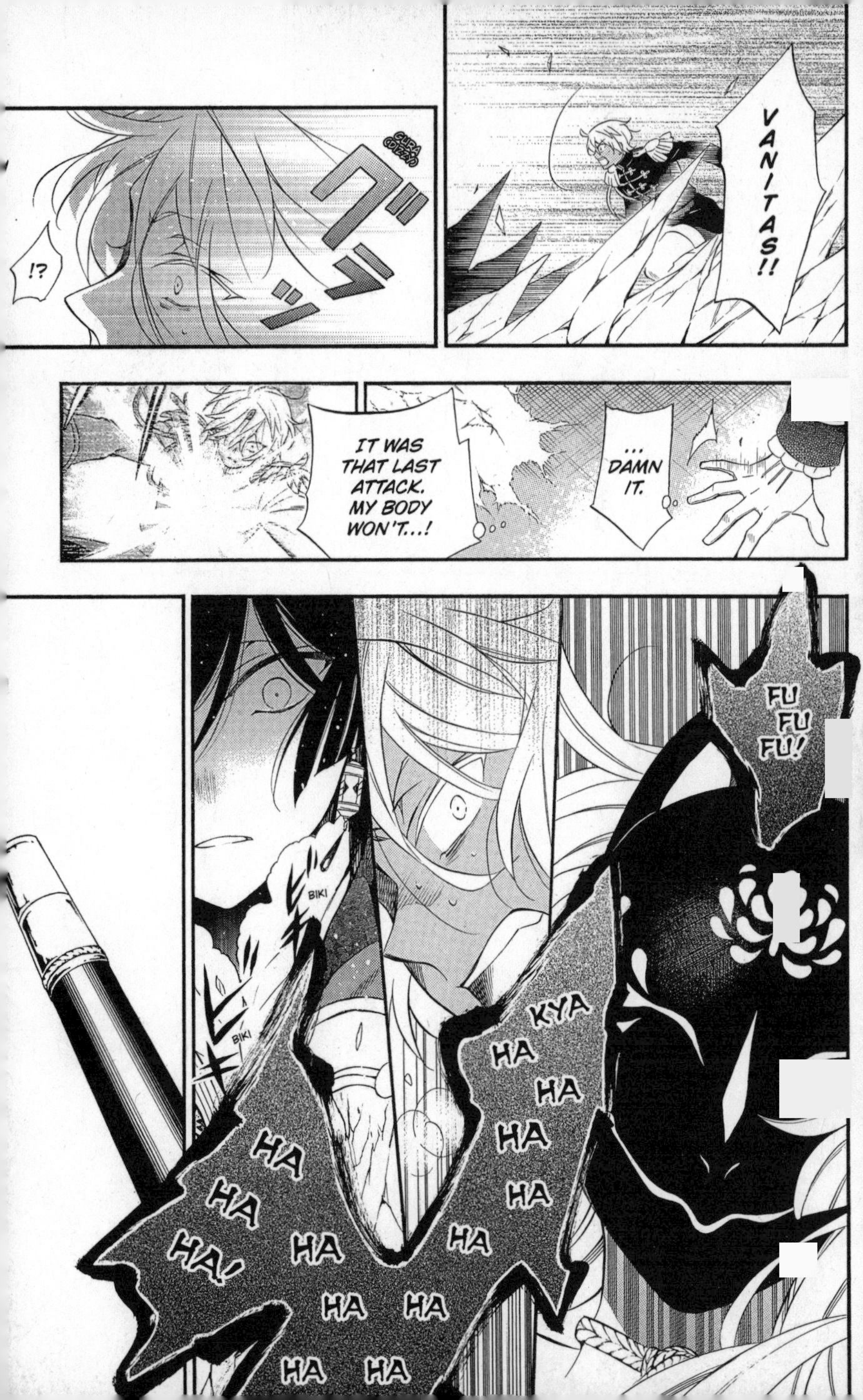
VANITAS!!
GUPA (DIZZY)
!?
...DAMN IT.
IT WAS THAT LAST ATTACK. MY BODY WON'T...!
FU FU FU!
KYA HA HA HA HA HA HA HA HA HA HA
BIKI
BIKI
HA HA HA!

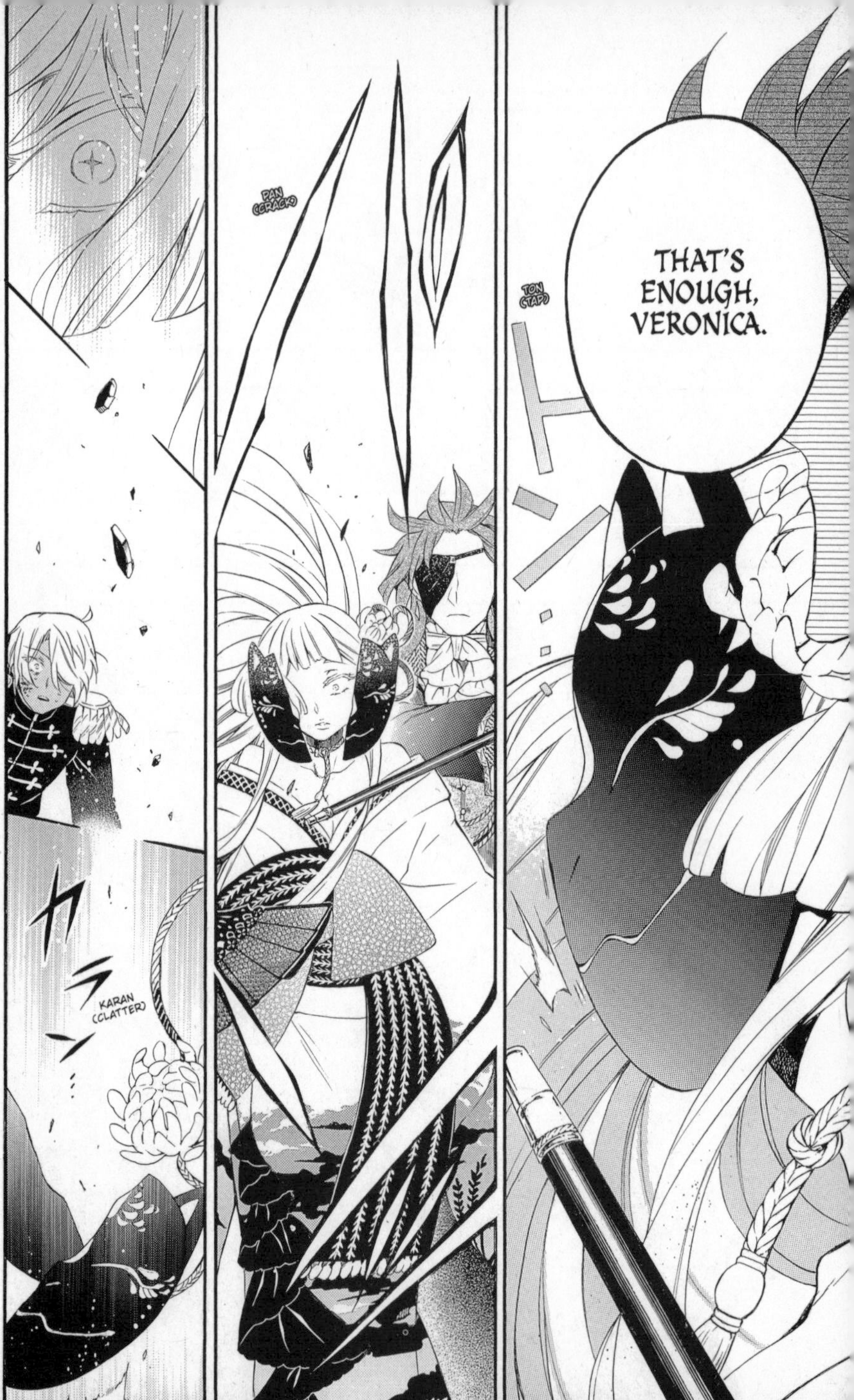
THAT'S ENOUGH, VERONICA.
TON (TAP)
PAN (CRACK)
KARAN (CLATTER)

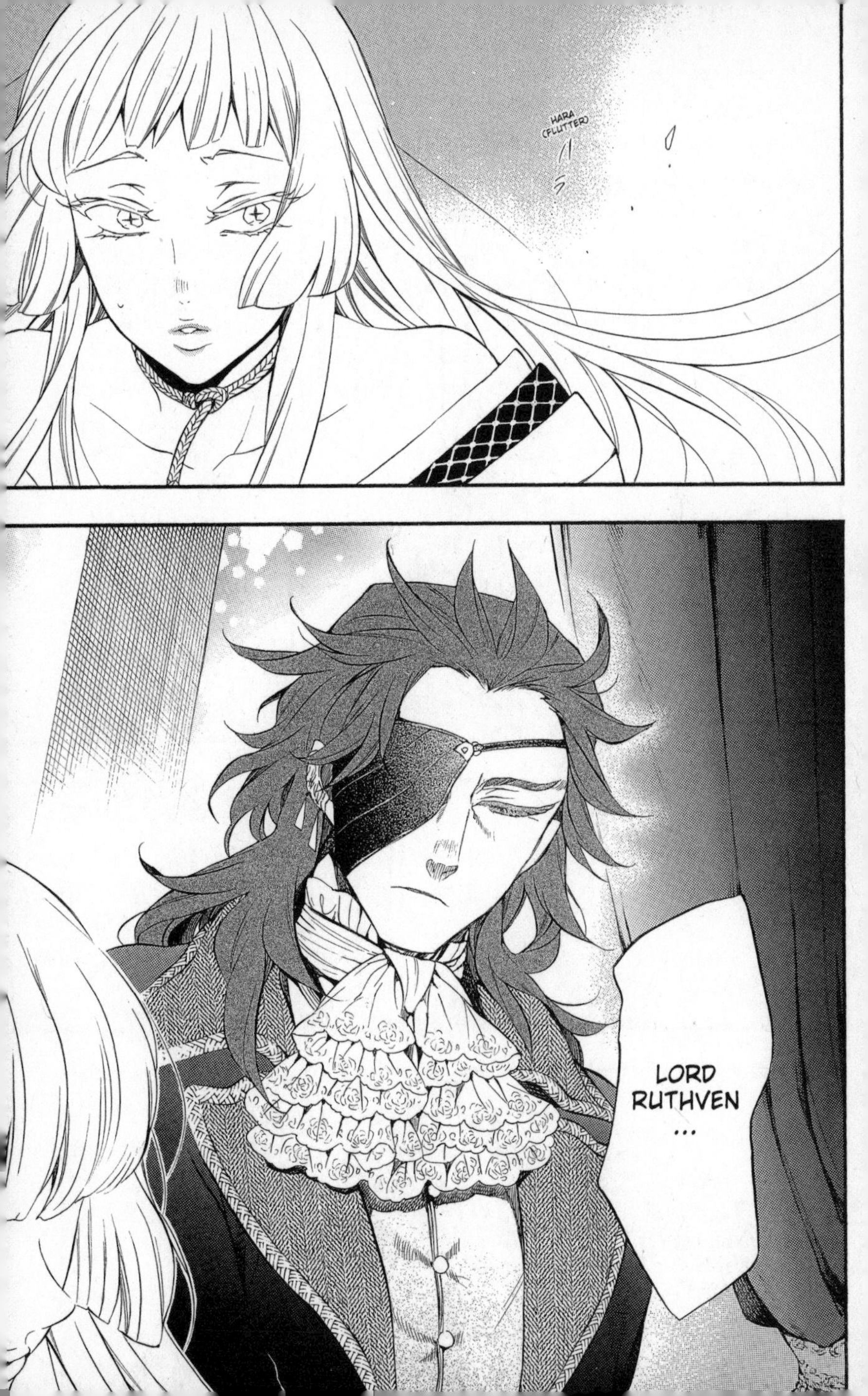
HARA (FLUTTER)
LORD RUTHVEN ...

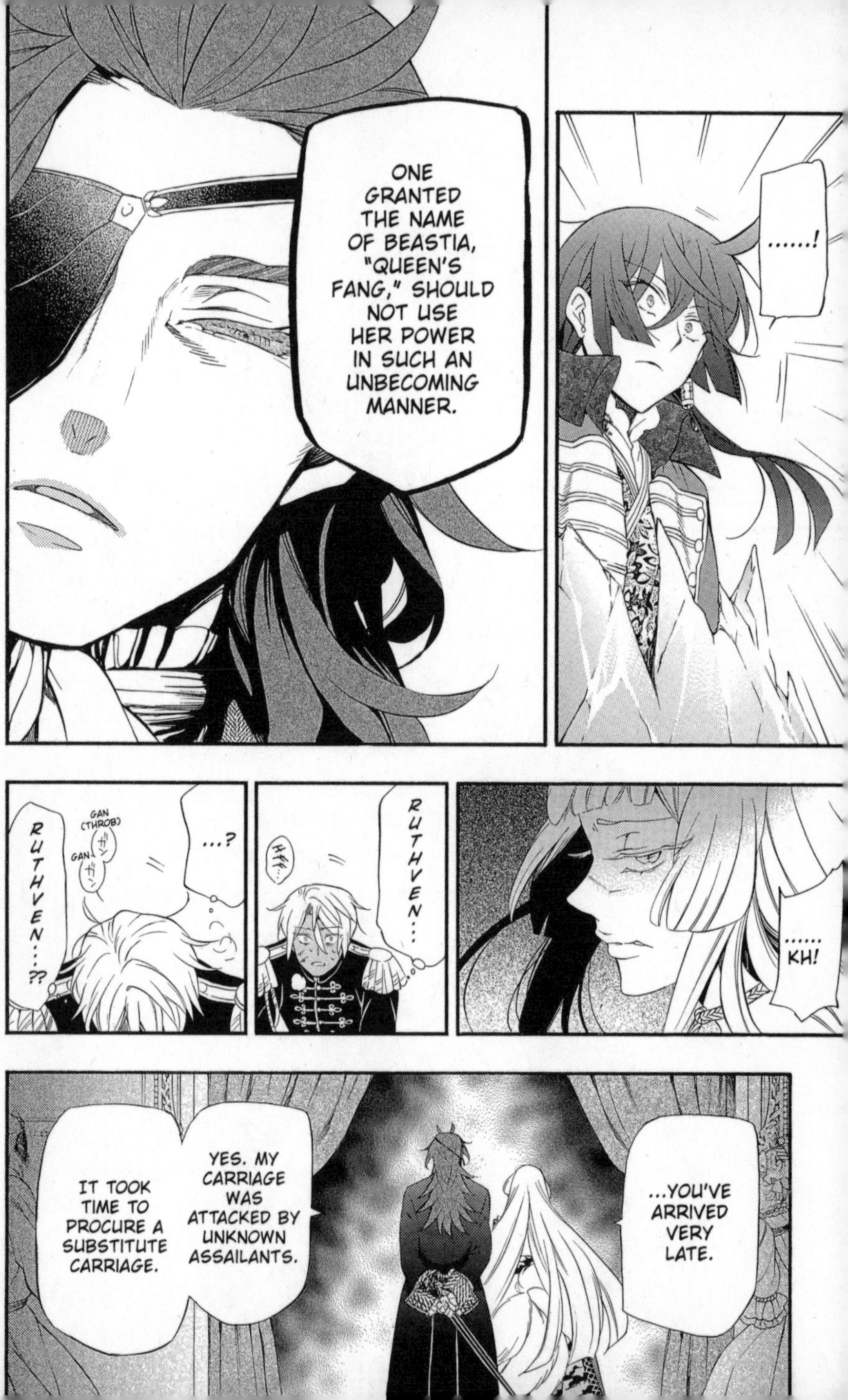
......!
ONE GRANTED THE NAME OF BEASTIA, "QUEEN'S FANG," SHOULD NOT USE HER POWER IN SUCH AN UNBECOMING MANNER.
......KH!
RUTHVEN...
...?
GAN (THROB)
ガン
GAN
ガン
RUTHVEN...??
...YOU'VE ARRIVED VERY LATE.
YES. MY CARRIAGE WAS ATTACKED BY UNKNOWN ASSAILANTS.
IT TOOK TIME TO PROCURE A SUBSTITUTE CARRIAGE.

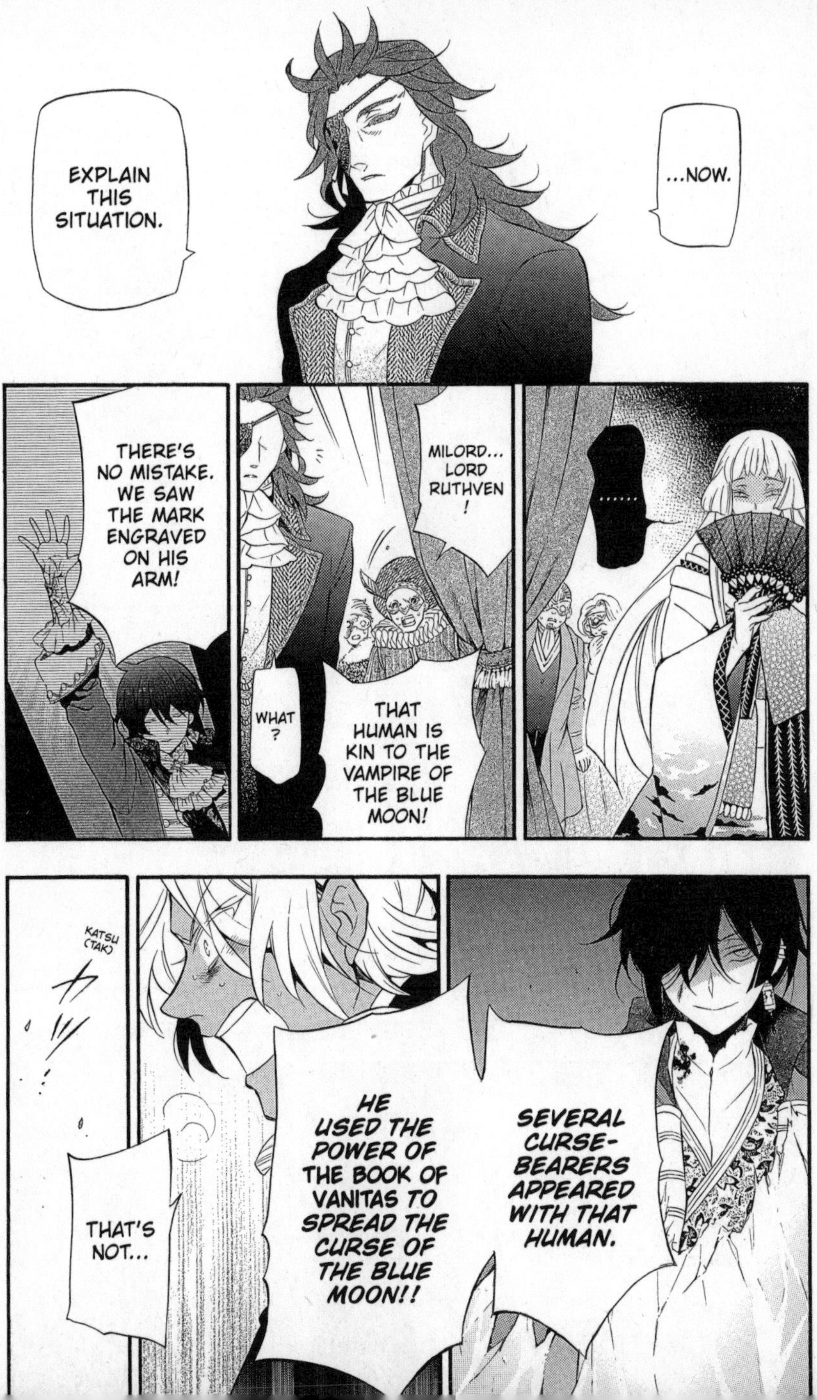
EXPLAIN THIS SITUATION.
...NOW.
......
MILORD... LORD RUTHVEN!
THAT HUMAN IS KIN TO THE VAMPIRE OF THE BLUE MOON!
WHAT?
THERE'S NO MISTAKE. WE SAW THE MARK ENGRAVED ON HIS ARM!
SEVERAL CURSE-BEARERS APPEARED WITH THAT HUMAN.
HE USED THE POWER OF THE BOOK OF VANITAS TO SPREAD THE CURSE OF THE BLUE MOON!!
KATSU (TAK)
THAT'S NOT...

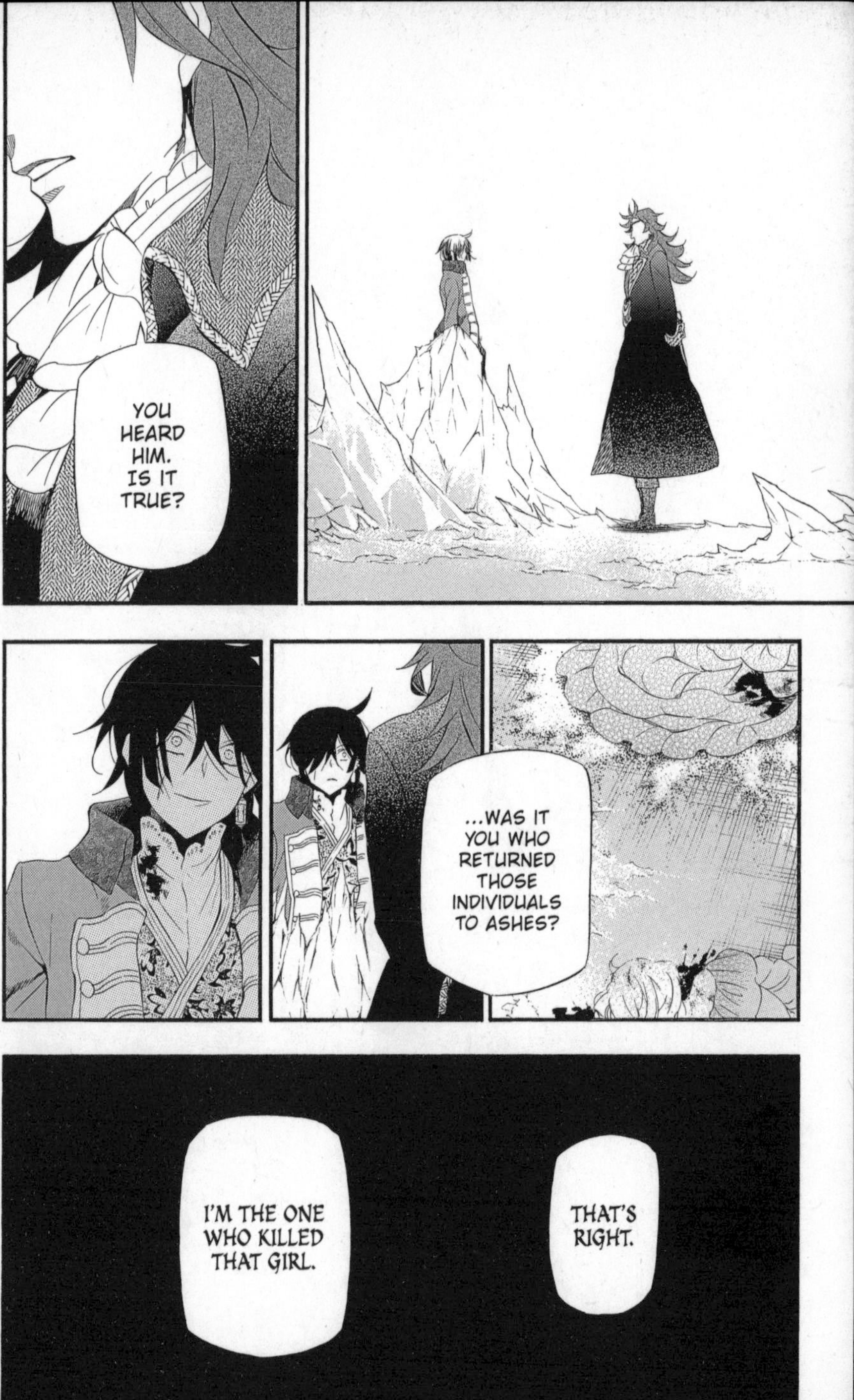
YOU HEARD HIM. IS IT TRUE?
...WAS IT YOU WHO RETURNED THOSE INDIVIDUALS TO ASHES?
THAT'S RIGHT.
I'M THE ONE WHO KILLED THAT GIRL.

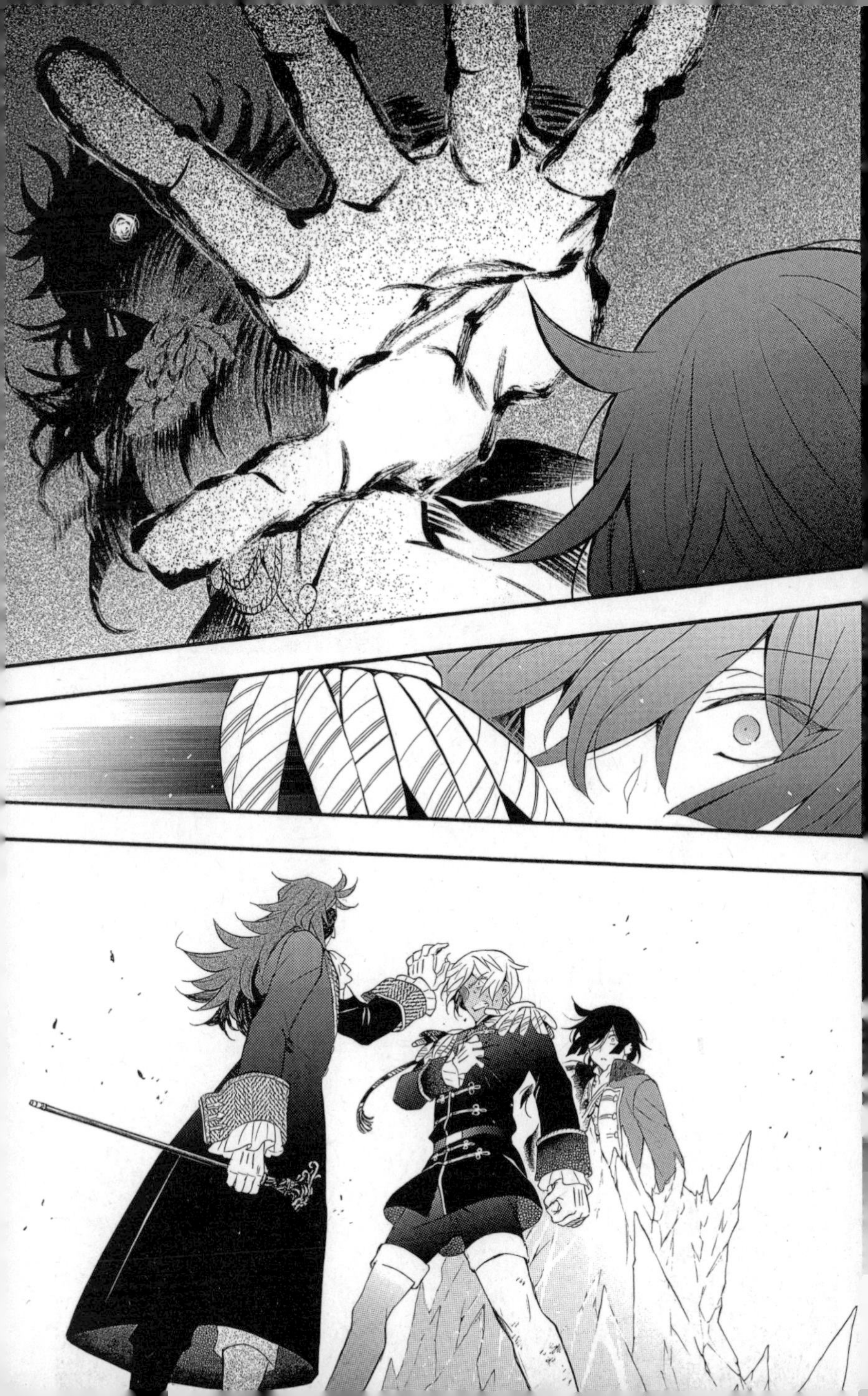

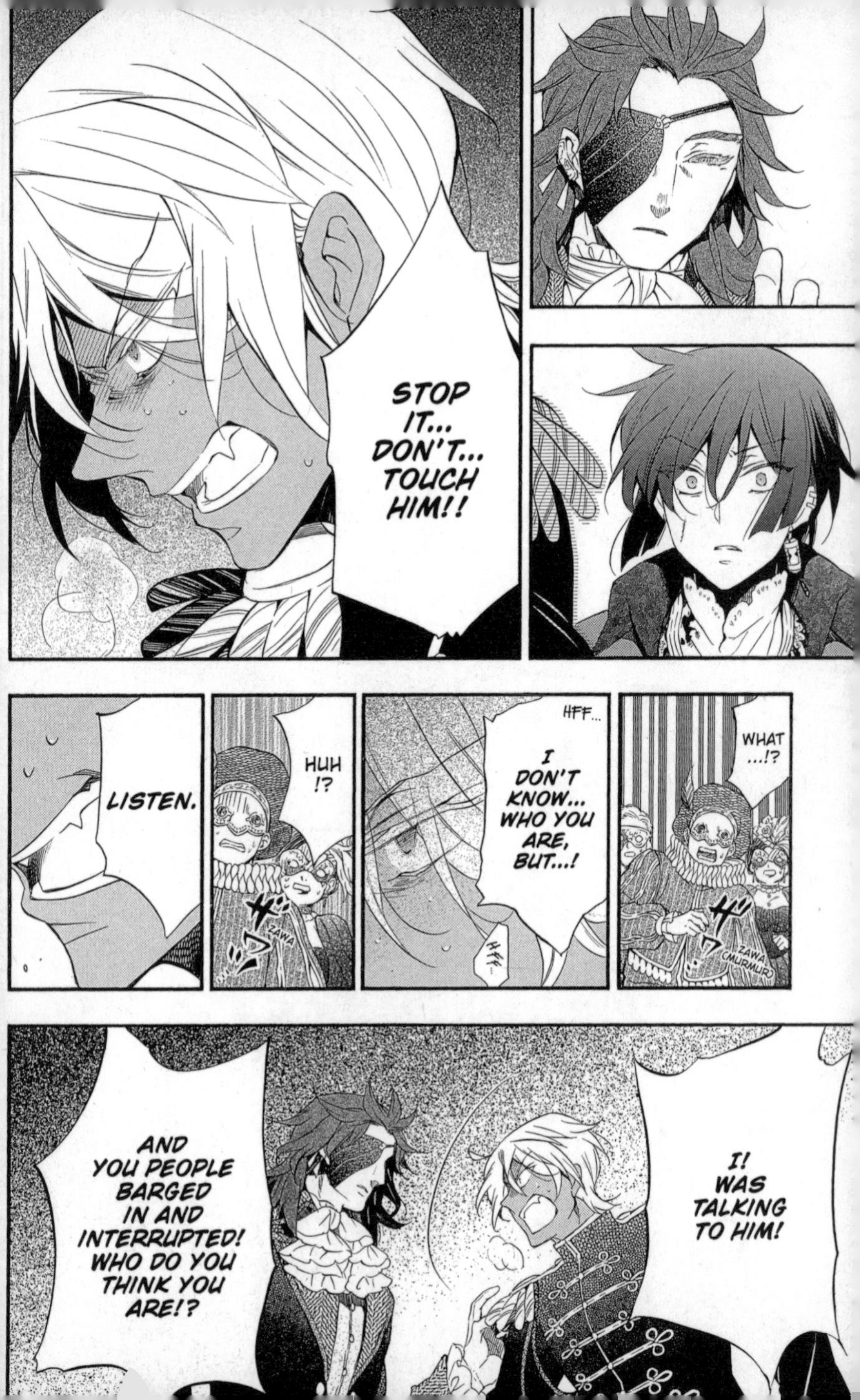
STOP IT... DON'T... TOUCH HIM!!
WHAT ...!?
ZAWA (MURMUR)
HFF...
I DON'T KNOW... WHO YOU ARE, BUT...!
HFF...
HUH !?
ZAWA
LISTEN.
I! WAS TALKING TO HIM!
AND YOU PEOPLE BARGED IN AND INTERRUPTED! WHO DO YOU THINK YOU ARE!?

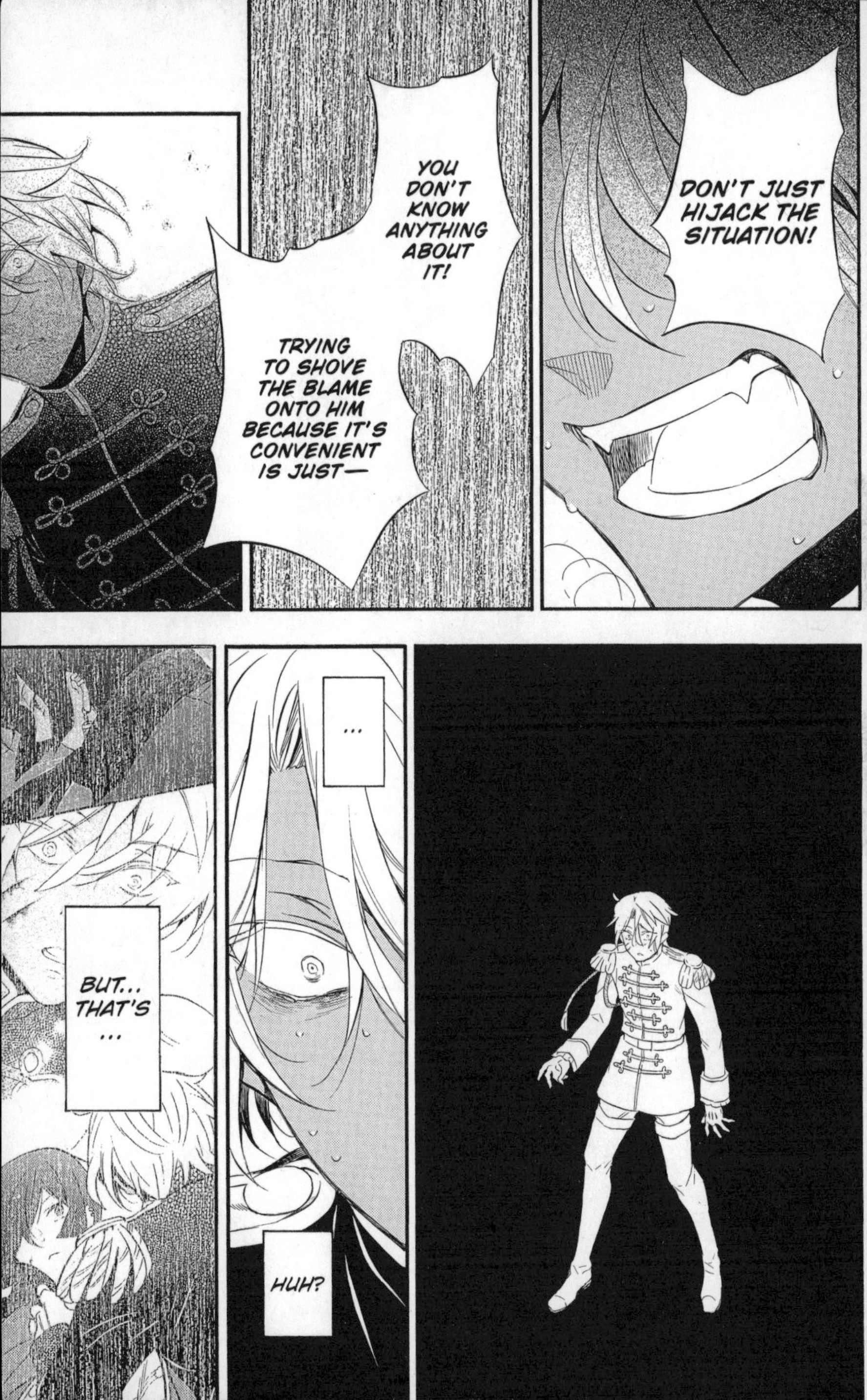
DON'T JUST HIJACK THE SITUATION!
YOU DON'T KNOW ANYTHING ABOUT IT!
TRYING TO SHOVE THE BLAME ONTO HIM BECAUSE IT'S CONVENIENT IS JUST—
...
HUH?
BUT... THAT'S ...

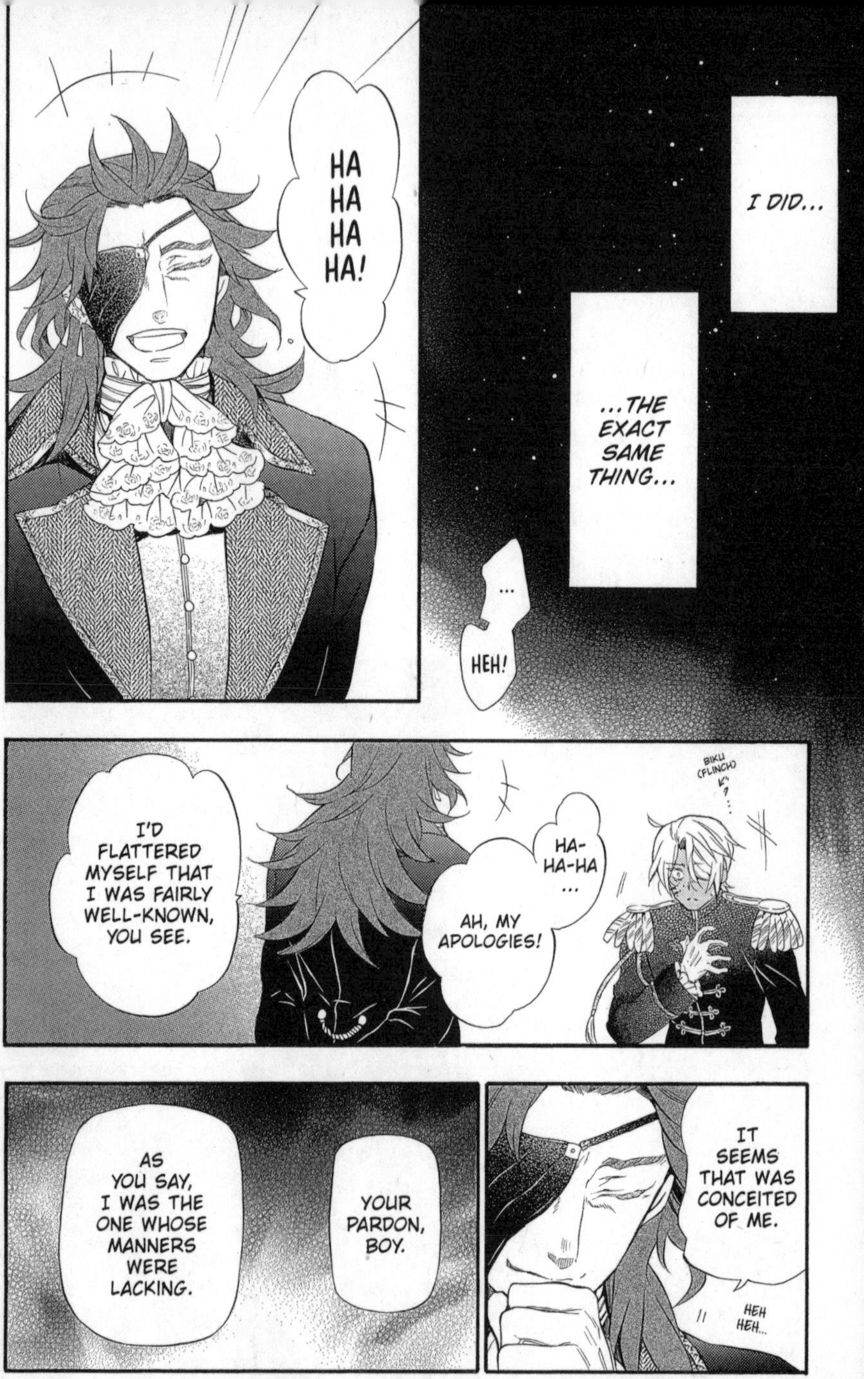
I DID...
...THE EXACT SAME THING...
...
HEH!
HA HA HA HA!
BIKU (FLINCH)
HA-HA-HA...
AH, MY APOLOGIES!
I'D FLATTERED MYSELF THAT I WAS FAIRLY WELL-KNOWN, YOU SEE.
IT SEEMS THAT WAS CONCEITED OF ME.
HEH HEH...
YOUR PARDON, BOY.
AS YOU SAY, I WAS THE ONE WHOSE MANNERS WERE LACKING.

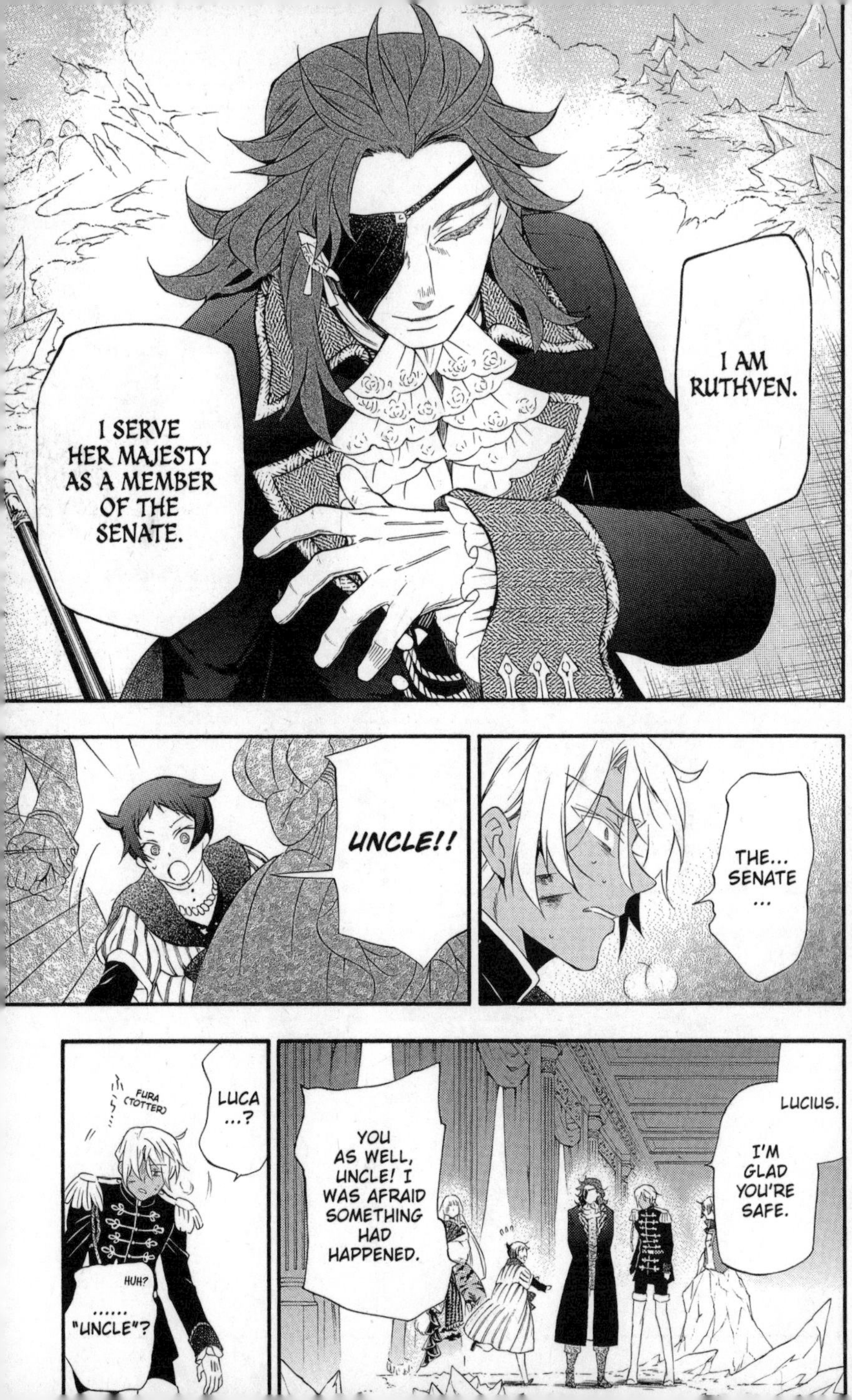
I AM RUTHVEN.
I SERVE HER MAJESTY AS A MEMBER OF THE SENATE.
THE... SENATE ...
UNCLE!!
LUCIUS.
I'M GLAD YOU'RE SAFE.
YOU AS WELL, UNCLE! I WAS AFRAID SOMETHING HAD HAPPENED.
LUCA ...?
FURA (TOTTER)
HUH?
...... "UNCLE"?

UH-OH.

NOÉ!!

DOSA
(WHUMP)

GURA
(STAGGER)

NOÉ...
WHAT IS
GOING ON
HERE......?

DON'T
...

SU
(SHUF)

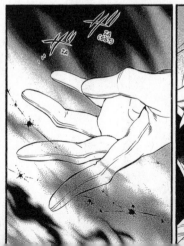

ZA
(SSST)

I'M
ONLY
MELTING
THE ICE.

HAVE
NO
FEAR.

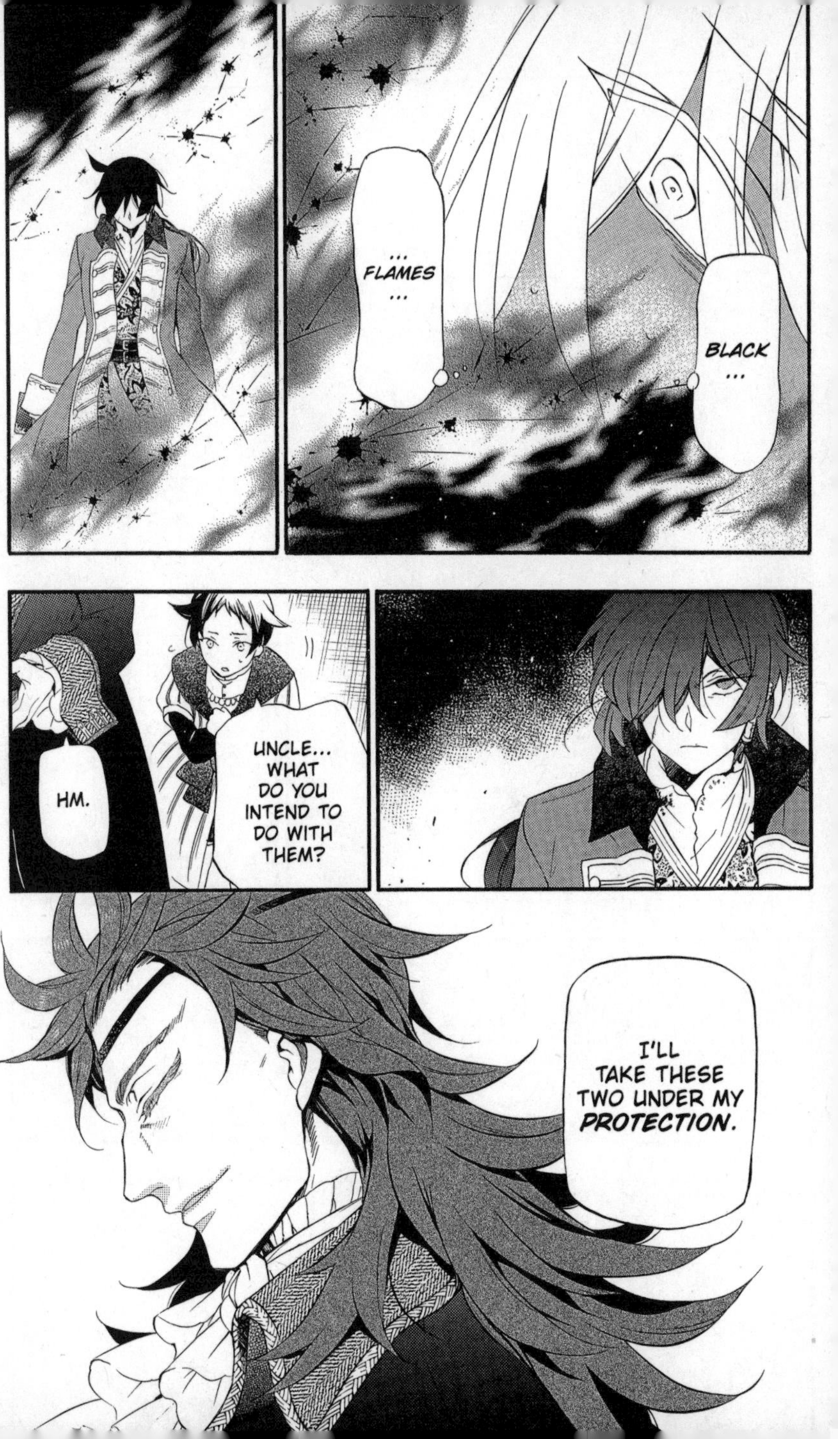
BLACK ...
... FLAMES ...
UNCLE... WHAT DO YOU INTEND TO DO WITH THEM?
HM.
I'LL TAKE THESE TWO UNDER MY *PROTECTION*.

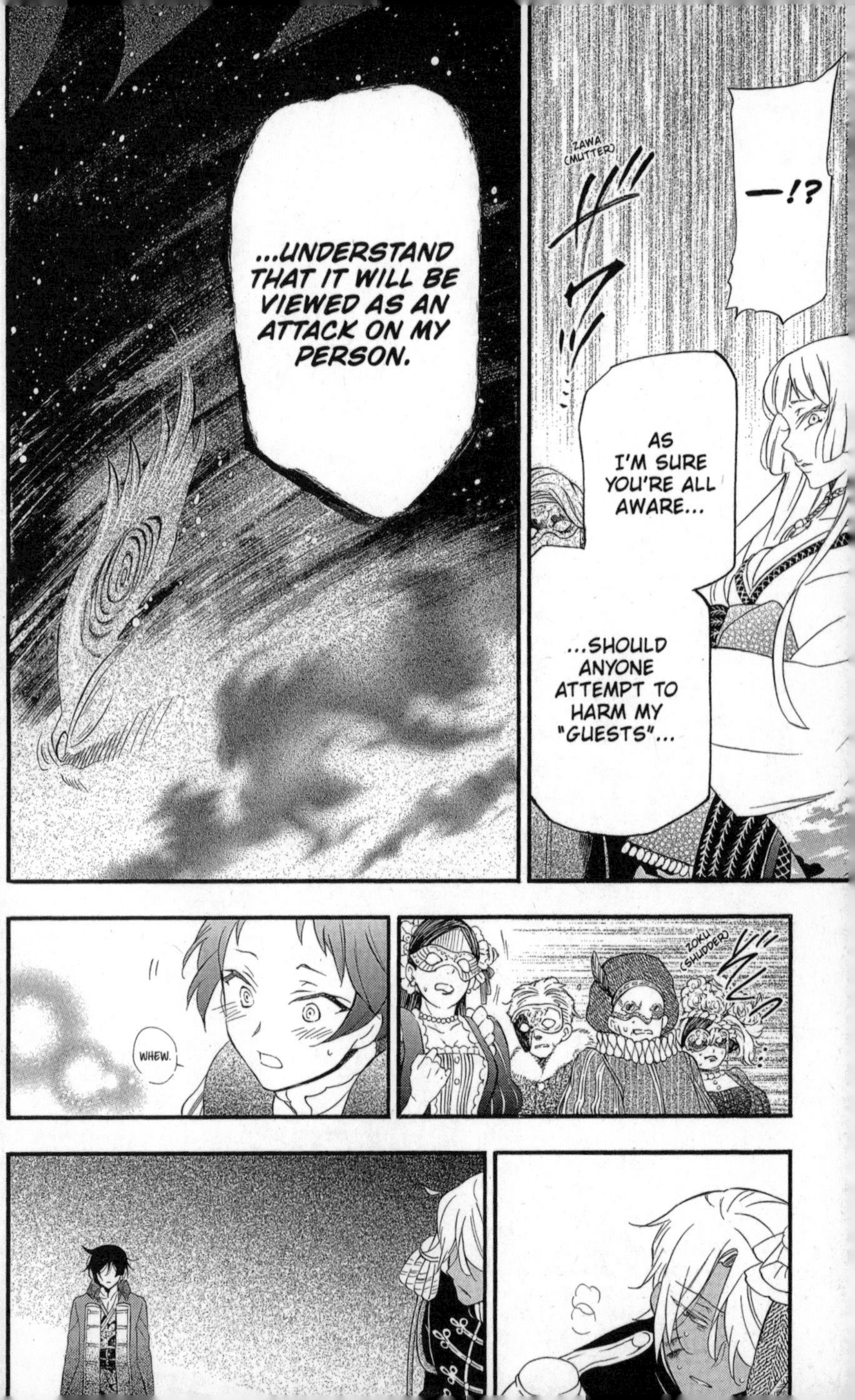
—!?
ZAWA (MUTTER)
AS I'M SURE YOU'RE ALL AWARE...
...SHOULD ANYONE ATTEMPT TO HARM MY "GUESTS"...
...UNDERSTAND THAT IT WILL BE VIEWED AS AN ATTACK ON MY PERSON.
ZOKU (SHUDDER)
WHEW.

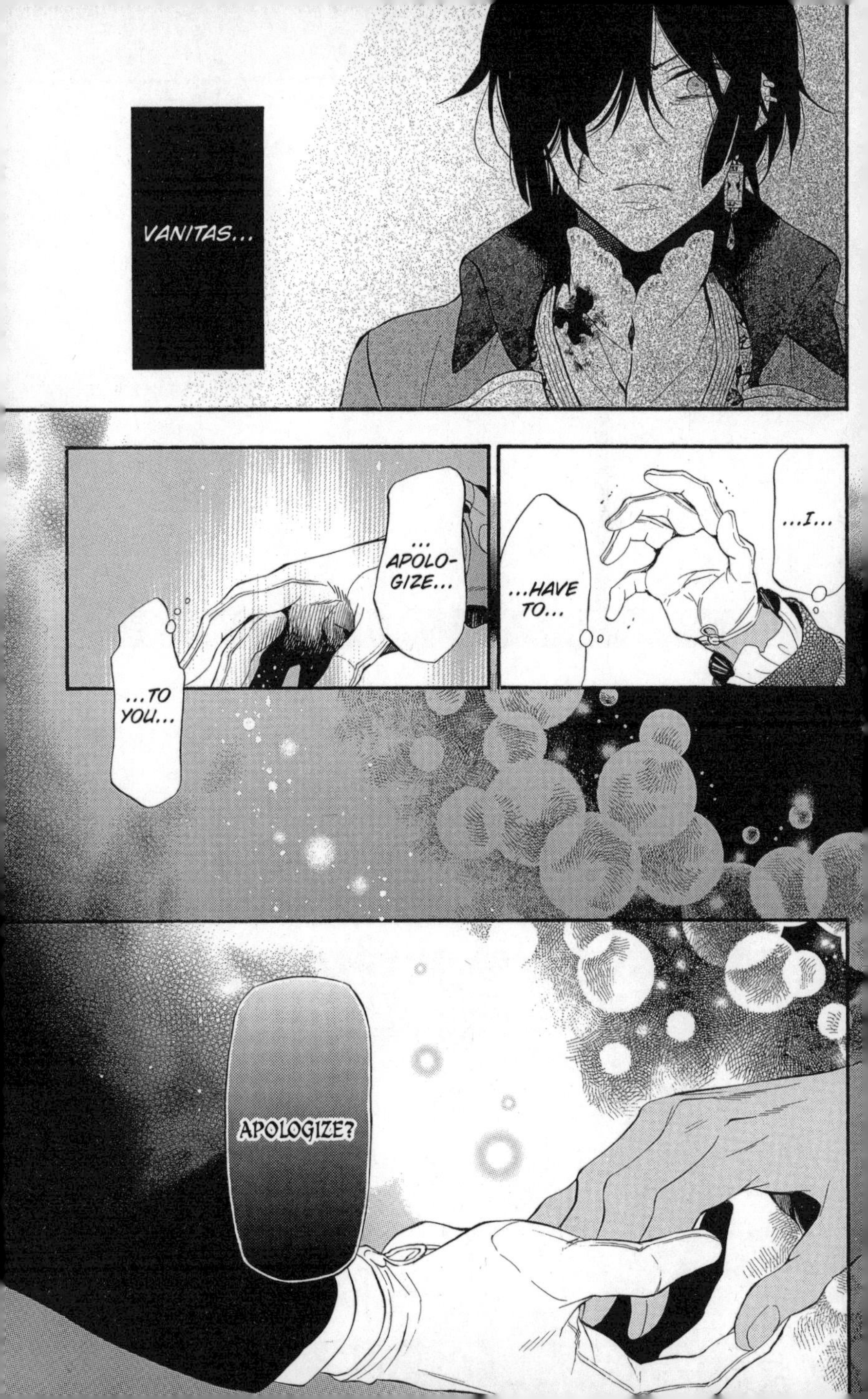
VANITAS...
...I...
...HAVE TO...
... APOLOGIZE...
...TO YOU...
APOLOGIZE?

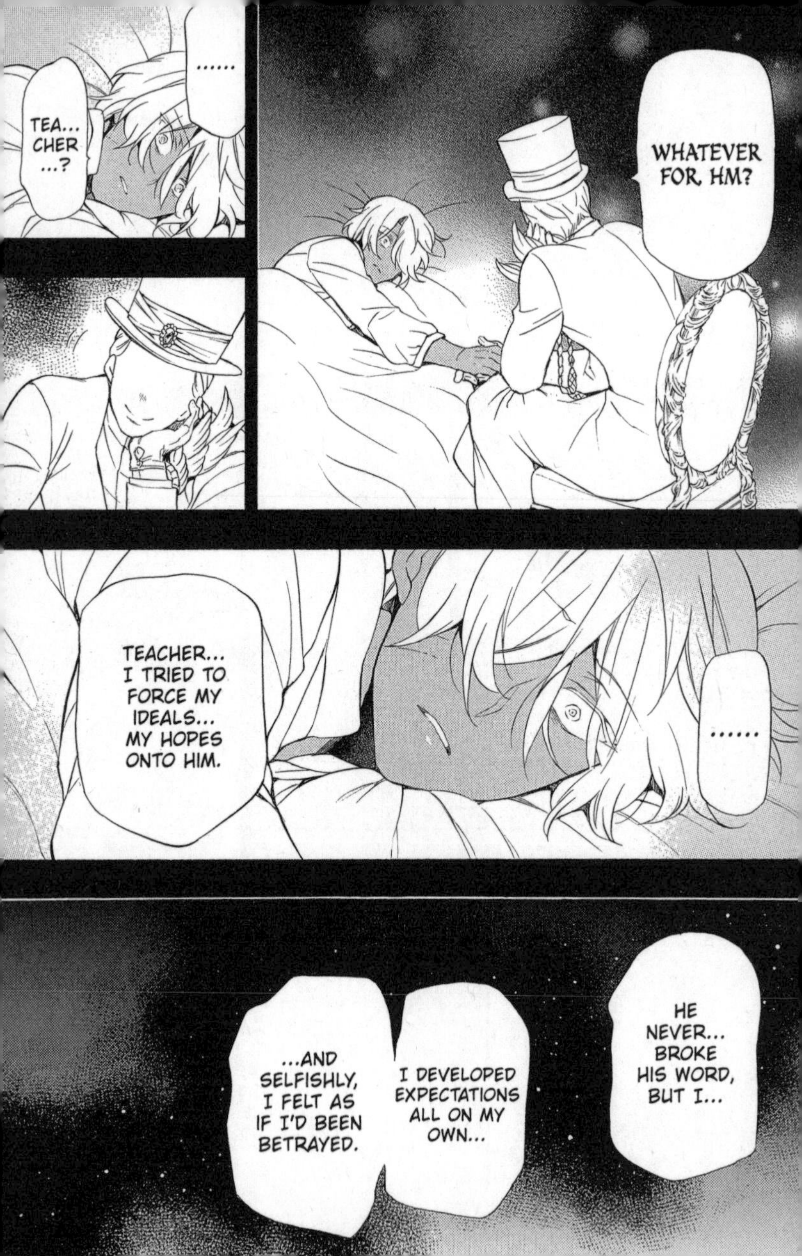
WHATEVER FOR, HM?
......
TEA... CHER ...?
......
TEACHER... I TRIED TO FORCE MY IDEALS... MY HOPES ONTO HIM.
HE NEVER... BROKE HIS WORD, BUT I...
I DEVELOPED EXPECTATIONS ALL ON MY OWN...
...AND SELFISHLY, I FELT AS IF I'D BEEN BETRAYED.

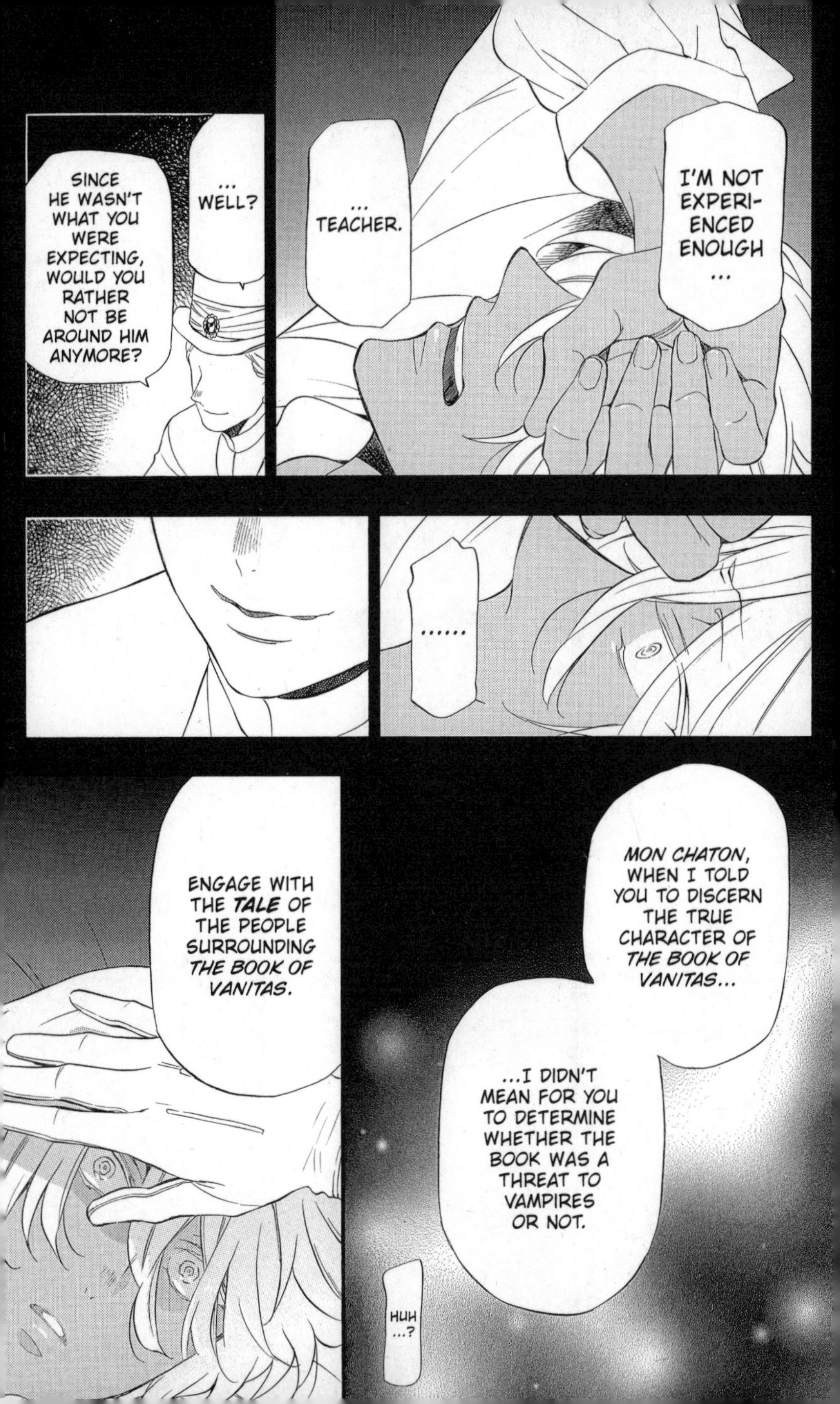
I'M NOT EXPERIENCED ENOUGH...
...TEACHER.
...WELL?
SINCE HE WASN'T WHAT YOU WERE EXPECTING, WOULD YOU RATHER NOT BE AROUND HIM ANYMORE?
......
MON CHATON, WHEN I TOLD YOU TO DISCERN THE TRUE CHARACTER OF *THE BOOK OF VANITAS*...
...I DIDN'T MEAN FOR YOU TO DETERMINE WHETHER THE BOOK WAS A THREAT TO VAMPIRES OR NOT.
ENGAGE WITH THE *TALE* OF THE PEOPLE SURROUNDING *THE BOOK OF VANITAS*.
HUH...?

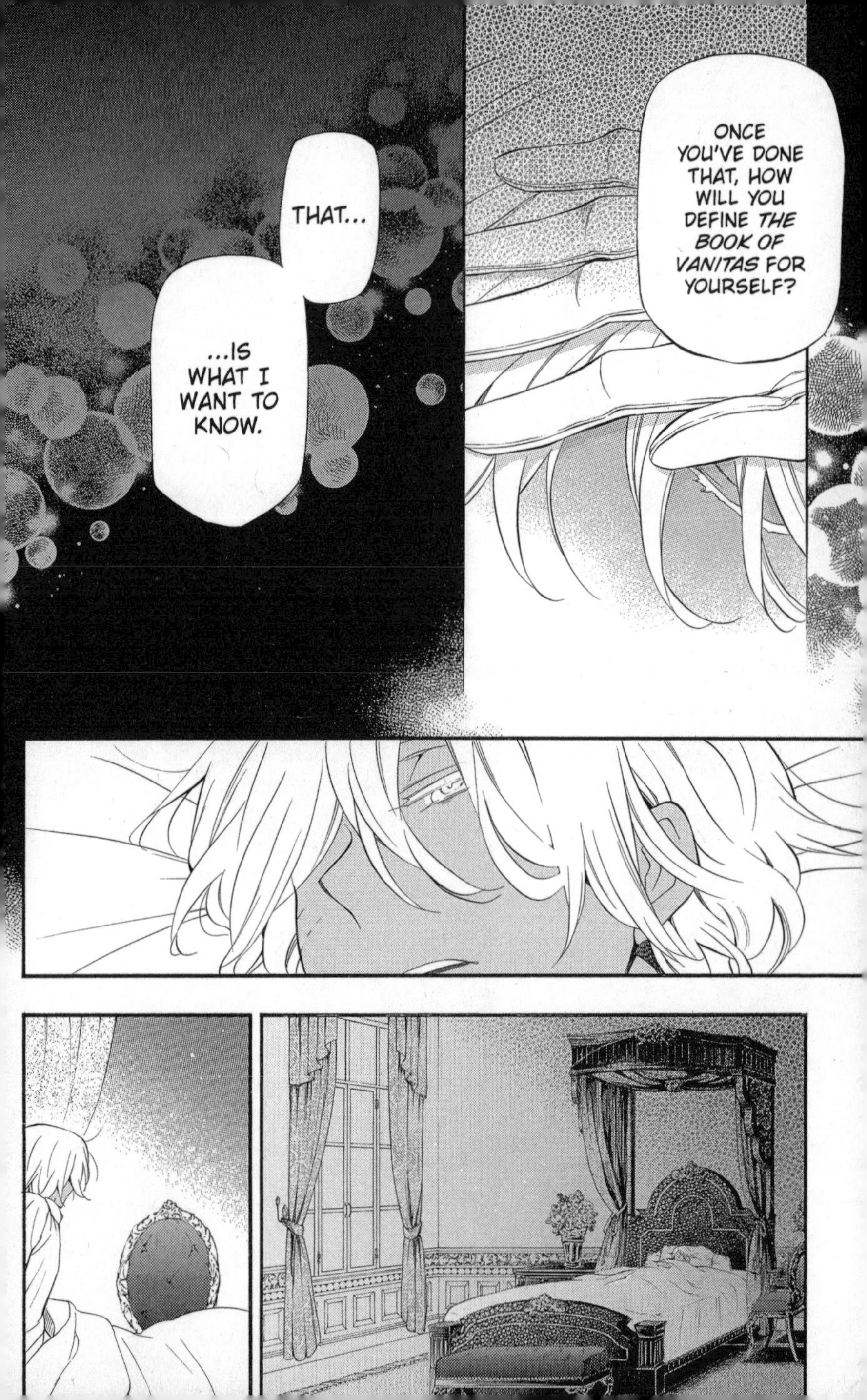
ONCE YOU'VE DONE THAT, HOW WILL YOU DEFINE *THE BOOK OF VANITAS* FOR YOURSELF?
THAT...
...IS WHAT I WANT TO KNOW.

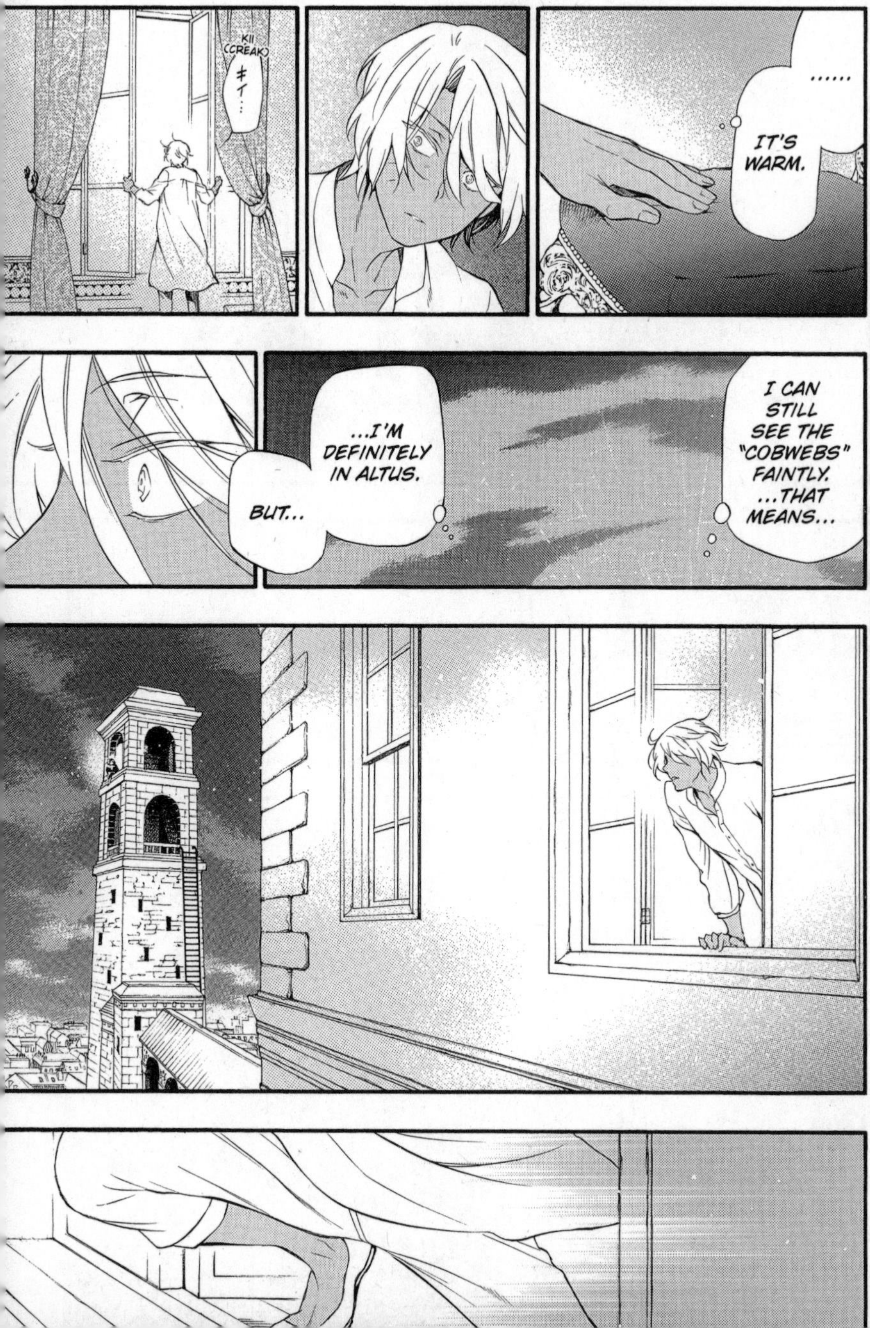
......
IT'S WARM.
KII (CREAK)
キイ…
I CAN STILL SEE THE "COBWEBS" FAINTLY. ...THAT MEANS...
...I'M DEFINITELY IN ALTUS.
BUT...

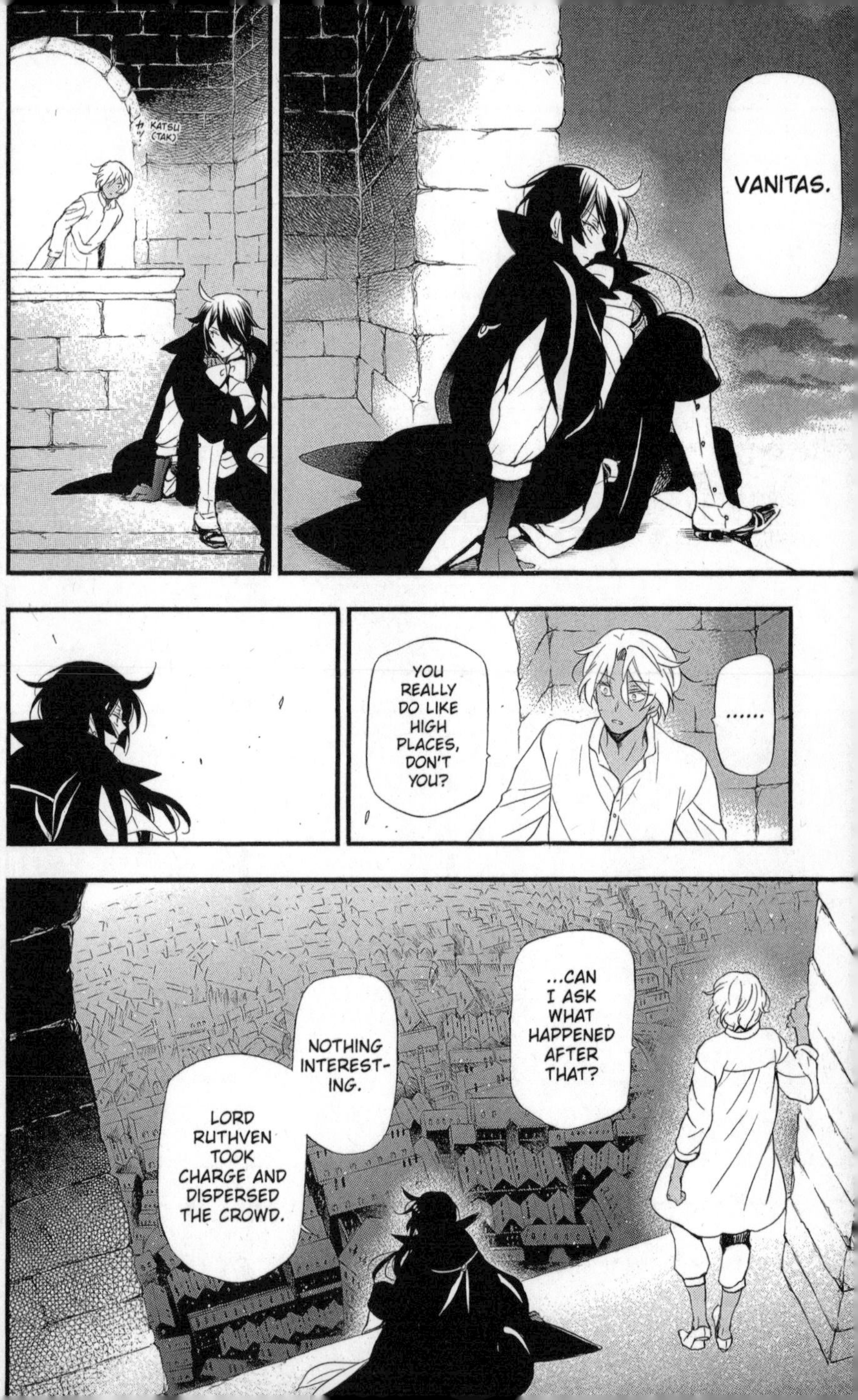
VANITAS.
KATSU (TAK)
......
YOU REALLY DO LIKE HIGH PLACES, DON'T YOU?
...CAN I ASK WHAT HAPPENED AFTER THAT?
NOTHING INTEREST-ING.
LORD RUTHVEN TOOK CHARGE AND DISPERSED THE CROWD.

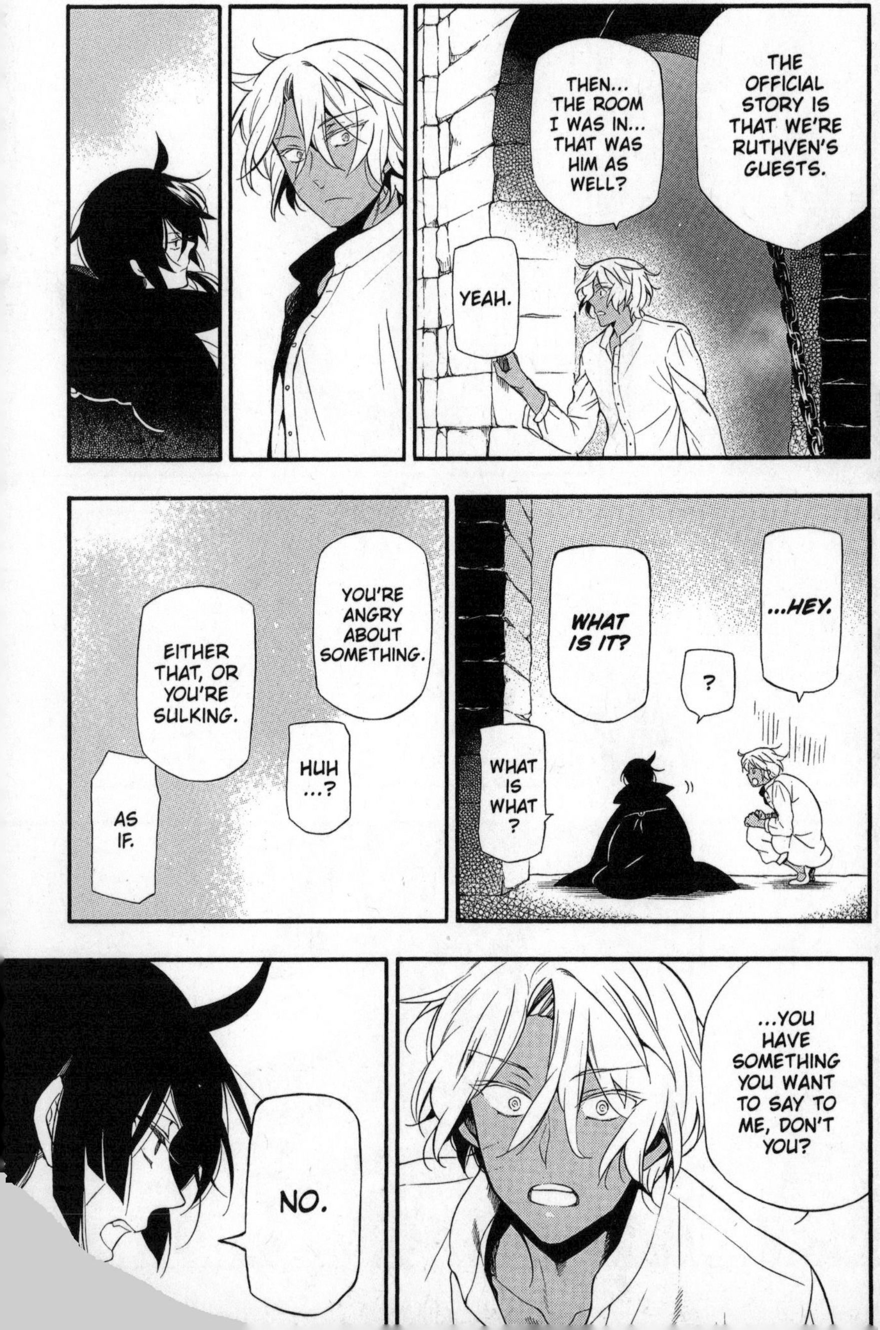
THE OFFICIAL STORY IS THAT WE'RE RUTHVEN'S GUESTS.
THEN... THE ROOM I WAS IN... THAT WAS HIM AS WELL?
YEAH.
...HEY.
?
WHAT IS IT?
WHAT IS WHAT?
YOU'RE ANGRY ABOUT SOMETHING.
HUH...?
EITHER THAT, OR YOU'RE SULKING.
AS IF.
...YOU HAVE SOMETHING YOU WANT TO SAY TO ME, DON'T YOU?
NO.

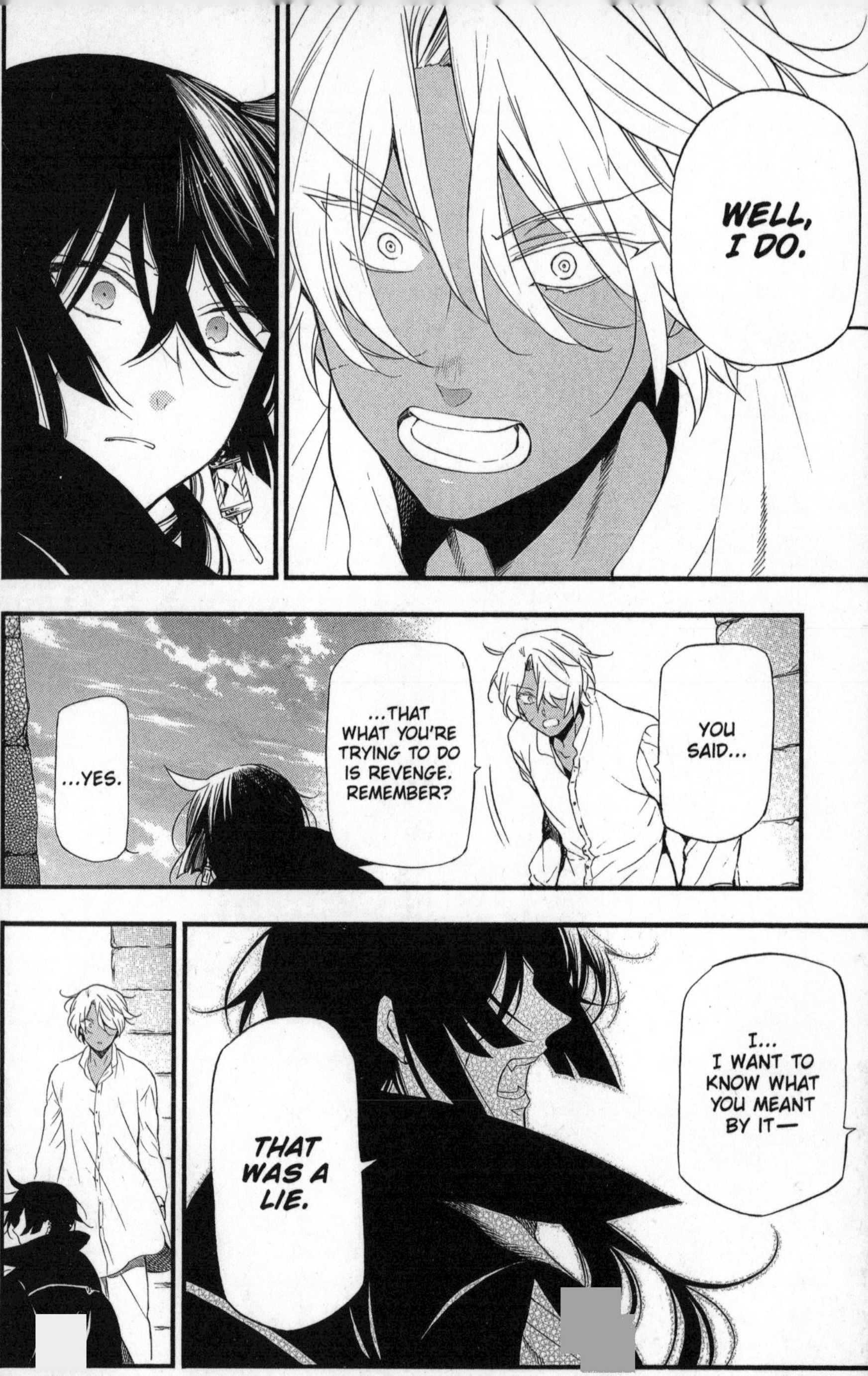
WELL, I DO.
YOU SAID...
...THAT WHAT YOU'RE TRYING TO DO IS REVENGE. REMEMBER?
...YES.
I... I WANT TO KNOW WHAT YOU MEANT BY IT—
THAT WAS A LIE.

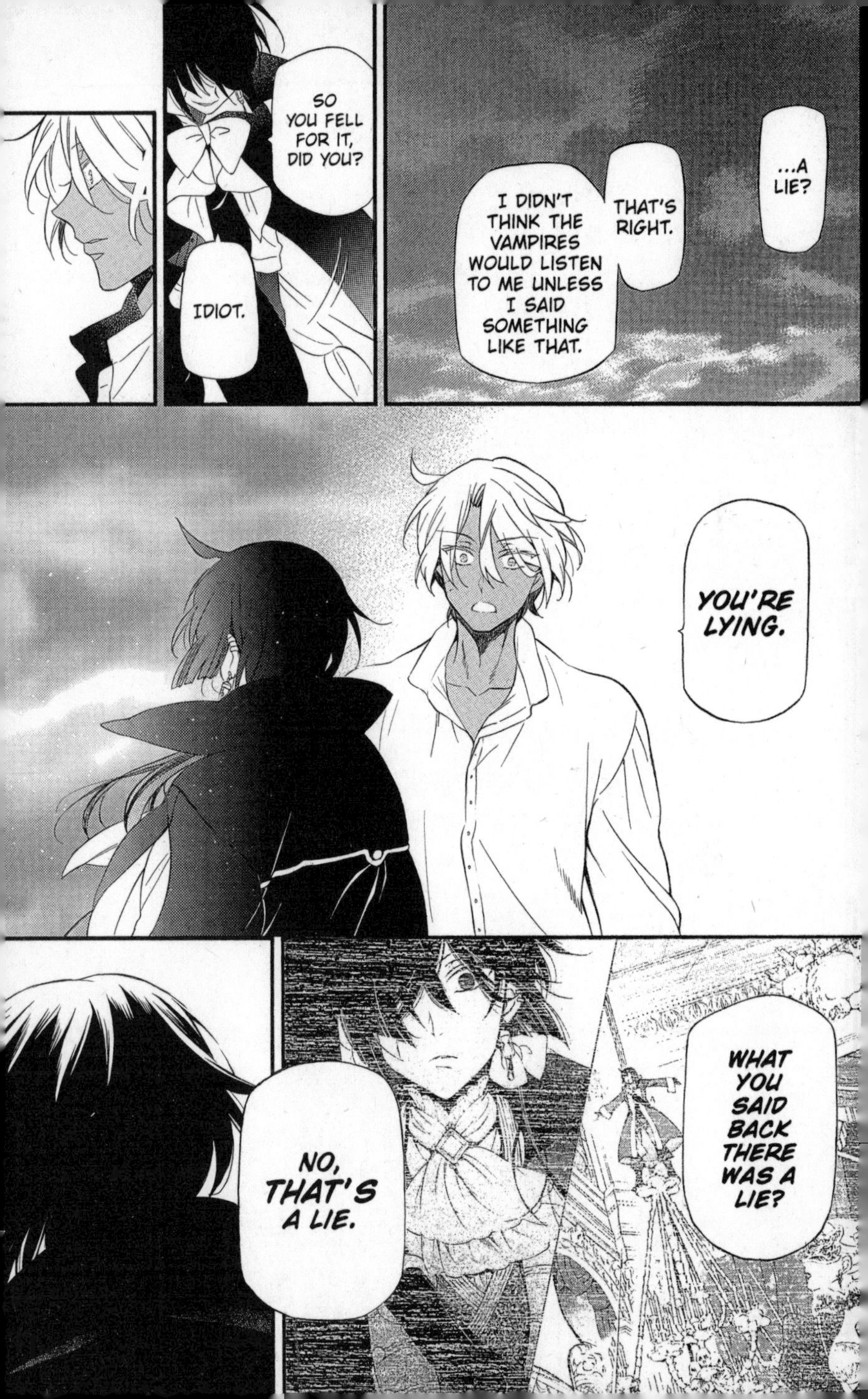
...A LIE?
THAT'S RIGHT.
I DIDN'T THINK THE VAMPIRES WOULD LISTEN TO ME UNLESS I SAID SOMETHING LIKE THAT.
SO YOU FELL FOR IT, DID YOU?
IDIOT.
YOU'RE LYING.
WHAT YOU SAID BACK THERE WAS A LIE?
NO, THAT'S A LIE.

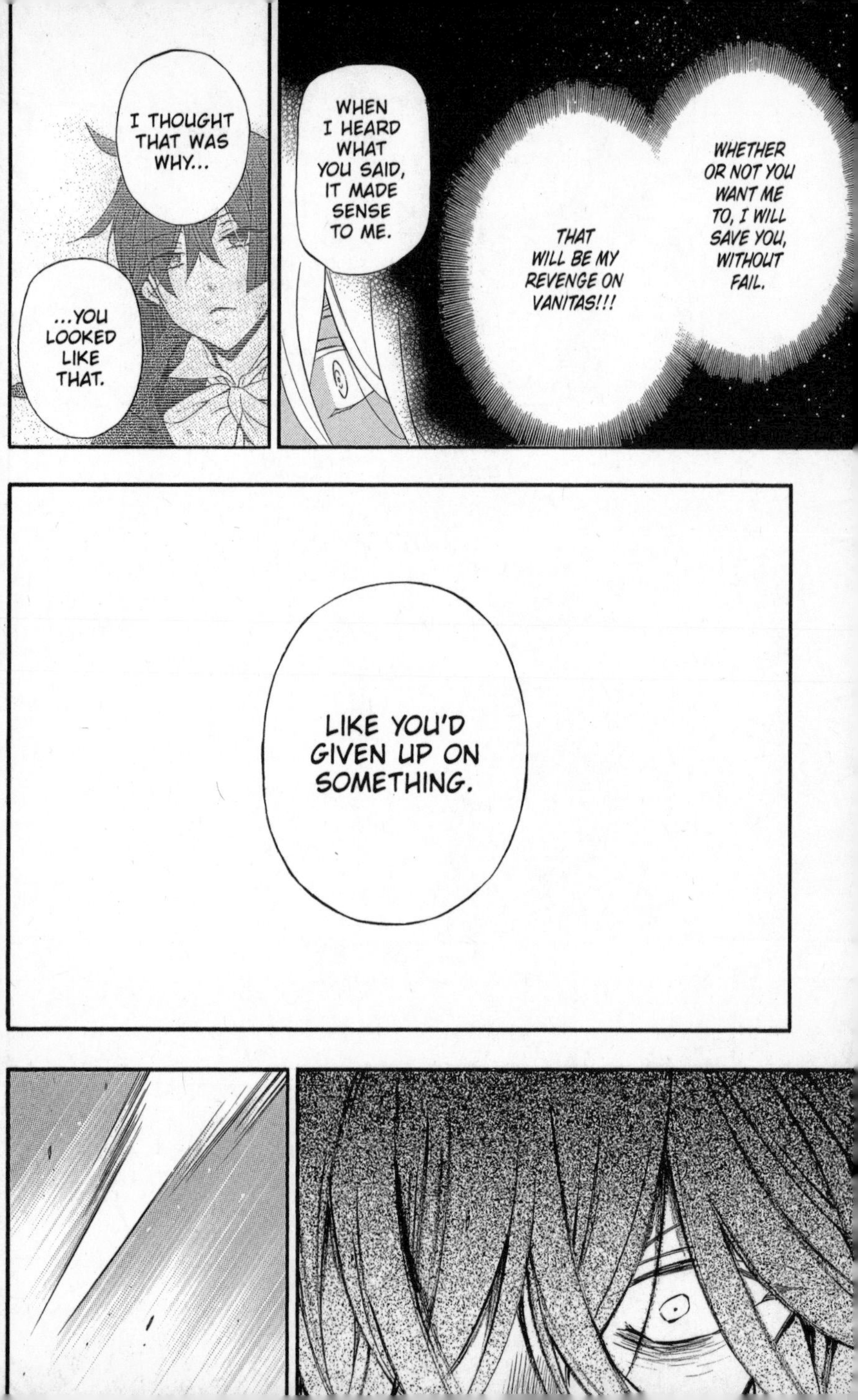
WHETHER OR NOT YOU WANT ME TO, I WILL SAVE YOU, WITHOUT FAIL.
THAT WILL BE MY REVENGE ON VANITAS!!!
WHEN I HEARD WHAT YOU SAID, IT MADE SENSE TO ME.
I THOUGHT THAT WAS WHY...
...YOU LOOKED LIKE THAT.
LIKE YOU'D GIVEN UP ON SOMETHING.

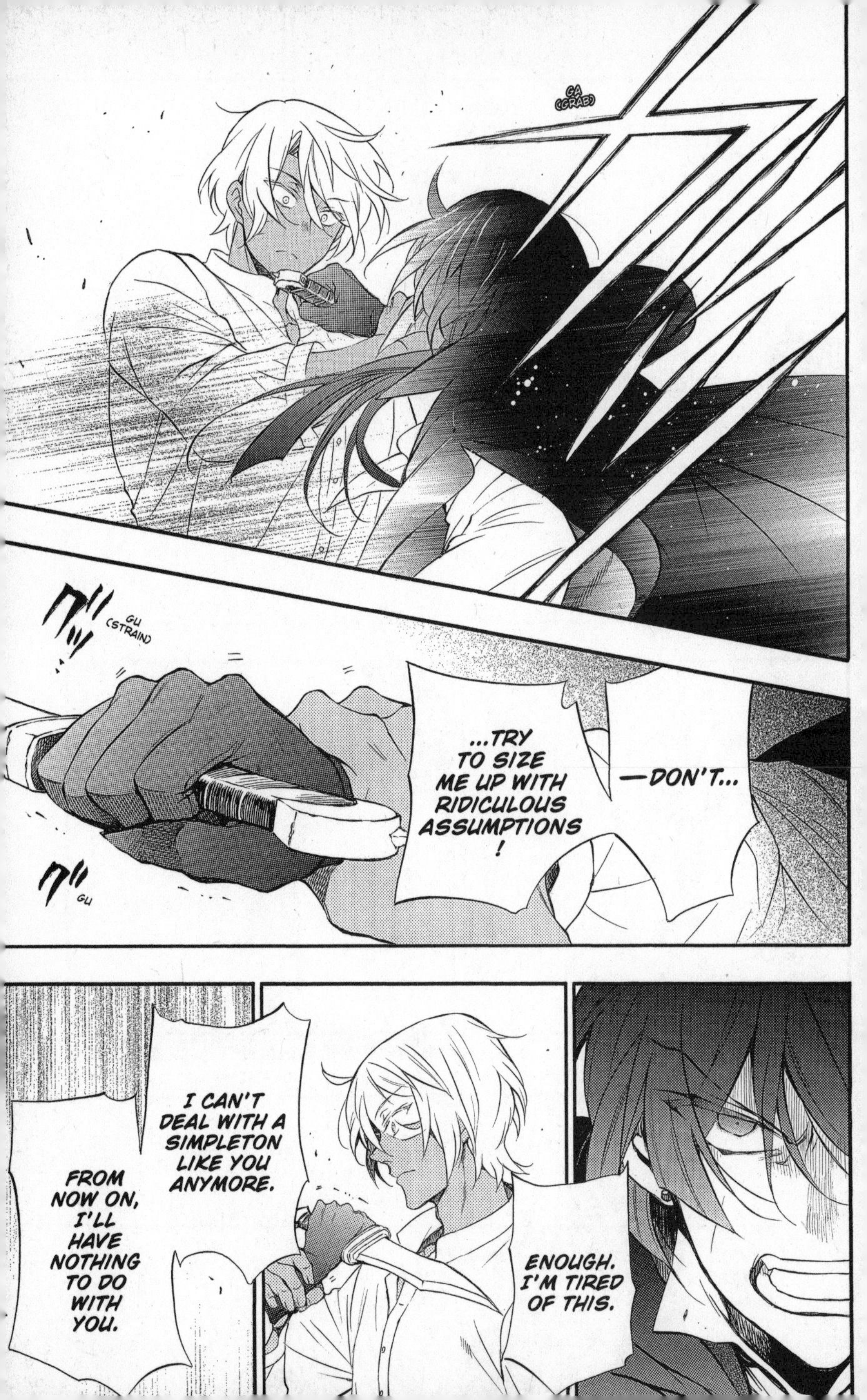
GA (GRAB)
—DON'T...
...TRY TO SIZE ME UP WITH RIDICULOUS ASSUMPTIONS!
GU (STRAIN)
GU
ENOUGH. I'M TIRED OF THIS.
I CAN'T DEAL WITH A SIMPLETON LIKE YOU ANYMORE.
FROM NOW ON, I'LL HAVE NOTHING TO DO WITH YOU.

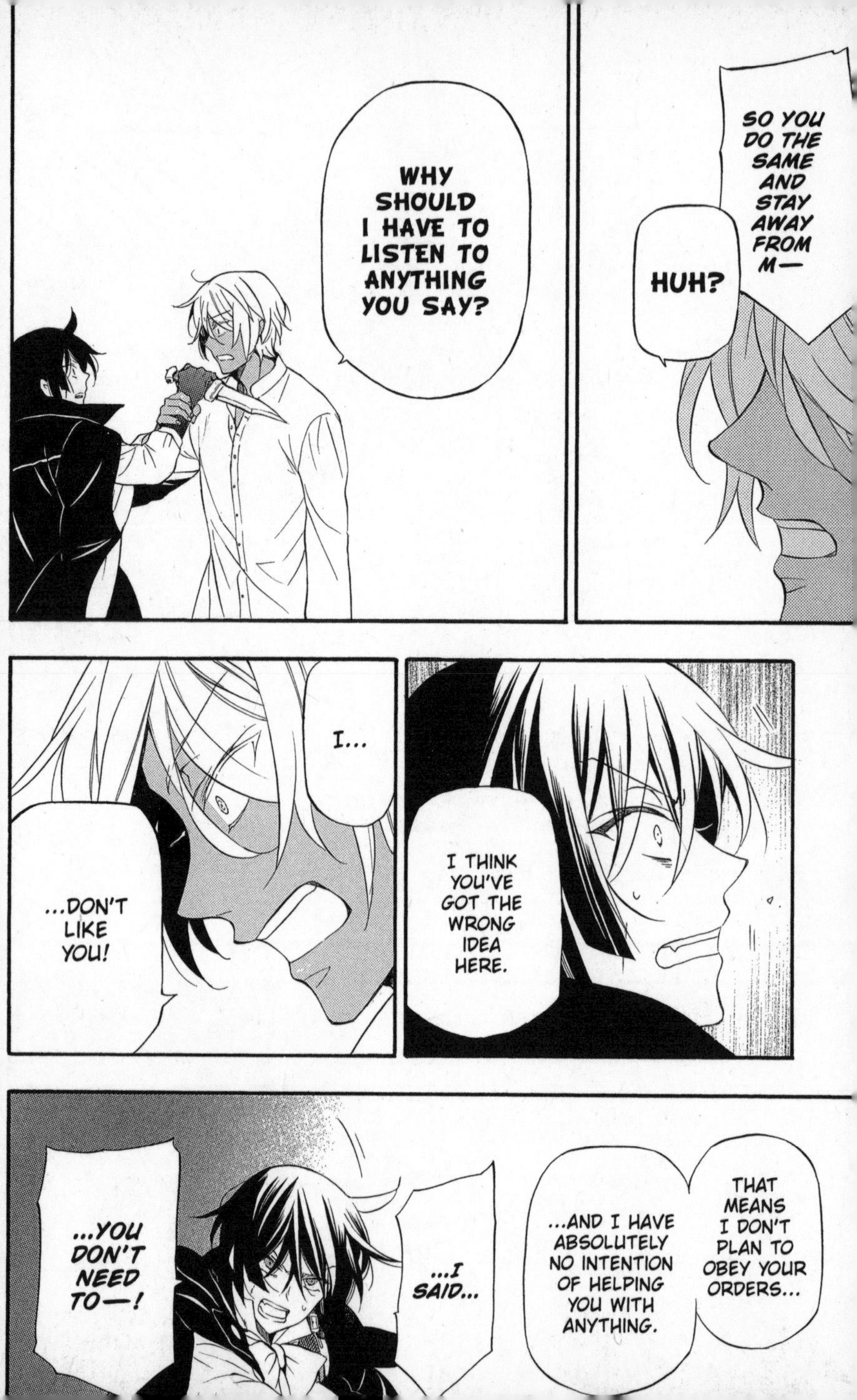
SO YOU DO THE SAME AND STAY AWAY FROM M—
HUH?
WHY SHOULD I HAVE TO LISTEN TO ANYTHING YOU SAY?
I THINK YOU'VE GOT THE WRONG IDEA HERE.
I...
...DON'T LIKE YOU!
THAT MEANS I DON'T PLAN TO OBEY YOUR ORDERS...
...AND I HAVE ABSOLUTELY NO INTENTION OF HELPING YOU WITH ANYTHING.
...I SAID...
...YOU DON'T NEED TO—!

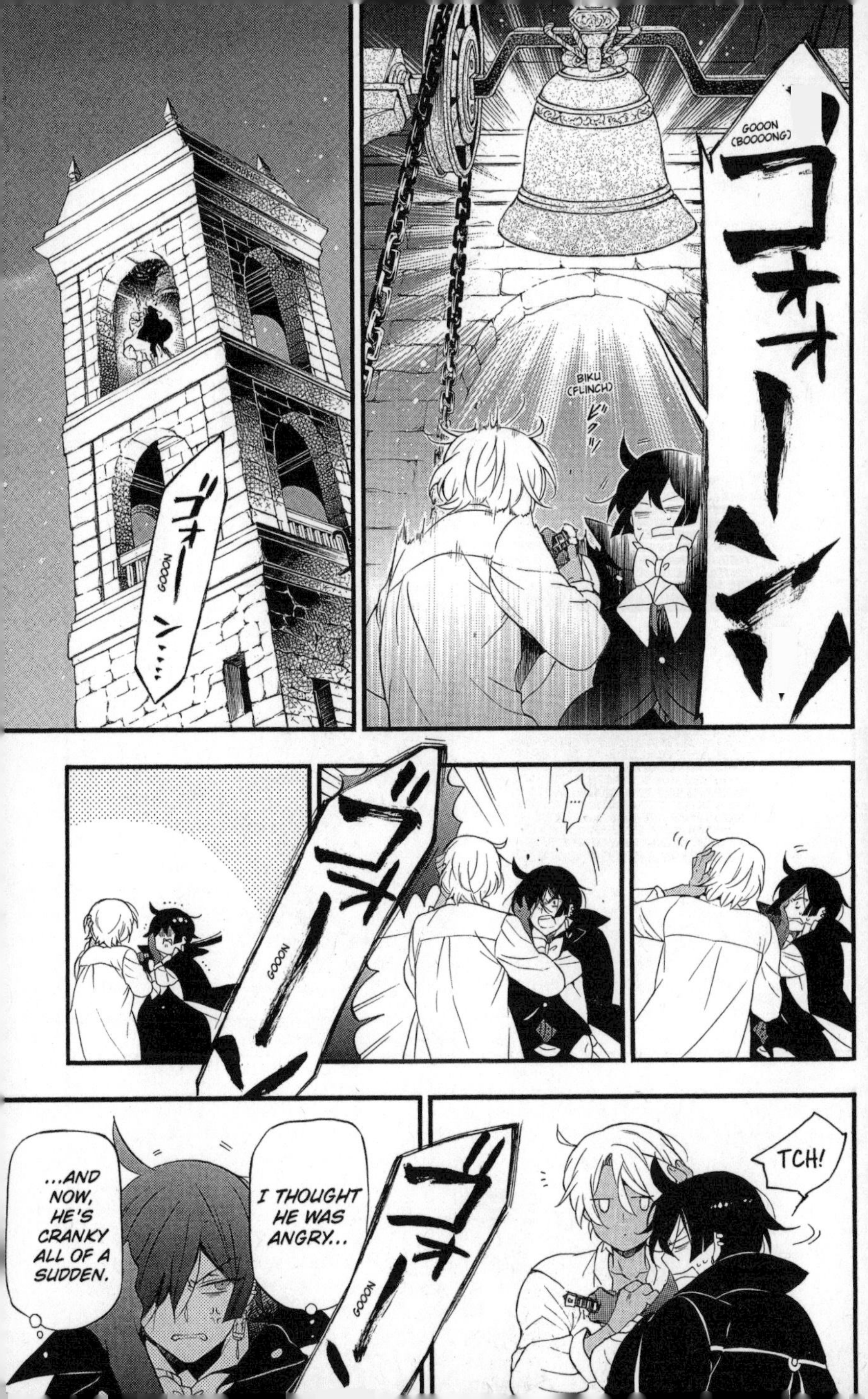

GOOON (BOOOONG)
BIKU (FLINCH)
ビクッ
GOOON
...
GOOON
TCH!
I THOUGHT HE WAS ANGRY...
...AND NOW, HE'S CRANKY ALL OF A SUDDEN.
GOOON

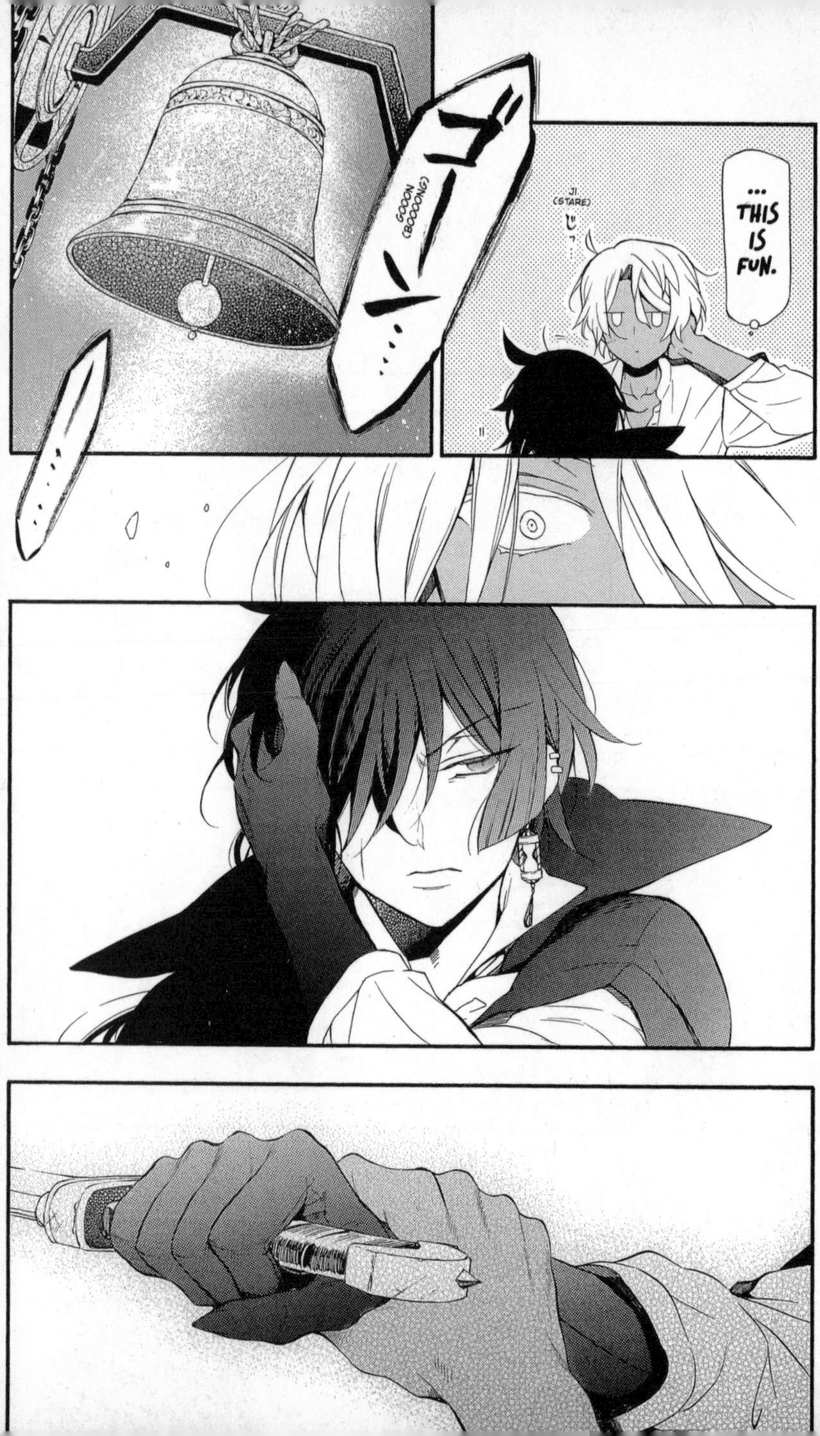

... THIS IS FUN.
JI (STARE)
じっ
GOOON (BOOOONG)
ゴーン……

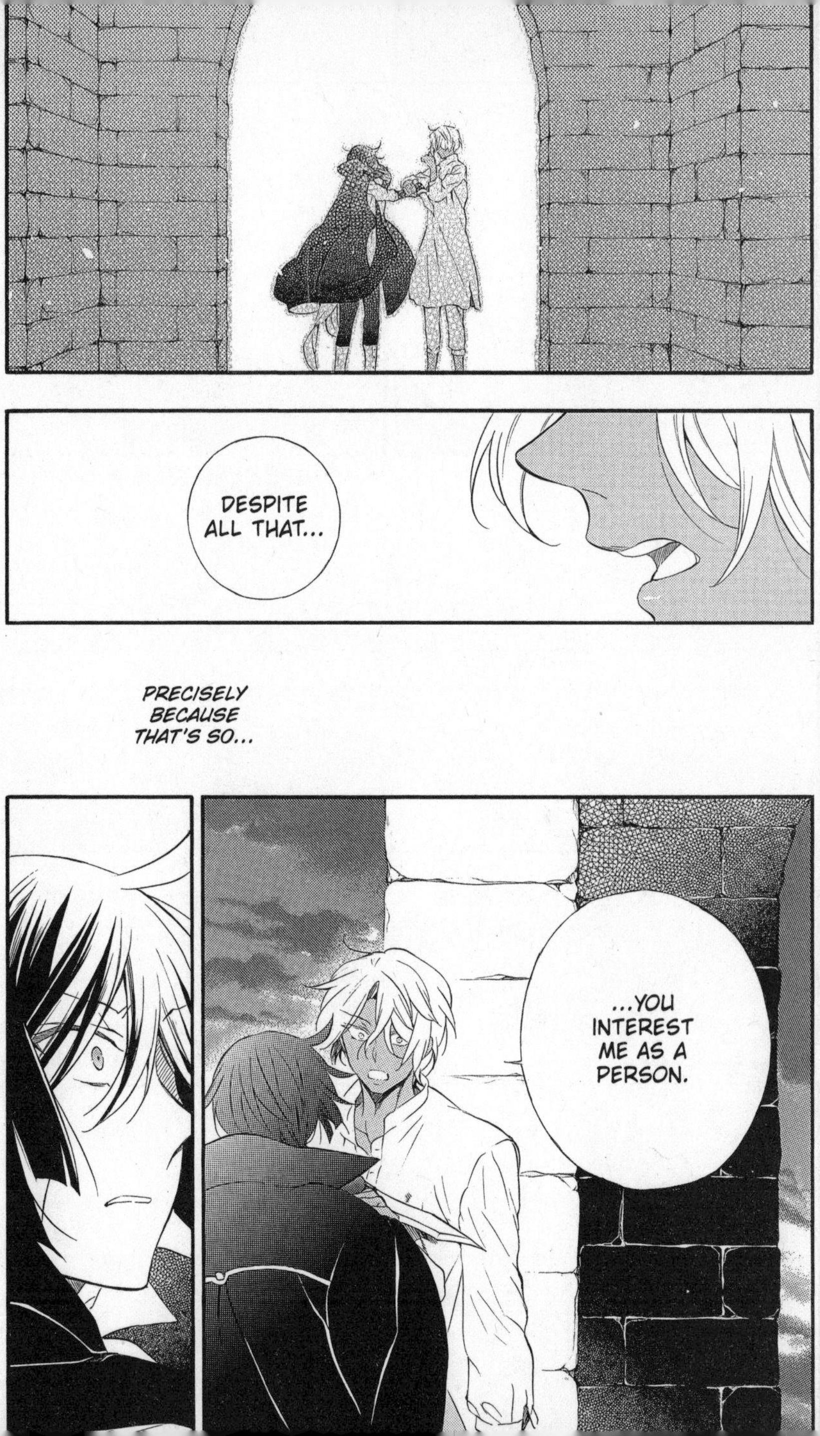
DESPITE ALL THAT...
PRECISELY BECAUSE THAT'S SO...
...YOU INTEREST ME AS A PERSON.

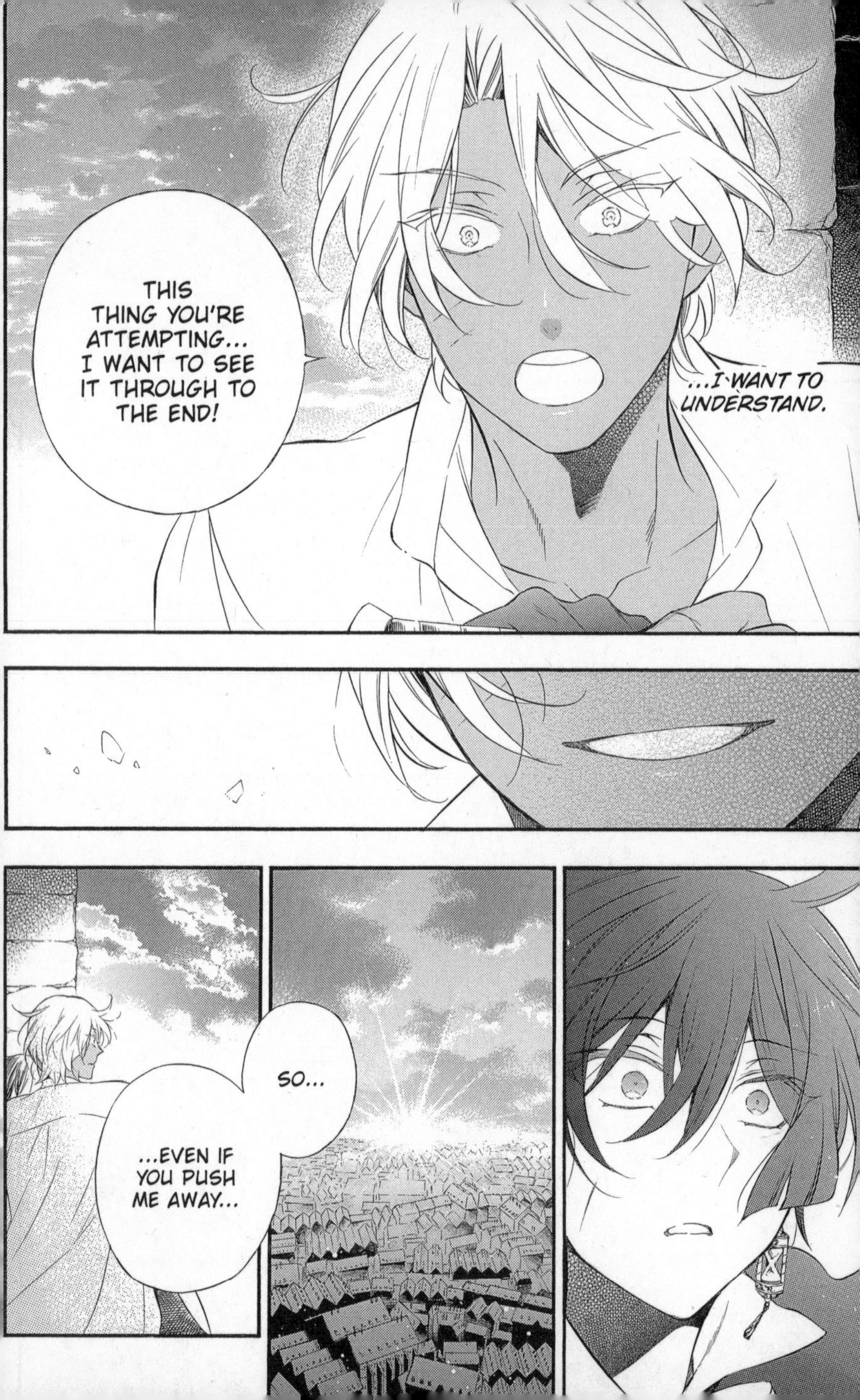
THIS THING YOU'RE ATTEMPTING... I WANT TO SEE IT THROUGH TO THE END!
...I WANT TO UNDERSTAND.
SO...
...EVEN IF YOU PUSH ME AWAY...

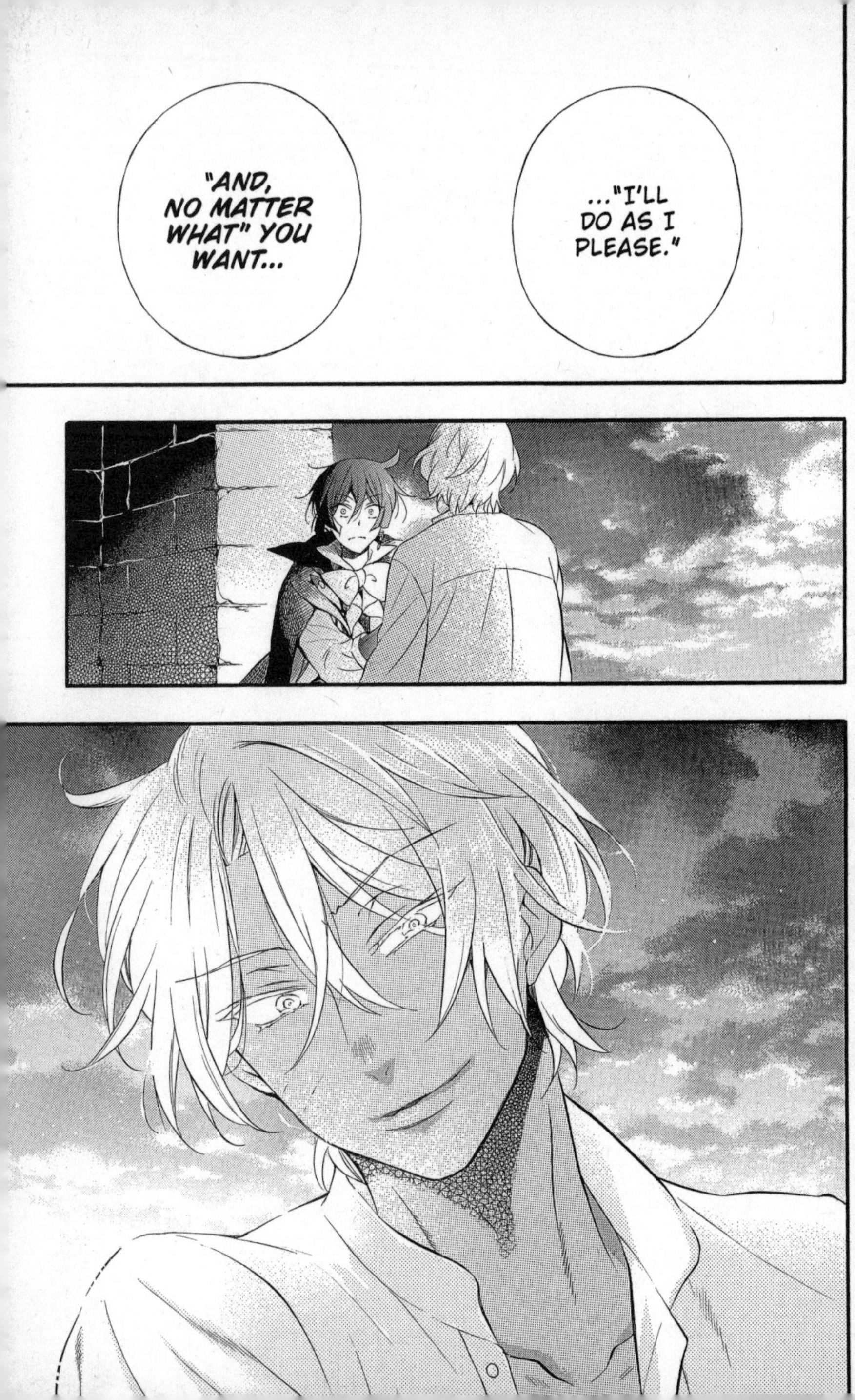
..."I'LL DO AS I PLEASE."
"AND, NO MATTER WHAT" YOU WANT...

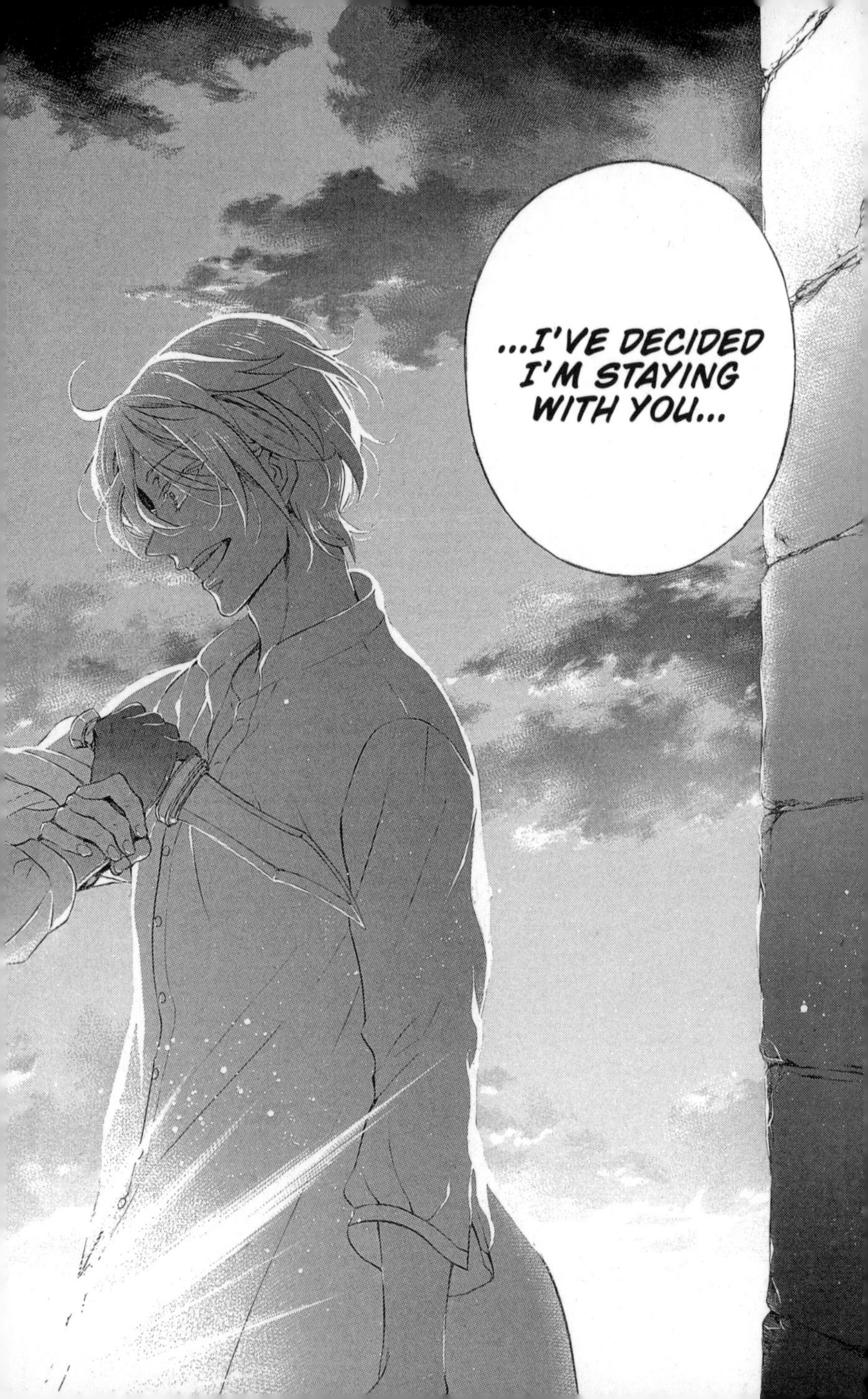
...I'VE DECIDED I'M STAYING WITH YOU...

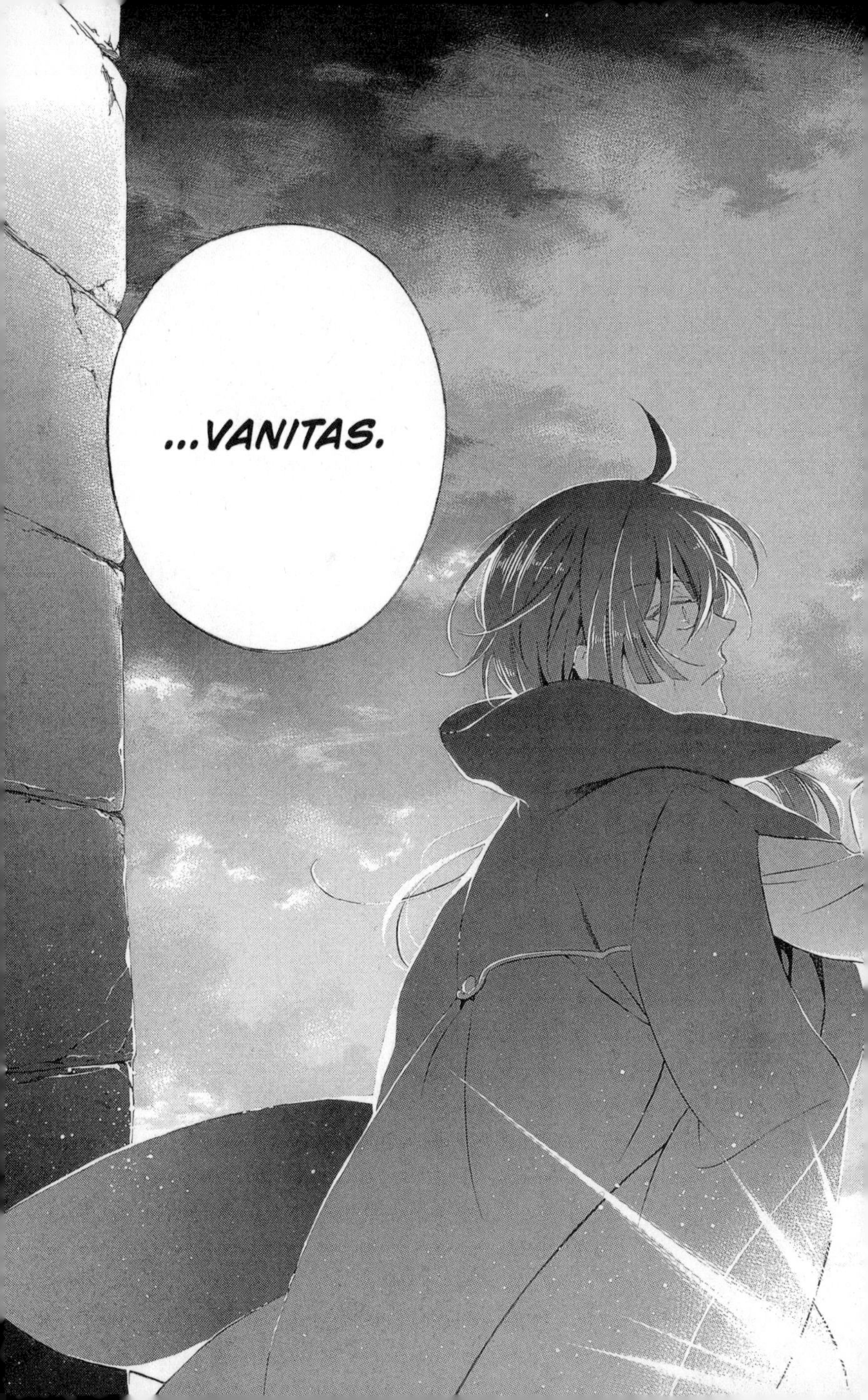
...VANITAS.

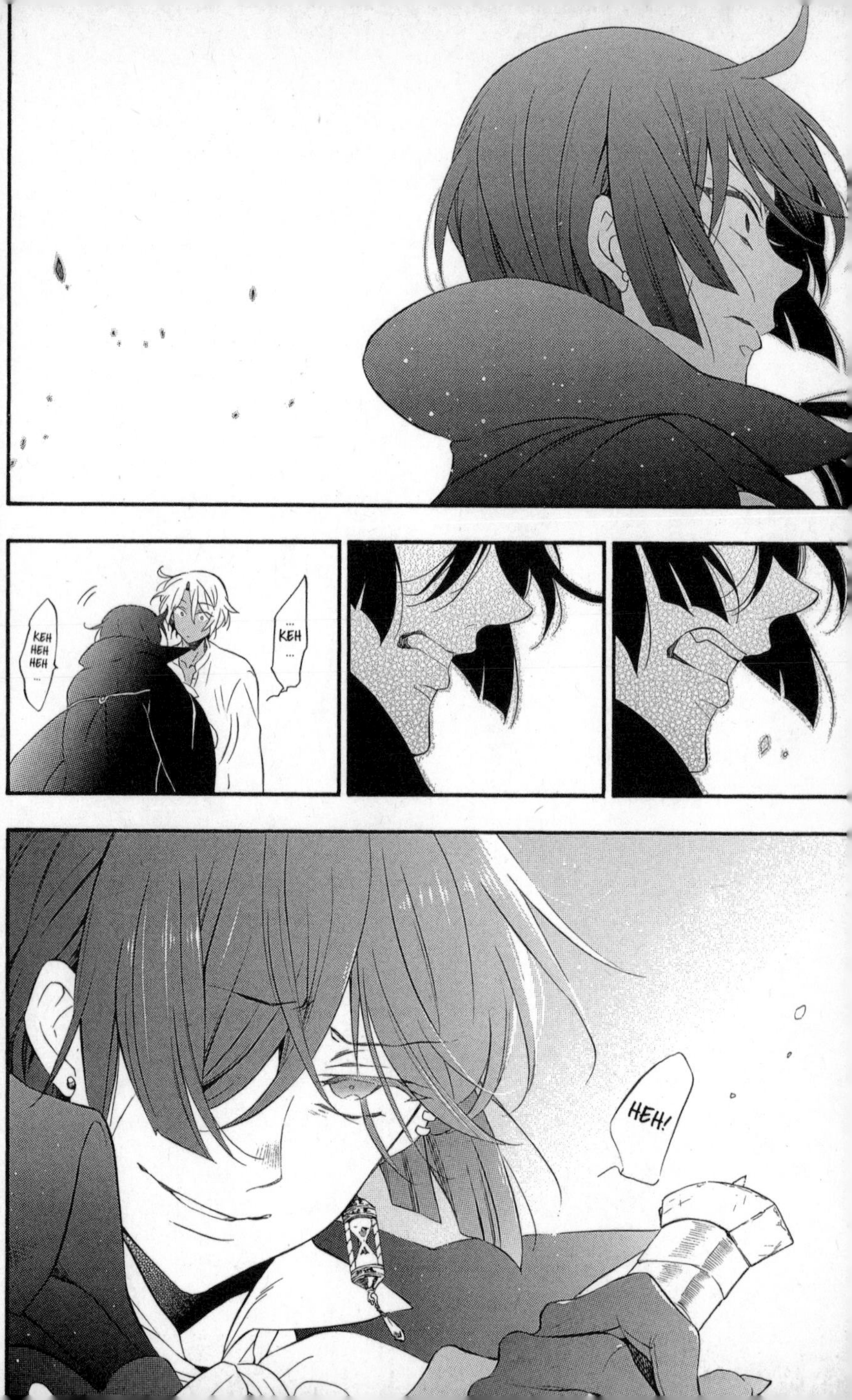
...KEH...
KEH HEH HEH...
HEH!

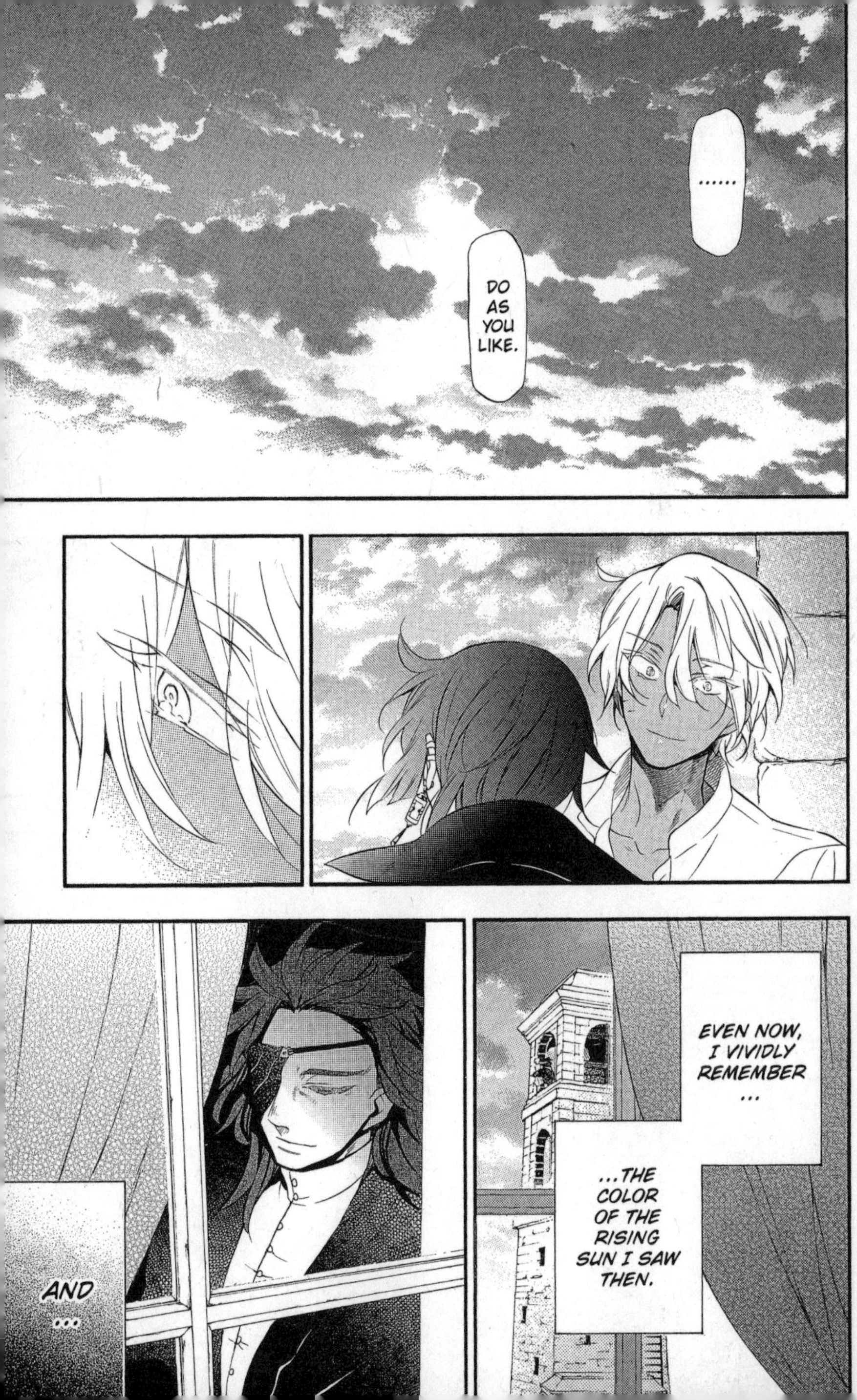
......
DO AS YOU LIKE.
EVEN NOW, I VIVIDLY REMEMBER ...
...THE COLOR OF THE RISING SUN I SAW THEN.
AND ...

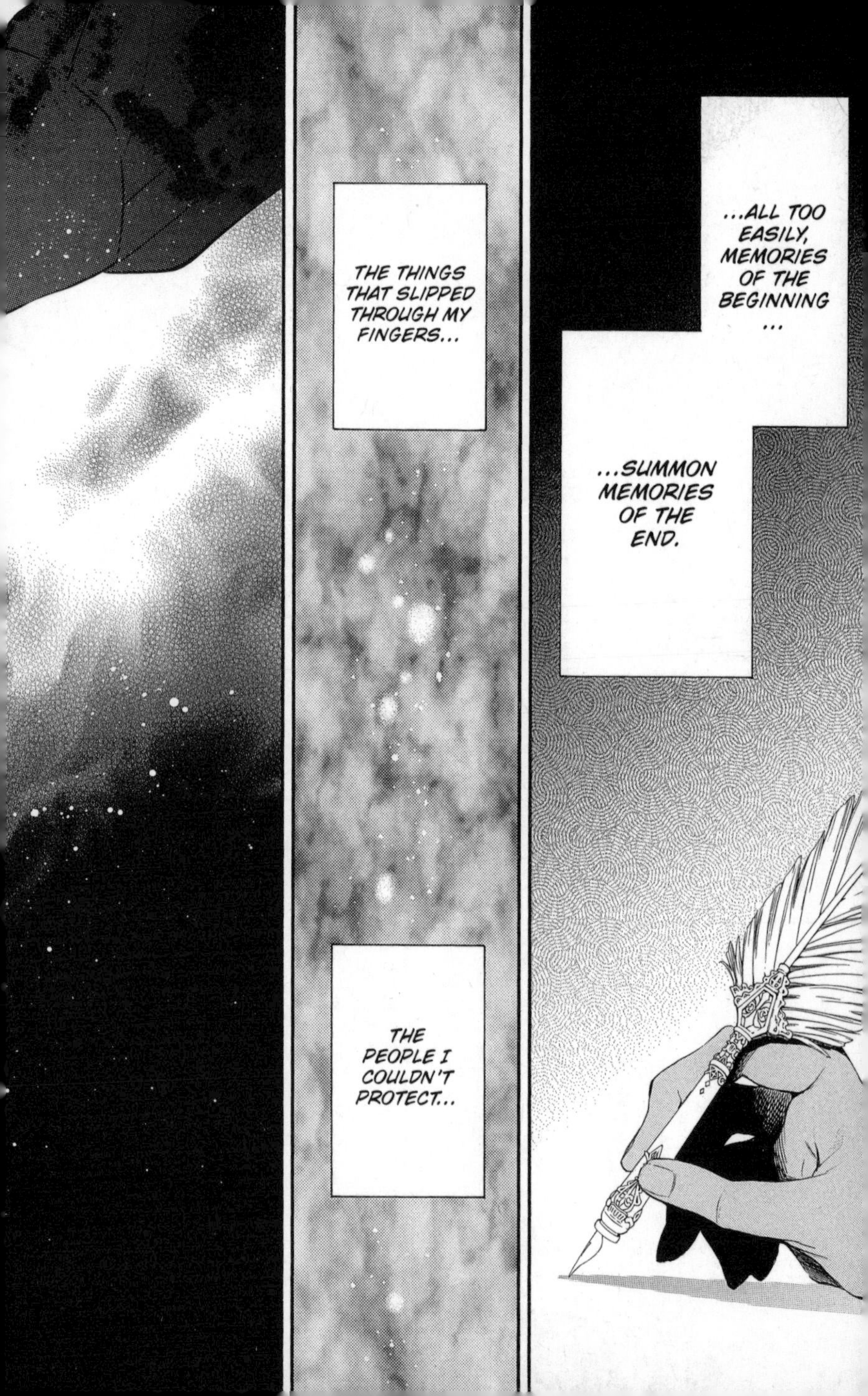
...ALL TOO EASILY, MEMORIES OF THE BEGINNING ...
...SUMMON MEMORIES OF THE END.
THE THINGS THAT SLIPPED THROUGH MY FINGERS...
THE PEOPLE I COULDN'T PROTECT...

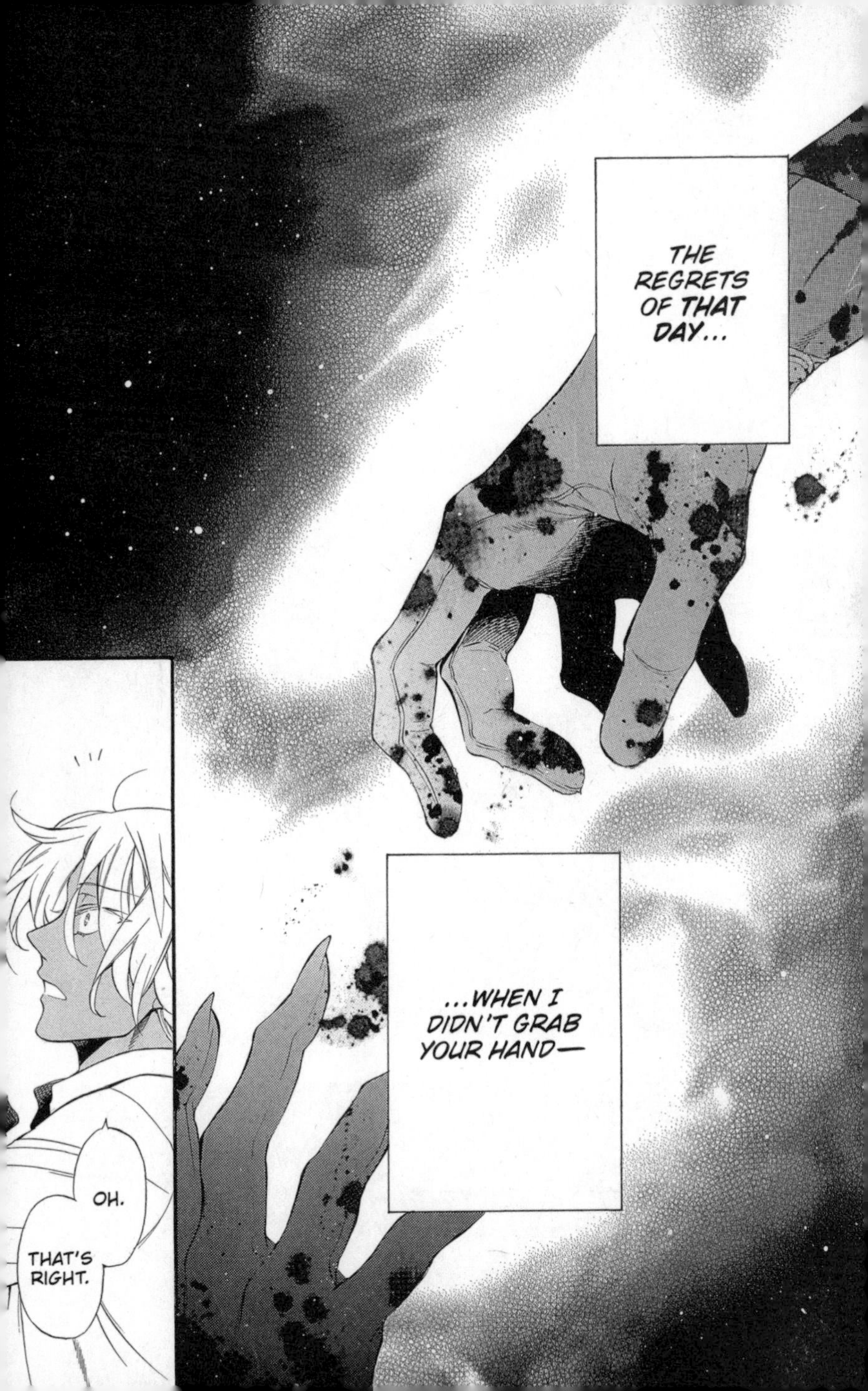
THE REGRETS OF THAT DAY...
...WHEN I DIDN'T GRAB YOUR HAND—
OH.
THAT'S RIGHT.

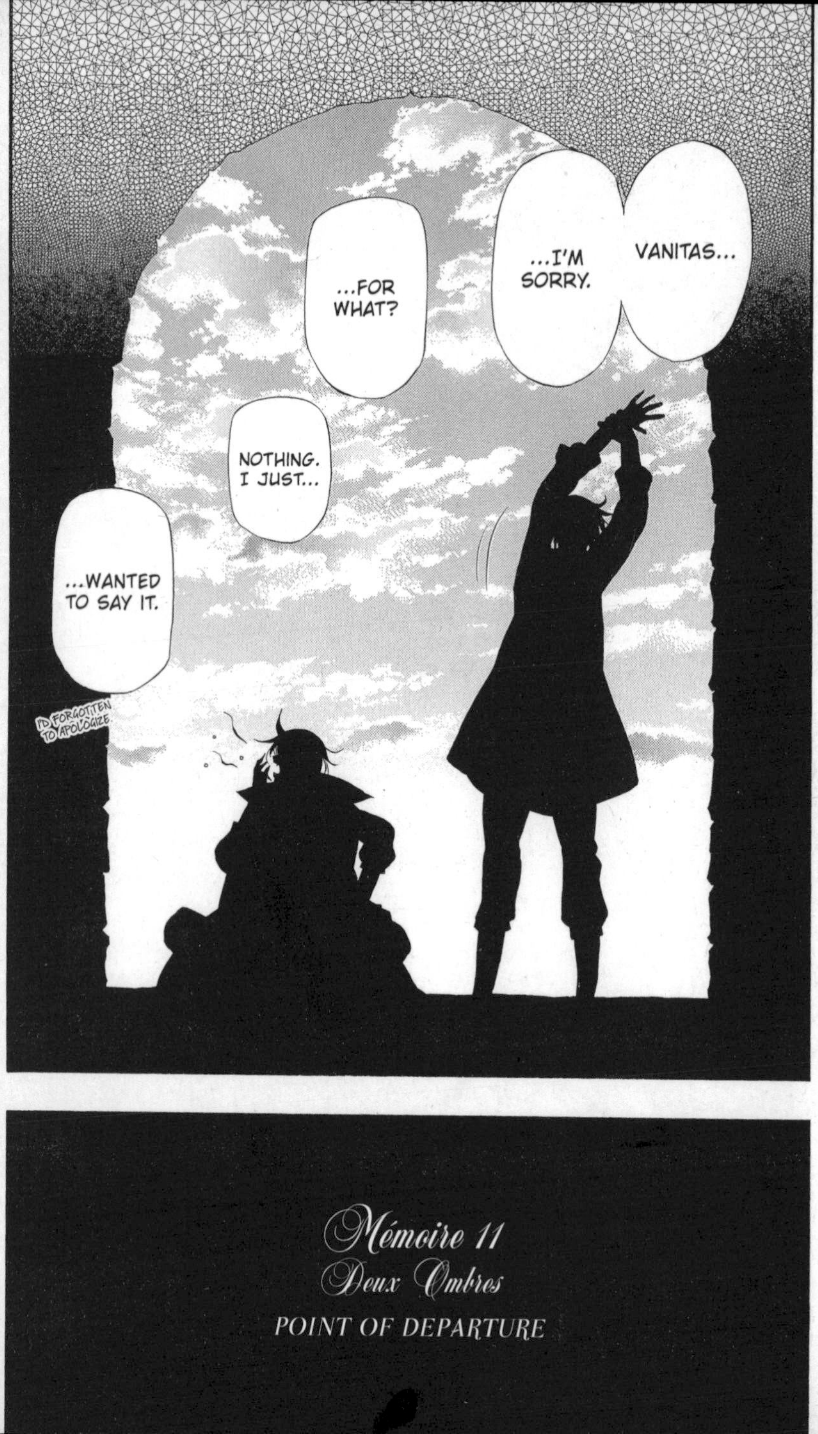
VANITAS...
...I'M SORRY.
...FOR WHAT?
NOTHING. I JUST...
...WANTED TO SAY IT.
I'D FORGOTTEN TO APOLOGIZE.

Mémoire 11

Deux Ombres

POINT OF DEPARTURE

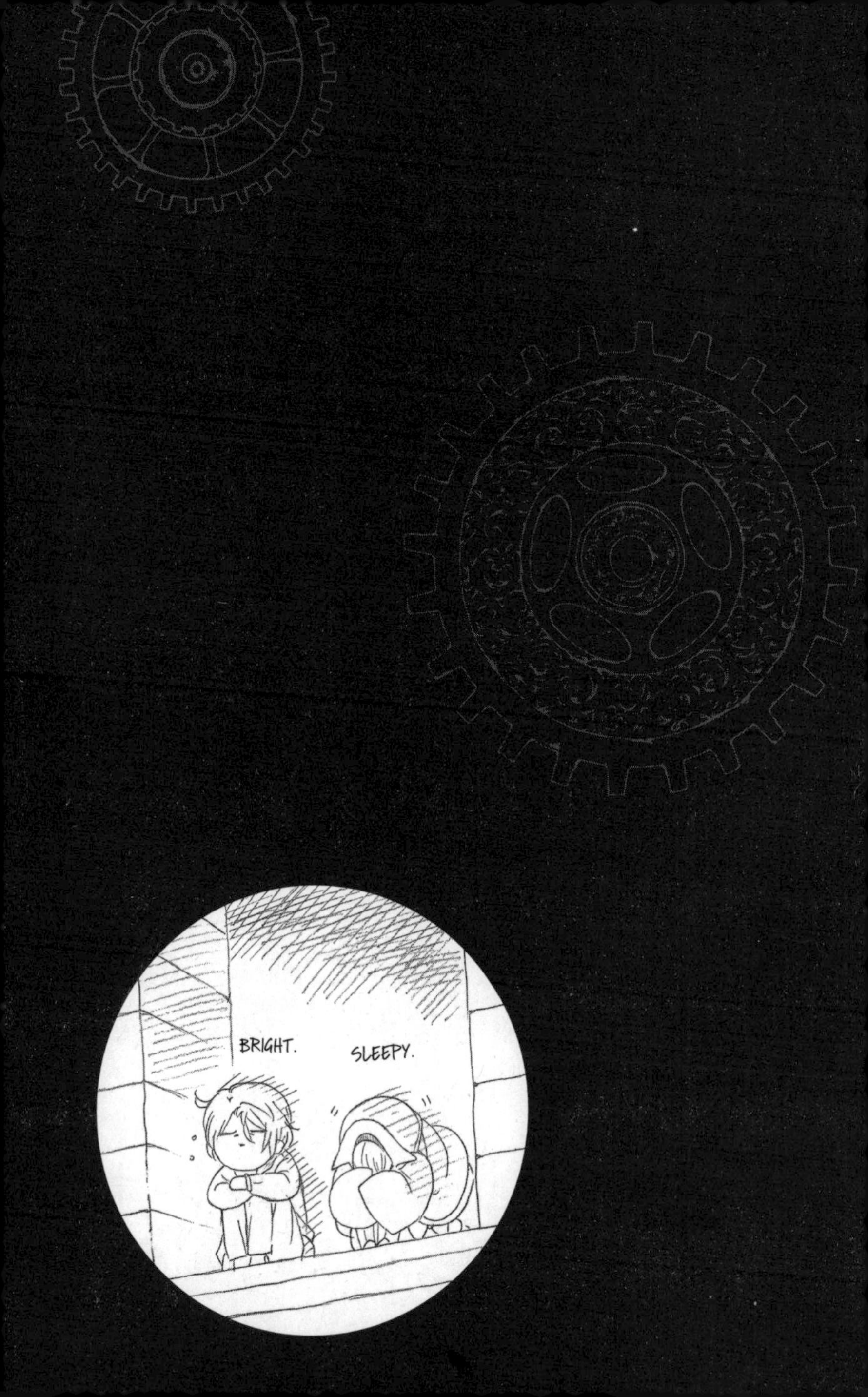
SLEEPY.
BRIGHT.

Les Mémoires de Vanitas

THE CASE STUDY OF
VANITAS

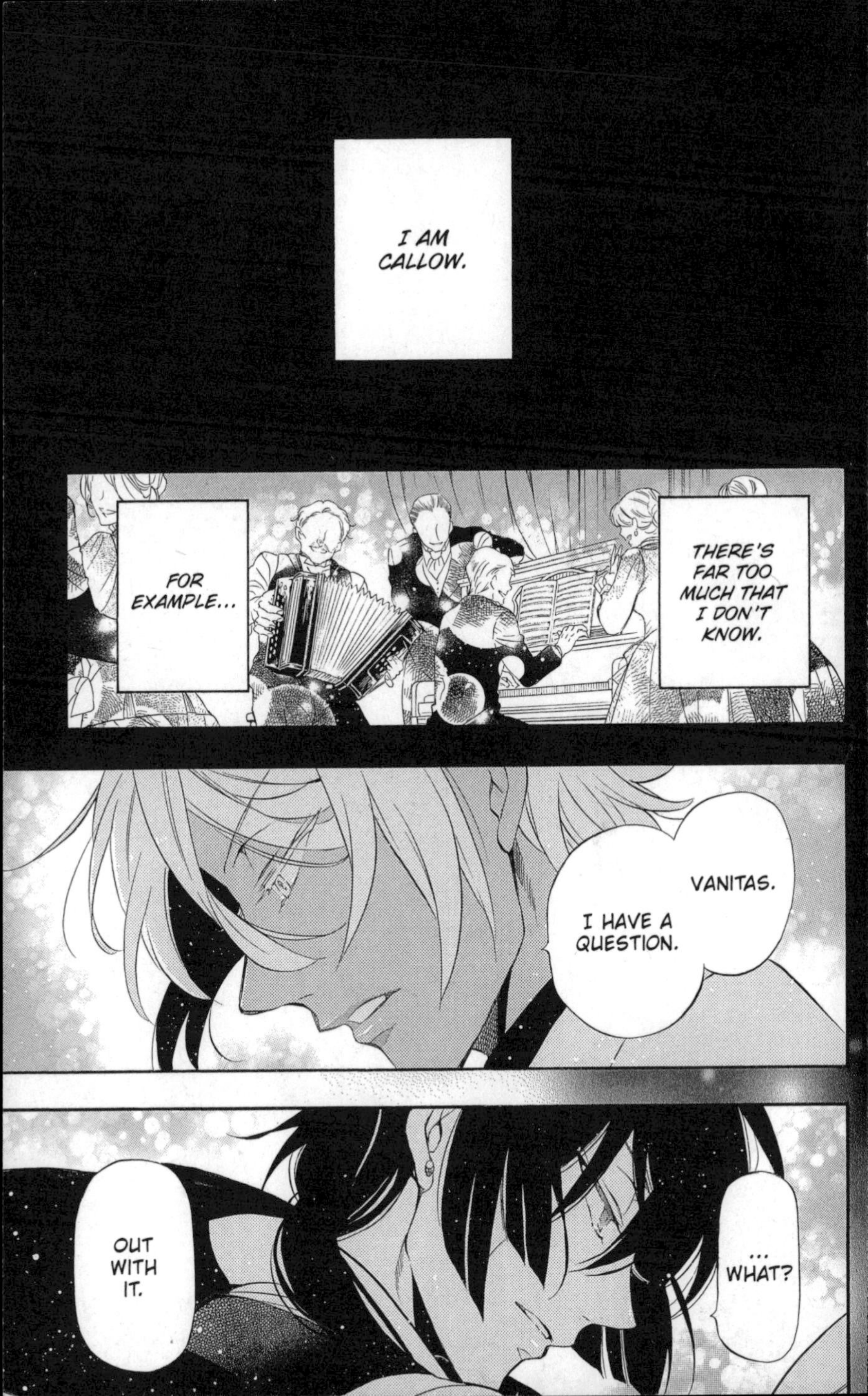
I AM CALLOW.
THERE'S FAR TOO MUCH THAT I DON'T KNOW.
FOR EXAMPLE...
VANITAS. I HAVE A QUESTION.
...WHAT?
OUT WITH IT.

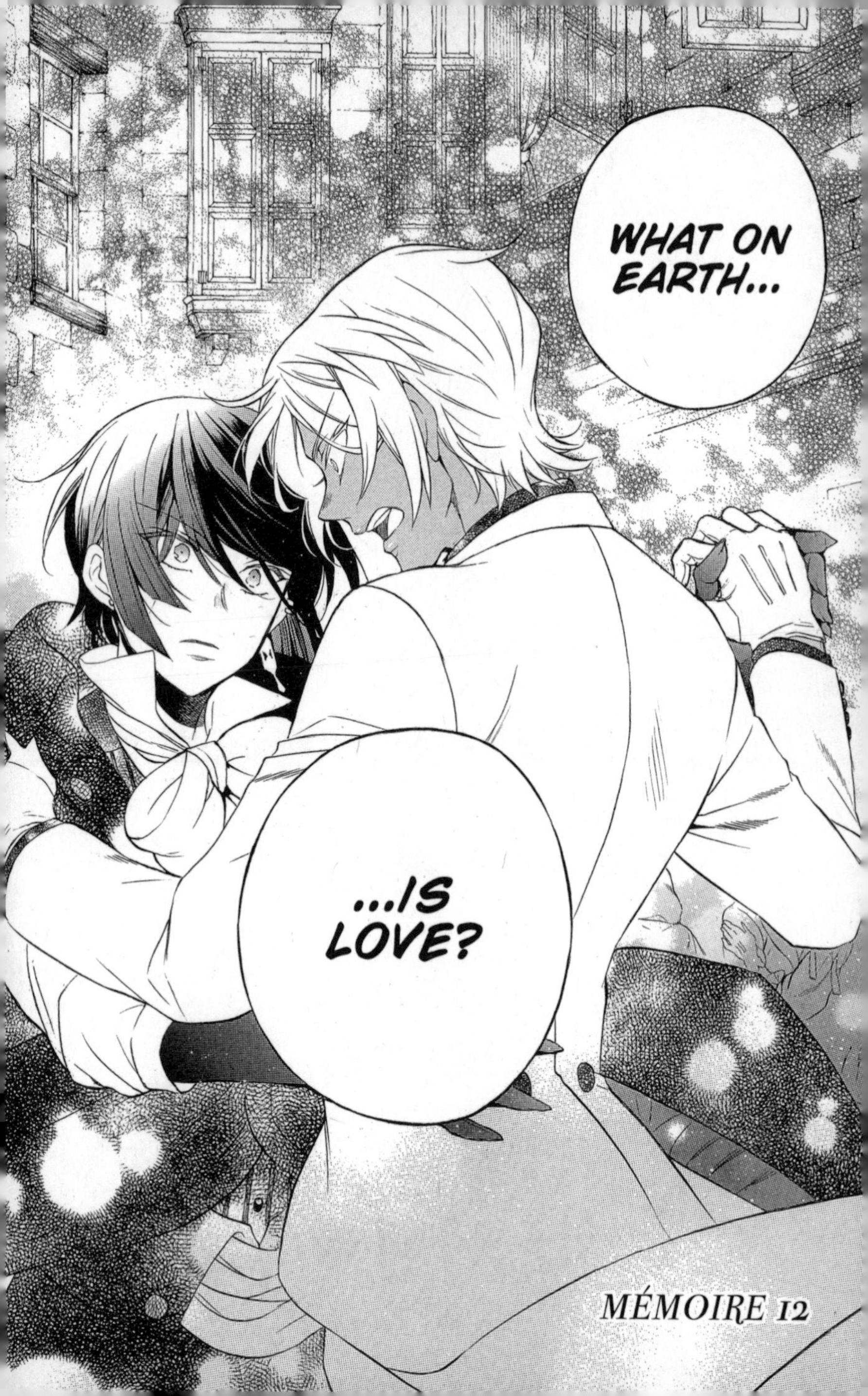
WHAT ON EARTH...
...IS LOVE?
MÉMOIRE 12

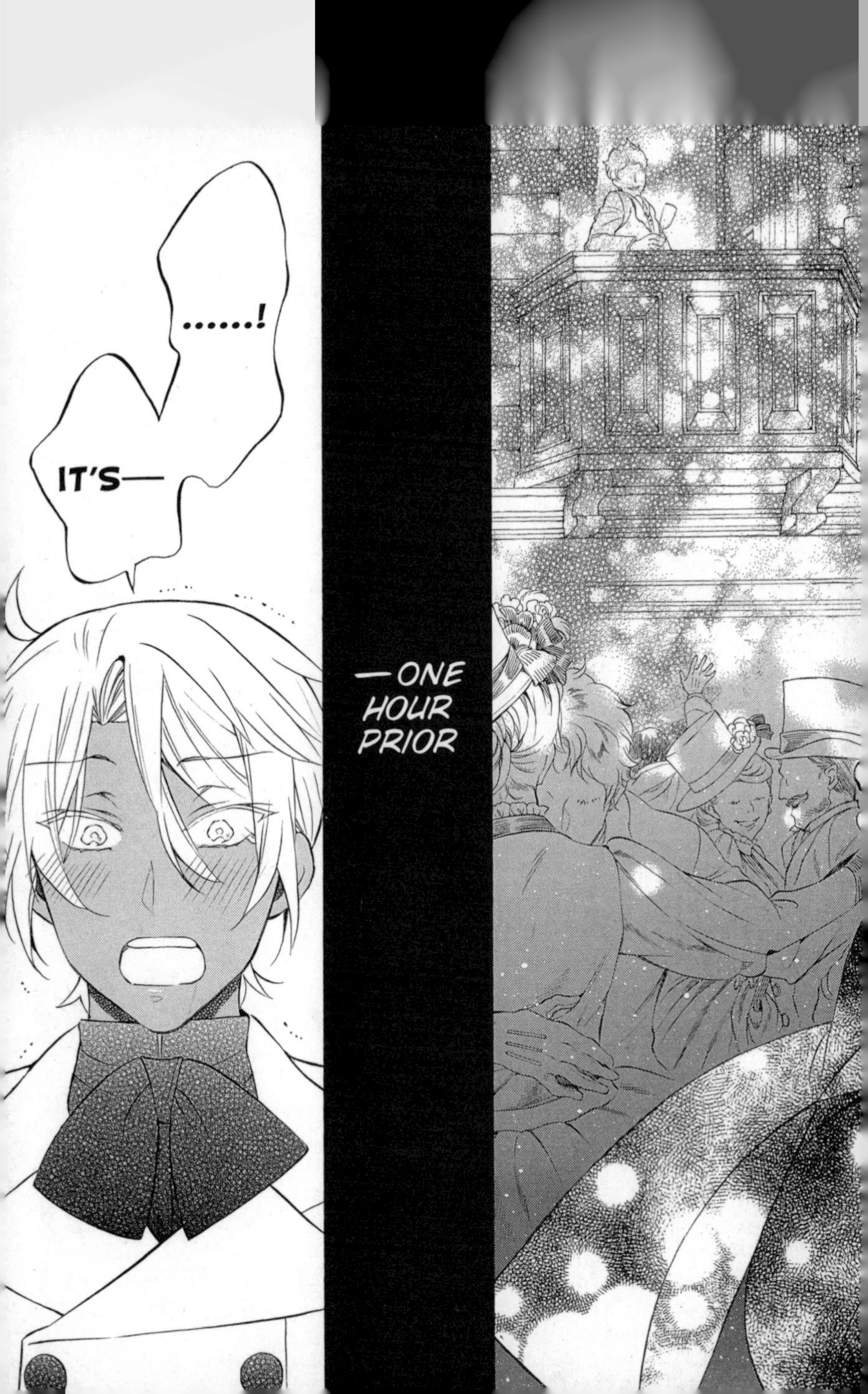
—ONE HOUR PRIOR
IT'S—
......!

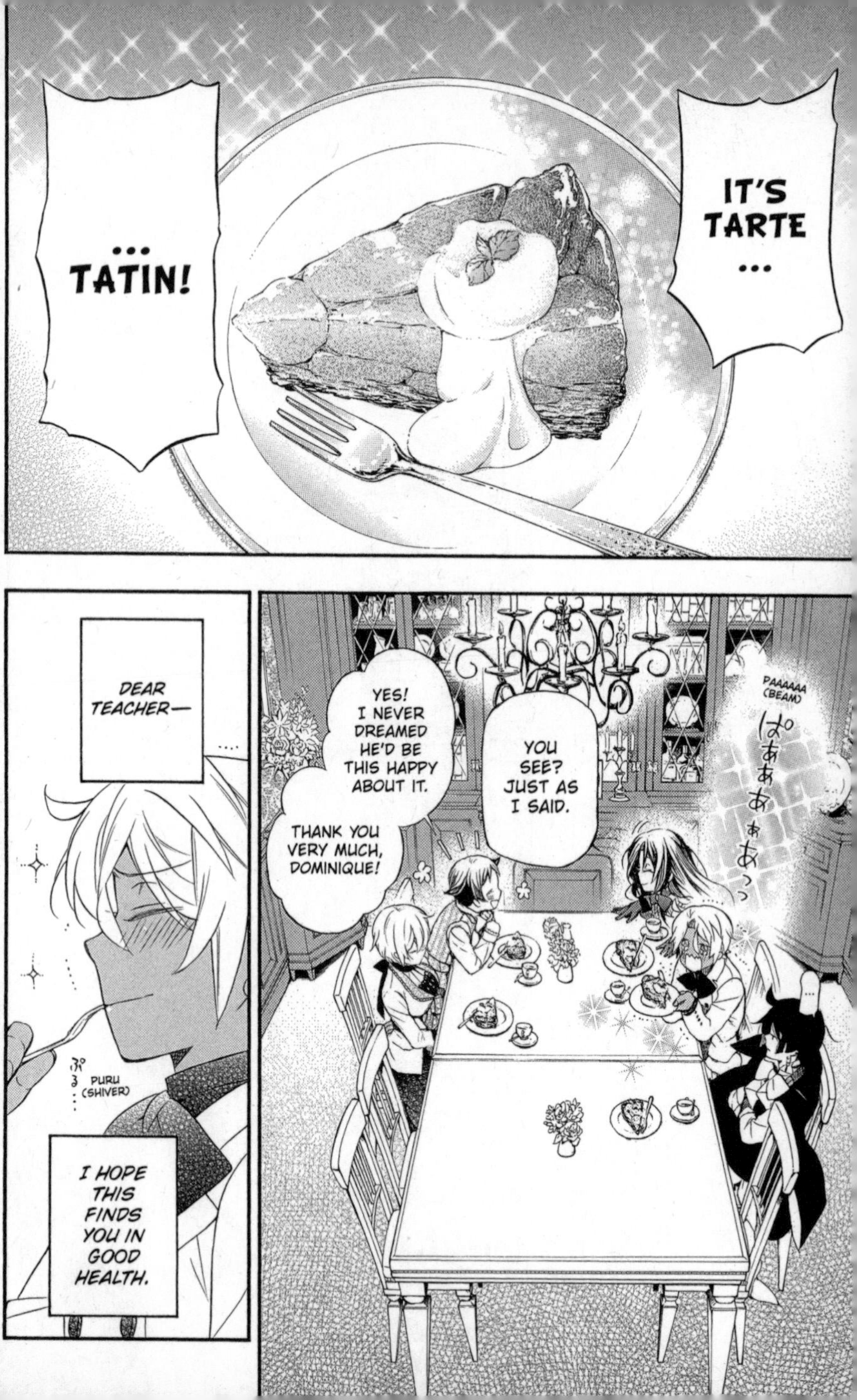
IT'S TARTE ...
... TATIN!
PAAAAAA (BEAM)
ぱあああぁあっ
YOU SEE? JUST AS I SAID.
YES! I NEVER DREAMED HE'D BE THIS HAPPY ABOUT IT.
THANK YOU VERY MUCH, DOMINIQUE!
DEAR TEACHER—
....
ぷる...
PURU (SHIVER)
I HOPE THIS FINDS YOU IN GOOD HEALTH.

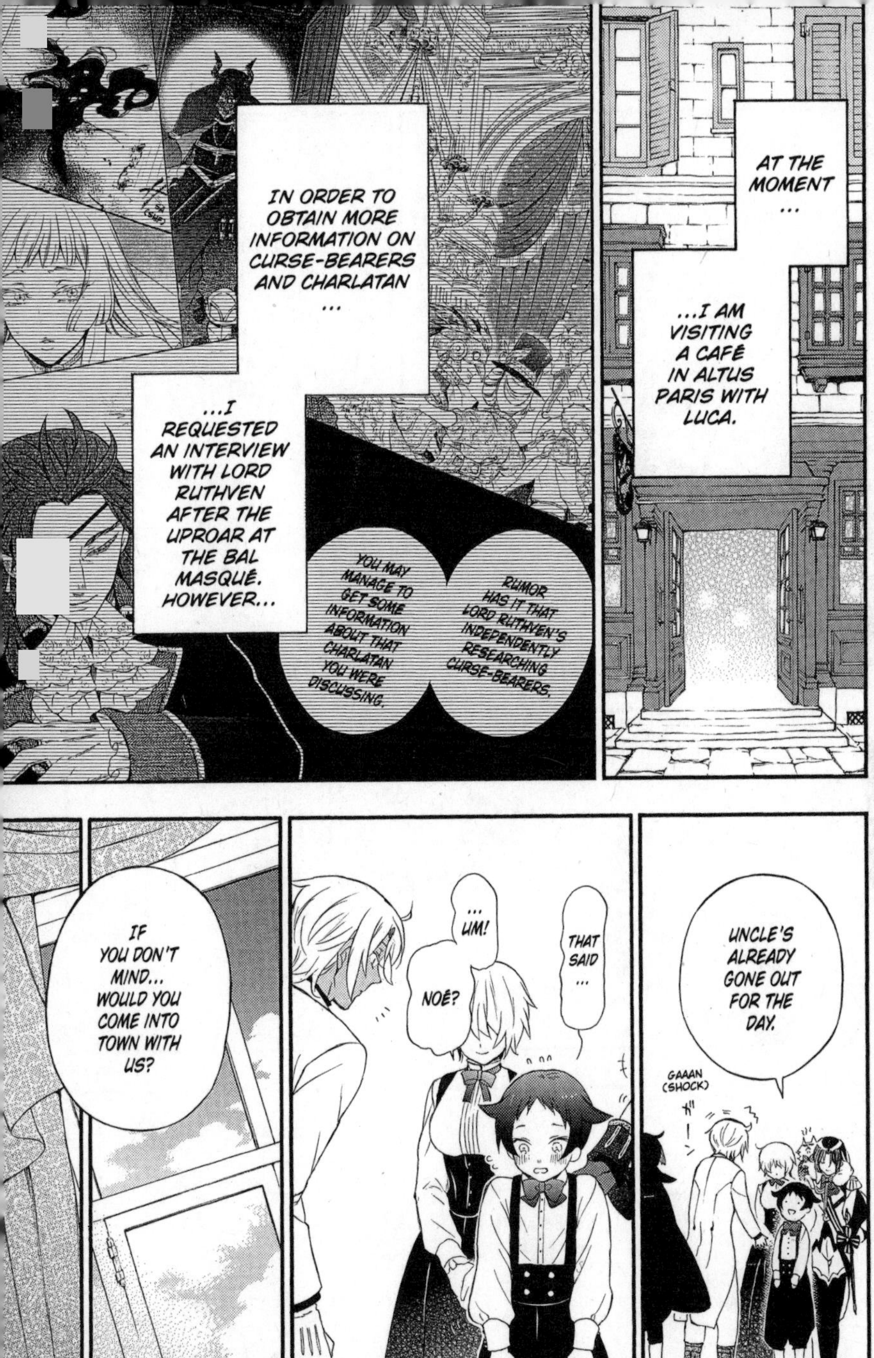
AT THE MOMENT ...
...I AM VISITING A CAFÉ IN ALTUS PARIS WITH LUCA.
IN ORDER TO OBTAIN MORE INFORMATION ON CURSE-BEARERS AND CHARLATAN ...
...I REQUESTED AN INTERVIEW WITH LORD RUTHVEN AFTER THE UPROAR AT THE BAL MASQUÉ. HOWEVER...
RUMOR HAS IT THAT LORD RUTHVEN'S INDEPENDENTLY RESEARCHING CURSE-BEARERS.
YOU MAY MANAGE TO GET SOME INFORMATION ABOUT THAT CHARLATAN YOU WERE DISCUSSING.
UNCLE'S ALREADY GONE OUT FOR THE DAY.
GAAAN (SHOCK)
THAT SAID ...
... UM!
NOÉ?
IF YOU DON'T MIND... WOULD YOU COME INTO TOWN WITH US?

SFX: MOGU (CHEW) MOGU

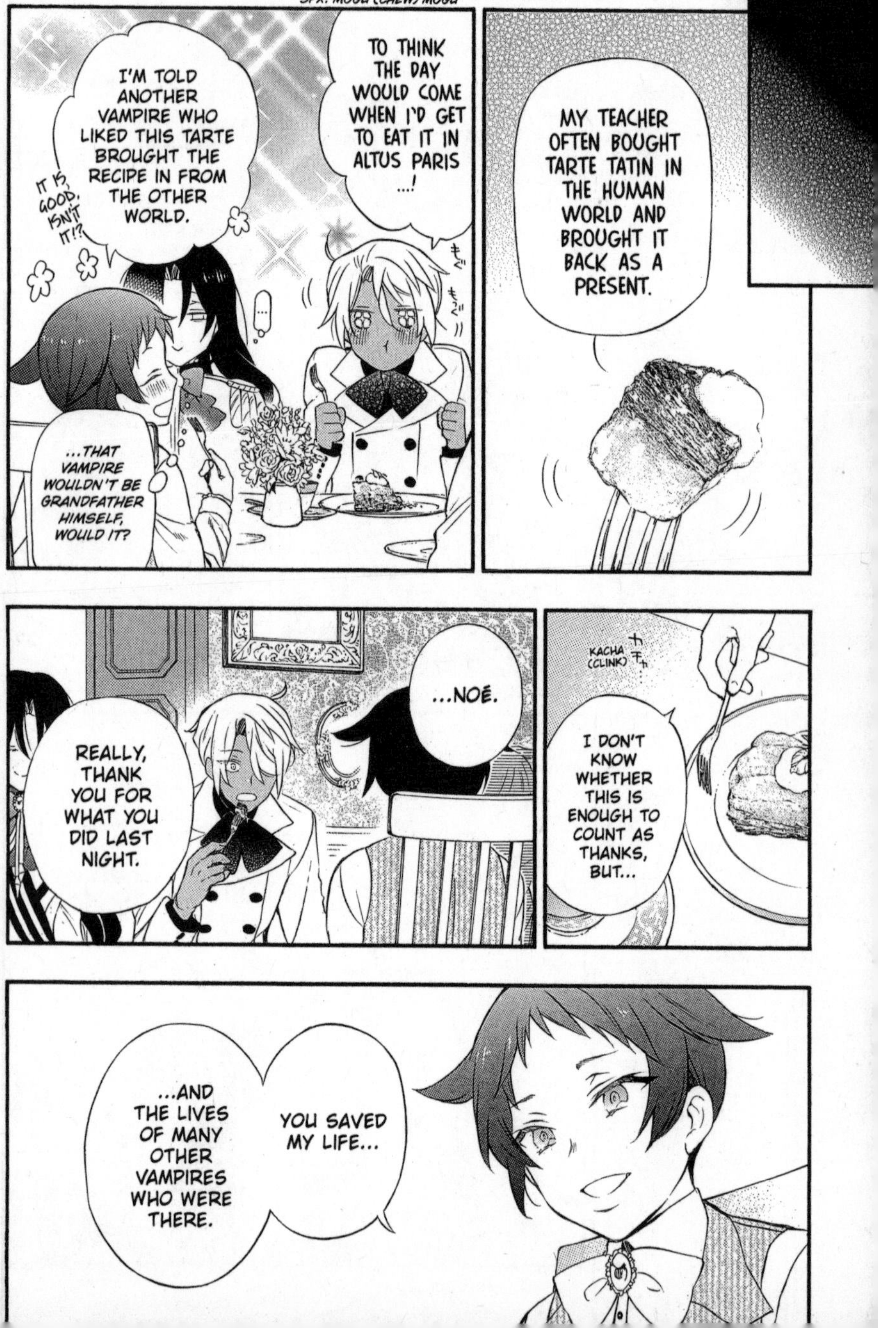
MY TEACHER OFTEN BOUGHT TARTE TATIN IN THE HUMAN WORLD AND BROUGHT IT BACK AS A PRESENT.
TO THINK THE DAY WOULD COME WHEN I'D GET TO EAT IT IN ALTUS PARIS ...!
もぐ もぐ
I'M TOLD ANOTHER VAMPIRE WHO LIKED THIS TARTE BROUGHT THE RECIPE IN FROM THE OTHER WORLD.
IT IS, GOOD, ISN'T IT!?
...
...THAT VAMPIRE WOULDN'T BE GRANDFATHER HIMSELF, WOULD IT?
KACHA (CLINK) カチャ
I DON'T KNOW WHETHER THIS IS ENOUGH TO COUNT AS THANKS, BUT...
...NOÉ.
REALLY, THANK YOU FOR WHAT YOU DID LAST NIGHT.
YOU SAVED MY LIFE...
...AND THE LIVES OF MANY OTHER VAMPIRES WHO WERE THERE.

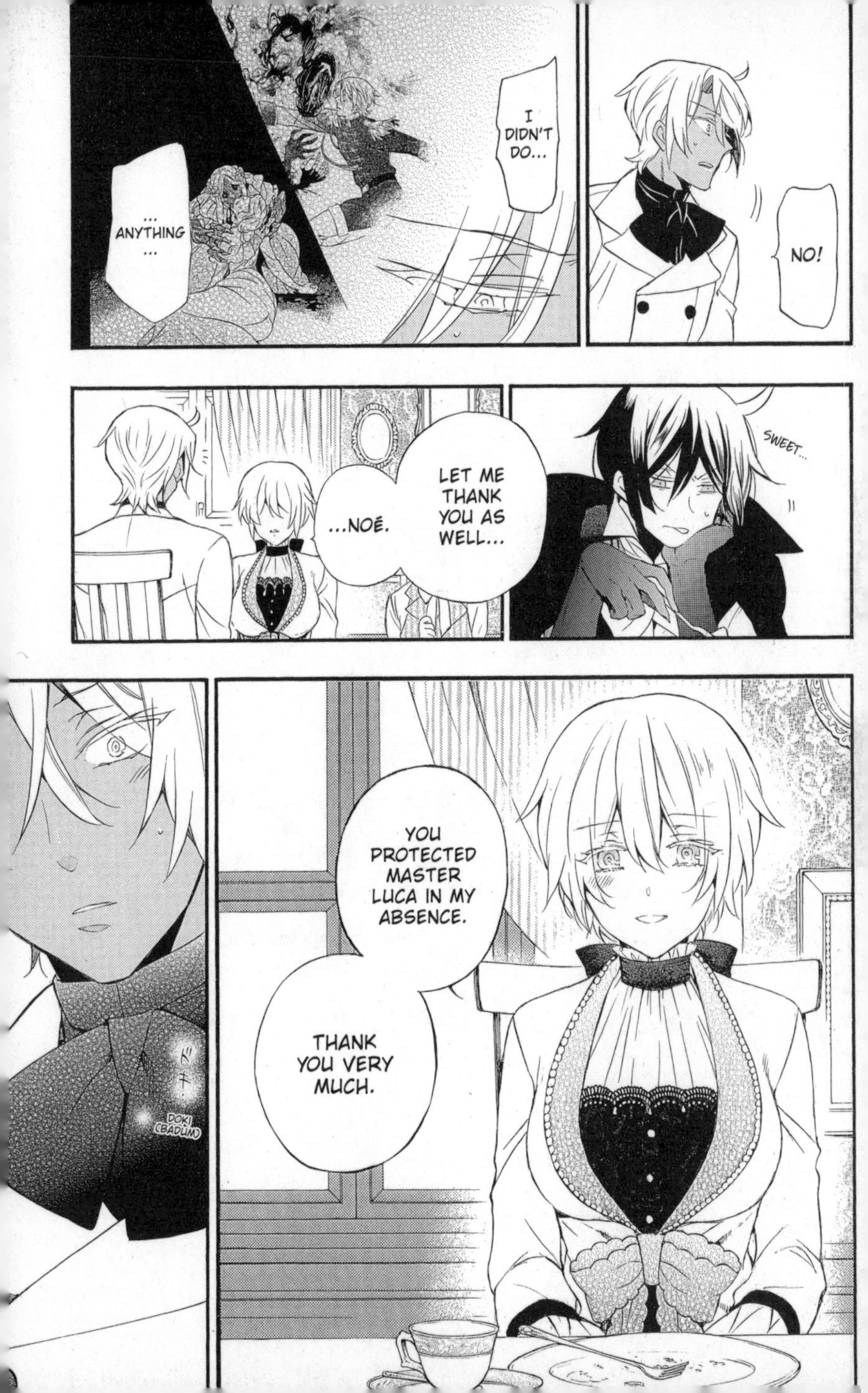
NO!
I DIDN'T DO...
... ANYTHING ...
SWEET...
LET ME THANK YOU AS WELL...
...NOÉ.
YOU PROTECTED MASTER LUCA IN MY ABSENCE.
THANK YOU VERY MUCH.
ドキ
DOKI (BADUM)

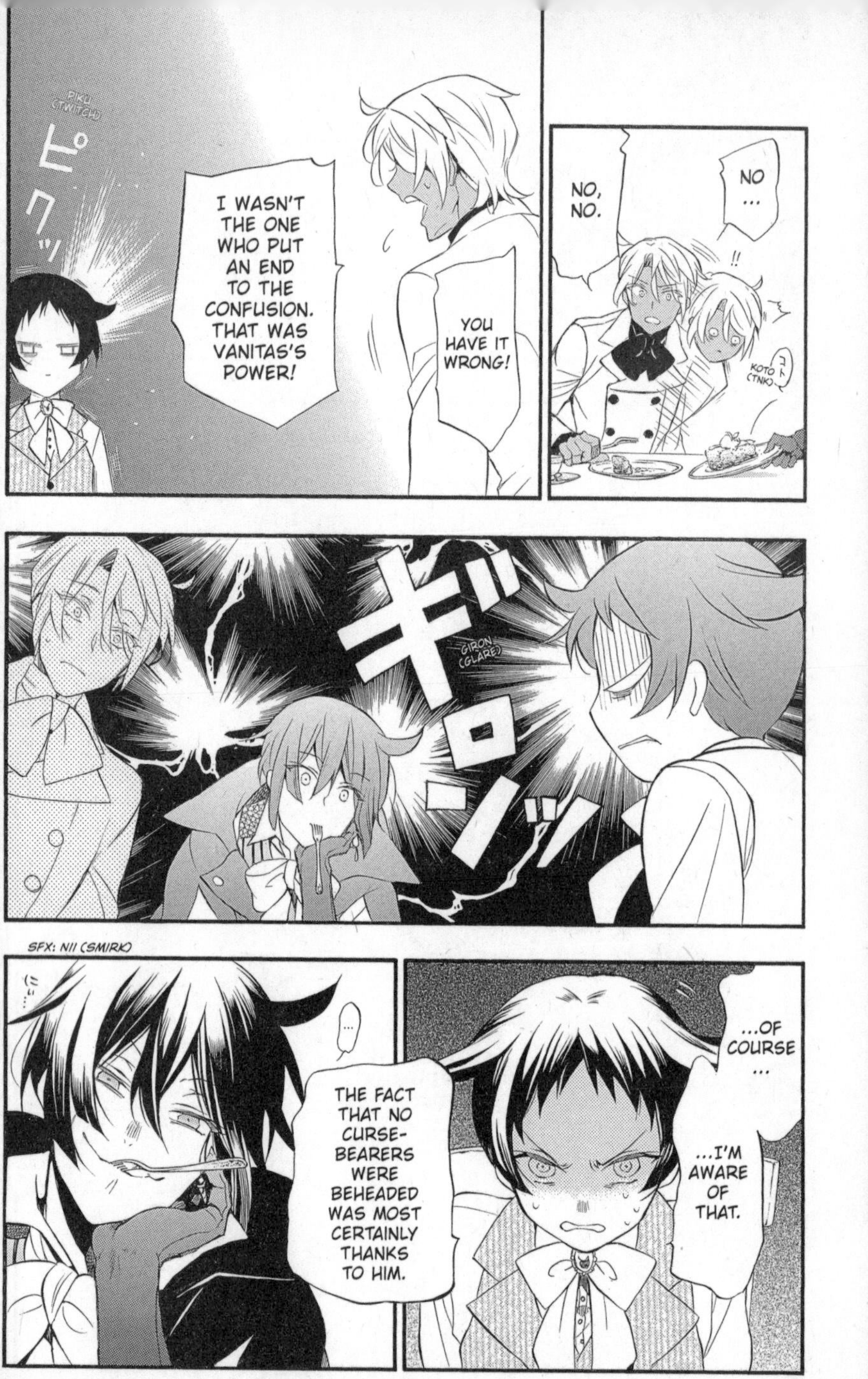
NO ...
NO, NO.
!!
KOTO (TNK)
コト
YOU HAVE IT WRONG!
I WASN'T THE ONE WHO PUT AN END TO THE CONFUSION. THAT WAS VANITAS'S POWER!
PIKU (TWITCH)
ピクッ
GIRON (GLARE)
ギロッ
...OF COURSE ...
...I'M AWARE OF THAT.
...
THE FACT THAT NO CURSE-BEARERS WERE BEHEADED WAS MOST CERTAINLY THANKS TO HIM.
SFX: NII (SMIRK)
にー...

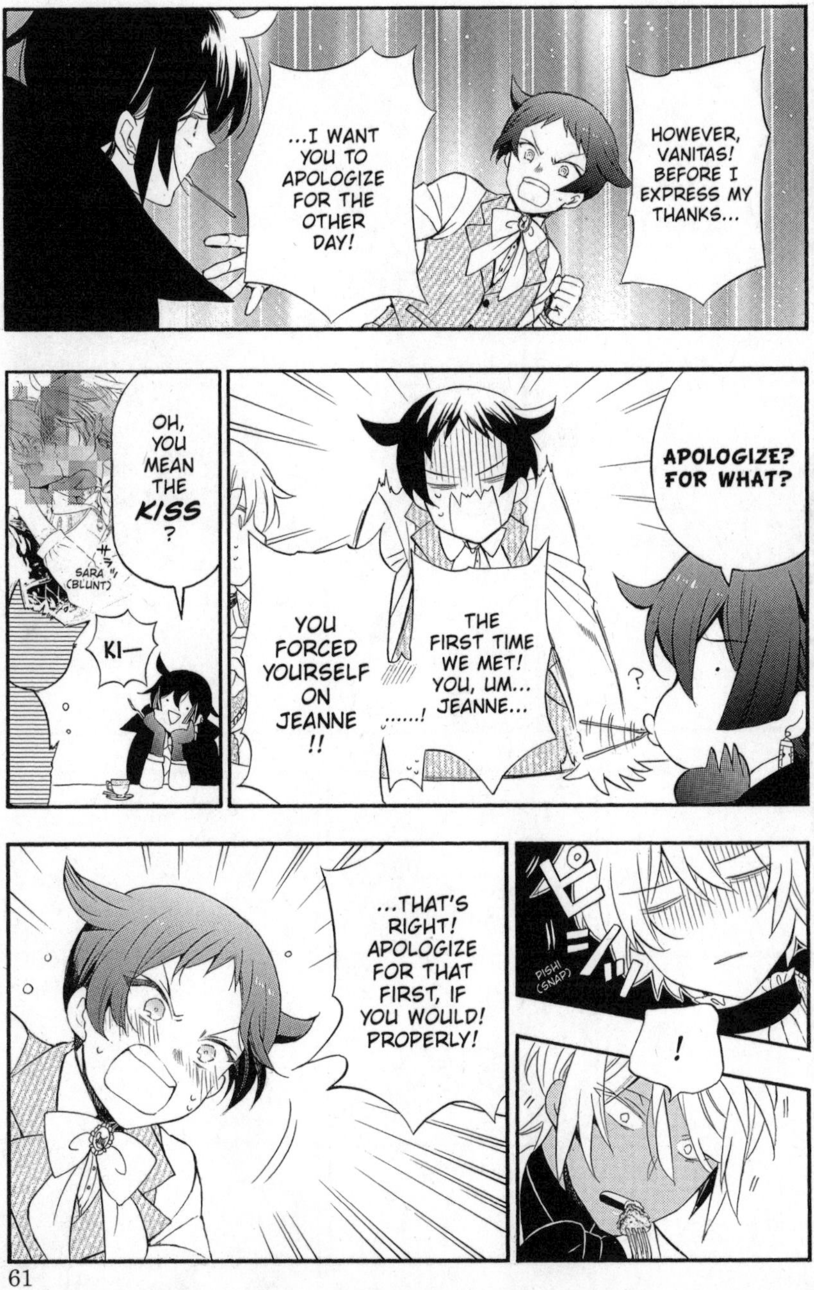

HOWEVER, VANITAS! BEFORE I EXPRESS MY THANKS...
...I WANT YOU TO APOLOGIZE FOR THE OTHER DAY!
APOLOGIZE? FOR WHAT?
?
THE FIRST TIME WE MET! YOU, UM... JEANNE...
......!
YOU FORCED YOURSELF ON JEANNE !!
OH, YOU MEAN THE KISS?
SARA (BLUNT)
KI—
PISHI (SNAP)
!
...THAT'S RIGHT! APOLOGIZE FOR THAT FIRST, IF YOU WOULD! PROPERLY!

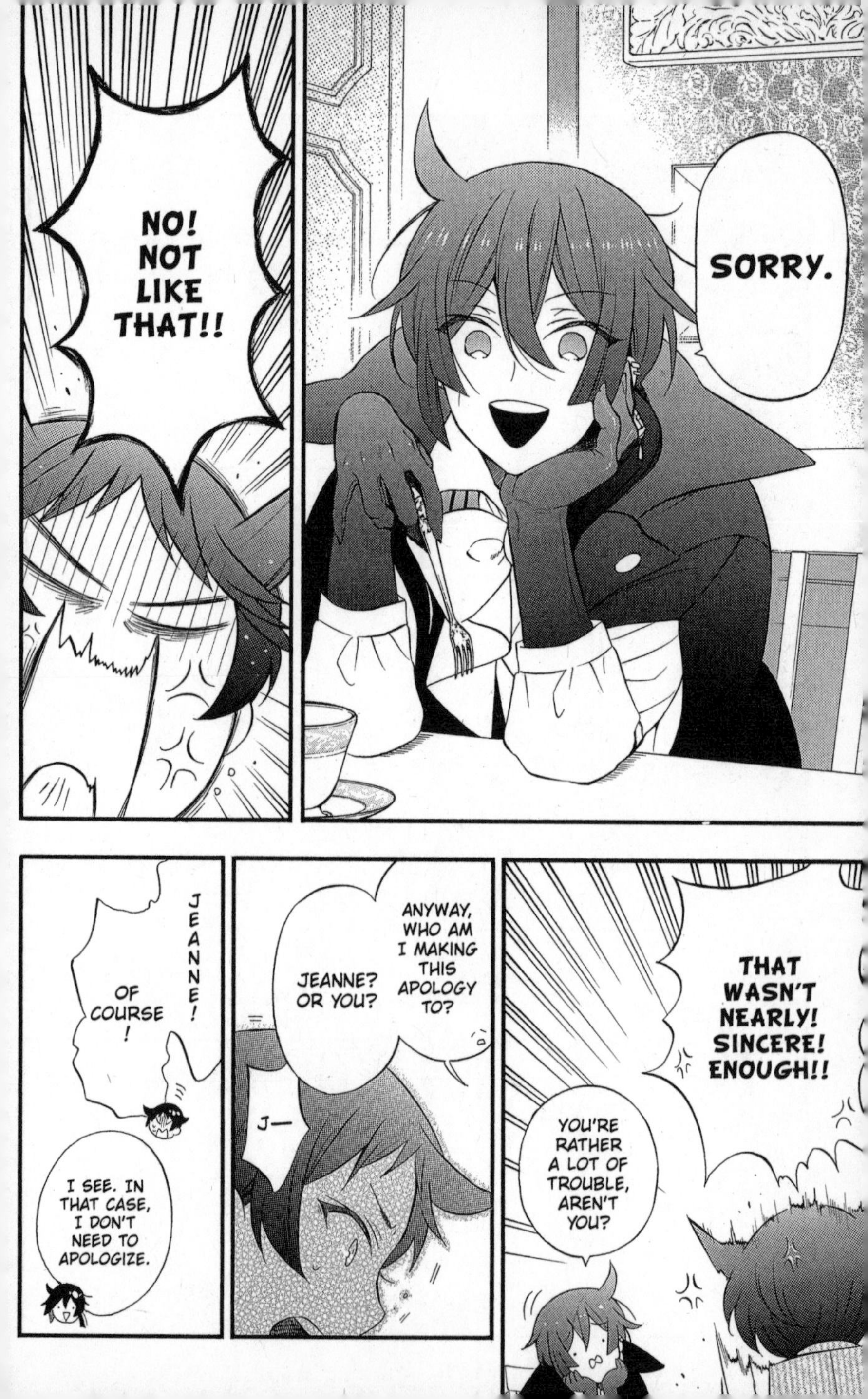
SORRY.
NO! NOT LIKE THAT!!
THAT WASN'T NEARLY! SINCERE! ENOUGH!!
YOU'RE RATHER A LOT OF TROUBLE, AREN'T YOU?
ANYWAY, WHO AM I MAKING THIS APOLOGY TO?
JEANNE? OR YOU?
J—
JEANNE!
OF COURSE!
I SEE. IN THAT CASE, I DON'T NEED TO APOLOGIZE.

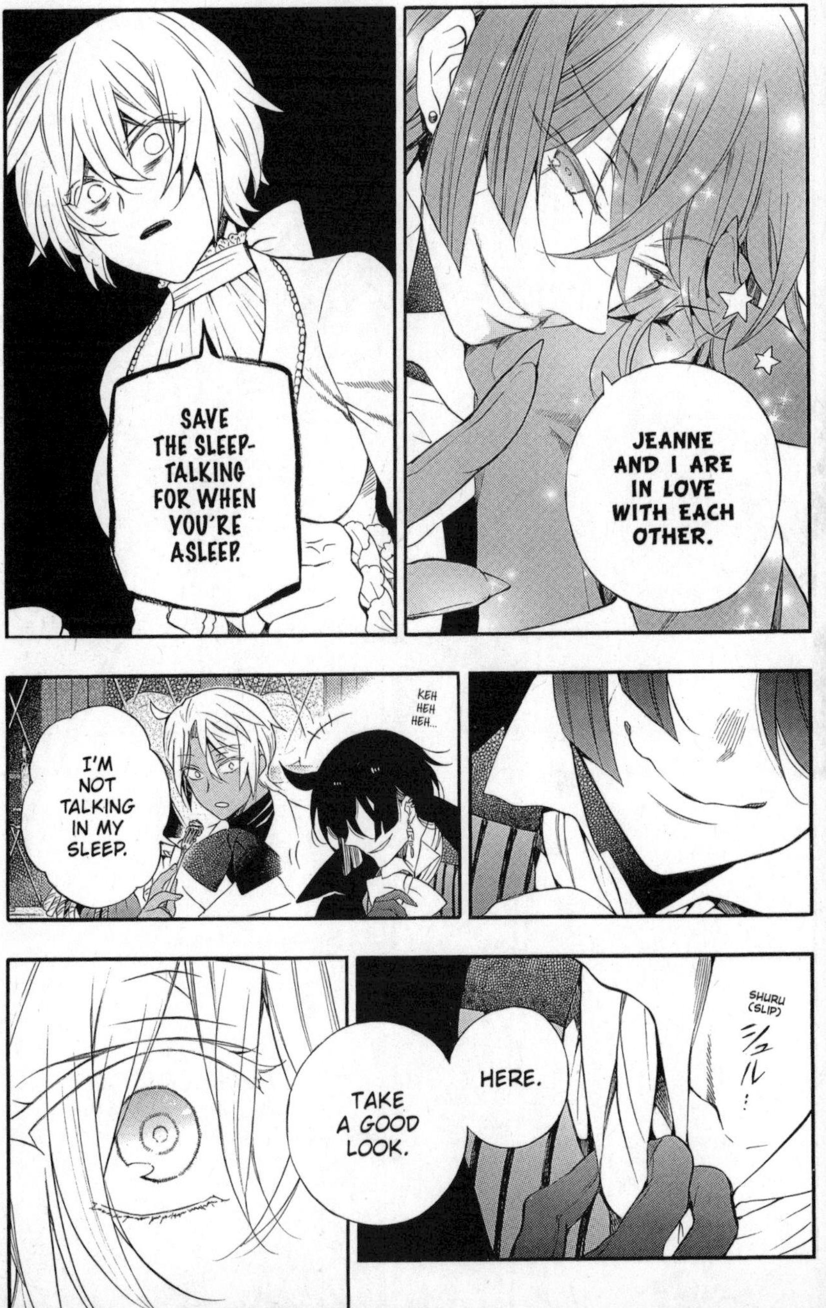
JEANNE AND I ARE IN LOVE WITH EACH OTHER.
SAVE THE SLEEP-TALKING FOR WHEN YOU'RE ASLEEP.
KEH HEH HEH...
I'M NOT TALKING IN MY SLEEP.
SHURU (SLIP)
シュル…
HERE.
TAKE A GOOD LOOK.

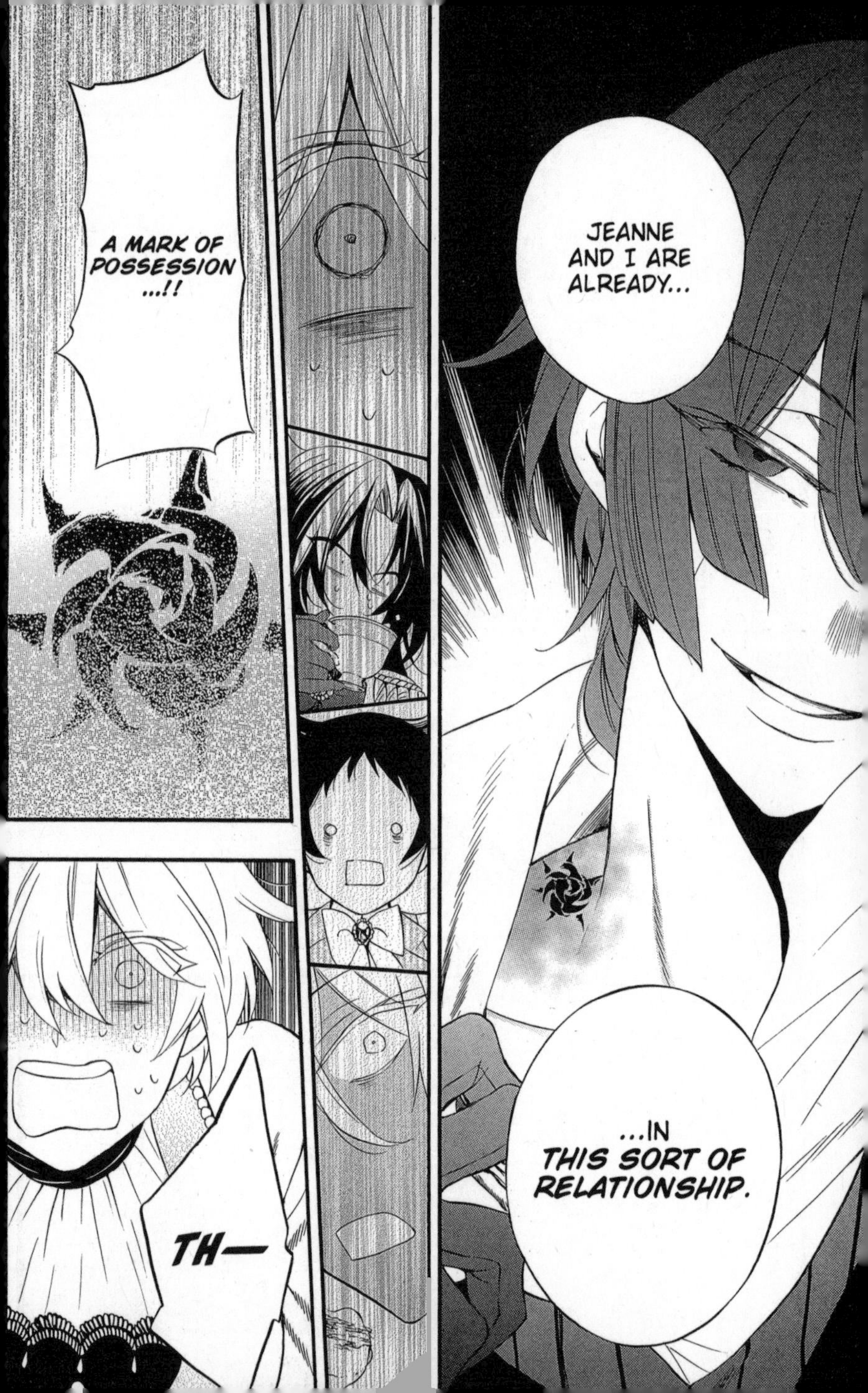
JEANNE AND I ARE ALREADY...
...IN THIS SORT OF RELATIONSHIP.
A MARK OF POSSESSION ...!!
TH—

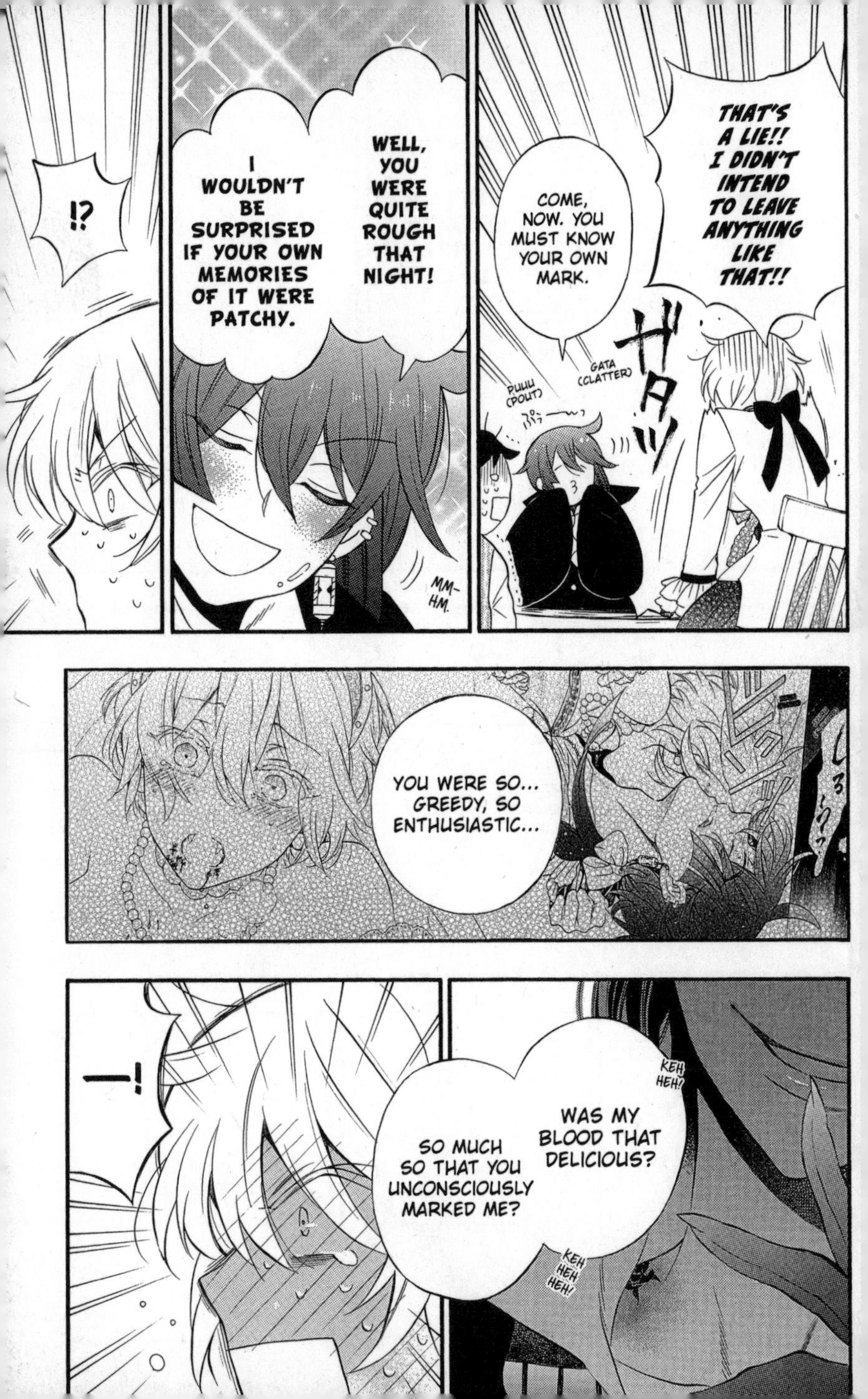
THAT'S A LIE!! I DIDN'T INTEND TO LEAVE ANYTHING LIKE THAT!!
GATA (CLATTER)
COME, NOW. YOU MUST KNOW YOUR OWN MARK.
PUUU (POUT)
WELL, YOU WERE QUITE ROUGH THAT NIGHT!
I WOULDN'T BE SURPRISED IF YOUR OWN MEMORIES OF IT WERE PATCHY.
MM-HM.
!?
YOU WERE SO... GREEDY, SO ENTHUSIASTIC...
KEH HEH!
WAS MY BLOOD THAT DELICIOUS?
SO MUCH SO THAT YOU UNCONSCIOUSLY MARKED ME?
KEH HEH HEH!
—!

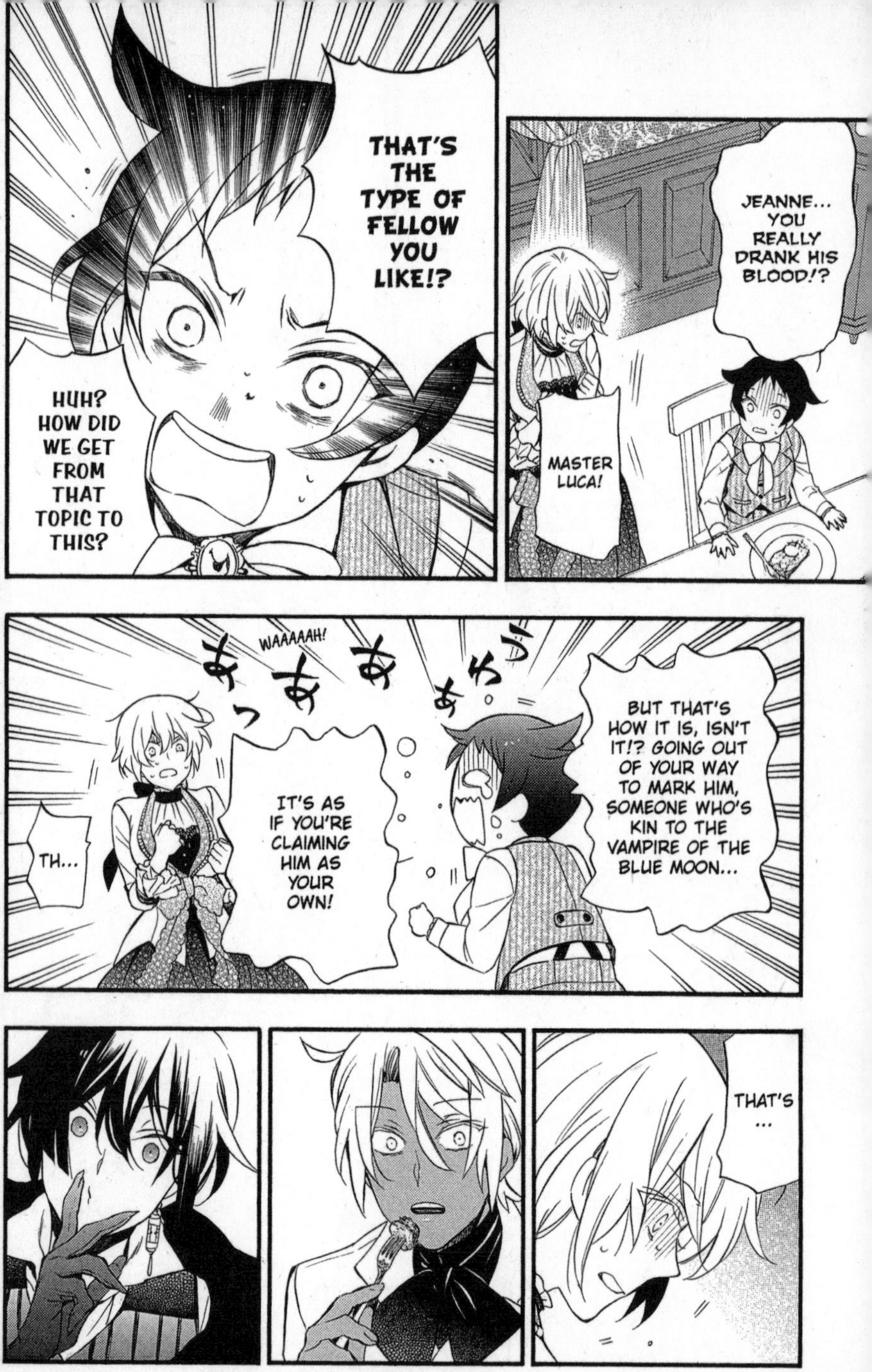
JEANNE... YOU REALLY DRANK HIS BLOOD!?
MASTER LUCA!
THAT'S THE TYPE OF FELLOW YOU LIKE!?
HUH? HOW DID WE GET FROM THAT TOPIC TO THIS?
BUT THAT'S HOW IT IS, ISN'T IT!? GOING OUT OF YOUR WAY TO MARK HIM, SOMEONE WHO'S KIN TO THE VAMPIRE OF THE BLUE MOON...
WAAAAAH!
IT'S AS IF YOU'RE CLAIMING HIM AS YOUR OWN!
TH...
THAT'S ...

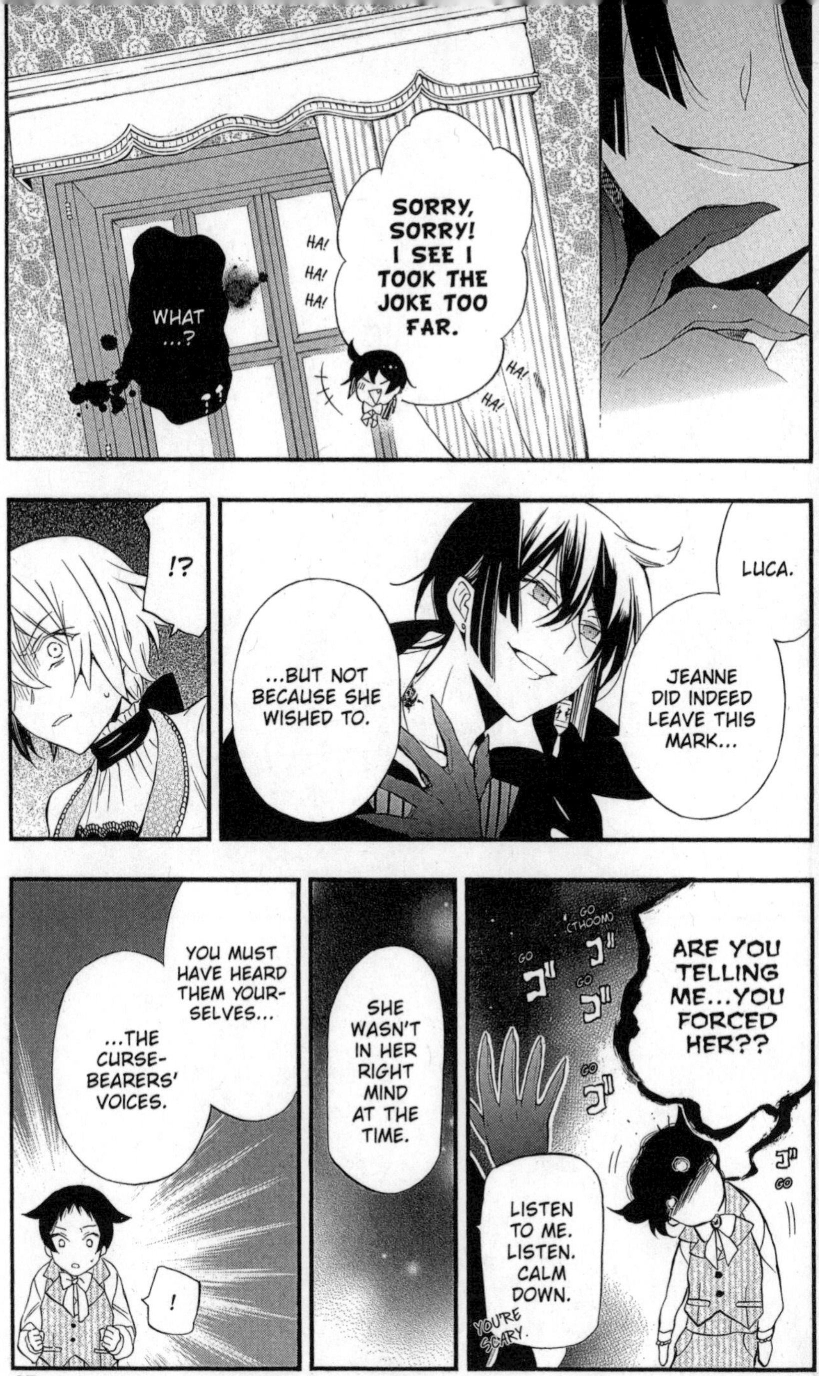
SORRY, SORRY! I SEE I TOOK THE JOKE TOO FAR.
HA! HA! HA!
WHAT ...?
HA! HA!
LUCA.
JEANNE DID INDEED LEAVE THIS MARK...
...BUT NOT BECAUSE SHE WISHED TO.
!?
ARE YOU TELLING ME...YOU FORCED HER??
GO (THOOM) ゴ
GO ゴ
GO ゴ
GO ゴ
GO ゴ
LISTEN TO ME. LISTEN. CALM DOWN.
YOU'RE SCARY.
SHE WASN'T IN HER RIGHT MIND AT THE TIME.
YOU MUST HAVE HEARD THEM YOUR-SELVES...
...THE CURSE-BEARERS' VOICES.
!

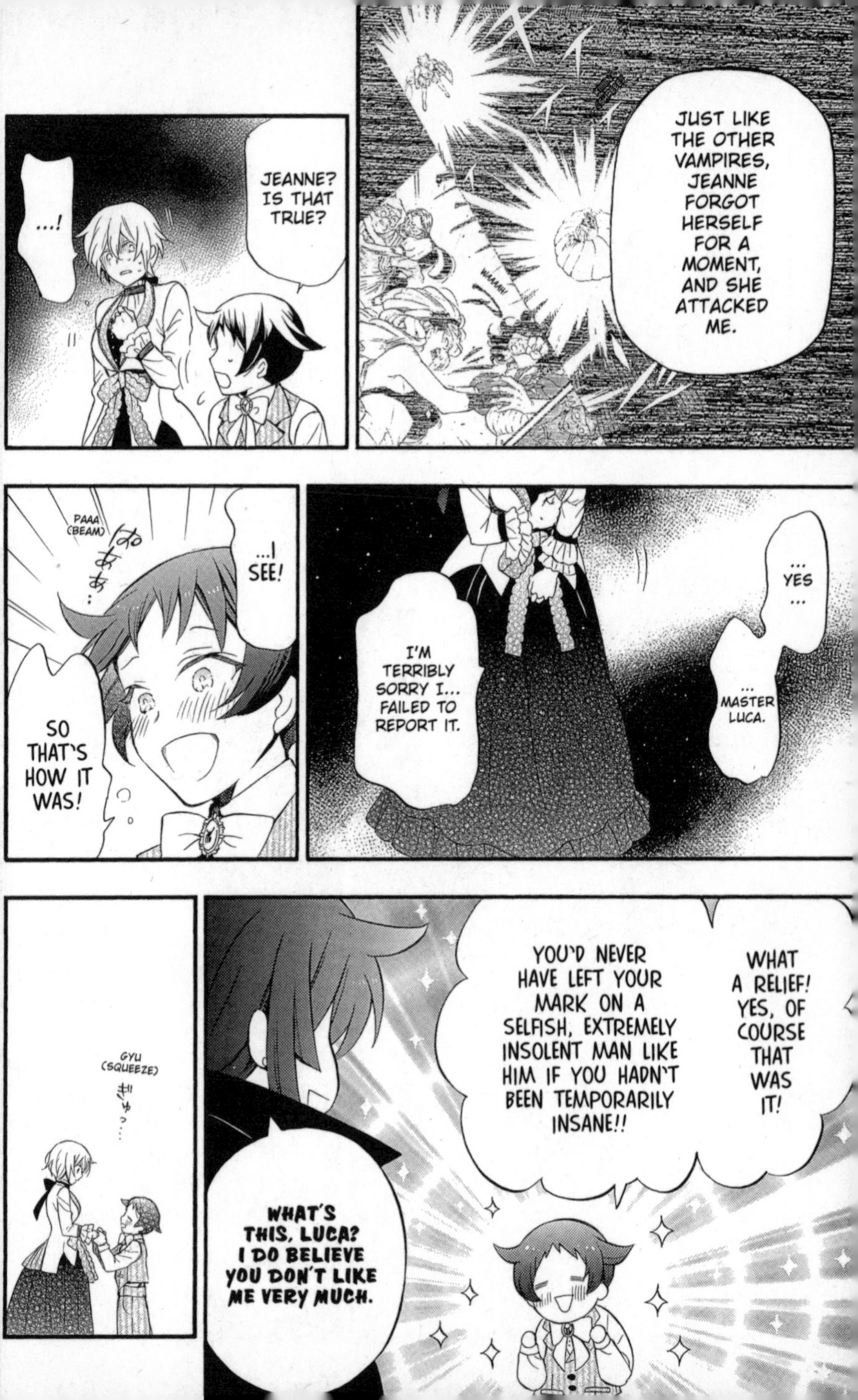
JUST LIKE THE OTHER VAMPIRES, JEANNE FORGOT HERSELF FOR A MOMENT, AND SHE ATTACKED ME.
JEANNE? IS THAT TRUE?
...!
... YES ...
... MASTER LUCA.
I'M TERRIBLY SORRY I... FAILED TO REPORT IT.
...I SEE!
PAAA (BEAM)
ぱぁぁ…
SO THAT'S HOW IT WAS!
WHAT A RELIEF! YES, OF COURSE THAT WAS IT!
YOU'D NEVER HAVE LEFT YOUR MARK ON A SELFISH, EXTREMELY INSOLENT MAN LIKE HIM IF YOU HADN'T BEEN TEMPORARILY INSANE!!
WHAT'S THIS, LUCA? I DO BELIEVE YOU DON'T LIKE ME VERY MUCH.
GYU (SQUEEZE)
ぎゅっ…

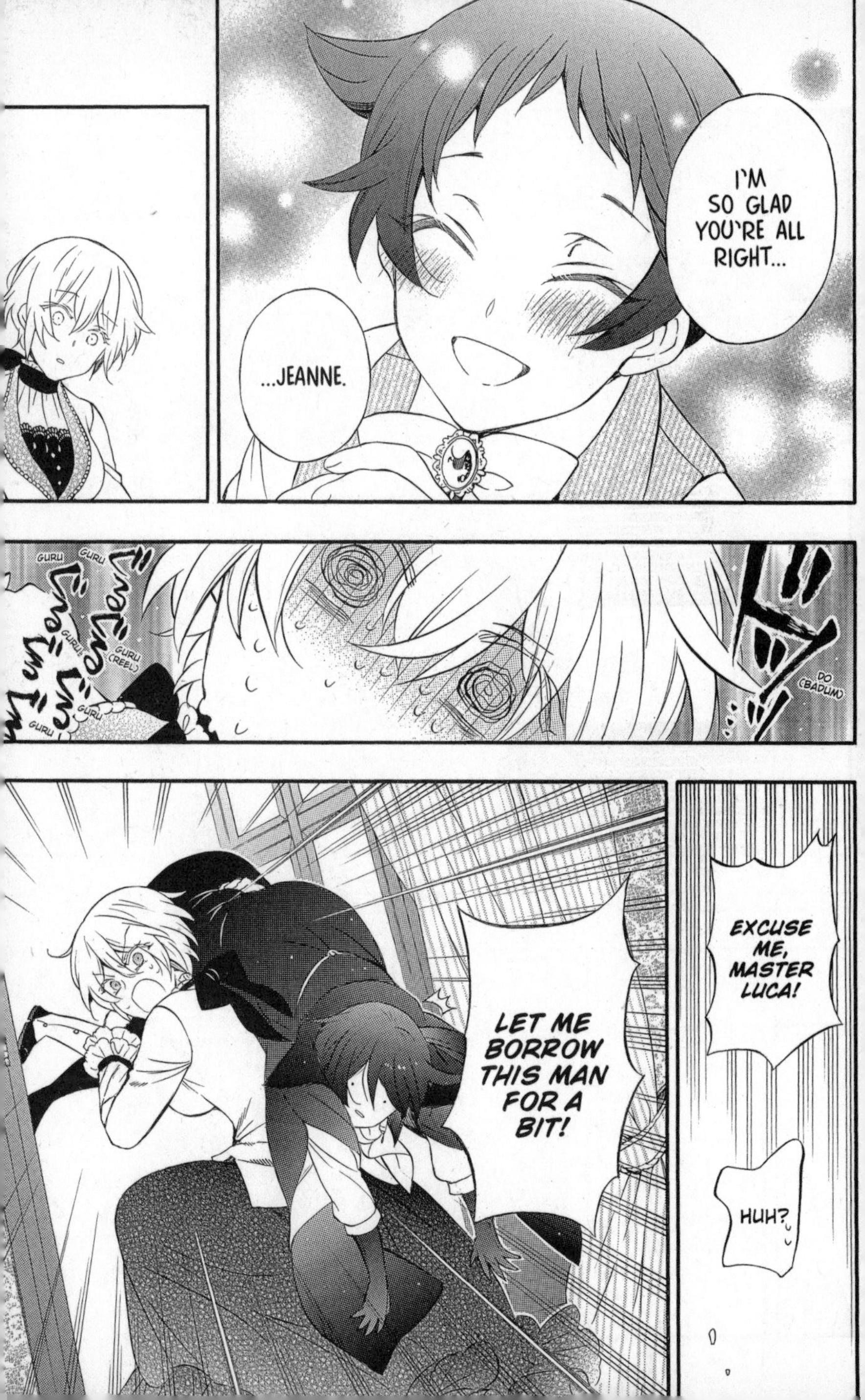
I'M SO GLAD YOU'RE ALL RIGHT...
...JEANNE.
DO (BADUM)
GURU GURU (REEL)
GURU GURU
GURU GURU
GURU GURU
EXCUSE ME, MASTER LUCA!
HUH?
LET ME BORROW THIS MAN FOR A BIT!

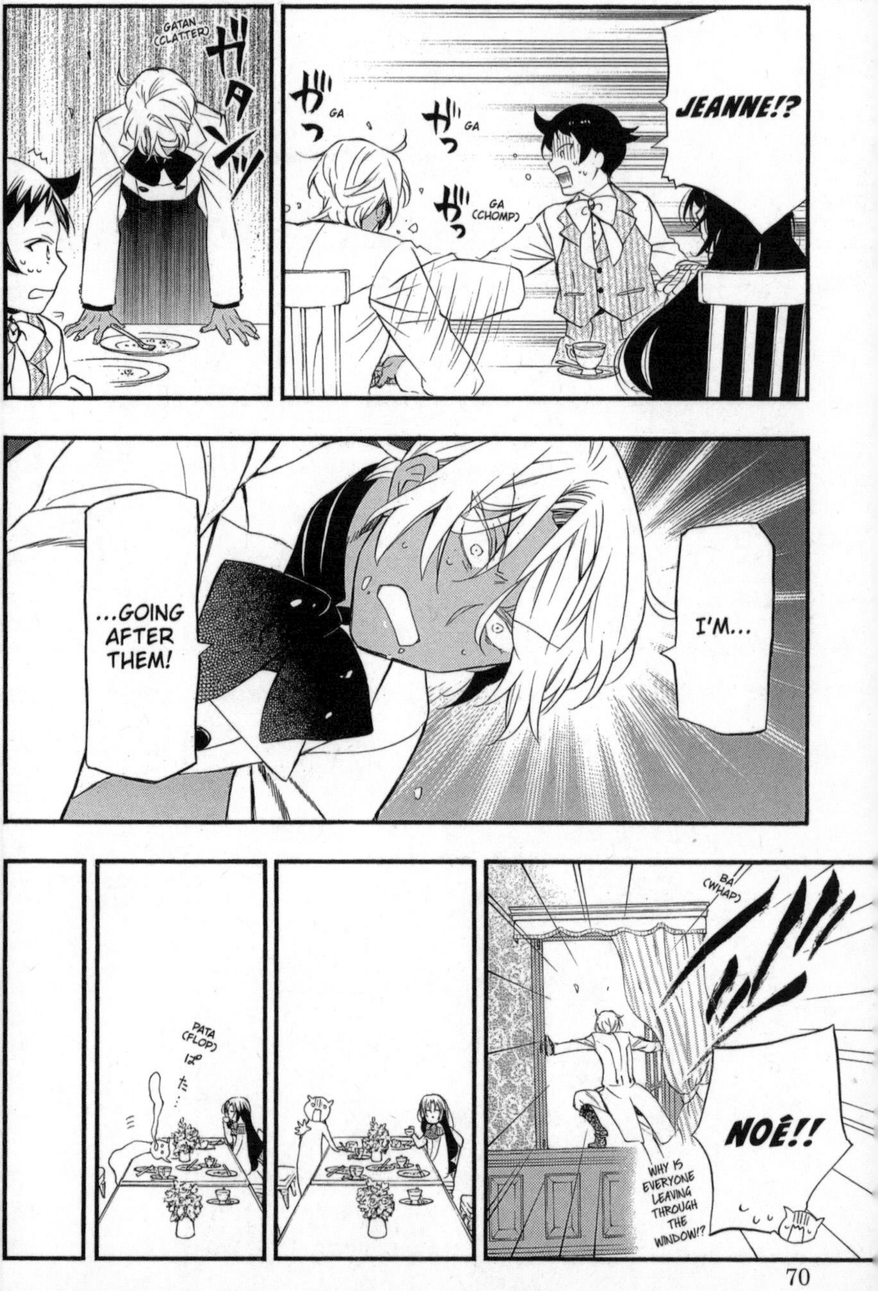
JEANNE!?
GA
GA
GA (CHOMP)
GATAN (CLATTER)
I'M...
...GOING AFTER THEM!
BA (WHAP)
NOÊ!!
WHY IS EVERYONE LEAVING THROUGH THE WINDOW!?
PATA (FLOP)

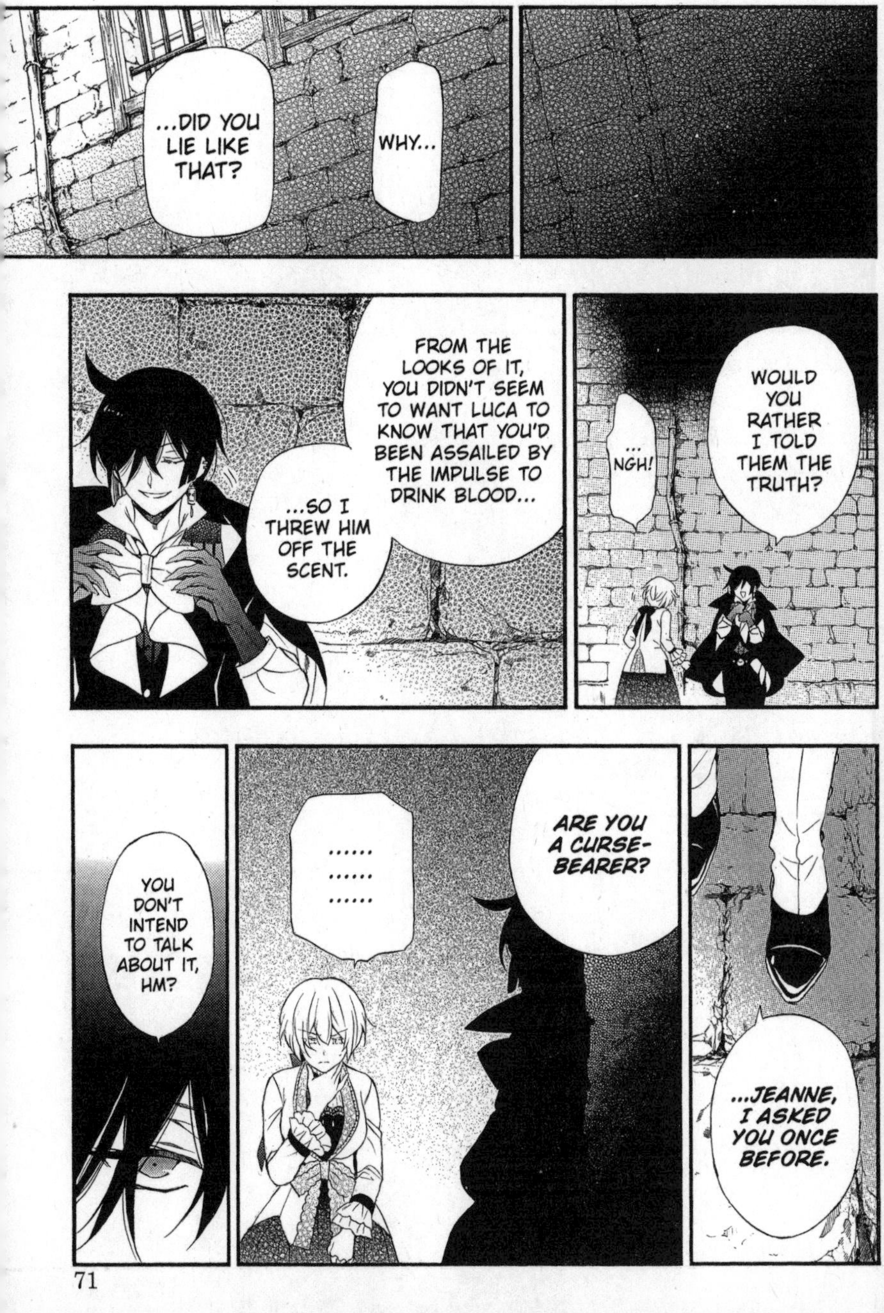
WHY...
...DID YOU LIE LIKE THAT?
WOULD YOU RATHER I TOLD THEM THE TRUTH?
...NGH!
FROM THE LOOKS OF IT, YOU DIDN'T SEEM TO WANT LUCA TO KNOW THAT YOU'D BEEN ASSAILED BY THE IMPULSE TO DRINK BLOOD...
...SO I THREW HIM OFF THE SCENT.
...JEANNE, I ASKED YOU ONCE BEFORE.
ARE YOU A CURSE-BEARER?
....
YOU DON'T INTEND TO TALK ABOUT IT, HM?

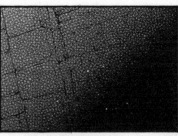

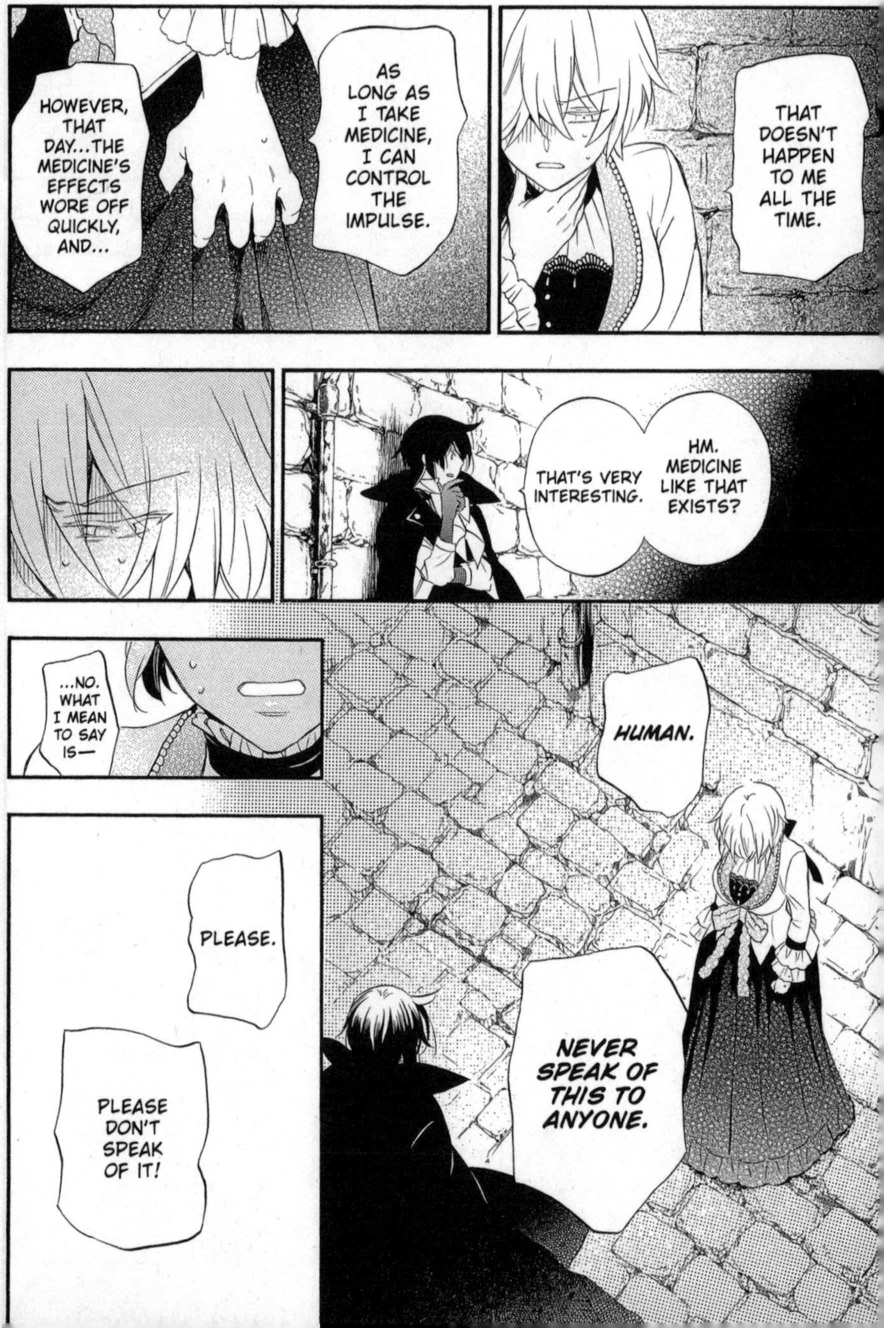

THAT DOESN'T HAPPEN TO ME ALL THE TIME.
AS LONG AS I TAKE MEDICINE, I CAN CONTROL THE IMPULSE.
HOWEVER, THAT DAY...THE MEDICINE'S EFFECTS WORE OFF QUICKLY, AND...
HM. MEDICINE LIKE THAT EXISTS?
THAT'S VERY INTERESTING.
HUMAN.
NEVER SPEAK OF THIS TO ANYONE.
...NO. WHAT I MEAN TO SAY IS—
PLEASE.
PLEASE DON'T SPEAK OF IT!

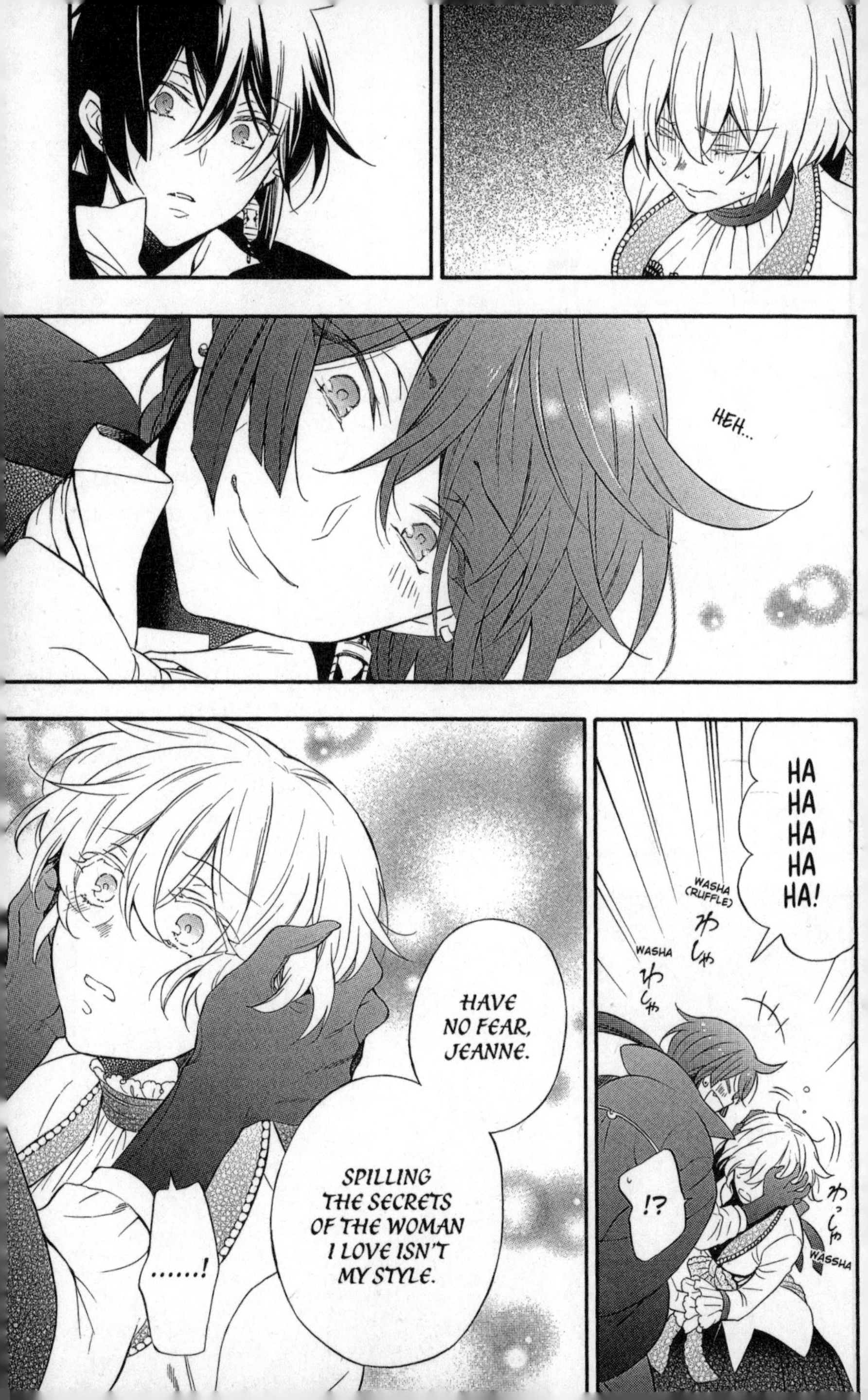
HEH...
HA HA HA HA HA!
WASHA (RUFFLE)
わしゃ
WASHA
わしゃ
!?
わっしゃ
WASSHA
HAVE NO FEAR, JEANNE.
SPILLING THE SECRETS OF THE WOMAN I LOVE ISN'T MY STYLE.
......!

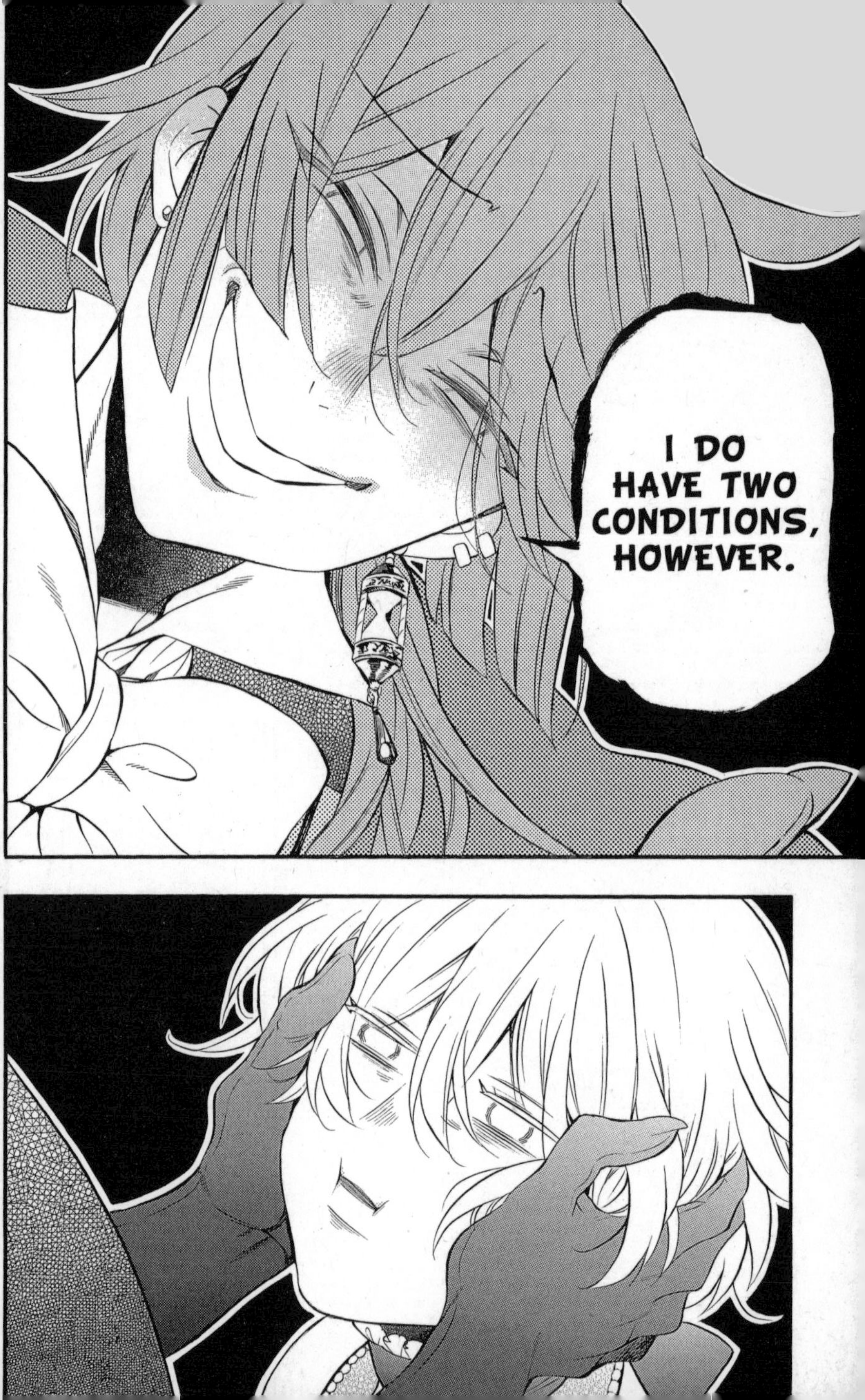
I DO HAVE TWO CONDITIONS, HOWEVER.

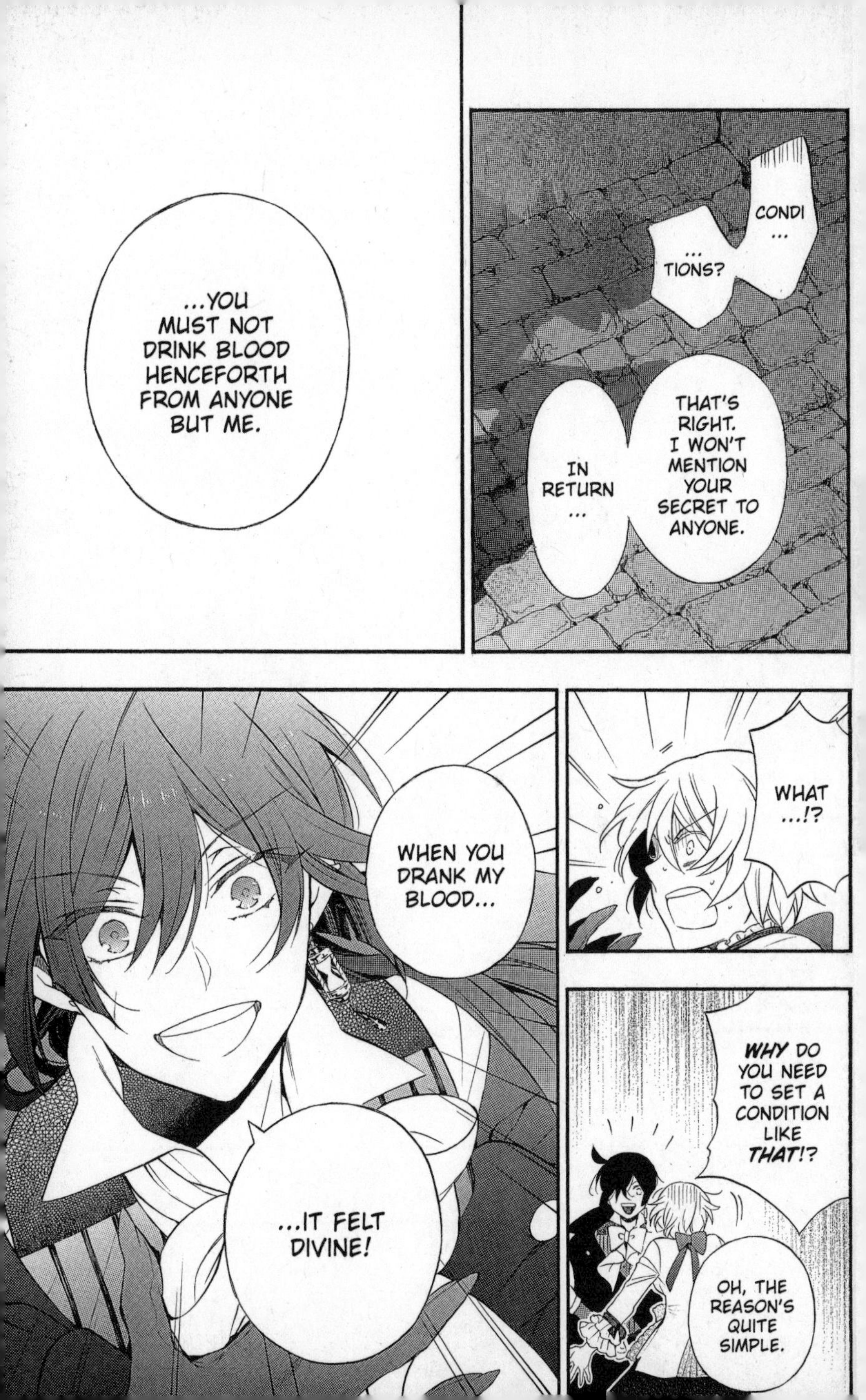
CONDI ...
... TIONS?
THAT'S RIGHT. I WON'T MENTION YOUR SECRET TO ANYONE.
IN RETURN ...
...YOU MUST NOT DRINK BLOOD HENCEFORTH FROM ANYONE BUT ME.
WHAT ...!?
WHY DO YOU NEED TO SET A CONDITION LIKE *THAT*!?
OH, THE REASON'S QUITE SIMPLE.
WHEN YOU DRANK MY BLOOD...
...IT FELT DIVINE!

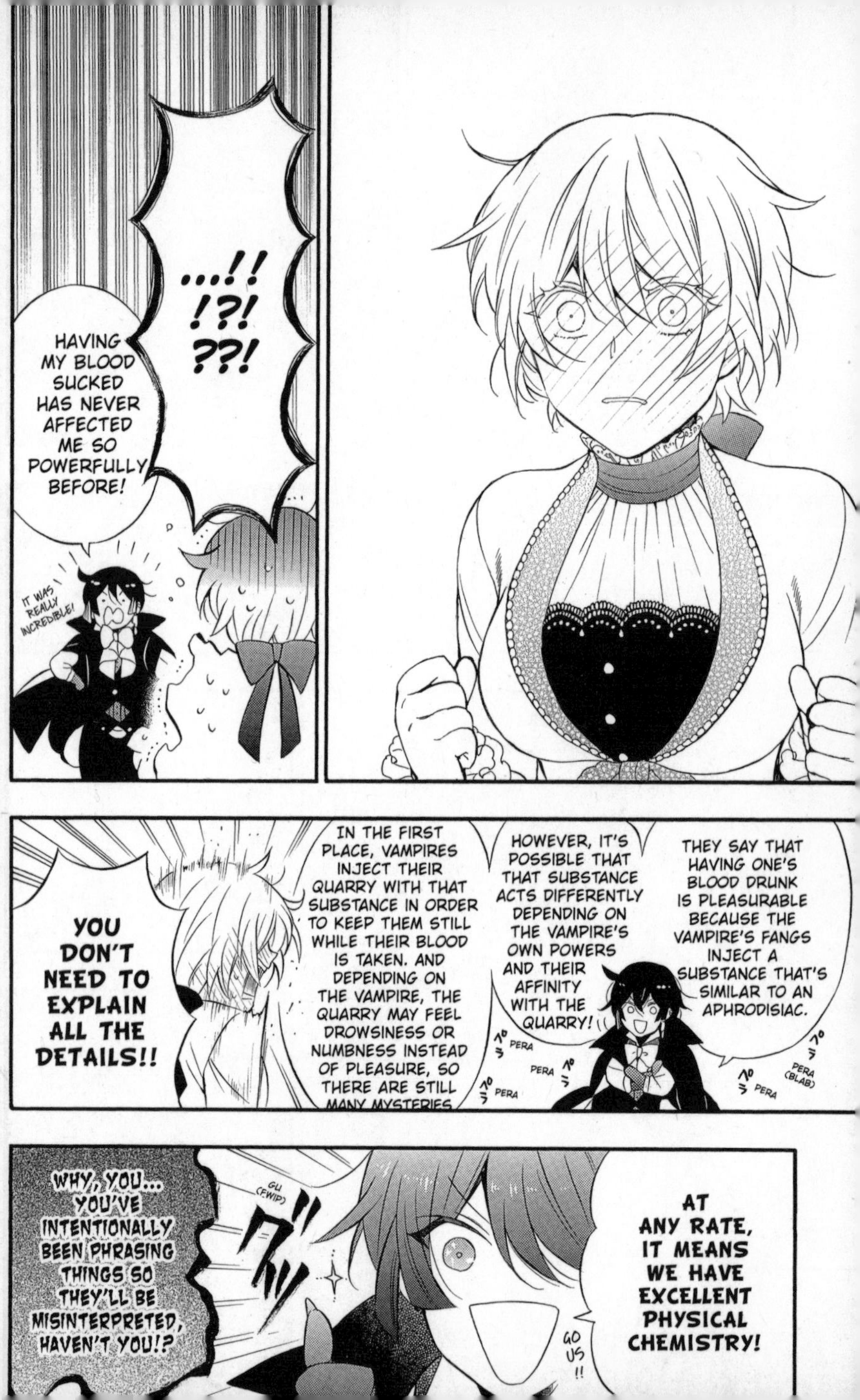
...!! !?! ??!
HAVING MY BLOOD SUCKED HAS NEVER AFFECTED ME SO POWERFULLY BEFORE!
IT WAS REALLY INCREDIBLE!
THEY SAY THAT HAVING ONE'S BLOOD DRUNK IS PLEASURABLE BECAUSE THE VAMPIRE'S FANGS INJECT A SUBSTANCE THAT'S SIMILAR TO AN APHRODISIAC.
PERA (BLAB)
PERA
HOWEVER, IT'S POSSIBLE THAT THAT SUBSTANCE ACTS DIFFERENTLY DEPENDING ON THE VAMPIRE'S OWN POWERS AND THEIR AFFINITY WITH THE QUARRY!
PERA
PERA
IN THE FIRST PLACE, VAMPIRES INJECT THEIR QUARRY WITH THAT SUBSTANCE IN ORDER TO KEEP THEM STILL WHILE THEIR BLOOD IS TAKEN. AND DEPENDING ON THE VAMPIRE, THE QUARRY MAY FEEL DROWSINESS OR NUMBNESS INSTEAD OF PLEASURE, SO THERE ARE STILL MANY MYSTERIES
PERA
YOU DON'T NEED TO EXPLAIN ALL THE DETAILS!!
AT ANY RATE, IT MEANS WE HAVE EXCELLENT PHYSICAL CHEMISTRY!
GO US!!
GU (FWIP)
WHY, YOU... YOU'VE INTENTIONALLY BEEN PHRASING THINGS SO THEY'LL BE MISINTERPRETED, HAVEN'T YOU!?

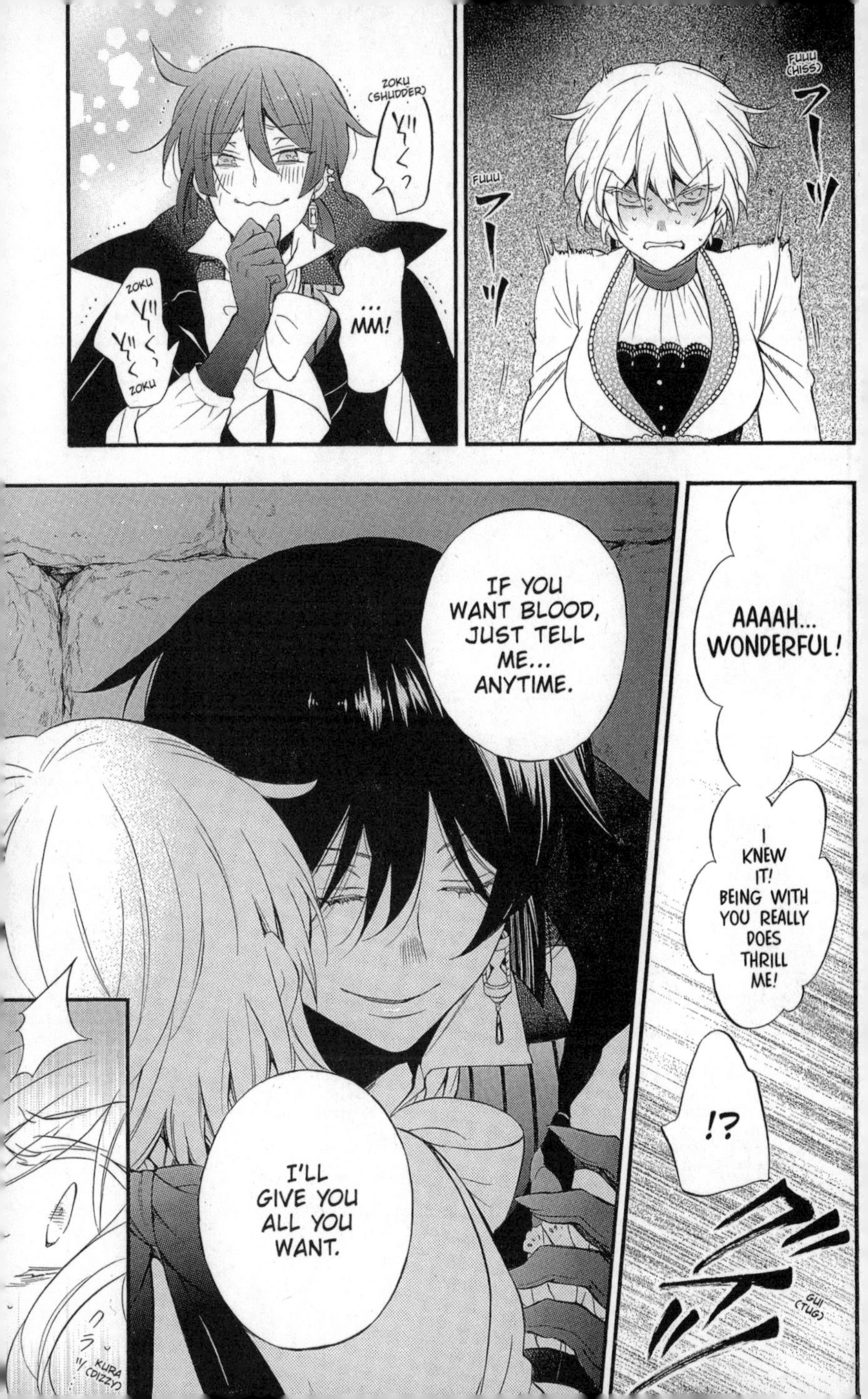
FUUU (HISS)
FUUU
ZOKU (SHUDDER)
...MM!
ZOKU
ZOKU
AAAAH... WONDERFUL!
I KNEW IT! BEING WITH YOU REALLY DOES THRILL ME!
!?
GUI (TUG)
IF YOU WANT BLOOD, JUST TELL ME... ANYTIME.
I'LL GIVE YOU ALL YOU WANT.
KURA (DIZZY)

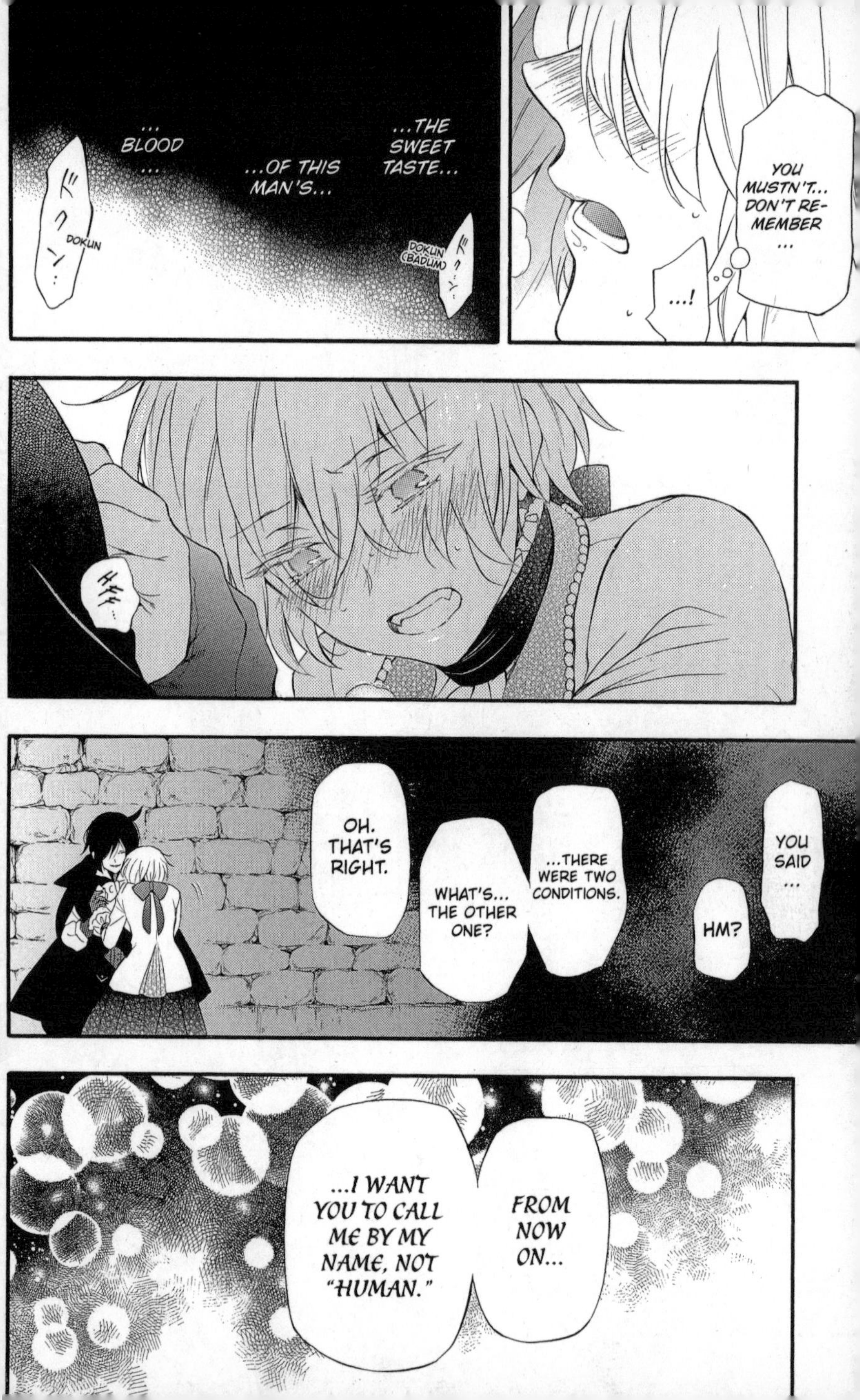
YOU MUSTN'T... DON'T RE-MEMBER...
...!
...THE SWEET TASTE...
DOKUN (BADUM)
...OF THIS MAN'S...
...BLOOD...
DOKUN
YOU SAID...
HM?
...THERE WERE TWO CONDITIONS.
WHAT'S... THE OTHER ONE?
OH. THAT'S RIGHT.
FROM NOW ON...
...I WANT YOU TO CALL ME BY MY NAME, NOT "HUMAN."

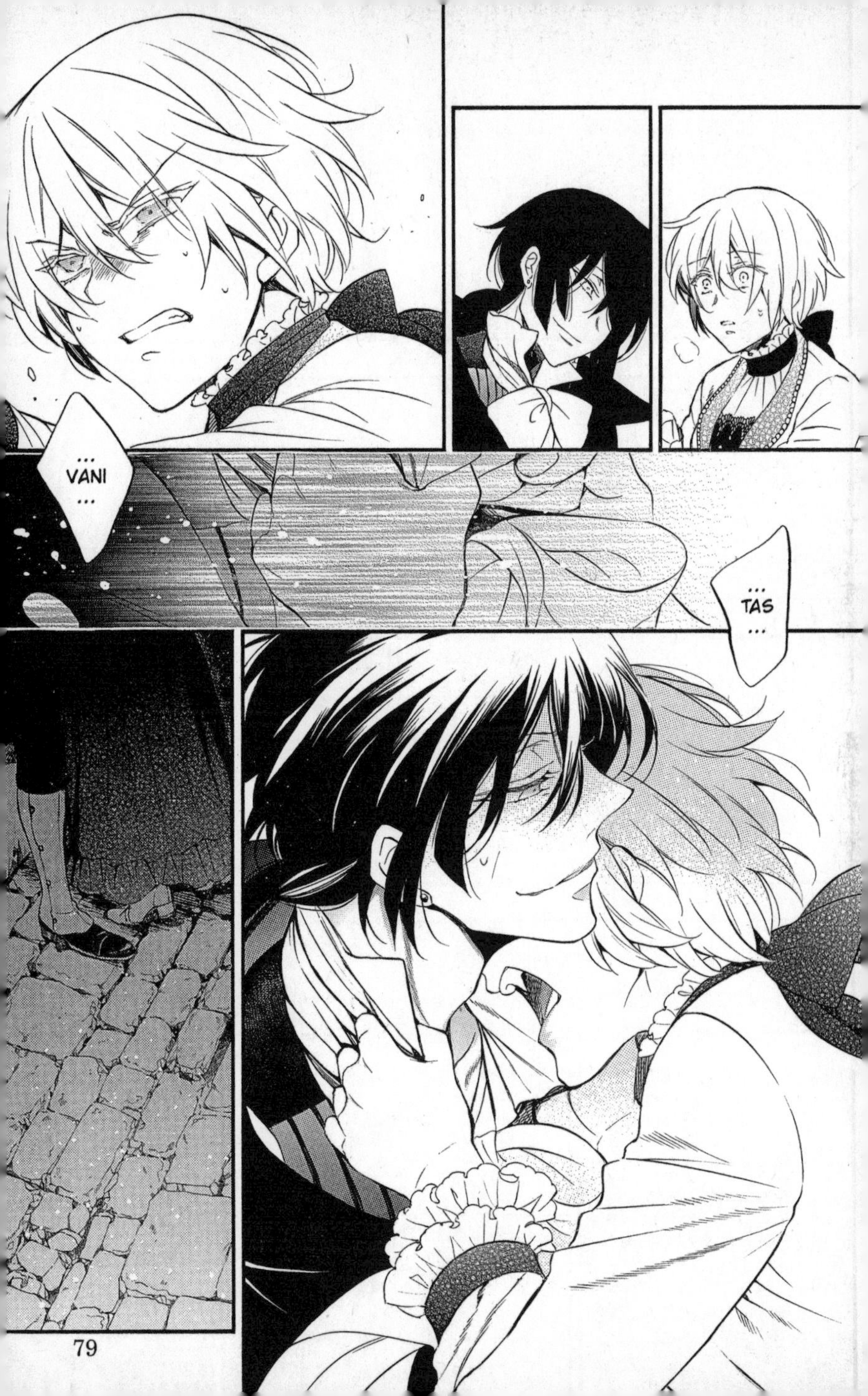
... VANI ...
... TAS ...

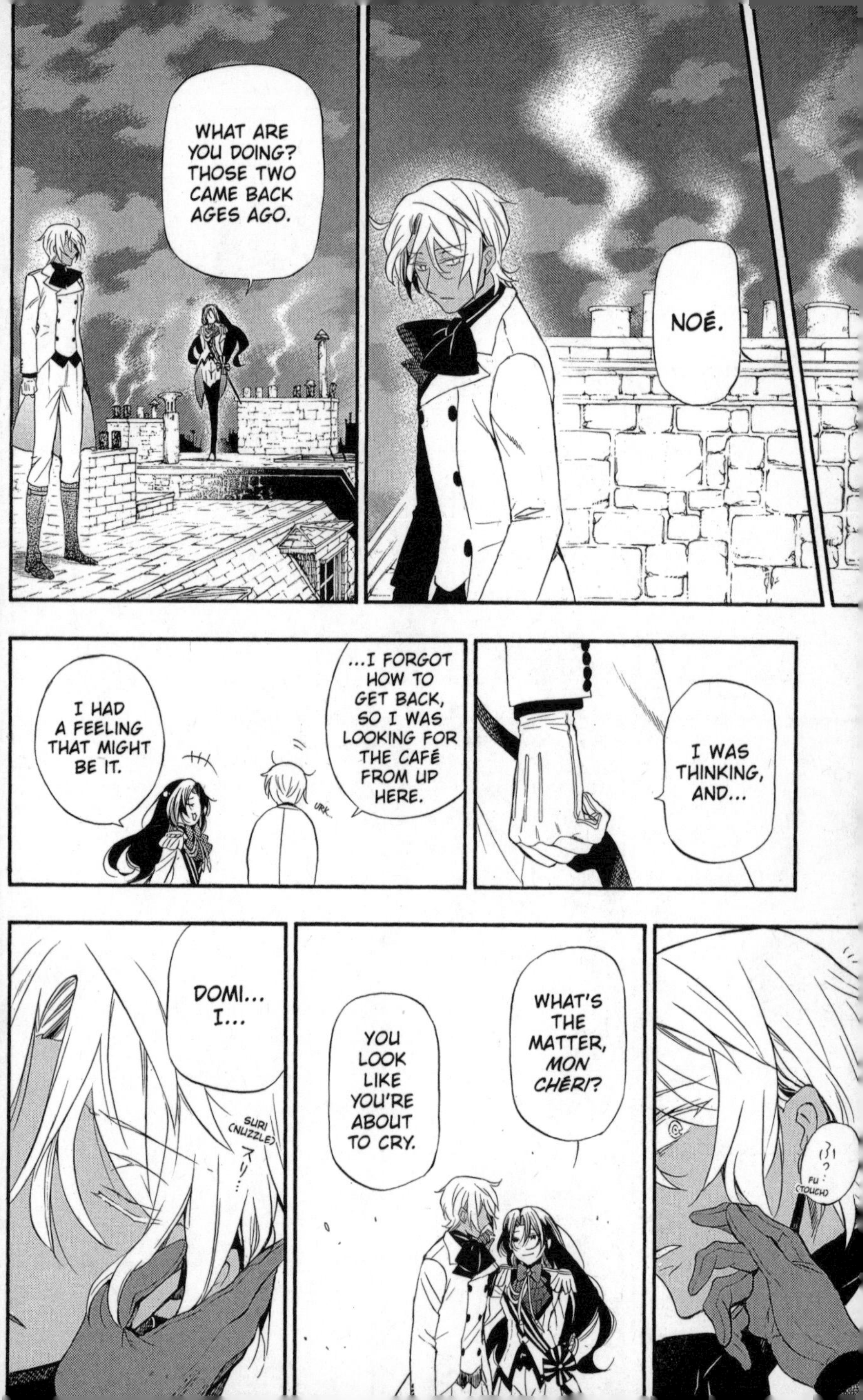
NOÉ.
WHAT ARE YOU DOING? THOSE TWO CAME BACK AGES AGO.
I WAS THINKING, AND...
...I FORGOT HOW TO GET BACK, SO I WAS LOOKING FOR THE CAFÉ FROM UP HERE.
URK
I HAD A FEELING THAT MIGHT BE IT.
ふ?
FU (TOUCH)
WHAT'S THE MATTER, *MON CHÉRI*?
YOU LOOK LIKE YOU'RE ABOUT TO CRY.
DOMI... I...
スリ…
SURI (NUZZLE)

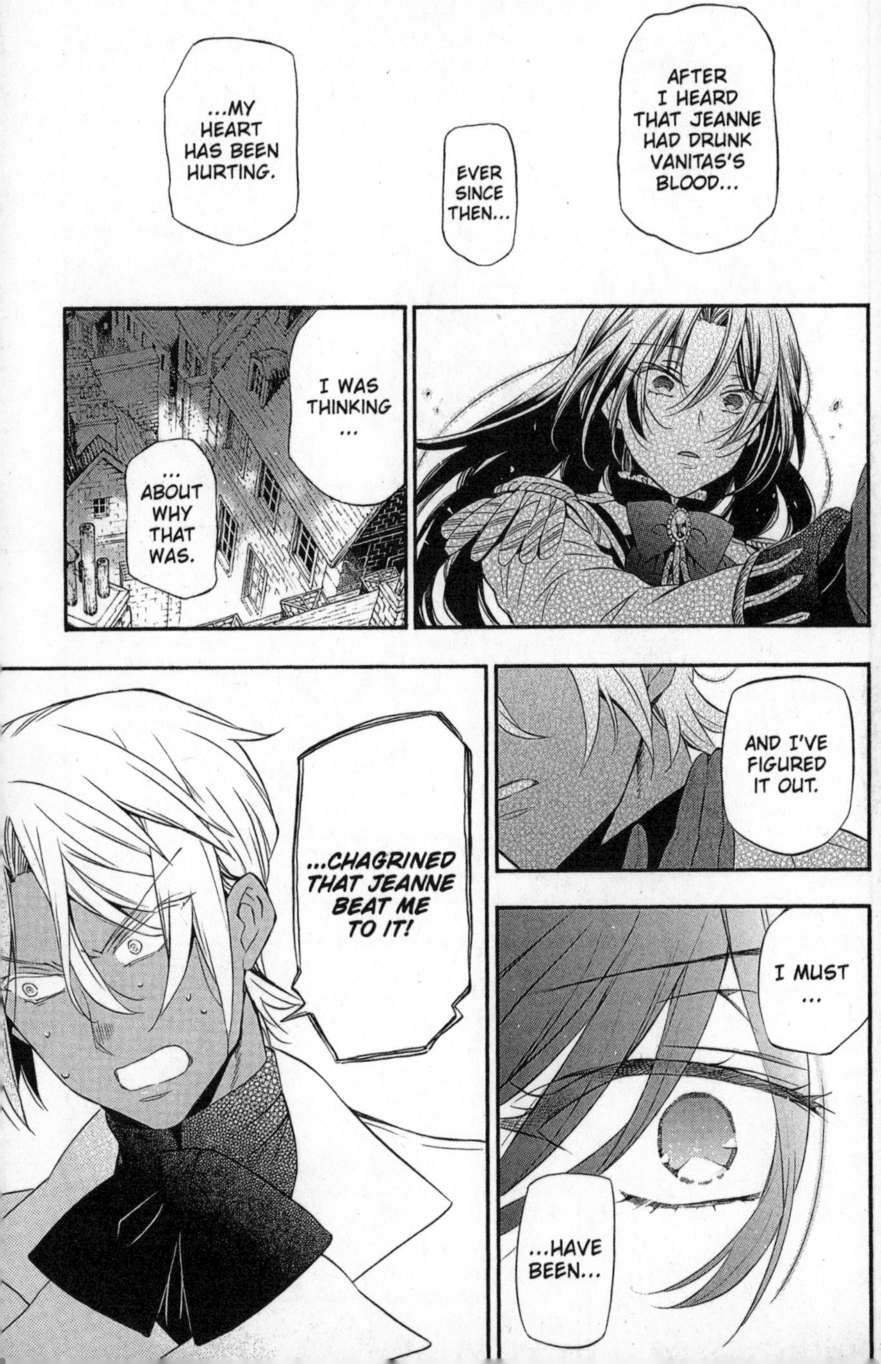
AFTER I HEARD THAT JEANNE HAD DRUNK VANITAS'S BLOOD...
EVER SINCE THEN...
...MY HEART HAS BEEN HURTING.
I WAS THINKING ...
... ABOUT WHY THAT WAS.
AND I'VE FIGURED IT OUT.
I MUST ...
...HAVE BEEN...
...CHAGRINED THAT JEANNE BEAT ME TO IT!

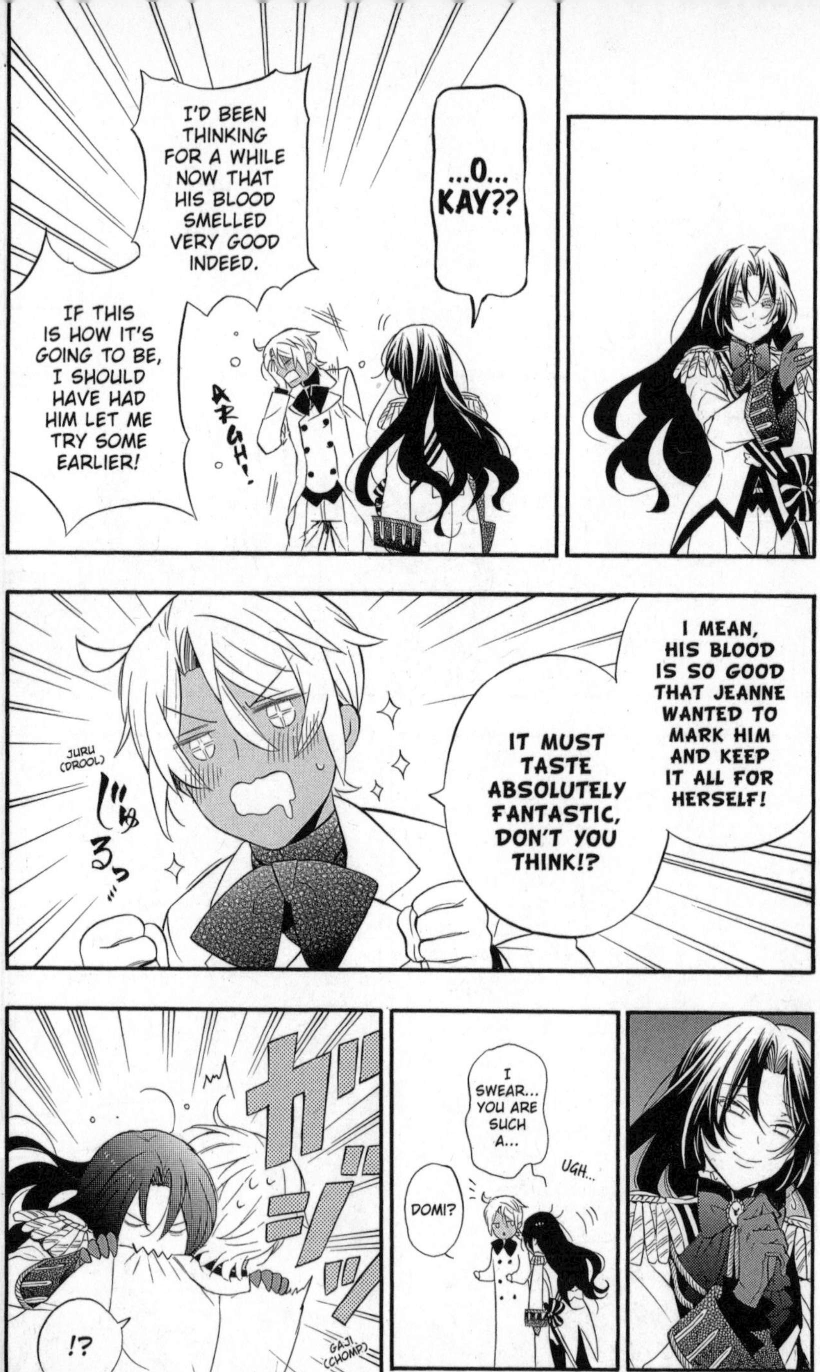
...O... KAY??
I'D BEEN THINKING FOR A WHILE NOW THAT HIS BLOOD SMELLED VERY GOOD INDEED.
IF THIS IS HOW IT'S GOING TO BE, I SHOULD HAVE HAD HIM LET ME TRY SOME EARLIER!
ARGH!
I MEAN, HIS BLOOD IS SO GOOD THAT JEANNE WANTED TO MARK HIM AND KEEP IT ALL FOR HERSELF!
IT MUST TASTE ABSOLUTELY FANTASTIC, DON'T YOU THINK!?
JURU (DROOL)
I SWEAR... YOU ARE SUCH A...
UGH...
DOMI?
GAJI (CHOMP)
!?

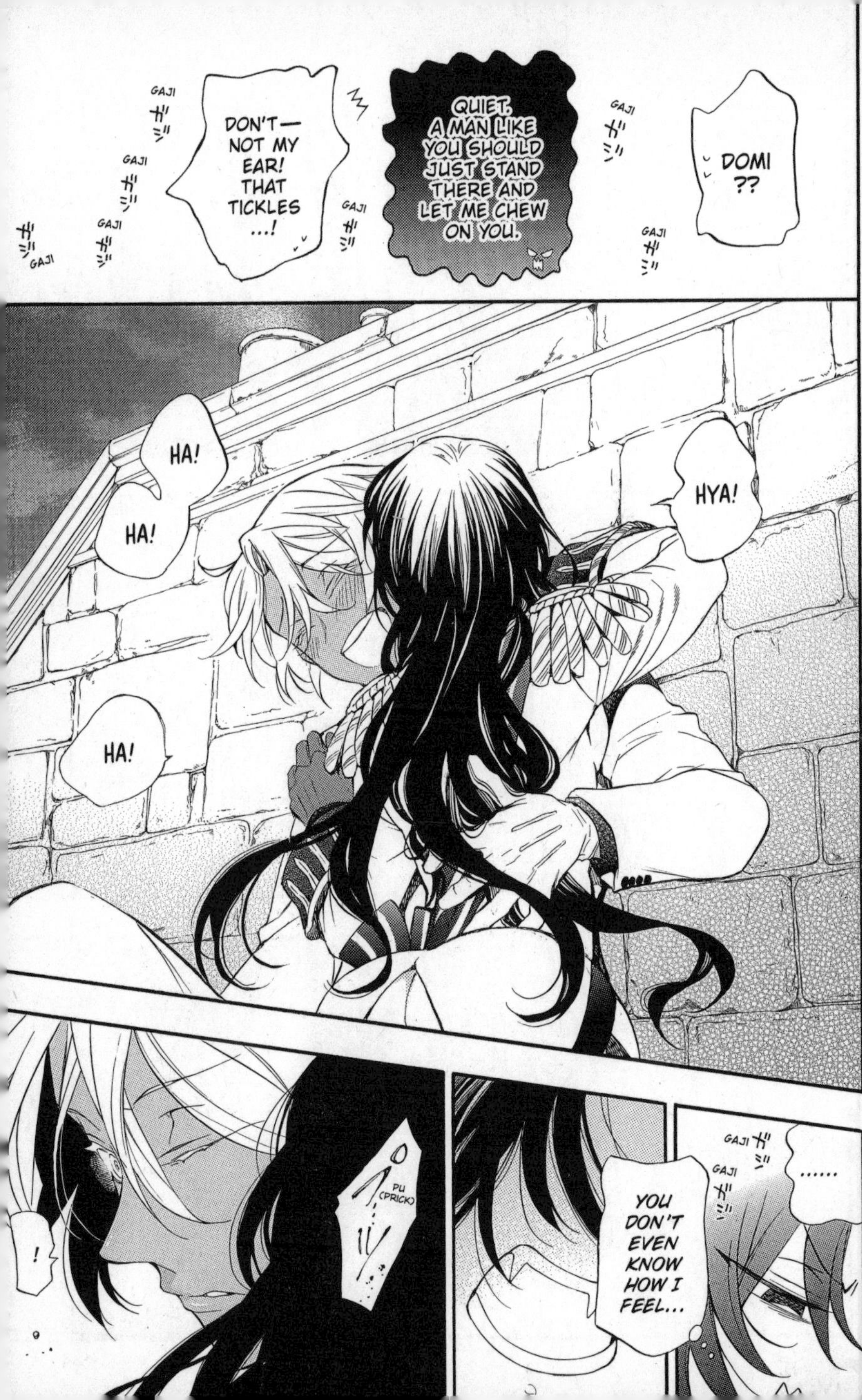
GAJI
DOMI ??
GAJI
QUIET. A MAN LIKE YOU SHOULD JUST STAND THERE AND LET ME CHEW ON YOU.
GAJI
DON'T— NOT MY EAR! THAT TICKLES ...!
GAJI
GAJI
GAJI
GAJI
HYA!
HA!
HA!
HA!
GAJI
GAJI
......
YOU DON'T EVEN KNOW HOW I FEEL...
PU (PRICK)
!
...

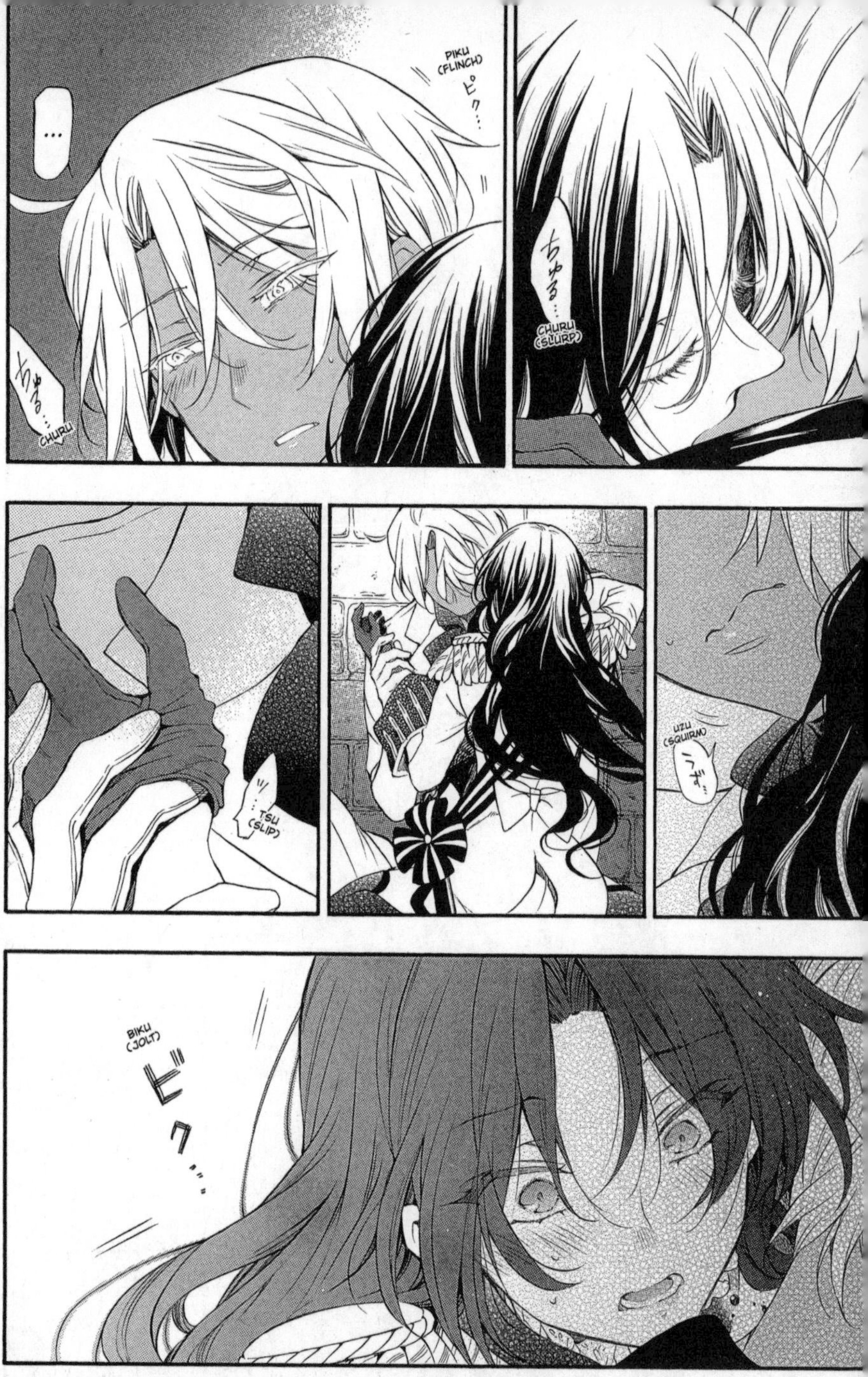
ちゅる…
CHURU (SLURP)
PIKU (FLINCH)
ピク…
…
ちゅる…
CHURU
UZU (SQUIRM)
うず…
ツ…
TSU (SLIP)
BIKU (JOLT)
ビク…

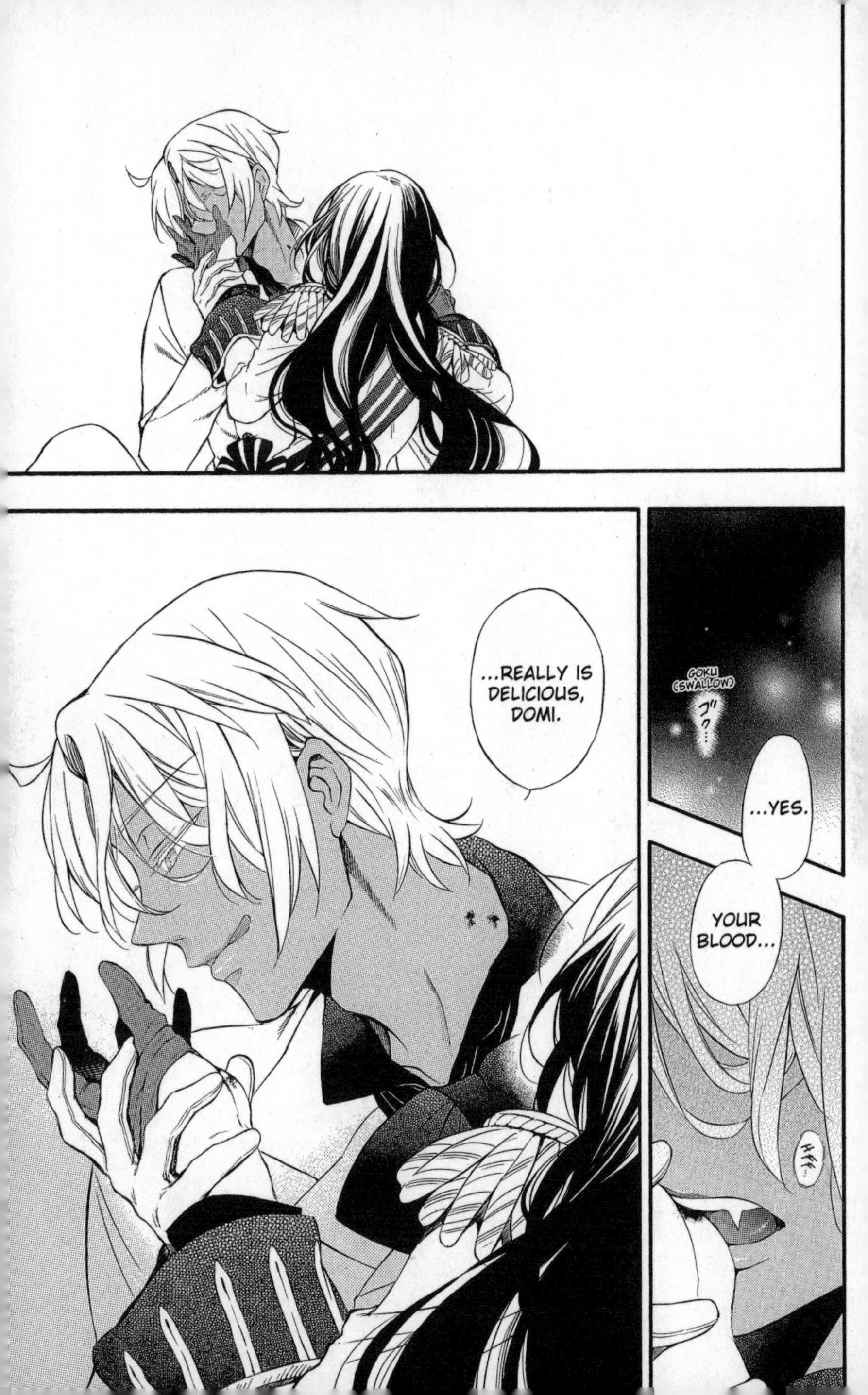
GOKU (SWALLOW)
ゴク…
...YES.
YOUR BLOOD...
Hff...
...REALLY IS DELICIOUS, DOMI.

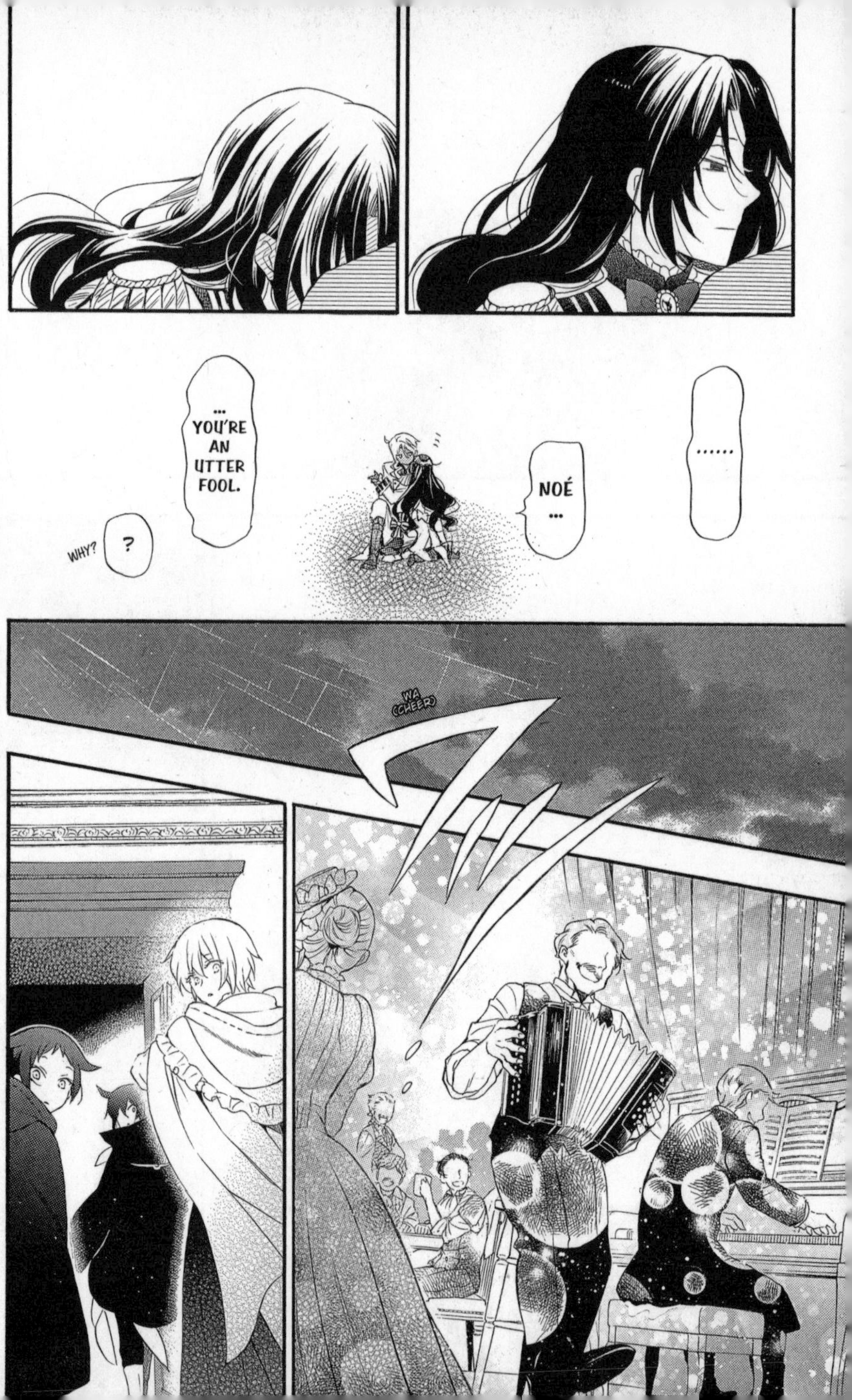
......
NOÉ ...
... YOU'RE AN UTTER FOOL.
?
WHY?
WA (CHEER)

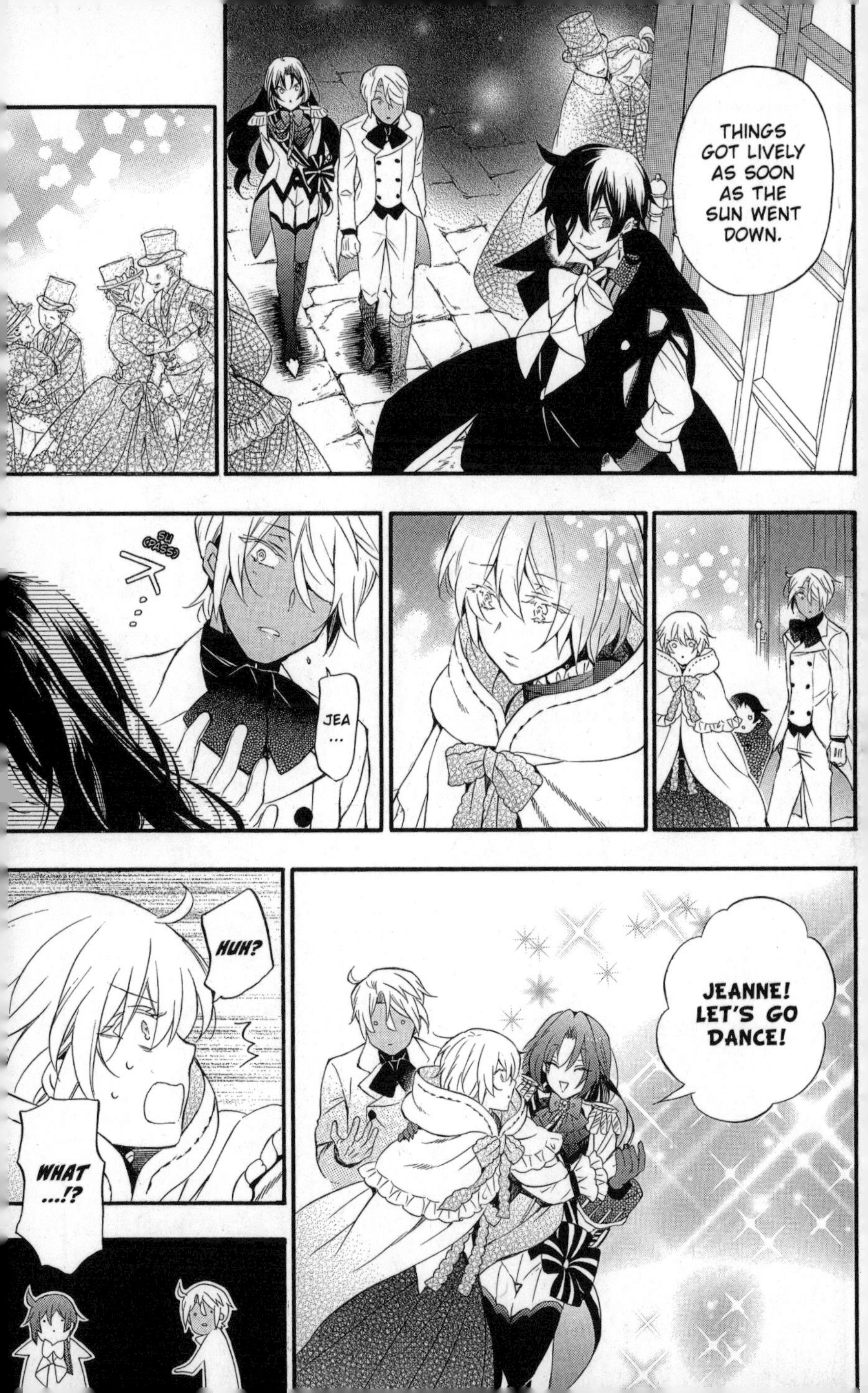
THINGS GOT LIVELY AS SOON AS THE SUN WENT DOWN.
SU (PASS)
JEA ...
JEANNE! LET'S GO DANCE!
HUH?
WHAT ....!?

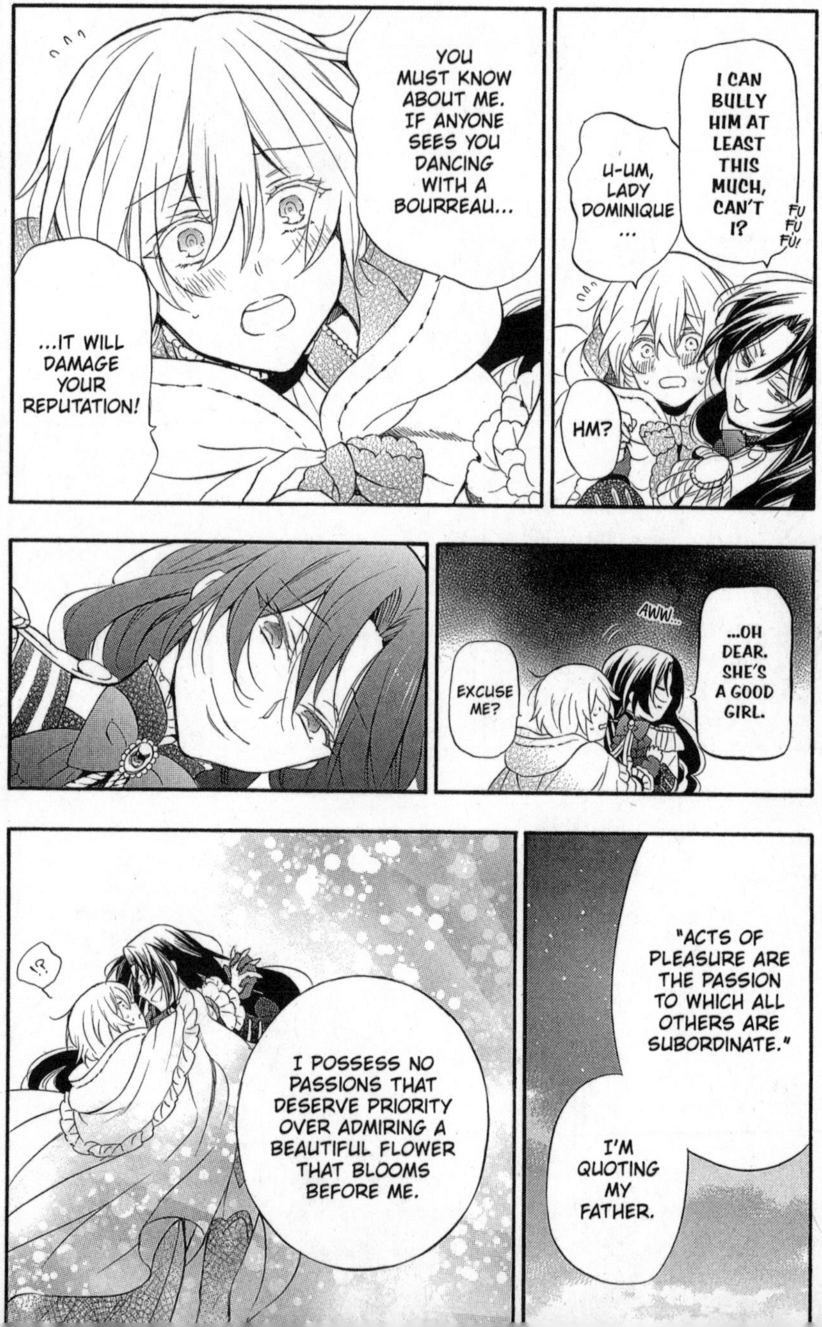
I CAN BULLY HIM AT LEAST THIS MUCH, CAN'T I?
FU FU FU!
U-UM, LADY DOMINIQUE...
HM?
YOU MUST KNOW ABOUT ME. IF ANYONE SEES YOU DANCING WITH A BOURREAU...
...IT WILL DAMAGE YOUR REPUTATION!
...OH DEAR. SHE'S A GOOD GIRL.
AWW...
EXCUSE ME?
"ACTS OF PLEASURE ARE THE PASSION TO WHICH ALL OTHERS ARE SUBORDINATE."
I'M QUOTING MY FATHER.
!?
I POSSESS NO PASSIONS THAT DESERVE PRIORITY OVER ADMIRING A BEAUTIFUL FLOWER THAT BLOOMS BEFORE ME.

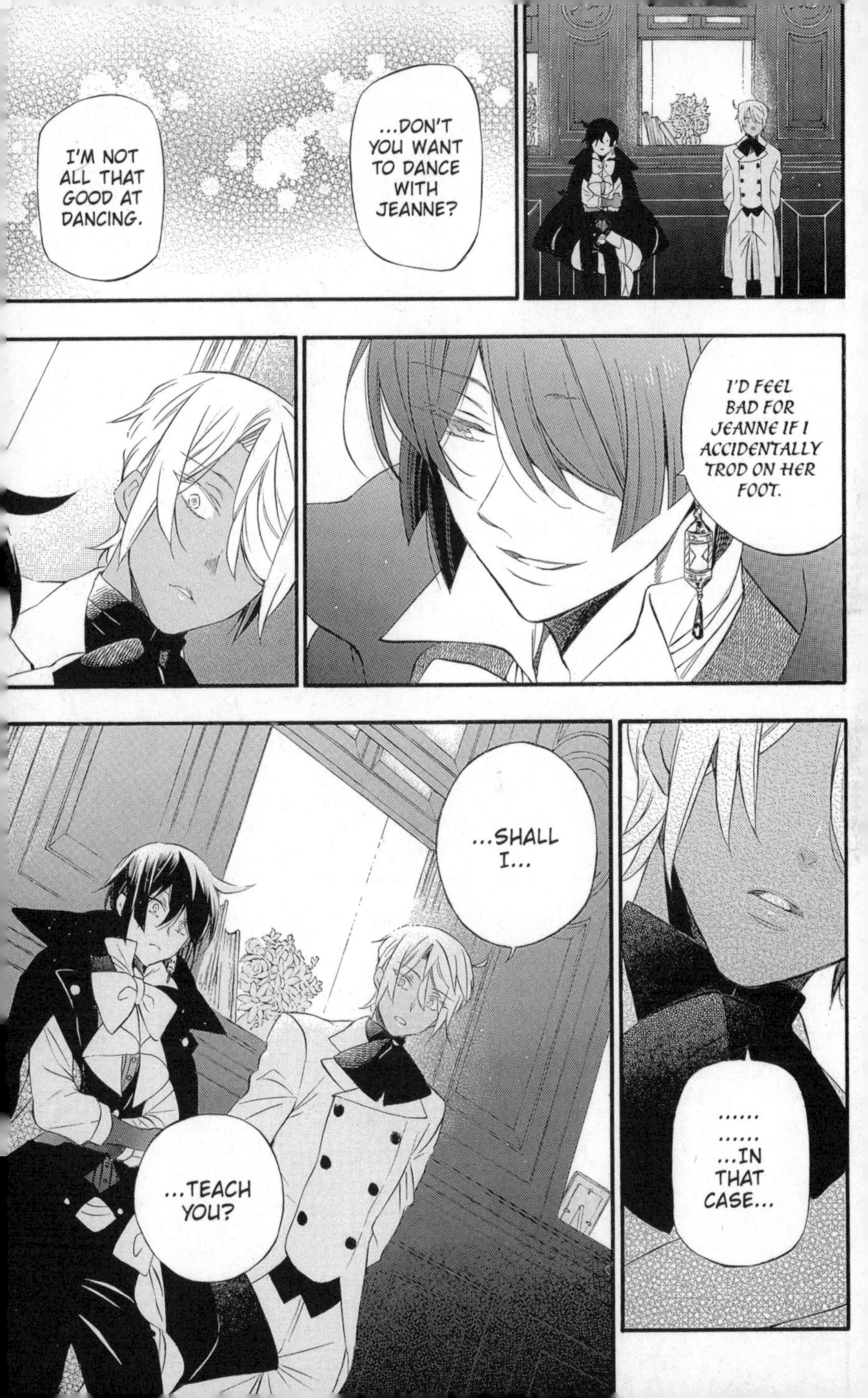
...DON'T YOU WANT TO DANCE WITH JEANNE?
I'M NOT ALL THAT GOOD AT DANCING.
I'D FEEL BAD FOR JEANNE IF I ACCIDENTALLY TROD ON HER FOOT.
....IN THAT CASE...
...SHALL I...
...TEACH YOU?

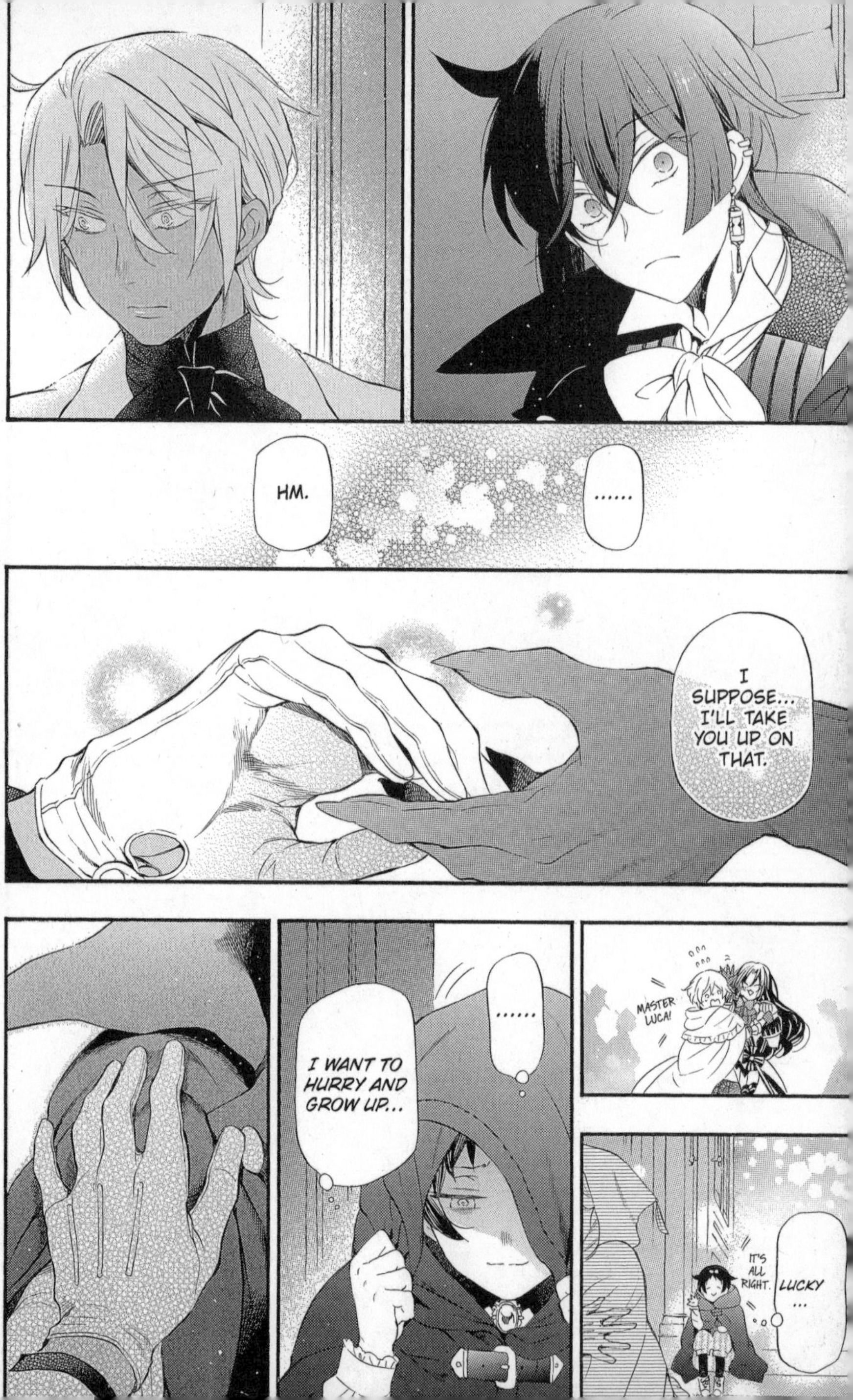
......
HM.
I SUPPOSE... I'LL TAKE YOU UP ON THAT.
MASTER LUCA!
LUCKY ...
IT'S ALL RIGHT.
......
I WANT TO HURRY AND GROW UP...

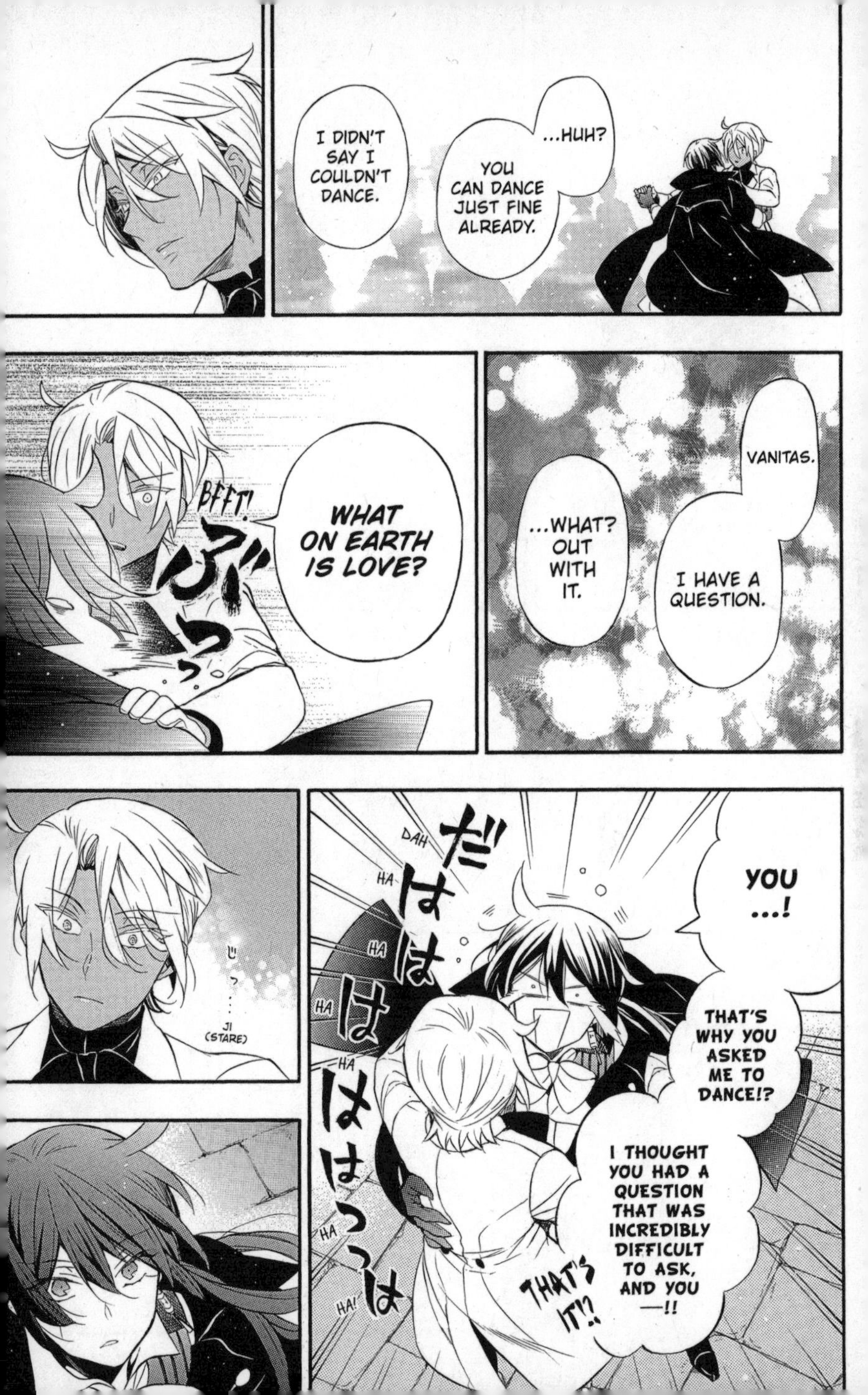
...HUH?
YOU CAN DANCE JUST FINE ALREADY.
I DIDN'T SAY I COULDN'T DANCE.
VANITAS.
I HAVE A QUESTION.
...WHAT? OUT WITH IT.
WHAT ON EARTH IS LOVE?
BFFT!
YOU ...!
THAT'S WHY YOU ASKED ME TO DANCE!?
I THOUGHT YOU HAD A QUESTION THAT WAS INCREDIBLY DIFFICULT TO ASK, AND YOU—!!
THAT'S IT!?
だははははっは
DAH HA HA HA HA HA HA!
じーっ…
JI (STARE)

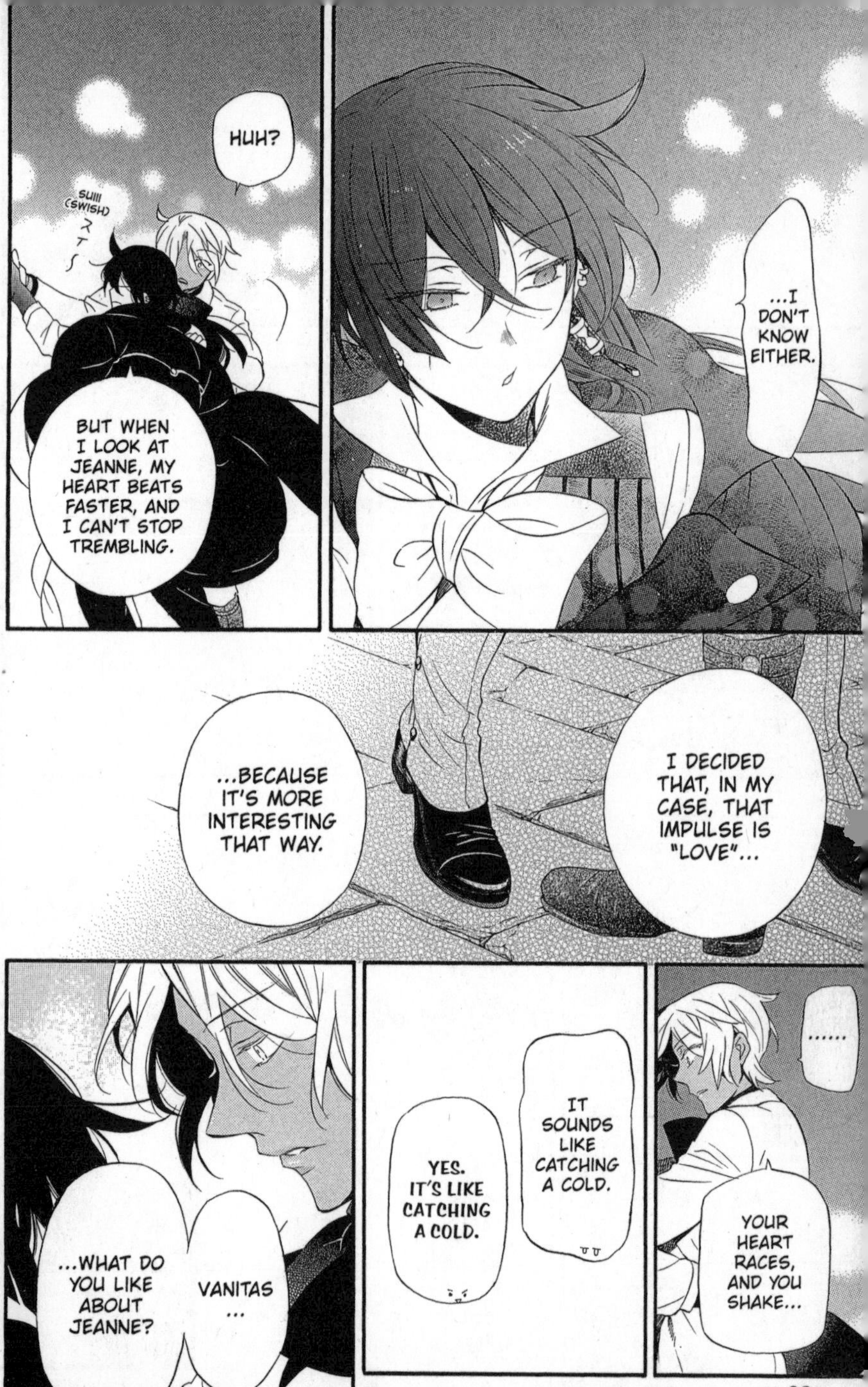
...I DON'T KNOW EITHER.
HUH?
SUIII (SWISH)
BUT WHEN I LOOK AT JEANNE, MY HEART BEATS FASTER, AND I CAN'T STOP TREMBLING.
I DECIDED THAT, IN MY CASE, THAT IMPULSE IS "LOVE"...
...BECAUSE IT'S MORE INTERESTING THAT WAY.
......
YOUR HEART RACES, AND YOU SHAKE...
IT SOUNDS LIKE CATCHING A COLD.
YES. IT'S LIKE CATCHING A COLD.
VANITAS...
...WHAT DO YOU LIKE ABOUT JEANNE?

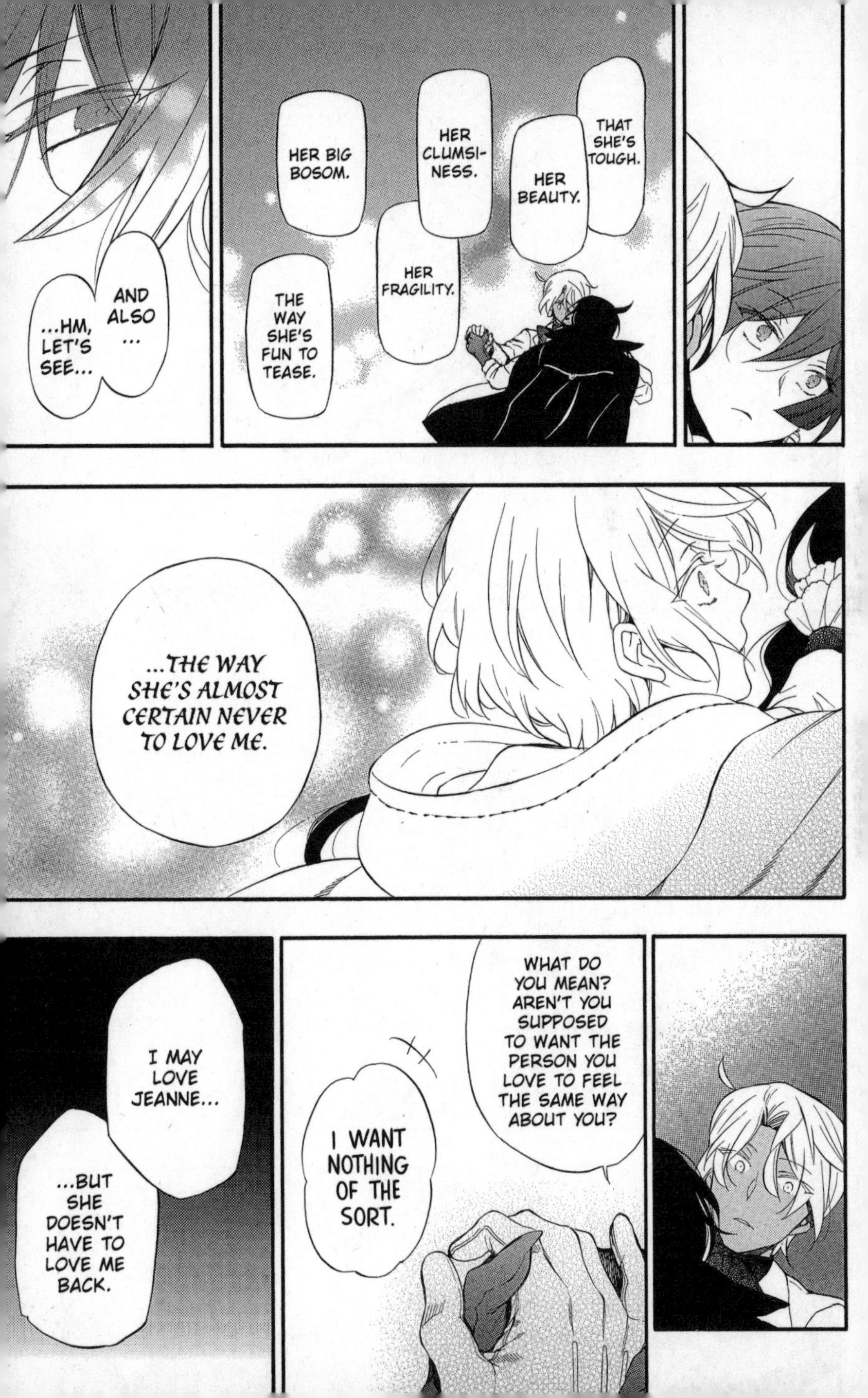
THAT SHE'S TOUGH.
HER BEAUTY.
HER CLUMSINESS.
HER BIG BOSOM.
HER FRAGILITY.
THE WAY SHE'S FUN TO TEASE.
AND ALSO ...
...HM, LET'S SEE...
...THE WAY SHE'S ALMOST CERTAIN NEVER TO LOVE ME.
WHAT DO YOU MEAN? AREN'T YOU SUPPOSED TO WANT THE PERSON YOU LOVE TO FEEL THE SAME WAY ABOUT YOU?
I WANT NOTHING OF THE SORT.
I MAY LOVE JEANNE...
...BUT SHE DOESN'T HAVE TO LOVE ME BACK.

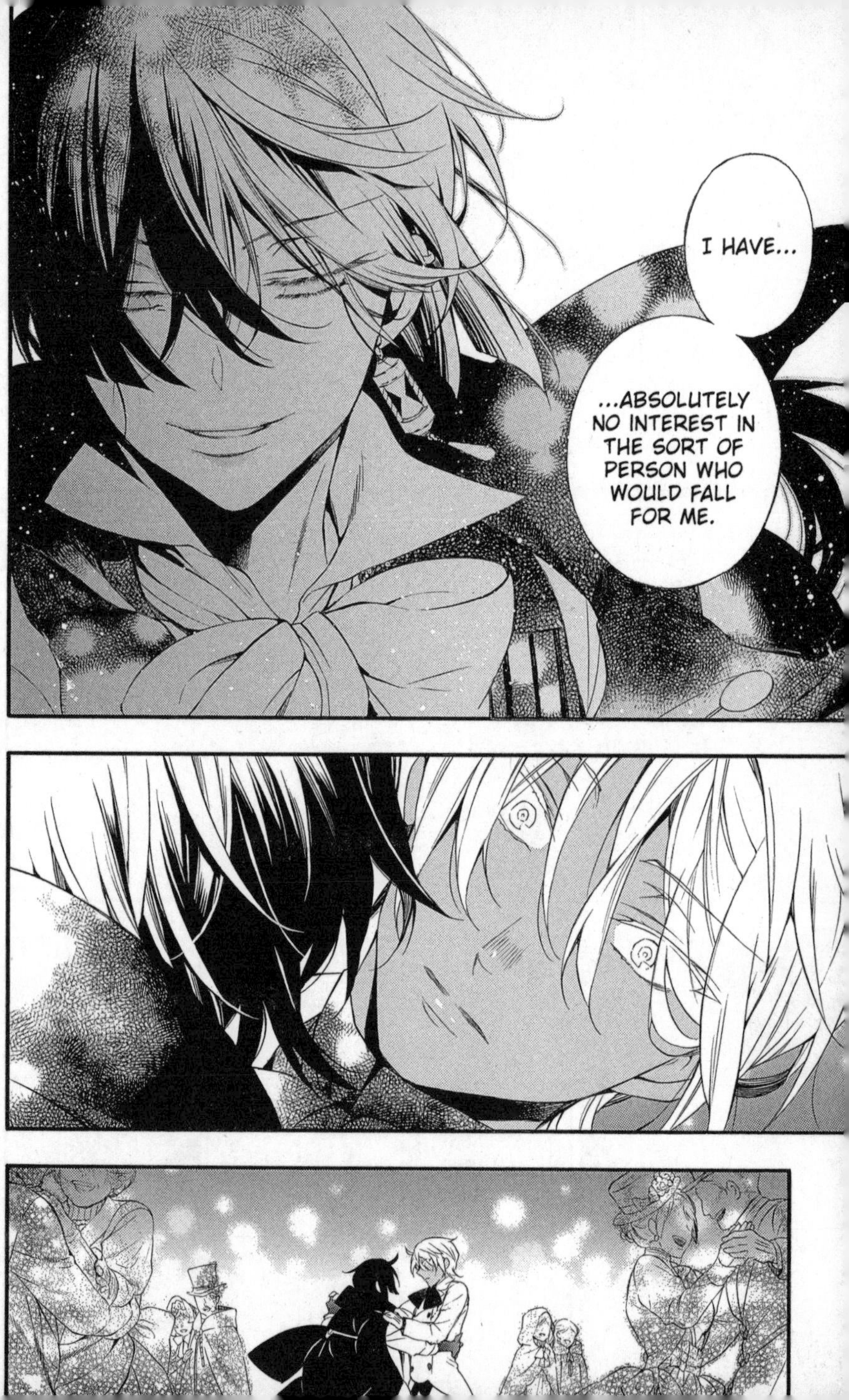
I HAVE...
...ABSOLUTELY NO INTEREST IN THE SORT OF PERSON WHO WOULD FALL FOR ME.

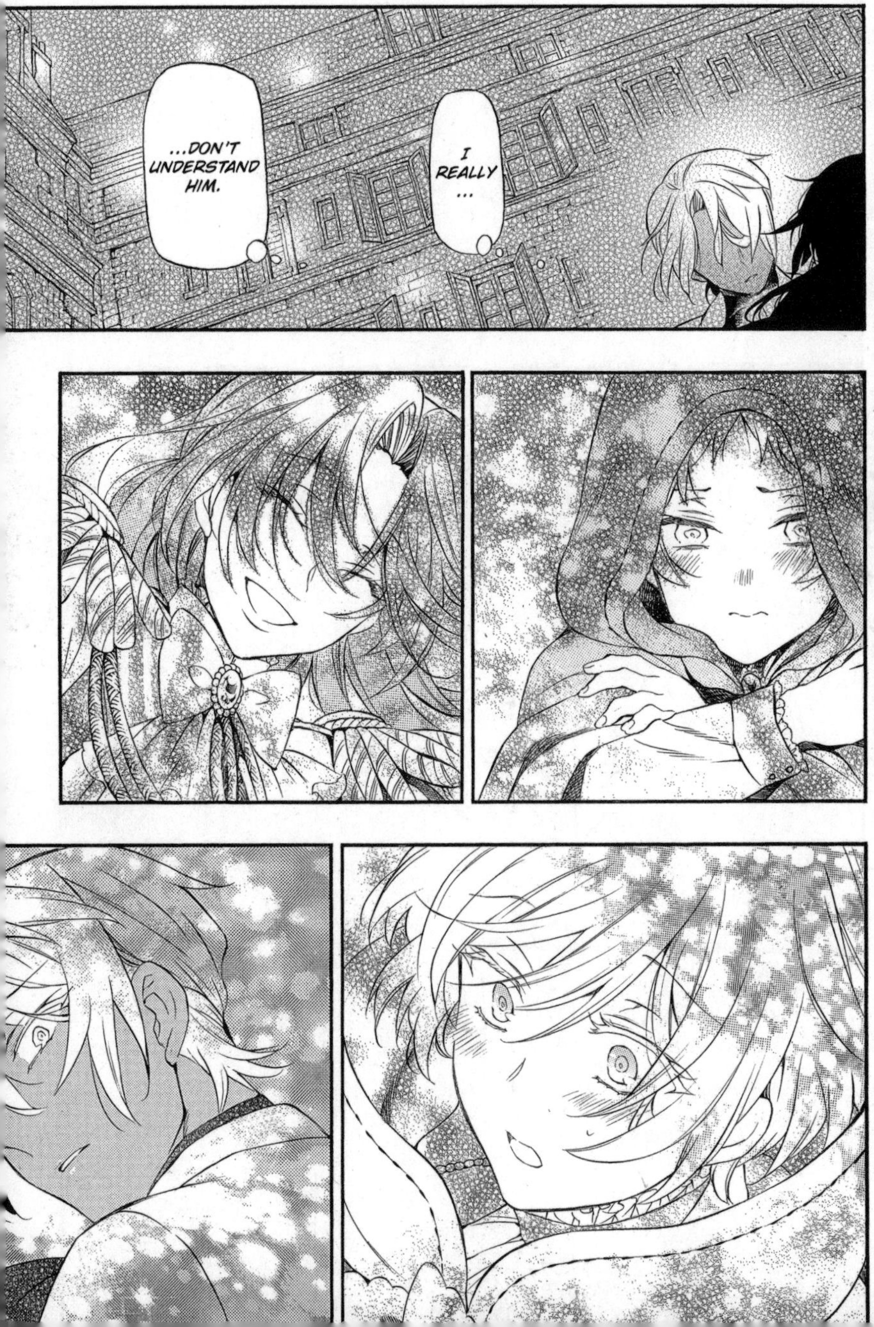
I REALLY ...
...DON'T UNDERSTAND HIM.

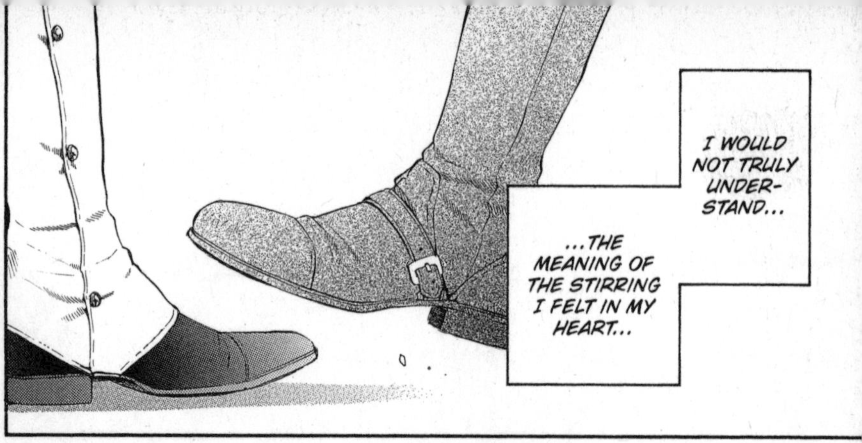
I WOULD NOT TRULY UNDER-STAND...
...THE MEANING OF THE STIRRING I FELT IN MY HEART...

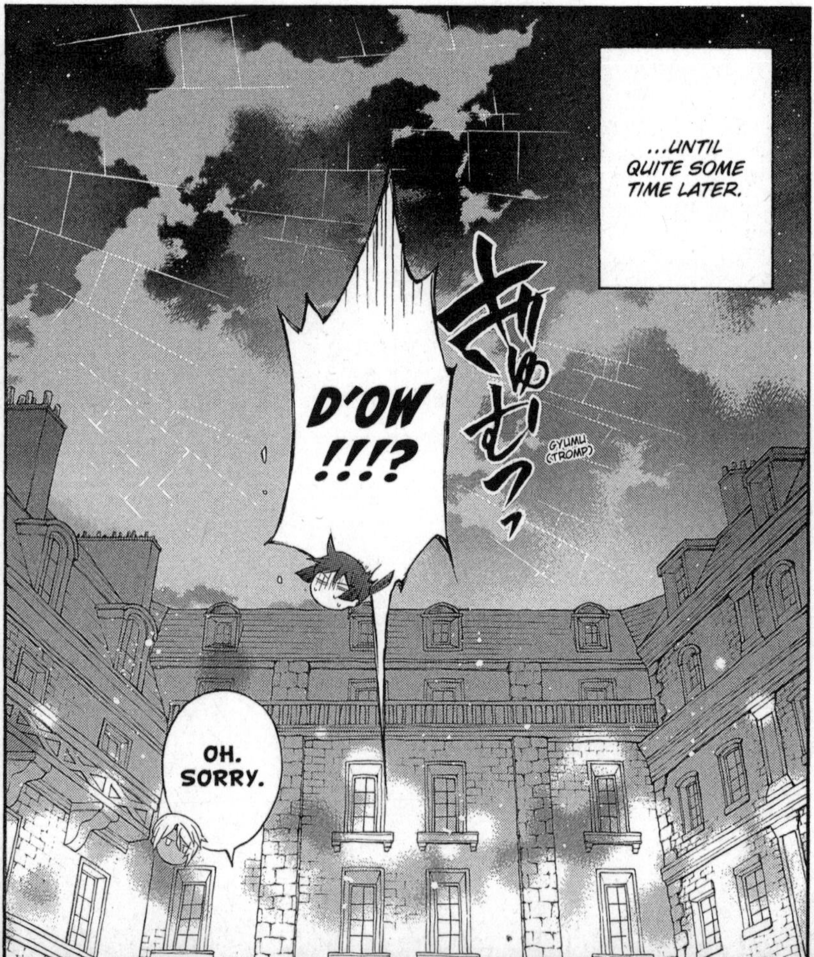
...UNTIL QUITE SOME TIME LATER.
ぎゅむっ
GYUMU (TROMP)
D'OW !!!?
OH. SORRY.

Mémoire 12 Pause

TARTE TATIN

An apple tart that was invented at the Hôtel Tatin in the town of Lamotte-Beuvron in France in the latter half of the 19th century, when the hotel's managers, the Tatin sisters, made a mistake.

Stéphanie, the older sister, forgot to put the tart crust in the pan and accidentally put the apples in the oven by themselves one day. Thinking fast, her younger sister, Caroline, laid the crust over the top and baked it, then inverted the whole thing onto a plate. That was the beginning of tarte Tatin, or so the story goes.

The tart became the hotel's specialty and later became popular across the Sologne region.

Parenthetically, the Hôtel Tatin is still in business.

IN THE WORLD OF VANITAS, TARTE TATIN WAS INVENTED
A LITTLE EARLIER THAN IT WAS IN OUR WORLD.

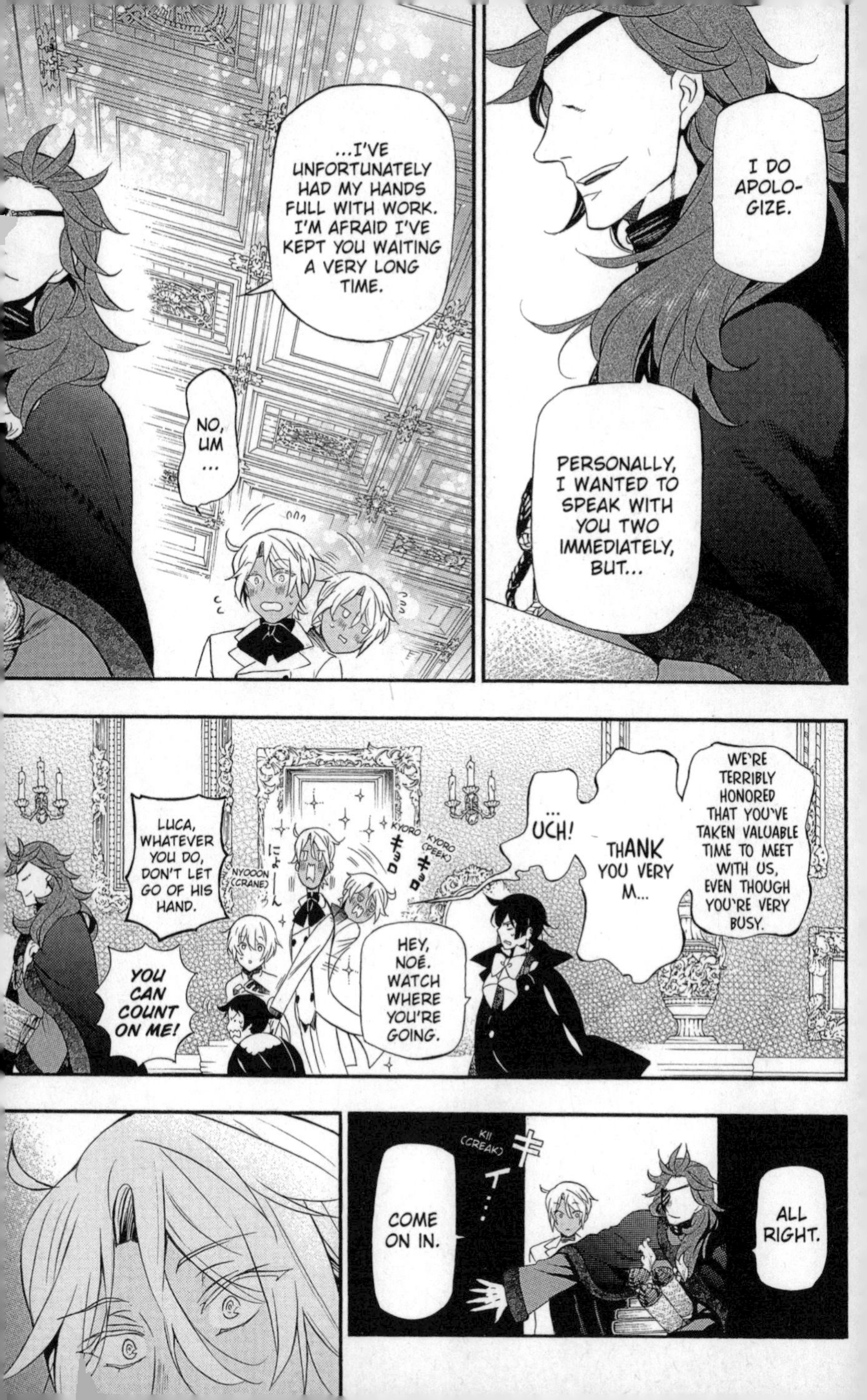
I DO APOLOGIZE.
PERSONALLY, I WANTED TO SPEAK WITH YOU TWO IMMEDIATELY, BUT...
...I'VE UNFORTUNATELY HAD MY HANDS FULL WITH WORK. I'M AFRAID I'VE KEPT YOU WAITING A VERY LONG TIME.
NO, UM ...
WE'RE TERRIBLY HONORED THAT YOU'VE TAKEN VALUABLE TIME TO MEET WITH US, EVEN THOUGH YOU'RE VERY BUSY.
THANK YOU VERY M...
...UCH!
KYORO KYORO (PEEK)
HEY, NOÉ. WATCH WHERE YOU'RE GOING.
NYOOON (CRANE)
LUCA, WHATEVER YOU DO, DON'T LET GO OF HIS HAND.
YOU CAN COUNT ON ME!
ALL RIGHT.
KII (CREAK)
COME ON IN.

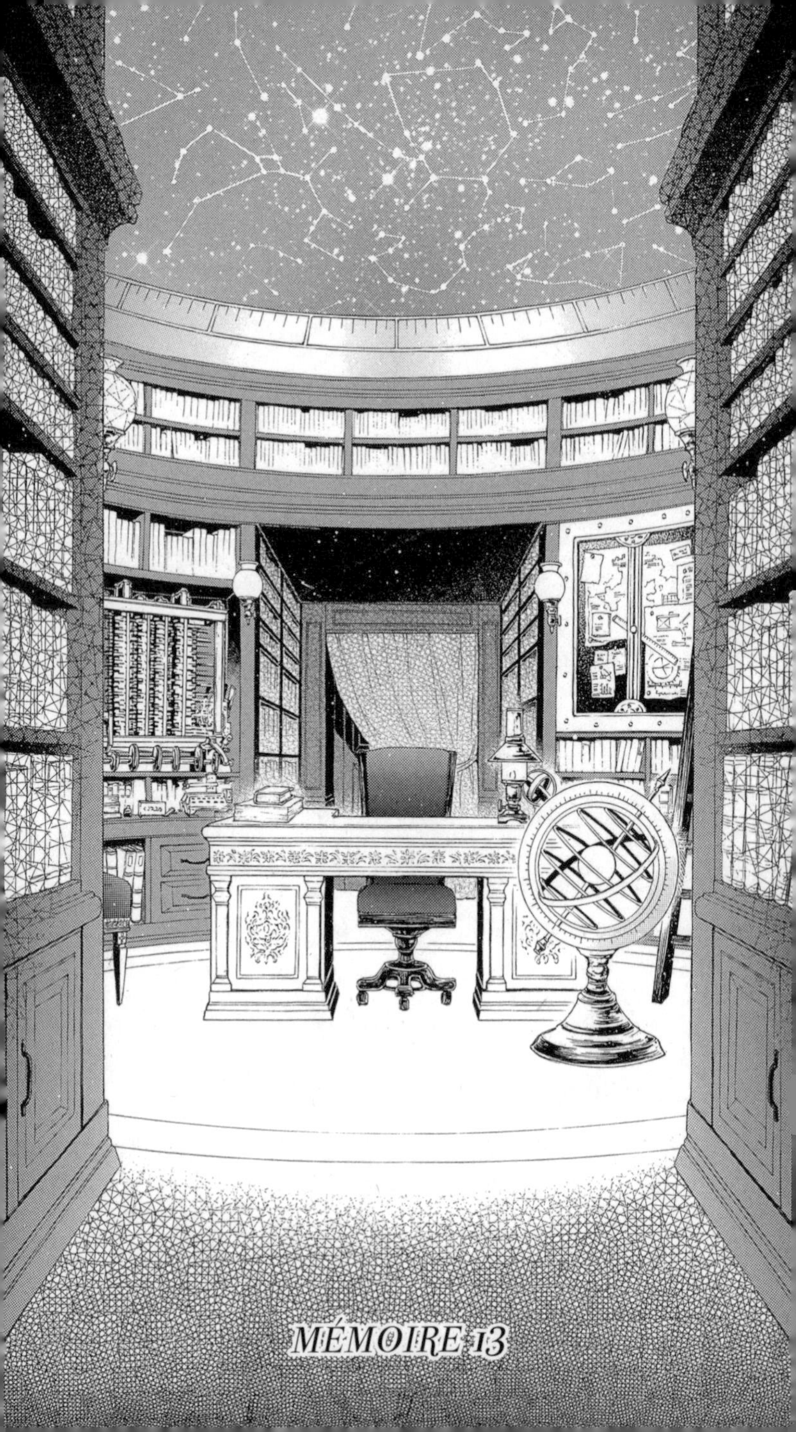
MÉMOIRE 13

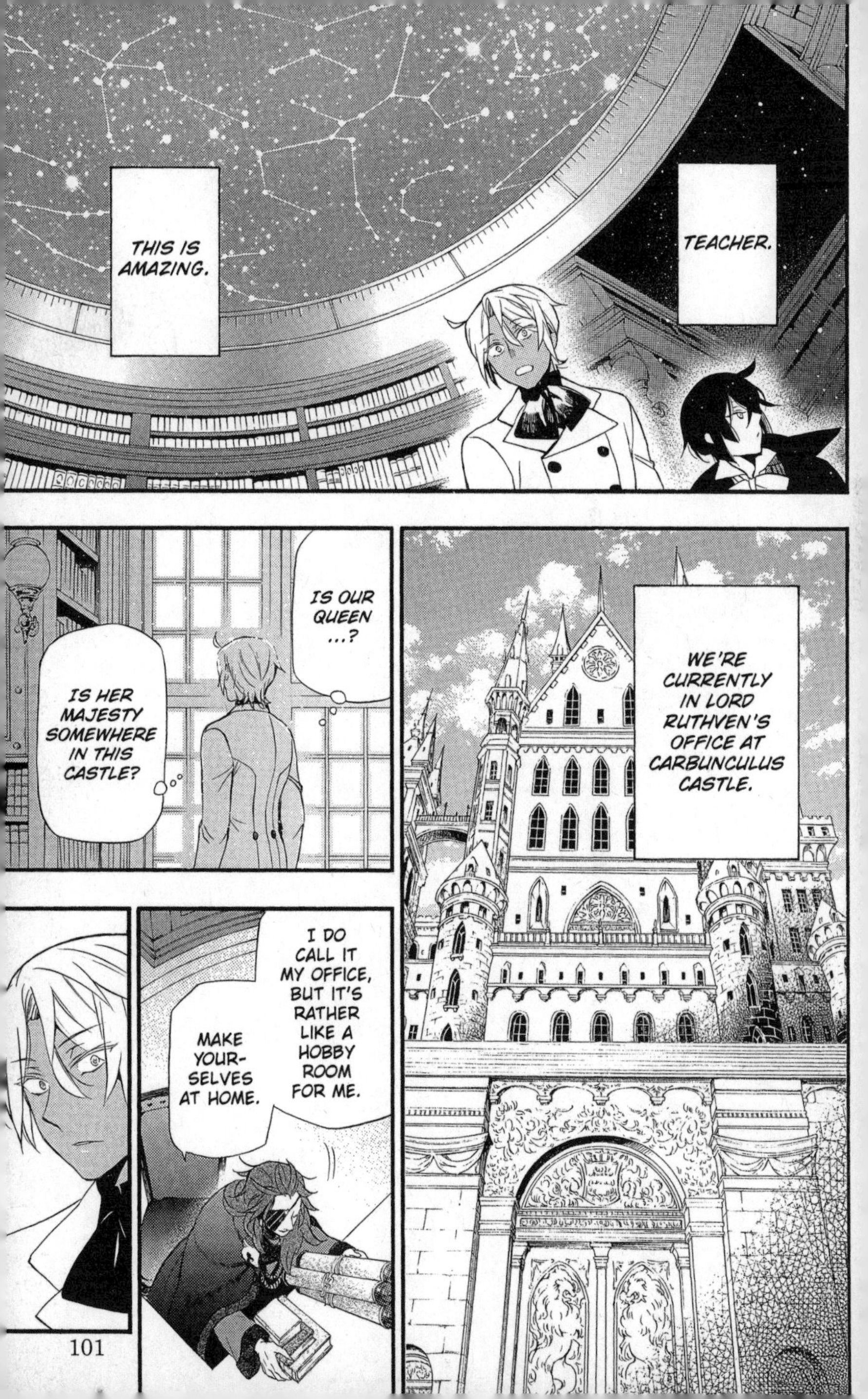
TEACHER.
THIS IS AMAZING.
WE'RE CURRENTLY IN LORD RUTHVEN'S OFFICE AT CARBUNCULUS CASTLE.
IS OUR QUEEN ...?
IS HER MAJESTY SOMEWHERE IN THIS CASTLE?
I DO CALL IT MY OFFICE, BUT IT'S RATHER LIKE A HOBBY ROOM FOR ME.
MAKE YOUR-SELVES AT HOME.

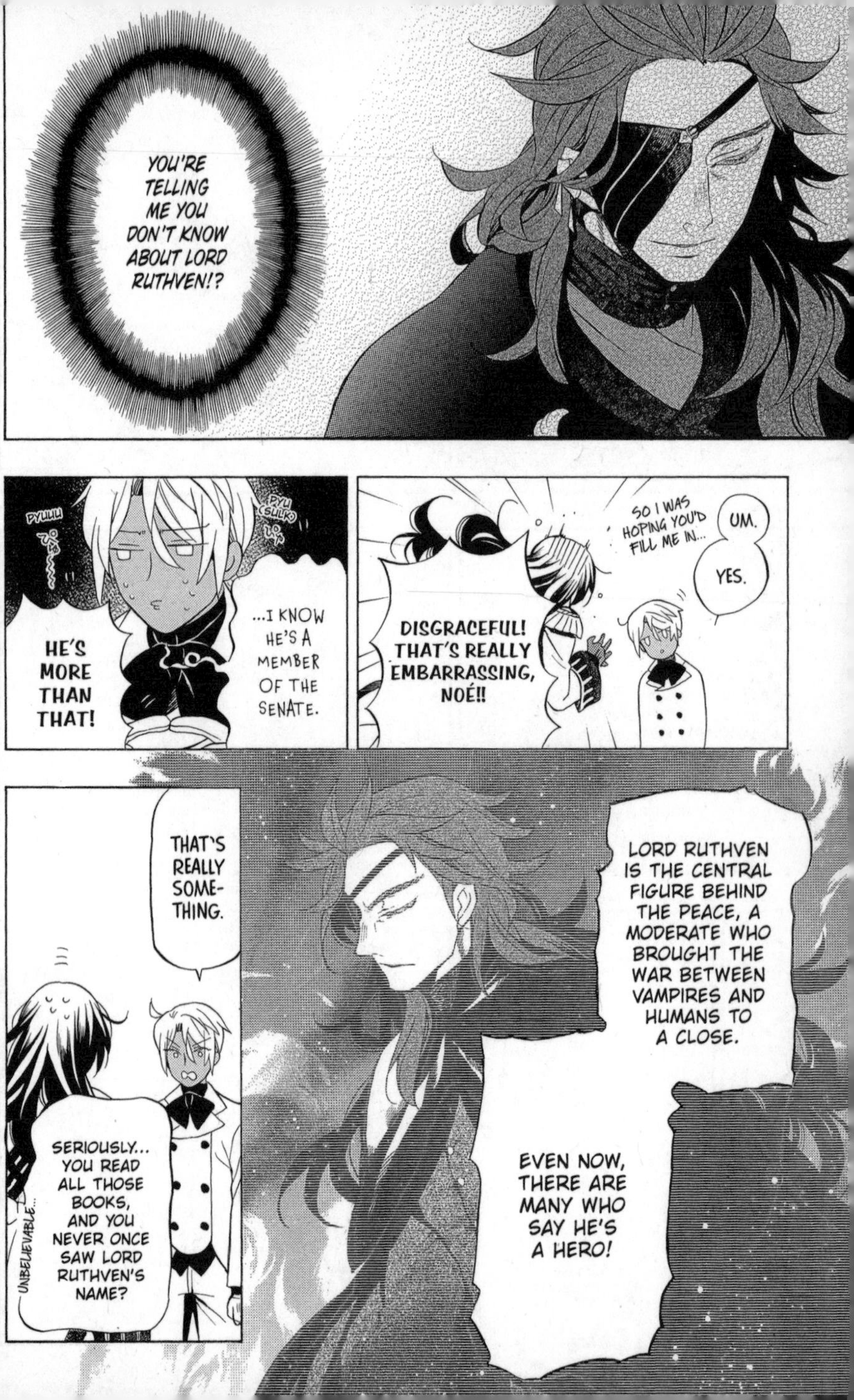
YOU'RE TELLING ME YOU DON'T KNOW ABOUT LORD RUTHVEN!?
UM.
YES.
SO I WAS HOPING YOU'D FILL ME IN...
DISGRACEFUL! THAT'S REALLY EMBARRASSING, NOÉ!!
PYU (SULK)
PYUUU
...I KNOW HE'S A MEMBER OF THE SENATE.
HE'S MORE THAN THAT!
LORD RUTHVEN IS THE CENTRAL FIGURE BEHIND THE PEACE, A MODERATE WHO BROUGHT THE WAR BETWEEN VAMPIRES AND HUMANS TO A CLOSE.
EVEN NOW, THERE ARE MANY WHO SAY HE'S A HERO!
THAT'S REALLY SOME-THING.
SERIOUSLY... YOU READ ALL THOSE BOOKS, AND YOU NEVER ONCE SAW LORD RUTHVEN'S NAME?
UNBELIEVABLE...

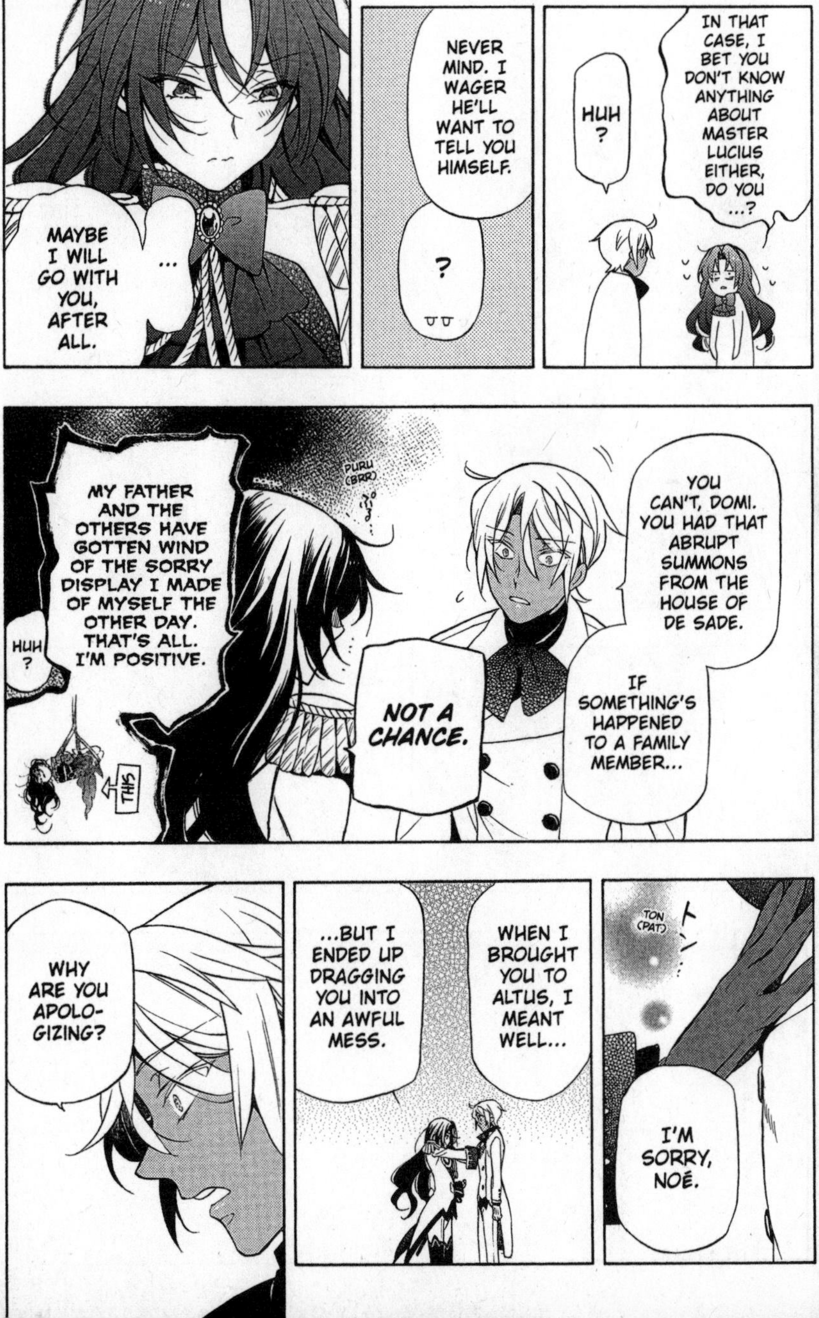
IN THAT CASE, I BET YOU DON'T KNOW ANYTHING ABOUT MASTER LUCIUS EITHER, DO YOU ...?
HUH?
NEVER MIND. I WAGER HE'LL WANT TO TELL YOU HIMSELF.
?
...
MAYBE I WILL GO WITH YOU, AFTER ALL.
YOU CAN'T, DOMI. YOU HAD THAT ABRUPT SUMMONS FROM THE HOUSE OF DE SADE.
IF SOMETHING'S HAPPENED TO A FAMILY MEMBER...
PURU (BRR)
NOT A CHANCE.
MY FATHER AND THE OTHERS HAVE GOTTEN WIND OF THE SORRY DISPLAY I MADE OF MYSELF THE OTHER DAY. THAT'S ALL. I'M POSITIVE.
HUH?
THIS
TON (PAT)
I'M SORRY, NOÉ.
WHEN I BROUGHT YOU TO ALTUS, I MEANT WELL...
...BUT I ENDED UP DRAGGING YOU INTO AN AWFUL MESS.
WHY ARE YOU APOLO-GIZING?

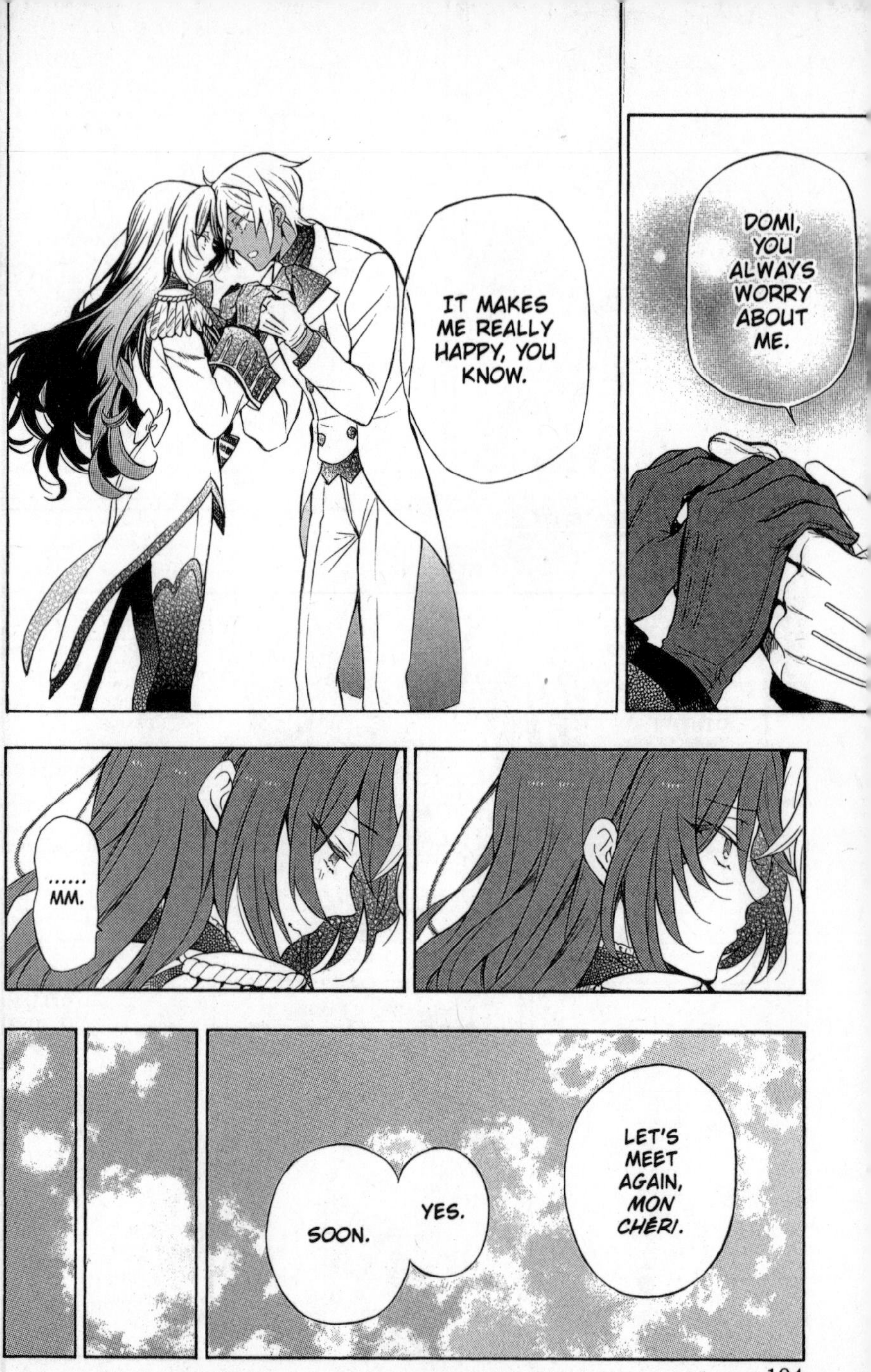
DOMI, YOU ALWAYS WORRY ABOUT ME.
IT MAKES ME REALLY HAPPY, YOU KNOW.
...... MM.
LET'S MEET AGAIN, *MON CHÉRI*.
YES.
SOON.

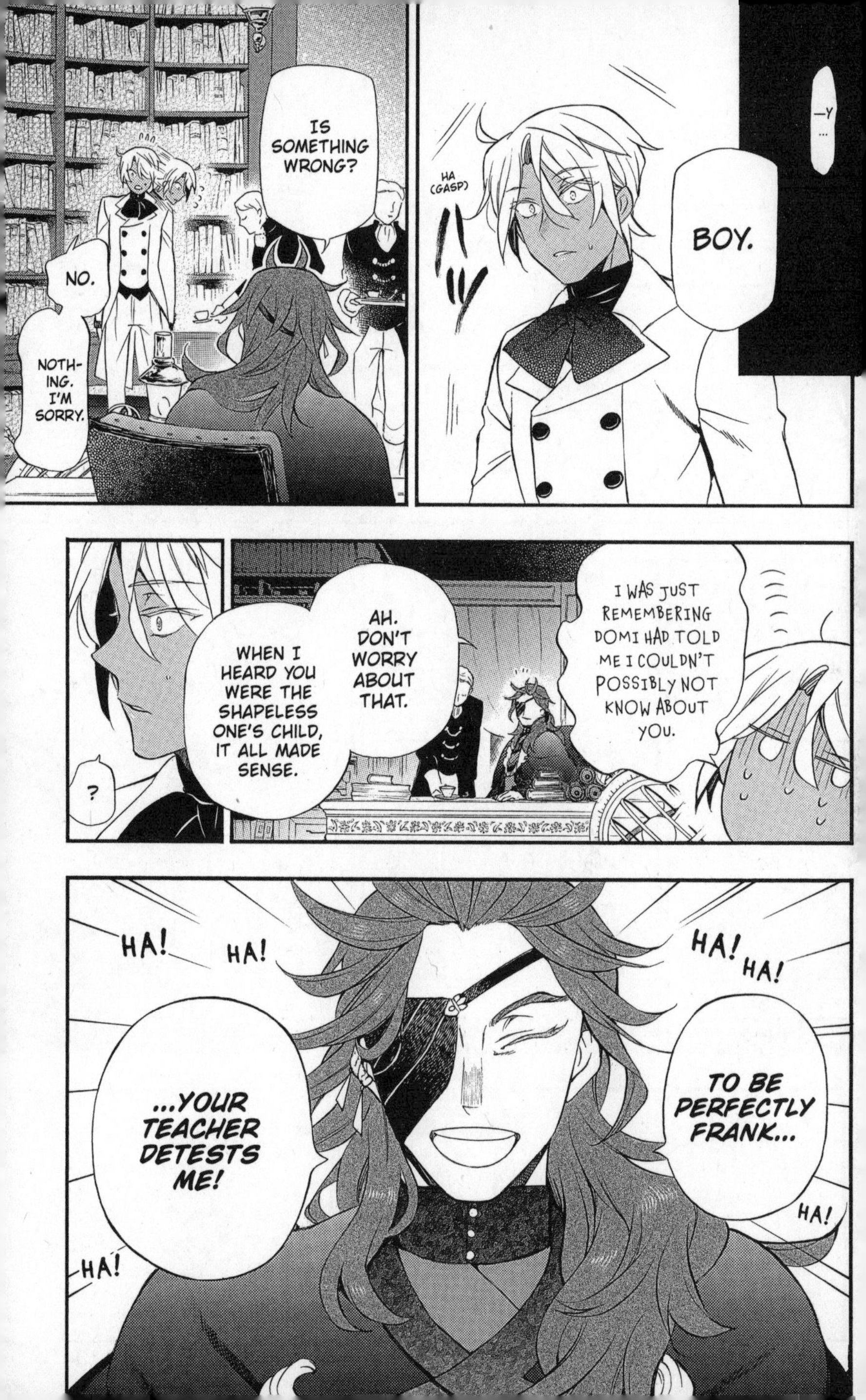
—Y ...
BOY.
HA (GASP)
IS SOMETHING WRONG?
NO.
NOTHING. I'M SORRY.
I WAS JUST REMEMBERING DOMI HAD TOLD ME I COULDN'T POSSIBLY NOT KNOW ABOUT YOU.
AH. DON'T WORRY ABOUT THAT.
WHEN I HEARD YOU WERE THE SHAPELESS ONE'S CHILD, IT ALL MADE SENSE.
?
HA! HA!
HA! HA!
TO BE PERFECTLY FRANK...
...YOUR TEACHER DETESTS ME!
HA!
HA!

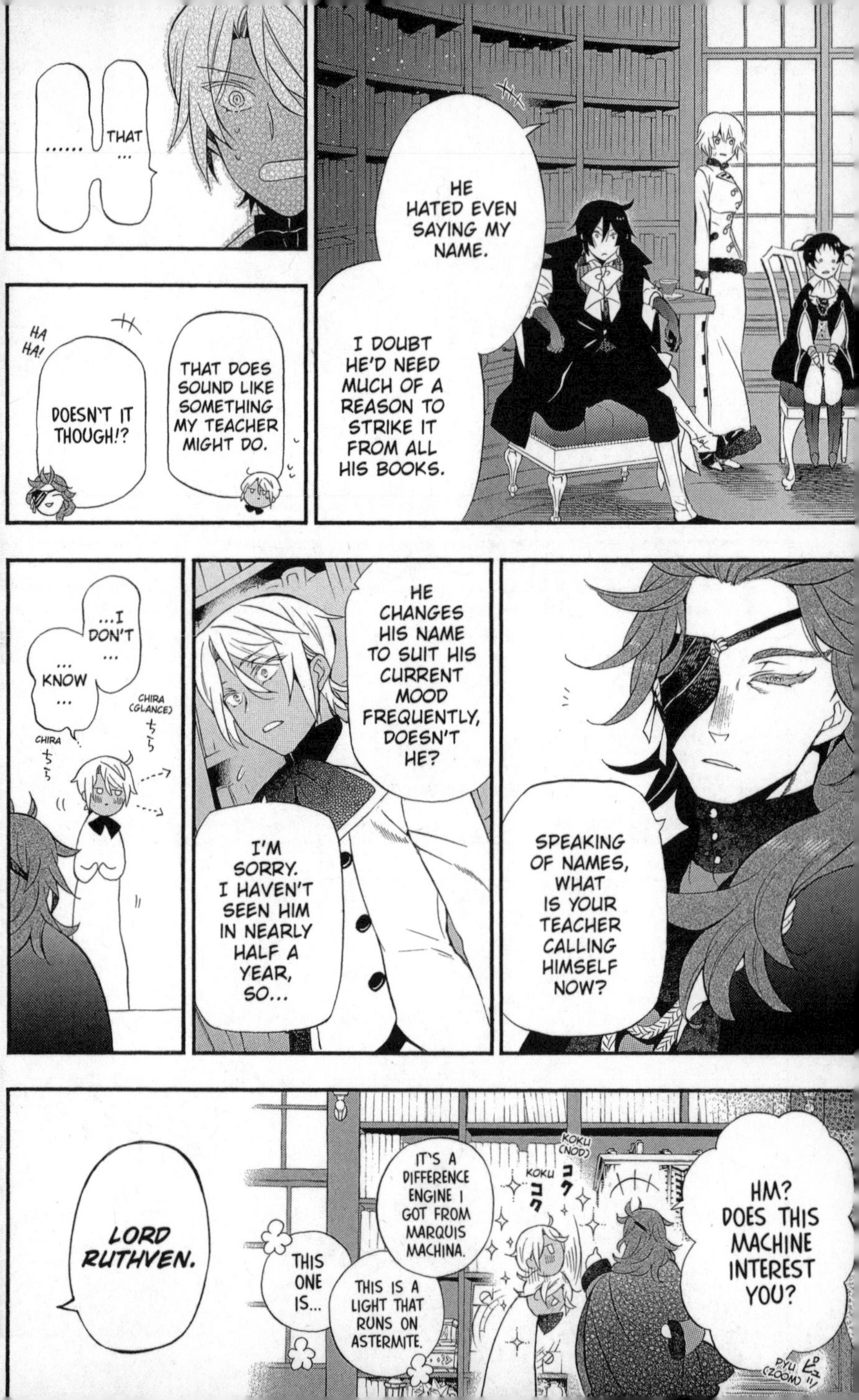

HE HATED EVEN SAYING MY NAME.
I DOUBT HE'D NEED MUCH OF A REASON TO STRIKE IT FROM ALL HIS BOOKS.
...... THAT ...
THAT DOES SOUND LIKE SOMETHING MY TEACHER MIGHT DO.
HA HA!
DOESN'T IT THOUGH!?
SPEAKING OF NAMES, WHAT IS YOUR TEACHER CALLING HIMSELF NOW?
HE CHANGES HIS NAME TO SUIT HIS CURRENT MOOD FREQUENTLY, DOESN'T HE?
I'M SORRY. I HAVEN'T SEEN HIM IN NEARLY HALF A YEAR, SO...
...I DON'T ... KNOW ...
CHIRA (GLANCE) ちら
CHIRA ちら
HM? DOES THIS MACHINE INTEREST YOU?
PYU (ZOOM) ピュ
KOKU (NOD) コク
KOKU コク
IT'S A DIFFERENCE ENGINE I GOT FROM MARQUIS MACHINA.
THIS IS A LIGHT THAT RUNS ON ASTERMITE.
THIS ONE IS...
LORD RUTHVEN.

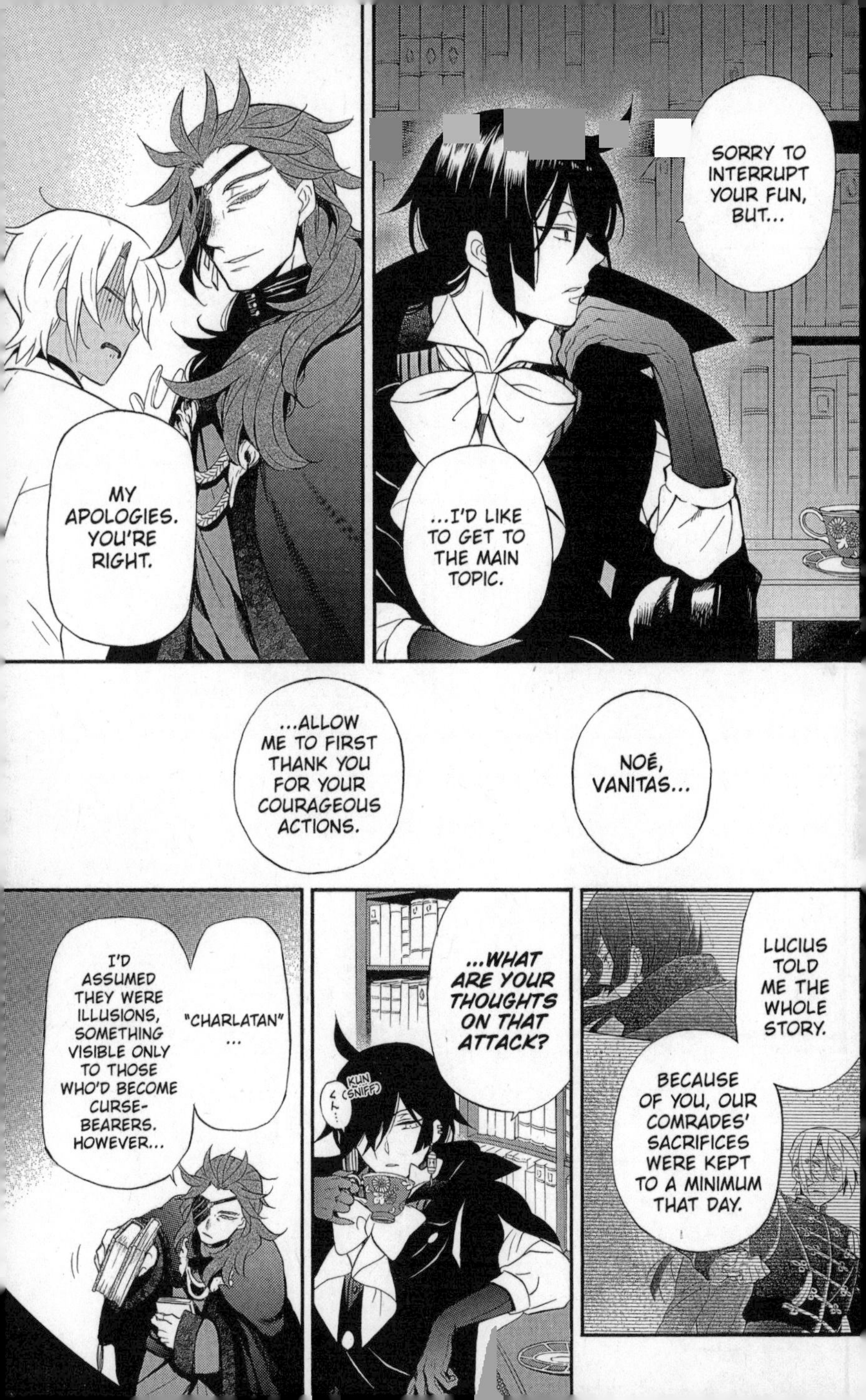
SORRY TO INTERRUPT YOUR FUN, BUT...
...I'D LIKE TO GET TO THE MAIN TOPIC.
MY APOLOGIES. YOU'RE RIGHT.
NOÉ, VANITAS...
...ALLOW ME TO FIRST THANK YOU FOR YOUR COURAGEOUS ACTIONS.
LUCIUS TOLD ME THE WHOLE STORY.
BECAUSE OF YOU, OUR COMRADES' SACRIFICES WERE KEPT TO A MINIMUM THAT DAY.
...WHAT ARE YOUR THOUGHTS ON THAT ATTACK?
くん…
KUN (SNIFF)
"CHARLATAN" ...
I'D ASSUMED THEY WERE ILLUSIONS, SOMETHING VISIBLE ONLY TO THOSE WHO'D BECOME CURSE-BEARERS. HOWEVER...

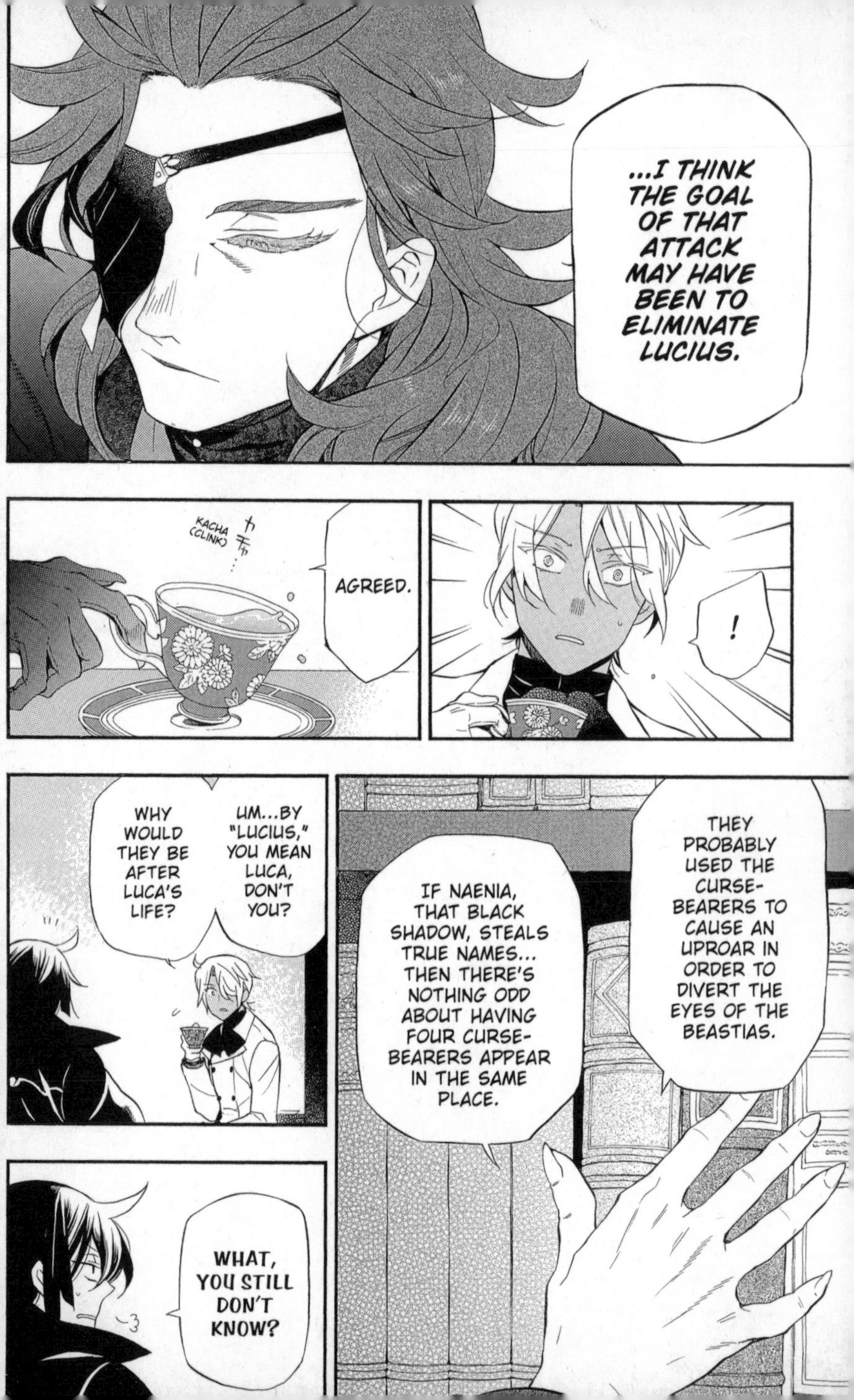
...I THINK THE GOAL OF THAT ATTACK MAY HAVE BEEN TO ELIMINATE LUCIUS.
!
AGREED.
KACHA (CLINK)
THEY PROBABLY USED THE CURSE-BEARERS TO CAUSE AN UPROAR IN ORDER TO DIVERT THE EYES OF THE BEASTIAS.
IF NAENIA, THAT BLACK SHADOW, STEALS TRUE NAMES... THEN THERE'S NOTHING ODD ABOUT HAVING FOUR CURSE-BEARERS APPEAR IN THE SAME PLACE.
UM...BY "LUCIUS," YOU MEAN LUCA, DON'T YOU?
WHY WOULD THEY BE AFTER LUCA'S LIFE?
WHAT, YOU STILL DON'T KNOW?

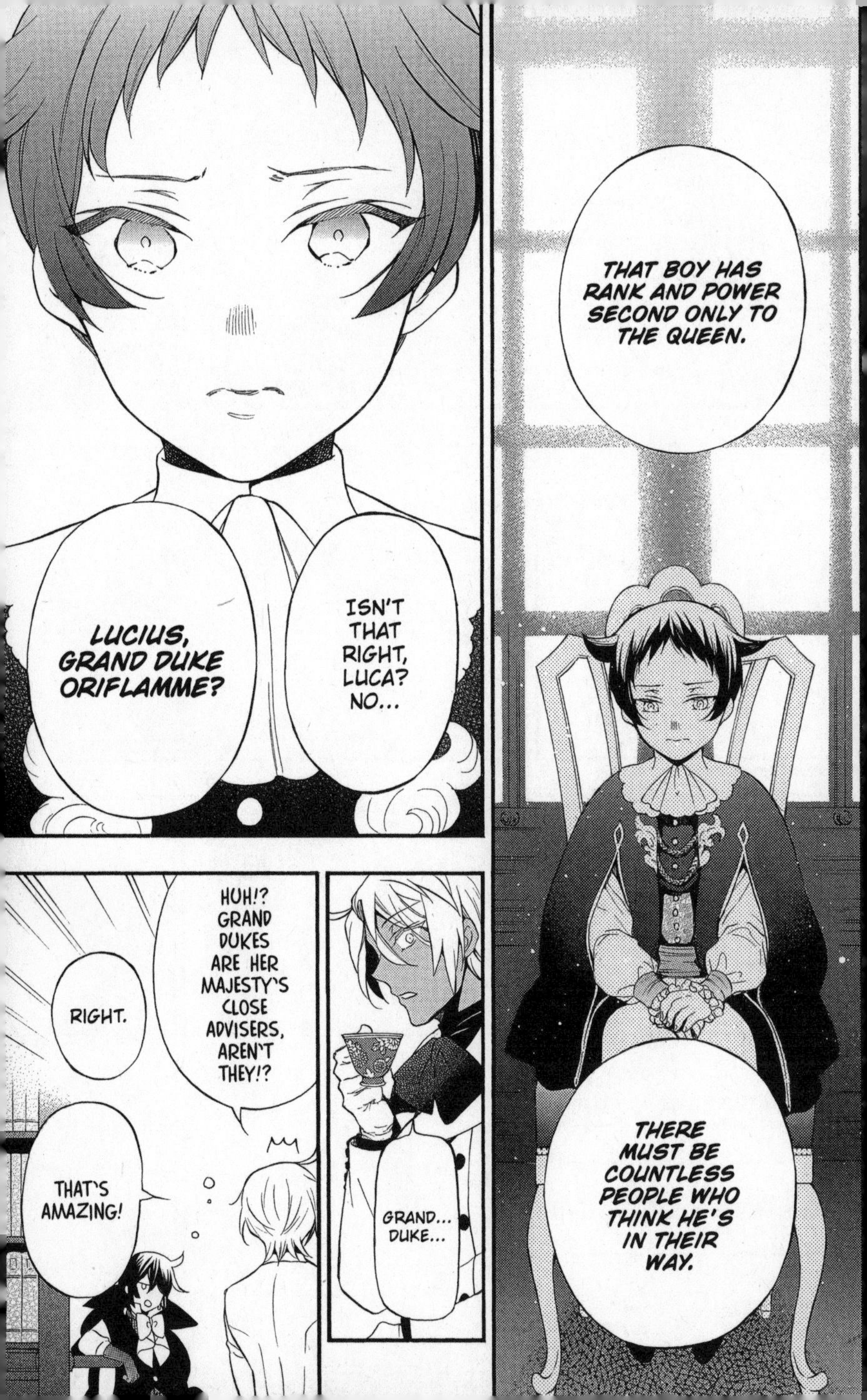
THAT BOY HAS RANK AND POWER SECOND ONLY TO THE QUEEN.
THERE MUST BE COUNTLESS PEOPLE WHO THINK HE'S IN THEIR WAY.
ISN'T THAT RIGHT, LUCA? NO...
LUCIUS, GRAND DUKE ORIFLAMME?
GRAND... DUKE...
HUH!? GRAND DUKES ARE HER MAJESTY'S CLOSE ADVISERS, AREN'T THEY!?
RIGHT.
THAT'S AMAZING!

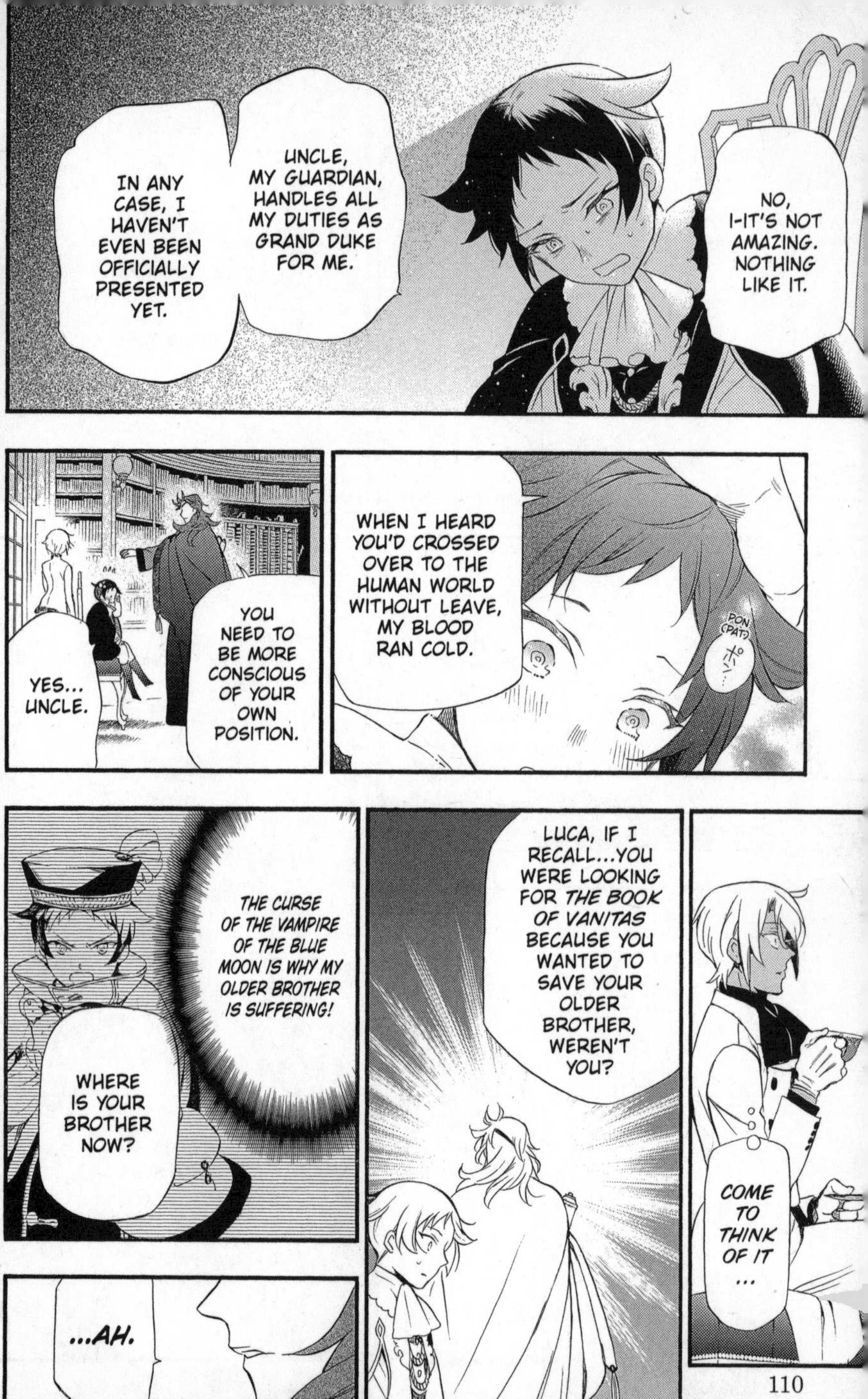
NO, I-IT'S NOT AMAZING. NOTHING LIKE IT.
UNCLE, MY GUARDIAN, HANDLES ALL MY DUTIES AS GRAND DUKE FOR ME.
IN ANY CASE, I HAVEN'T EVEN BEEN OFFICIALLY PRESENTED YET.
WHEN I HEARD YOU'D CROSSED OVER TO THE HUMAN WORLD WITHOUT LEAVE, MY BLOOD RAN COLD.
PON (PAT)
ポン…
YOU NEED TO BE MORE CONSCIOUS OF YOUR OWN POSITION.
YES... UNCLE.
COME TO THINK OF IT ...
LUCA, IF I RECALL...YOU WERE LOOKING FOR *THE BOOK OF VANITAS* BECAUSE YOU WANTED TO SAVE YOUR OLDER BROTHER, WEREN'T YOU?
THE CURSE OF THE VAMPIRE OF THE BLUE MOON IS WHY MY OLDER BROTHER IS SUFFERING!
WHERE IS YOUR BROTHER NOW?
...AH.

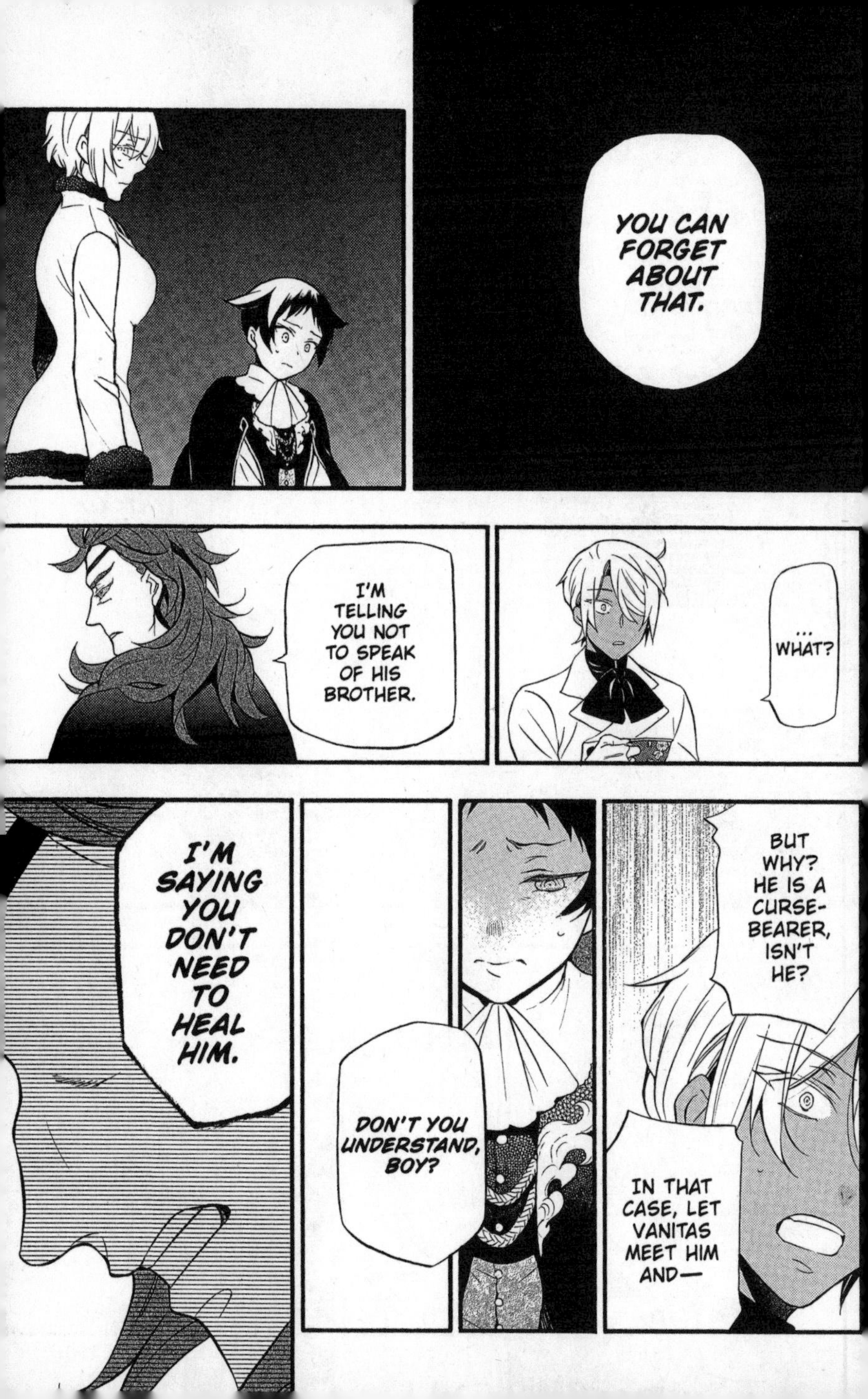
YOU CAN FORGET ABOUT THAT.
... WHAT?
I'M TELLING YOU NOT TO SPEAK OF HIS BROTHER.
BUT WHY? HE IS A CURSE-BEARER, ISN'T HE?
IN THAT CASE, LET VANITAS MEET HIM AND—
DON'T YOU UNDERSTAND, BOY?
I'M SAYING YOU DON'T NEED TO HEAL HIM.

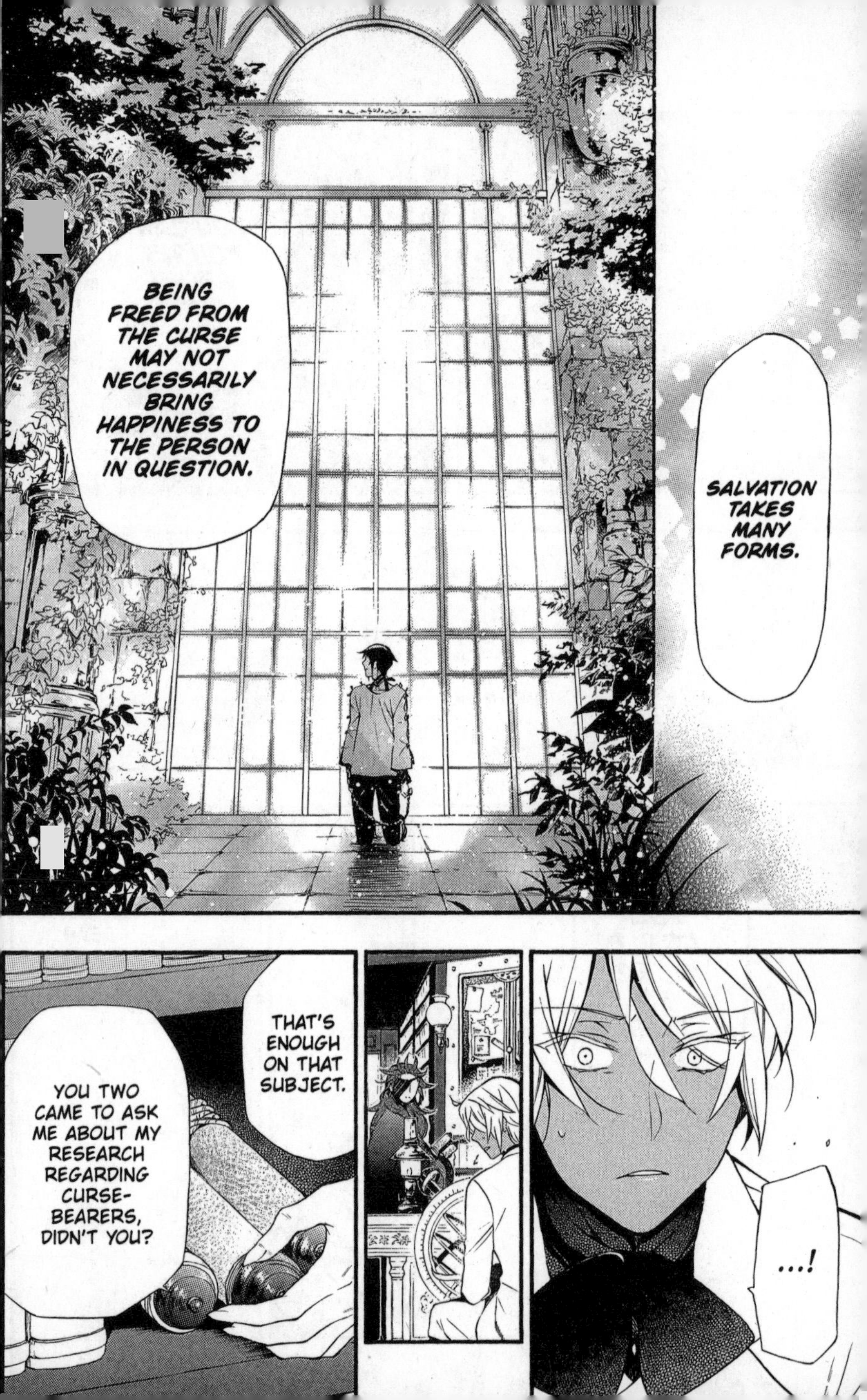
SALVATION TAKES MANY FORMS.
BEING FREED FROM THE CURSE MAY NOT NECESSARILY BRING HAPPINESS TO THE PERSON IN QUESTION.
...!
THAT'S ENOUGH ON THAT SUBJECT.
YOU TWO CAME TO ASK ME ABOUT MY RESEARCH REGARDING CURSE-BEARERS, DIDN'T YOU?

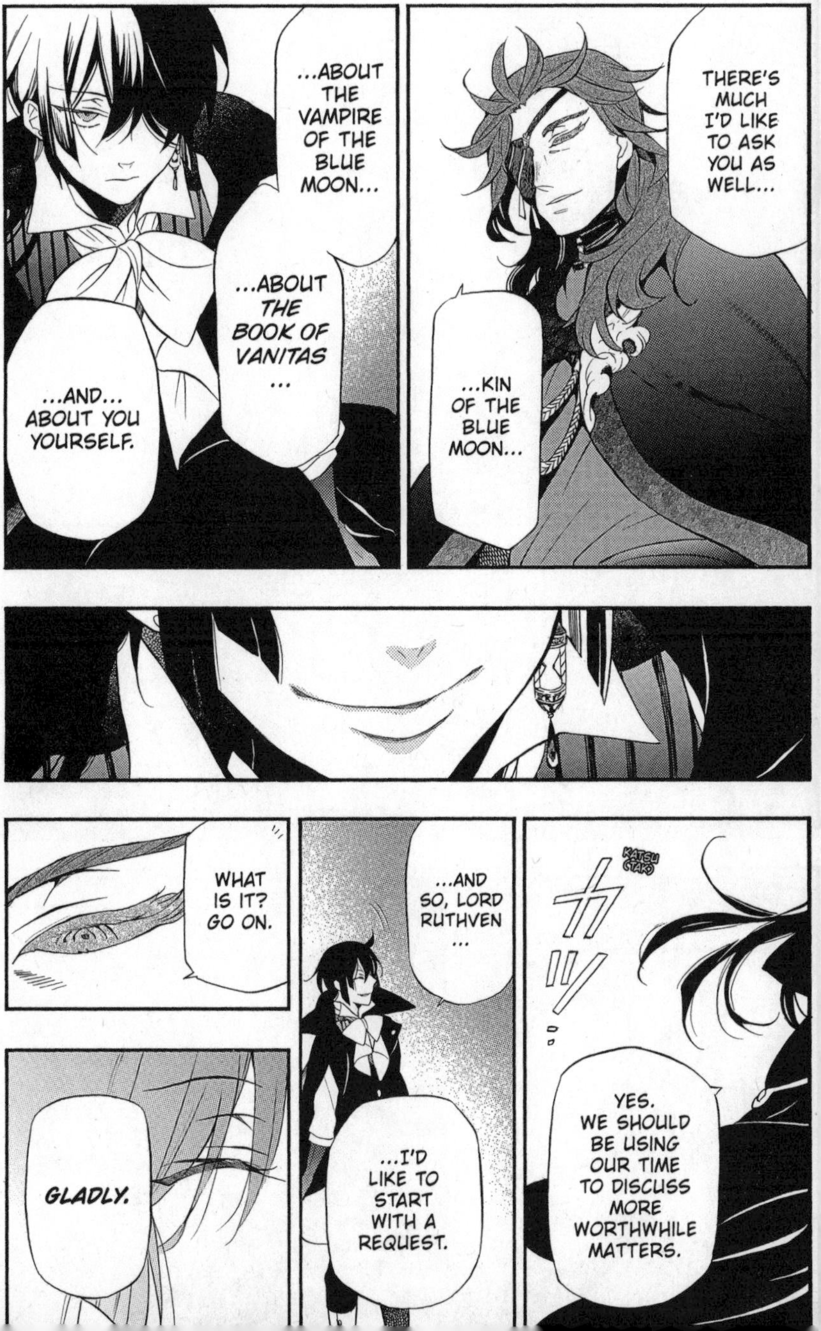
THERE'S MUCH I'D LIKE TO ASK YOU AS WELL...
...KIN OF THE BLUE MOON...
...ABOUT THE VAMPIRE OF THE BLUE MOON...
...ABOUT *THE BOOK OF VANITAS* ...
...AND... ABOUT YOU YOURSELF.
KATSU (TAK)
YES. WE SHOULD BE USING OUR TIME TO DISCUSS MORE WORTHWHILE MATTERS.
...AND SO, LORD RUTHVEN ...
...I'D LIKE TO START WITH A REQUEST.
WHAT IS IT? GO ON.
GLADLY.

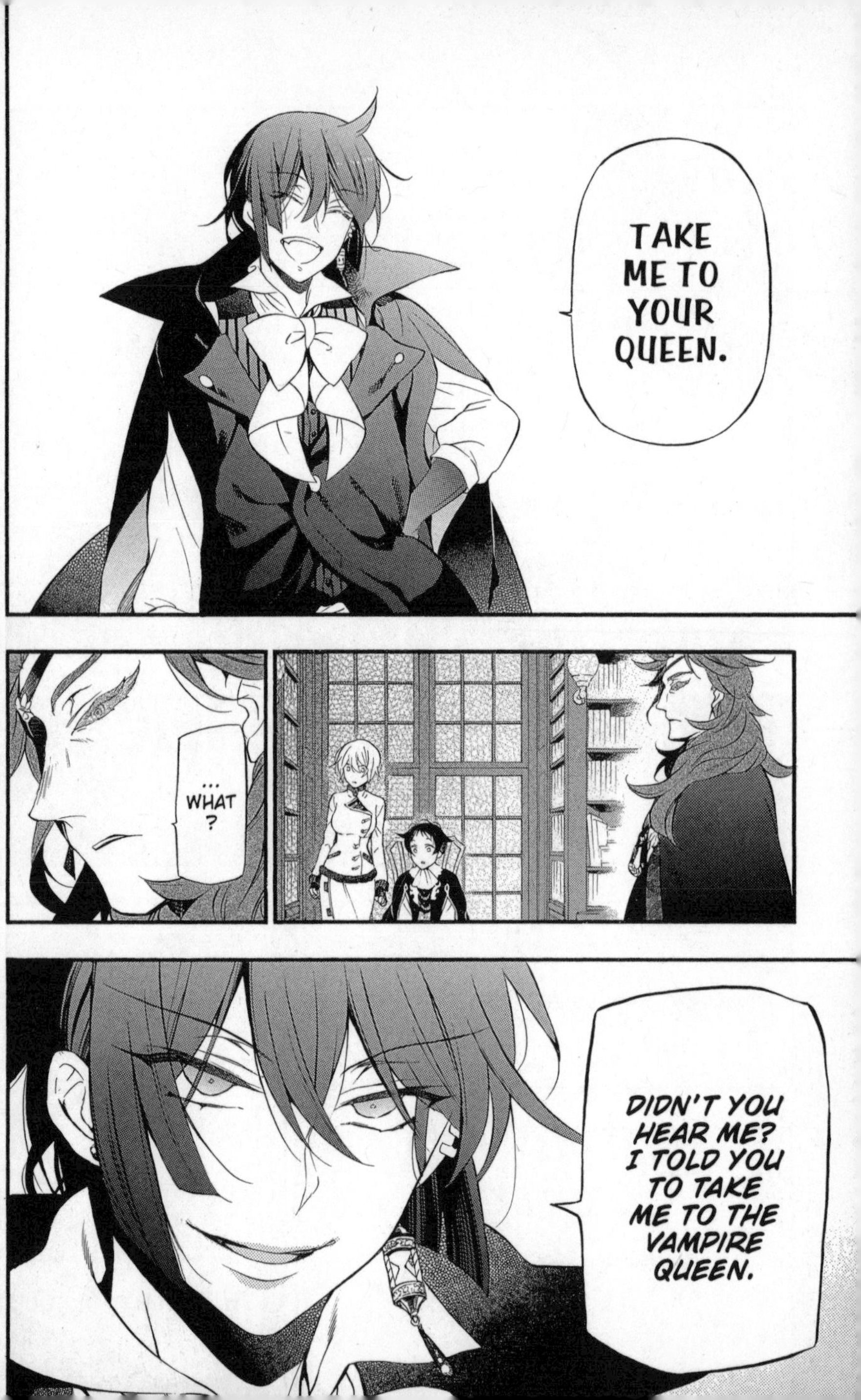
TAKE ME TO YOUR QUEEN.
...WHAT?
DIDN'T YOU HEAR ME? I TOLD YOU TO TAKE ME TO THE VAMPIRE QUEEN.

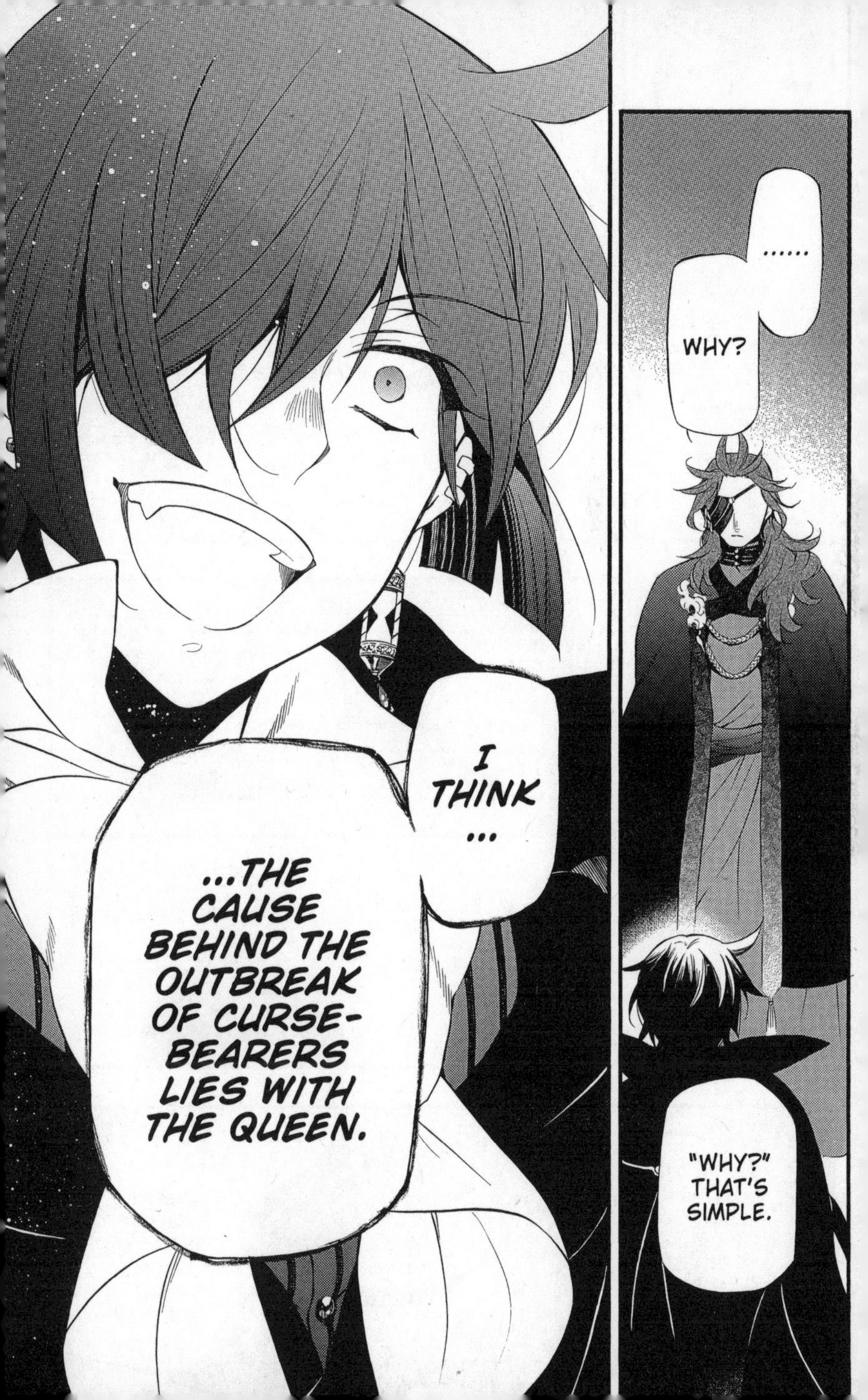
......
WHY?
"WHY?" THAT'S SIMPLE.
I THINK...
...THE CAUSE BEHIND THE OUTBREAK OF CURSE-BEARERS LIES WITH THE QUEEN.

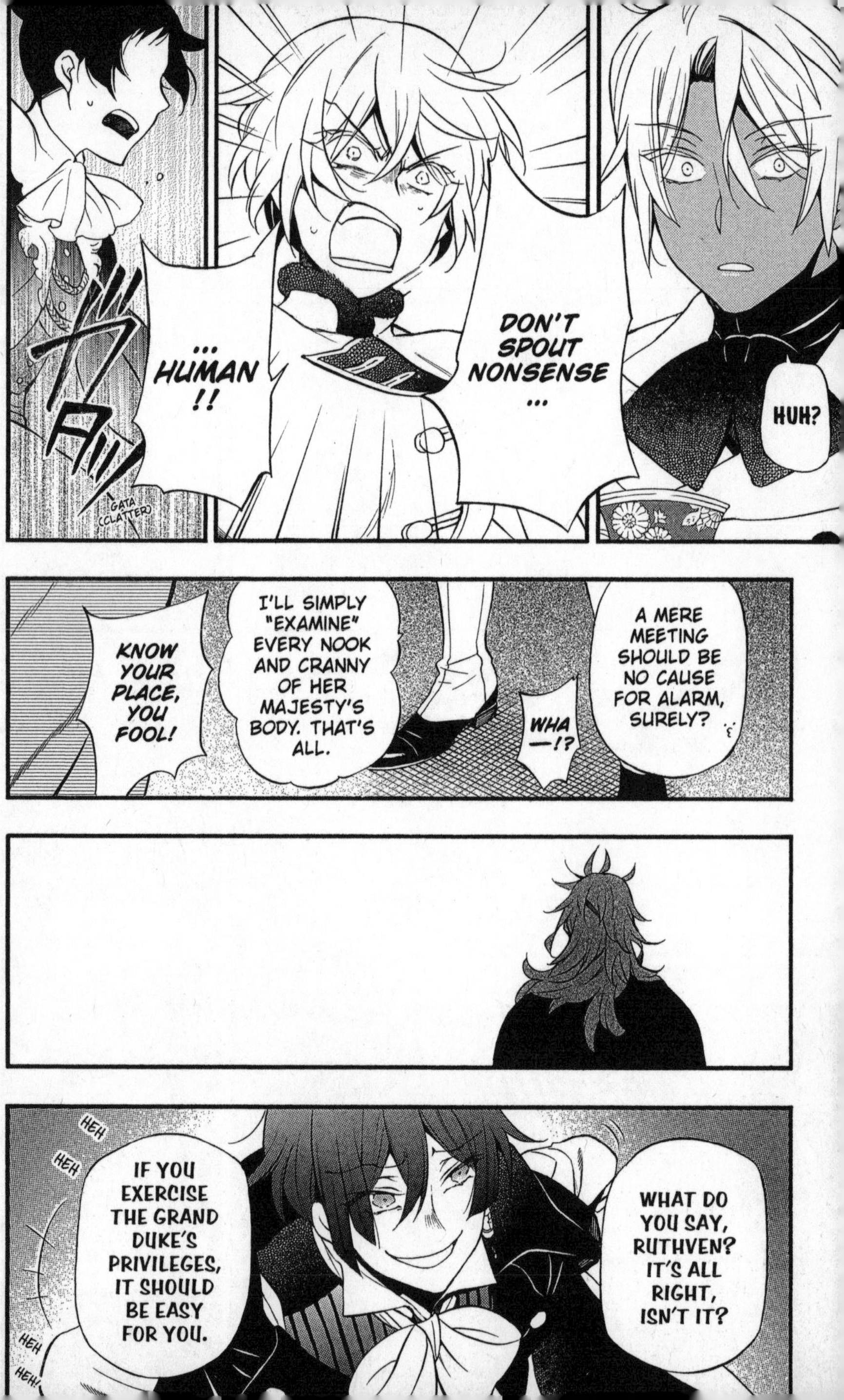
HUH?
DON'T SPOUT NONSENSE ...
... HUMAN !!
GATA (CLATTER)
A MERE MEETING SHOULD BE NO CAUSE FOR ALARM, SURELY?
WHA —!?
I'LL SIMPLY "EXAMINE" EVERY NOOK AND CRANNY OF HER MAJESTY'S BODY. THAT'S ALL.
KNOW YOUR PLACE, YOU FOOL!
WHAT DO YOU SAY, RUTHVEN? IT'S ALL RIGHT, ISN'T IT?
IF YOU EXERCISE THE GRAND DUKE'S PRIVILEGES, IT SHOULD BE EASY FOR YOU.
HEH
HEH
HEH
HEH!

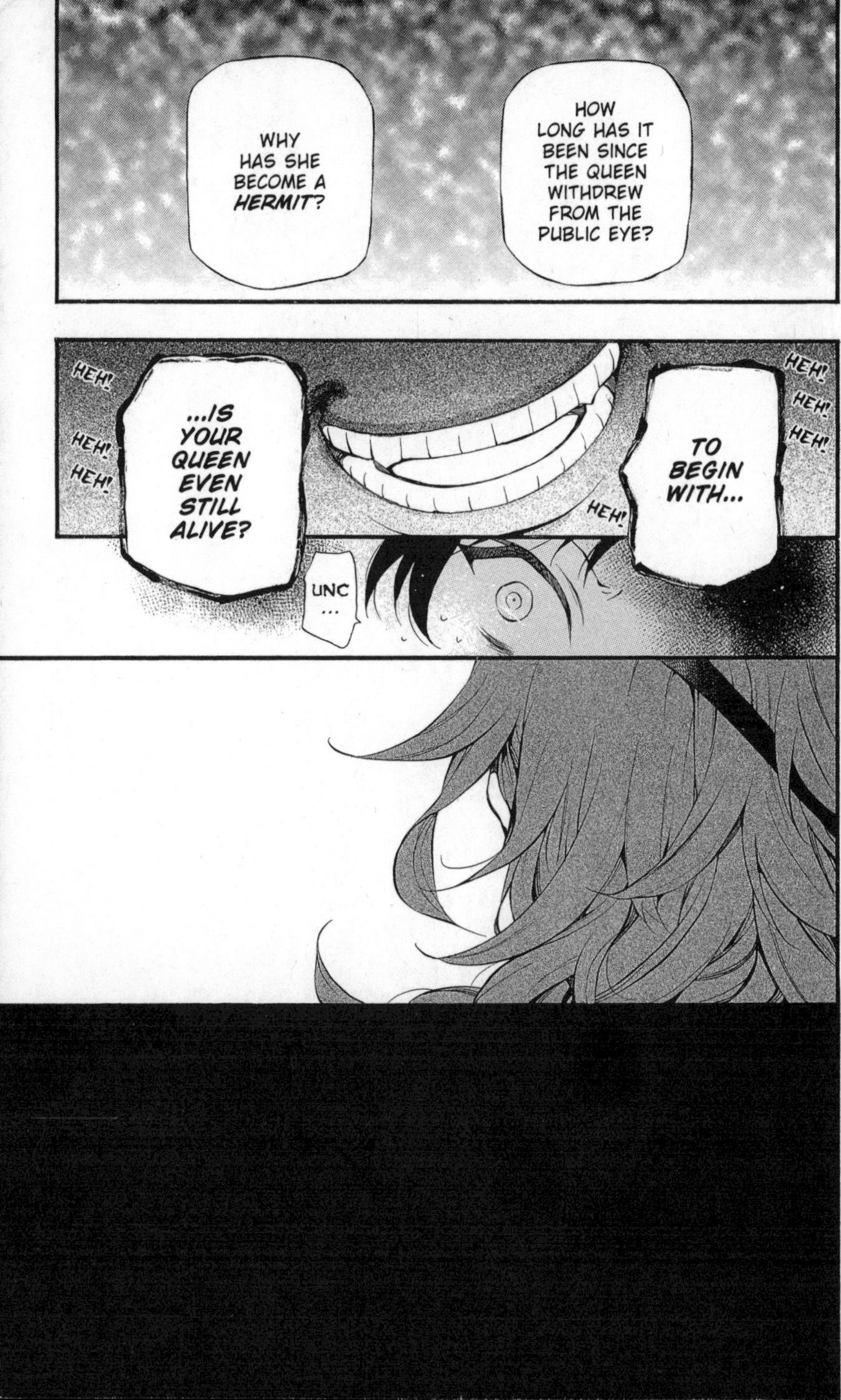
HOW LONG HAS IT BEEN SINCE THE QUEEN WITHDREW FROM THE PUBLIC EYE?
WHY HAS SHE BECOME A *HERMIT*?
HEH! HEH! HEH!
TO BEGIN WITH...
HEH!
HEH!
HEH! HEH!
...IS YOUR QUEEN EVEN STILL ALIVE?
UNC...

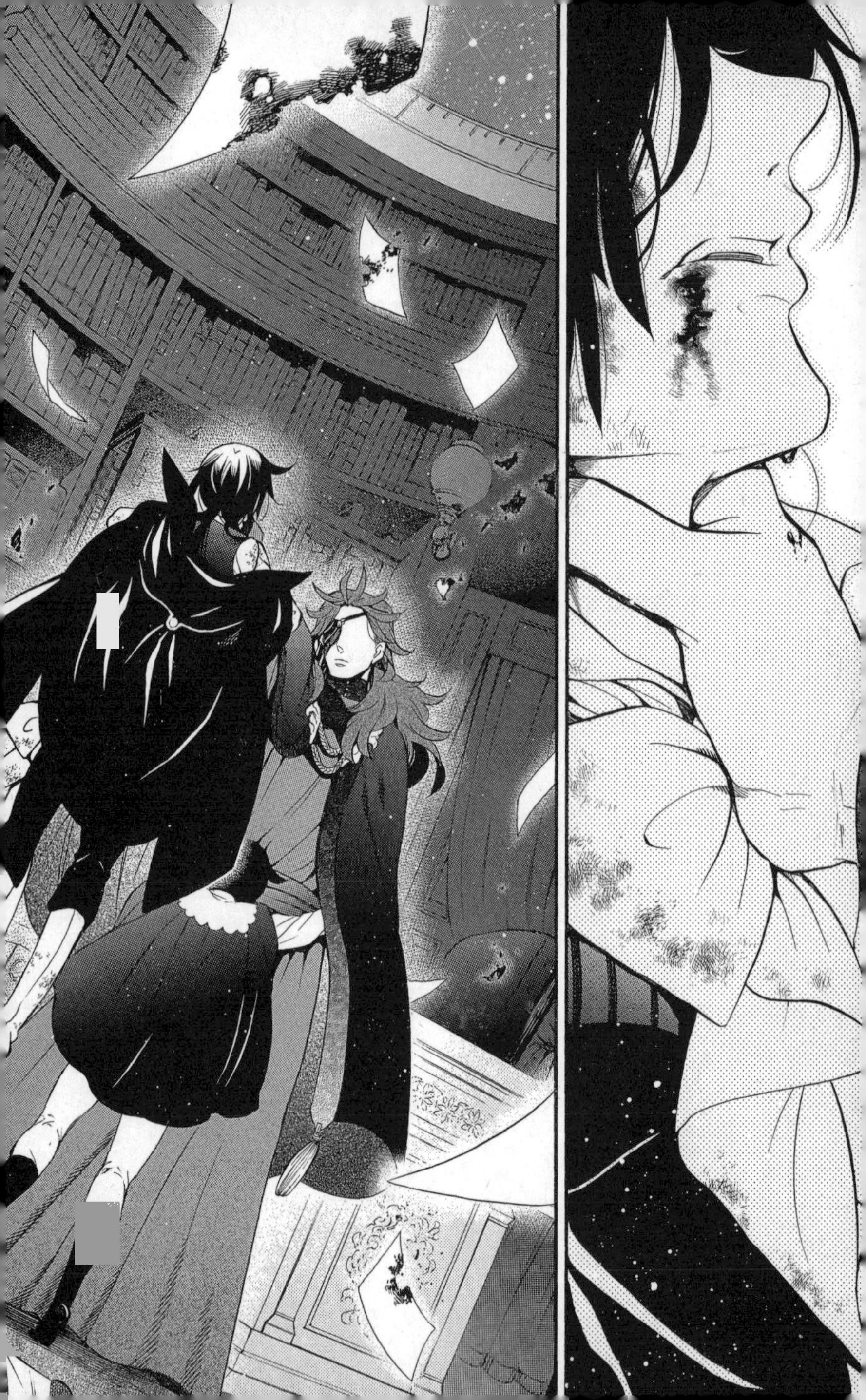

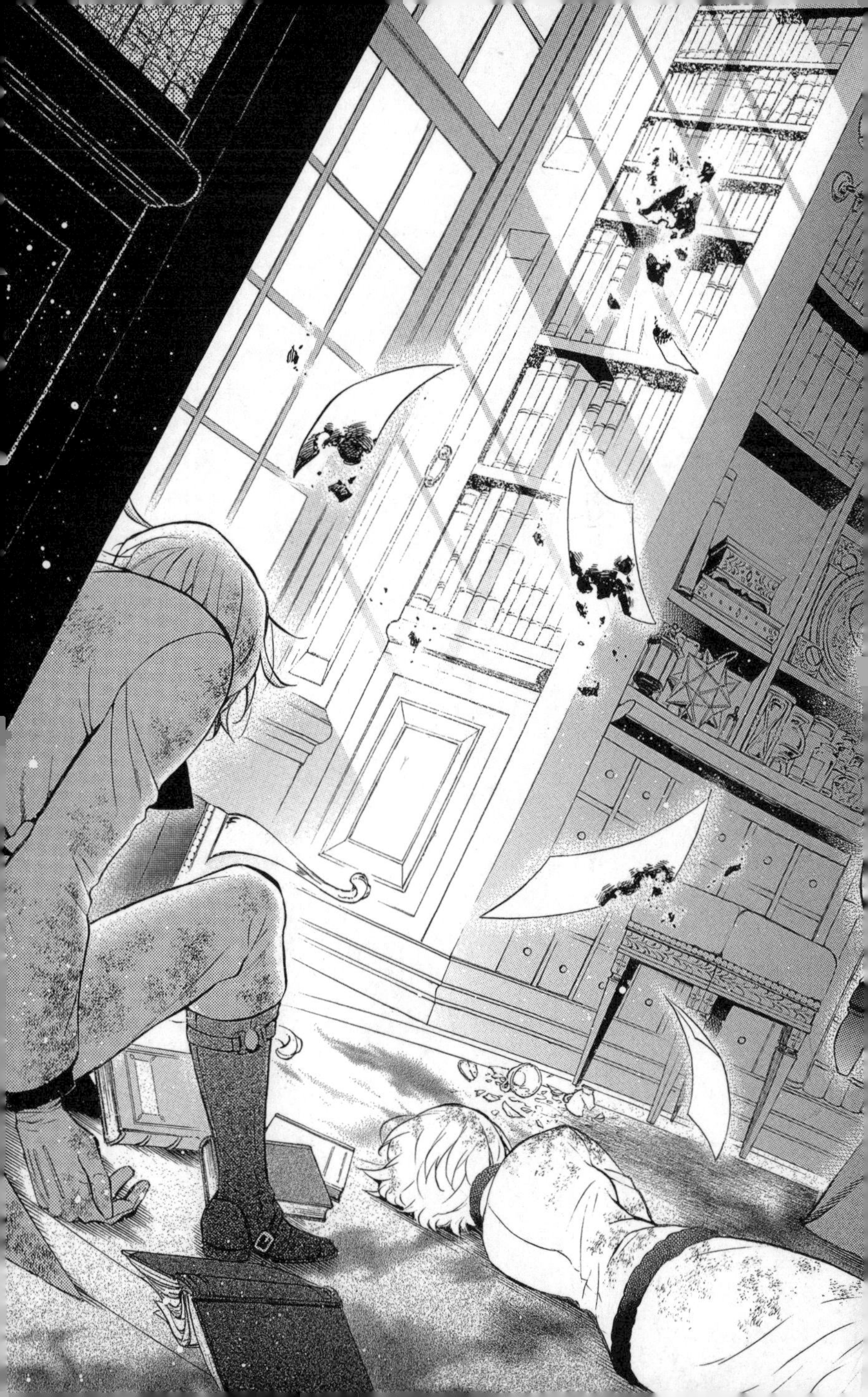

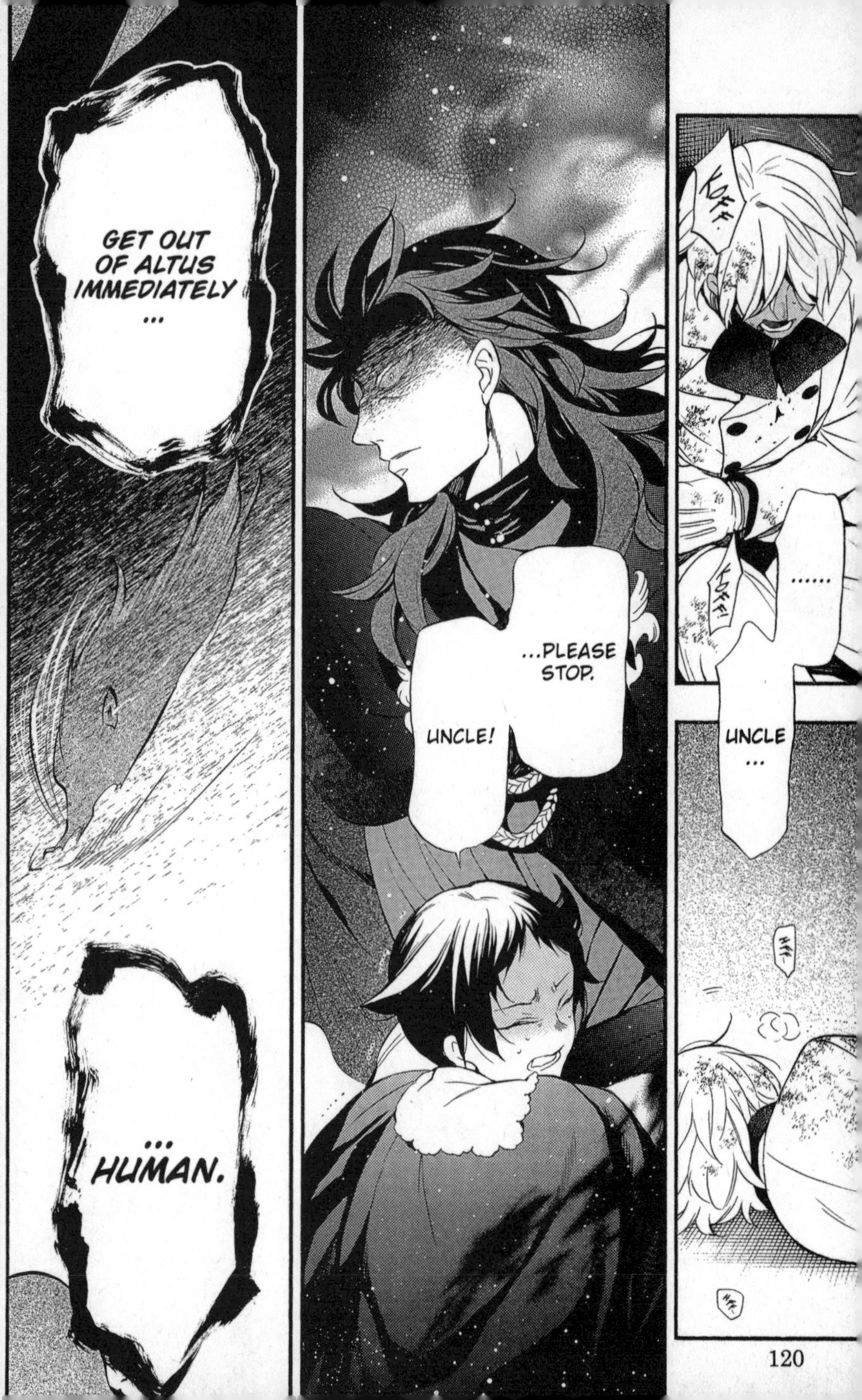
KOFF.
......
KOFF!
UNCLE...
HFF
HFF
...PLEASE STOP.
UNCLE!
GET OUT OF ALTUS IMMEDIATELY...
...HUMAN.

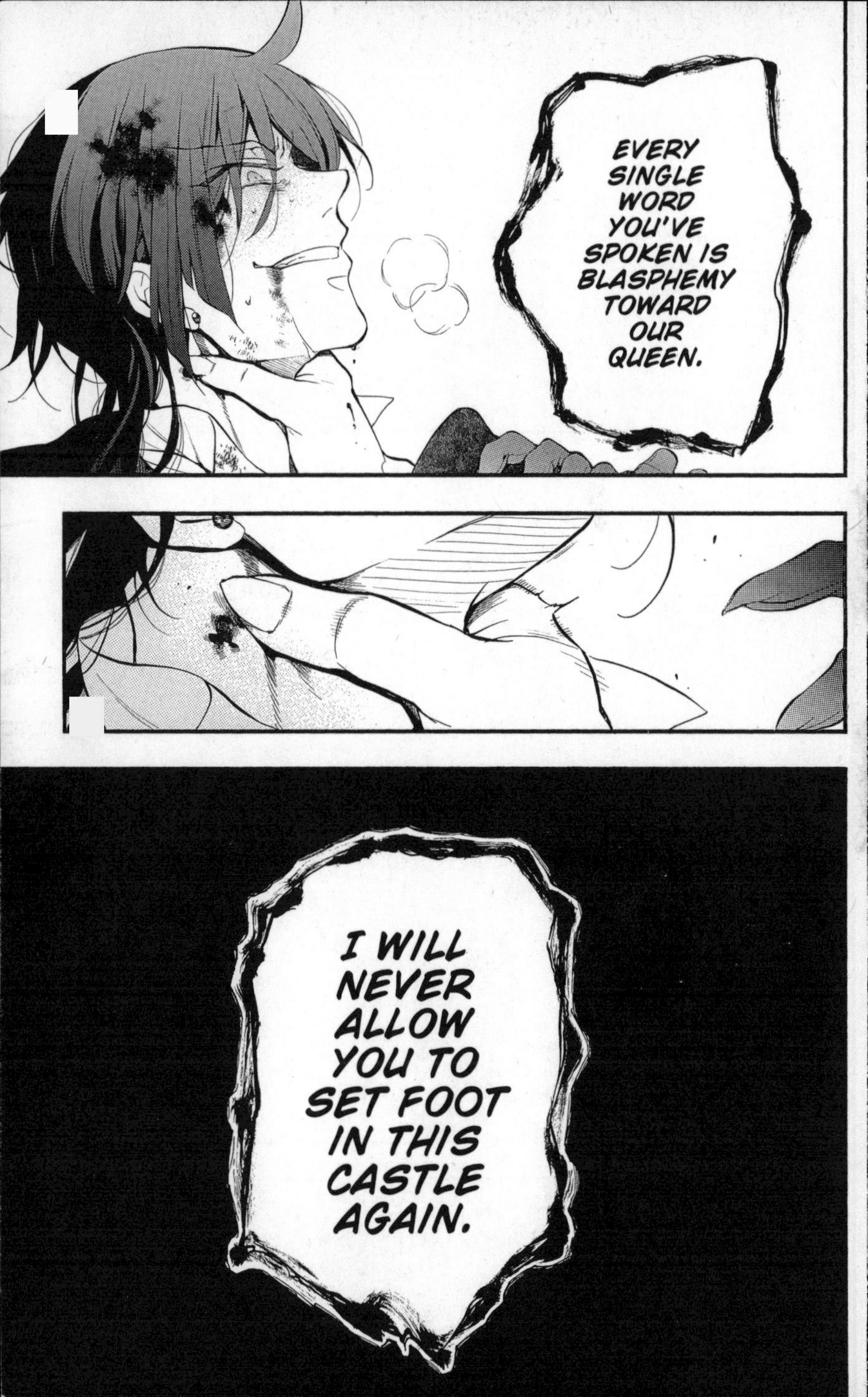
EVERY SINGLE WORD YOU'VE SPOKEN IS BLASPHEMY TOWARD OUR QUEEN.
I WILL NEVER ALLOW YOU TO SET FOOT IN THIS CASTLE AGAIN.

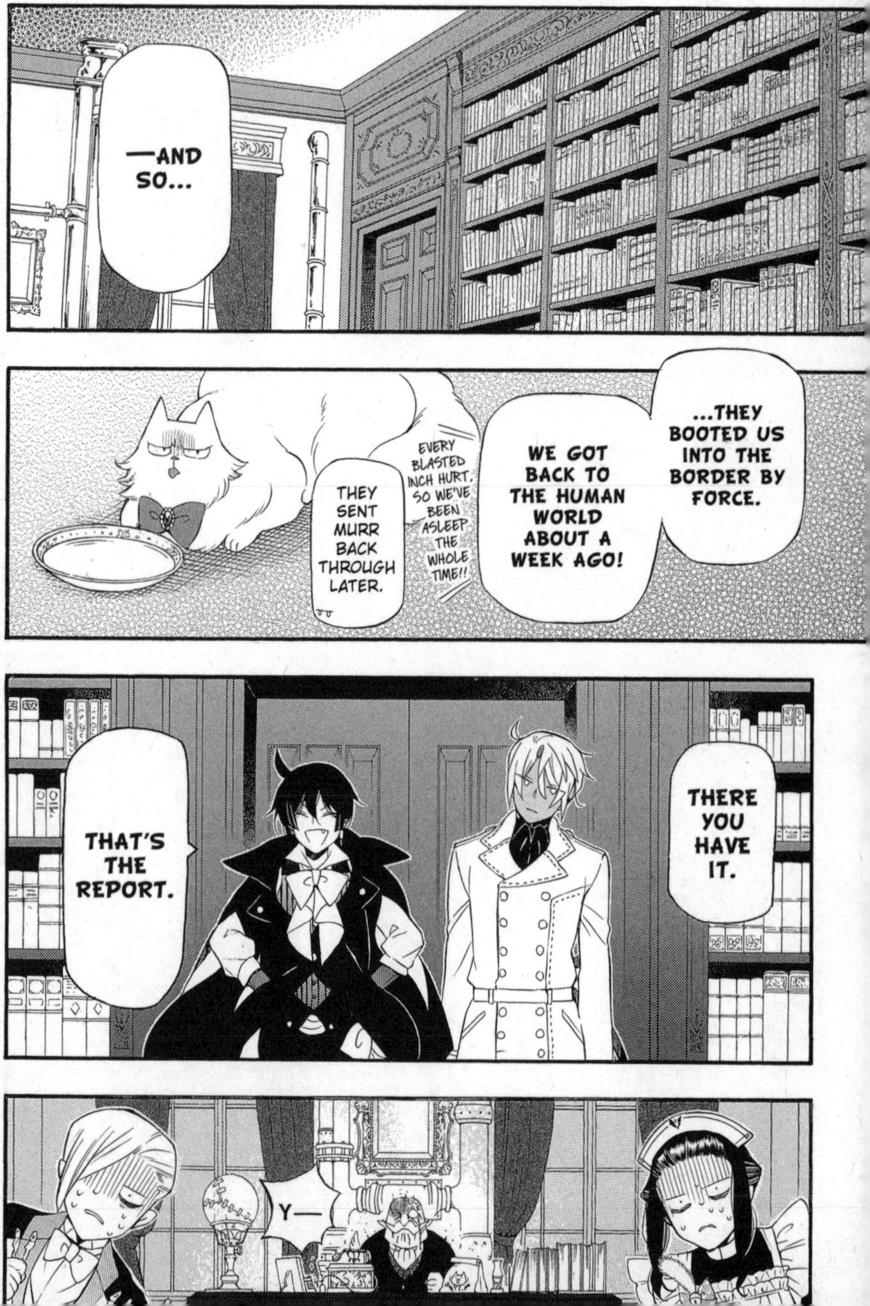
—AND SO...
...THEY BOOTED US INTO THE BORDER BY FORCE.
WE GOT BACK TO THE HUMAN WORLD ABOUT A WEEK AGO!
EVERY BLASTED INCH HURT, SO WE'VE BEEN ASLEEP THE WHOLE TIME!!
THEY SENT MURR BACK THROUGH LATER.
THERE YOU HAVE IT.
THAT'S THE REPORT.
Y—

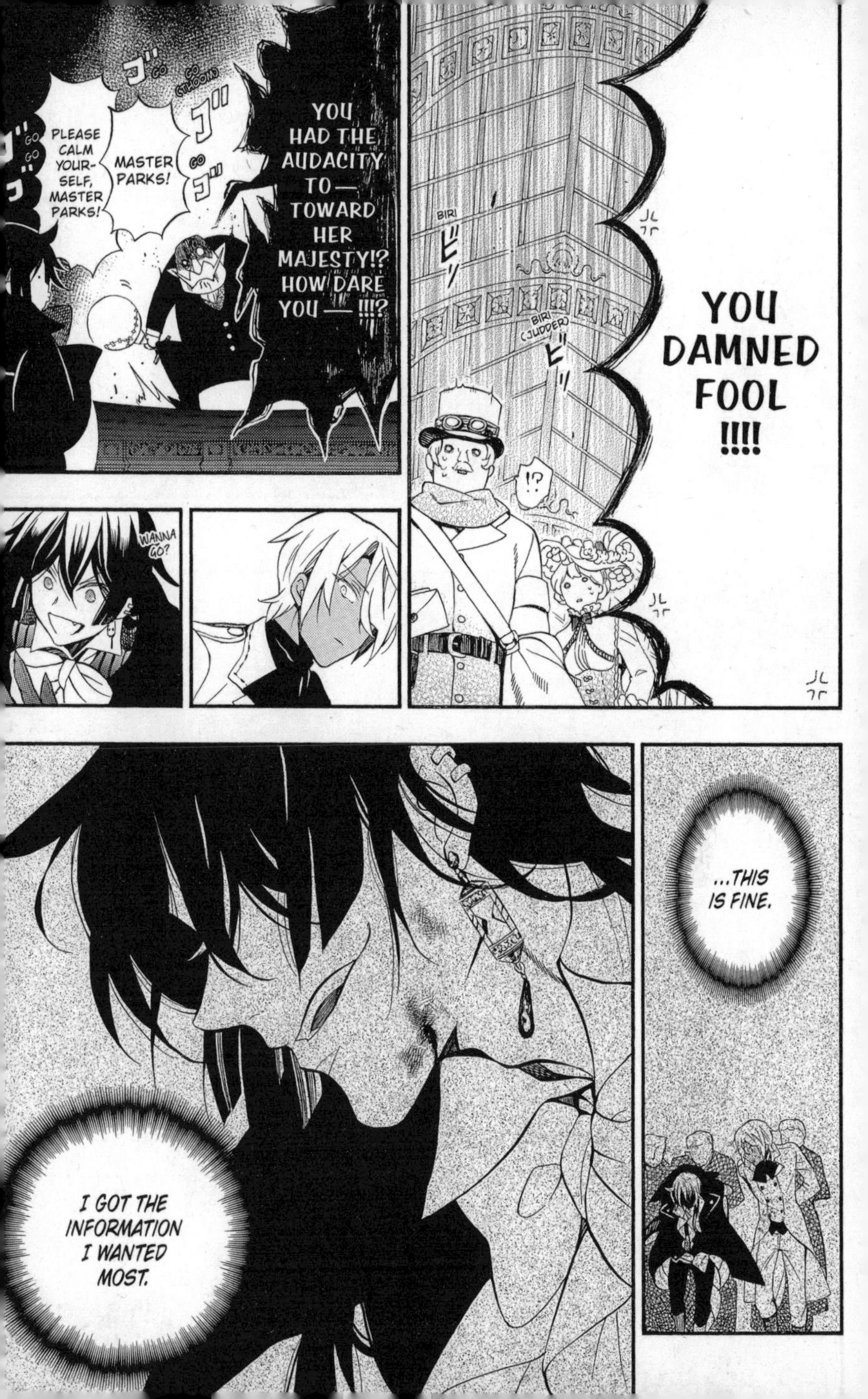

BIRI
BIRI (JUDDER)
YOU DAMNED FOOL !!!!
!?
GO
GO (SHOOM)
GO
GO GO
YOU HAD THE AUDACITY TO— TOWARD HER MAJESTY!? HOW DARE YOU—!!!?
MASTER PARKS!
PLEASE CALM YOUR-SELF, MASTER PARKS!
WANNA GO?
...THIS IS FINE.
I GOT THE INFORMATION I WANTED MOST.

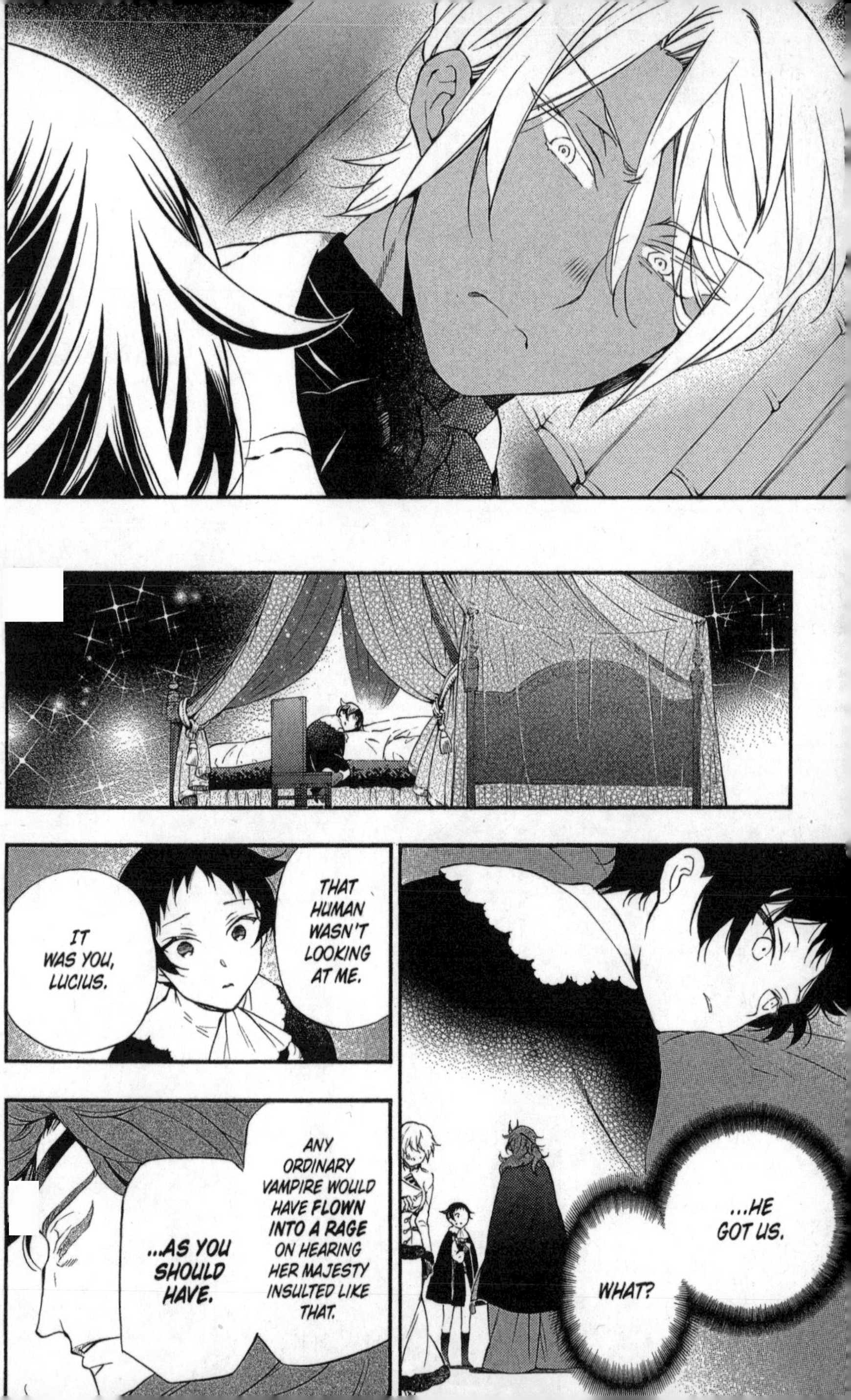
...HE GOT US.
WHAT?
THAT HUMAN WASN'T LOOKING AT ME.
IT WAS YOU, LUCIUS.
ANY ORDINARY VAMPIRE WOULD HAVE FLOWN INTO A RAGE ON HEARING HER MAJESTY INSULTED LIKE THAT.
...AS YOU SHOULD HAVE.

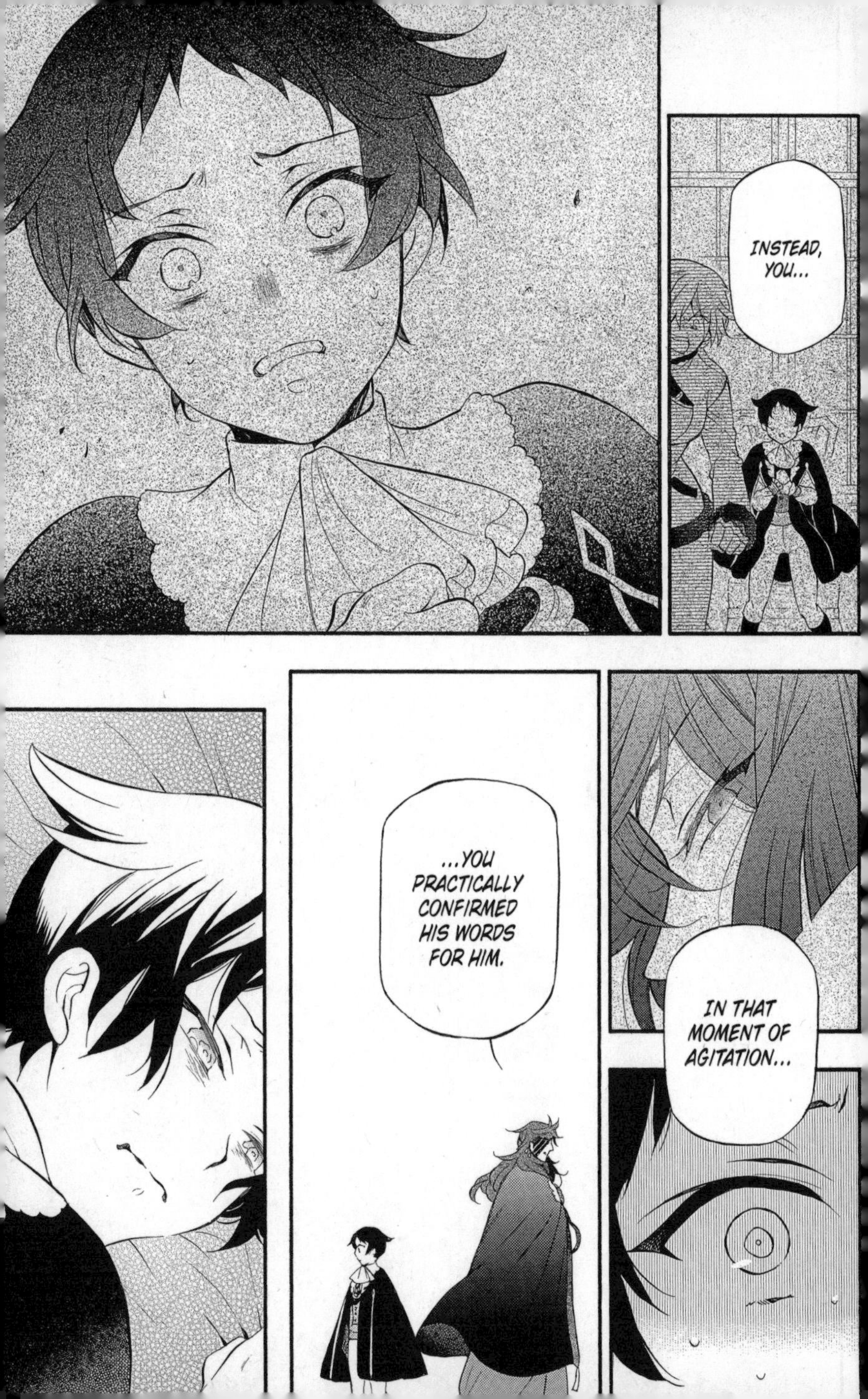
INSTEAD, YOU...
IN THAT MOMENT OF AGITATION...
...YOU PRACTICALLY CONFIRMED HIS WORDS FOR HIM.

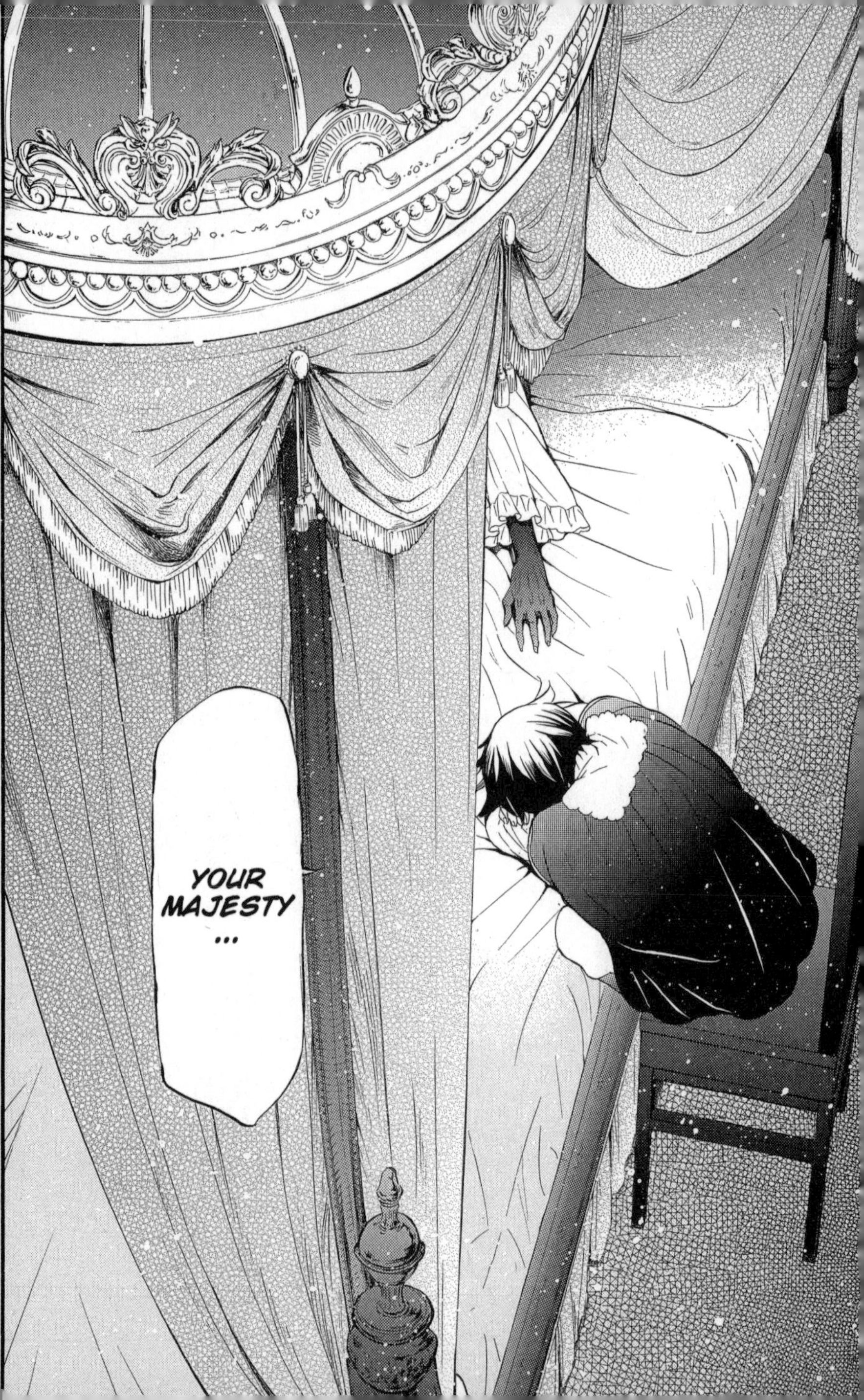
YOUR MAJESTY ...

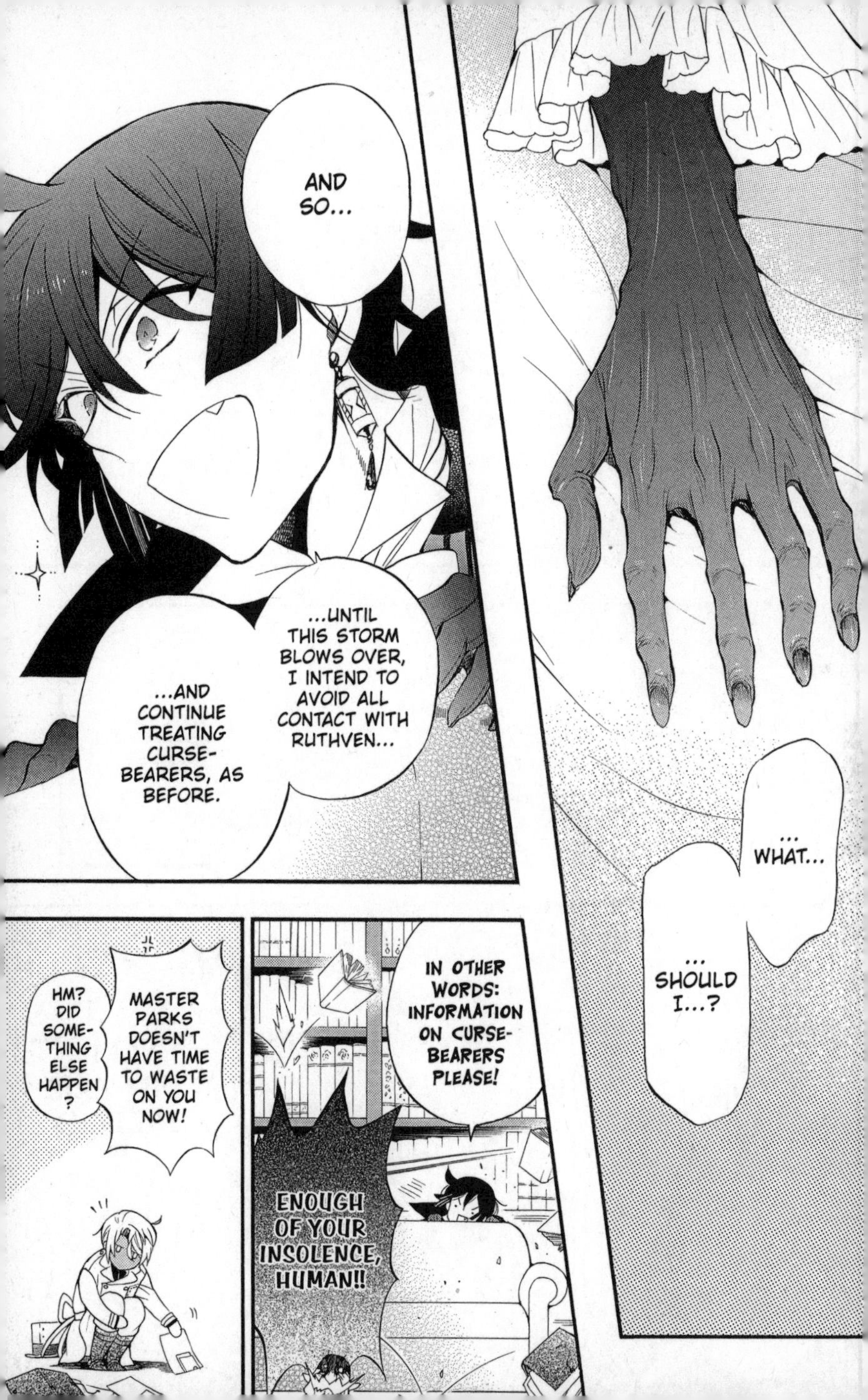
...WHAT...
...SHOULD I...?
AND SO...
...UNTIL THIS STORM BLOWS OVER, I INTEND TO AVOID ALL CONTACT WITH RUTHVEN...
...AND CONTINUE TREATING CURSE-BEARERS, AS BEFORE.
IN OTHER WORDS: INFORMATION ON CURSE-BEARERS PLEASE!
ENOUGH OF YOUR INSOLENCE, HUMAN!!
MASTER PARKS DOESN'T HAVE TIME TO WASTE ON YOU NOW!
HM? DID SOME-THING ELSE HAPPEN?

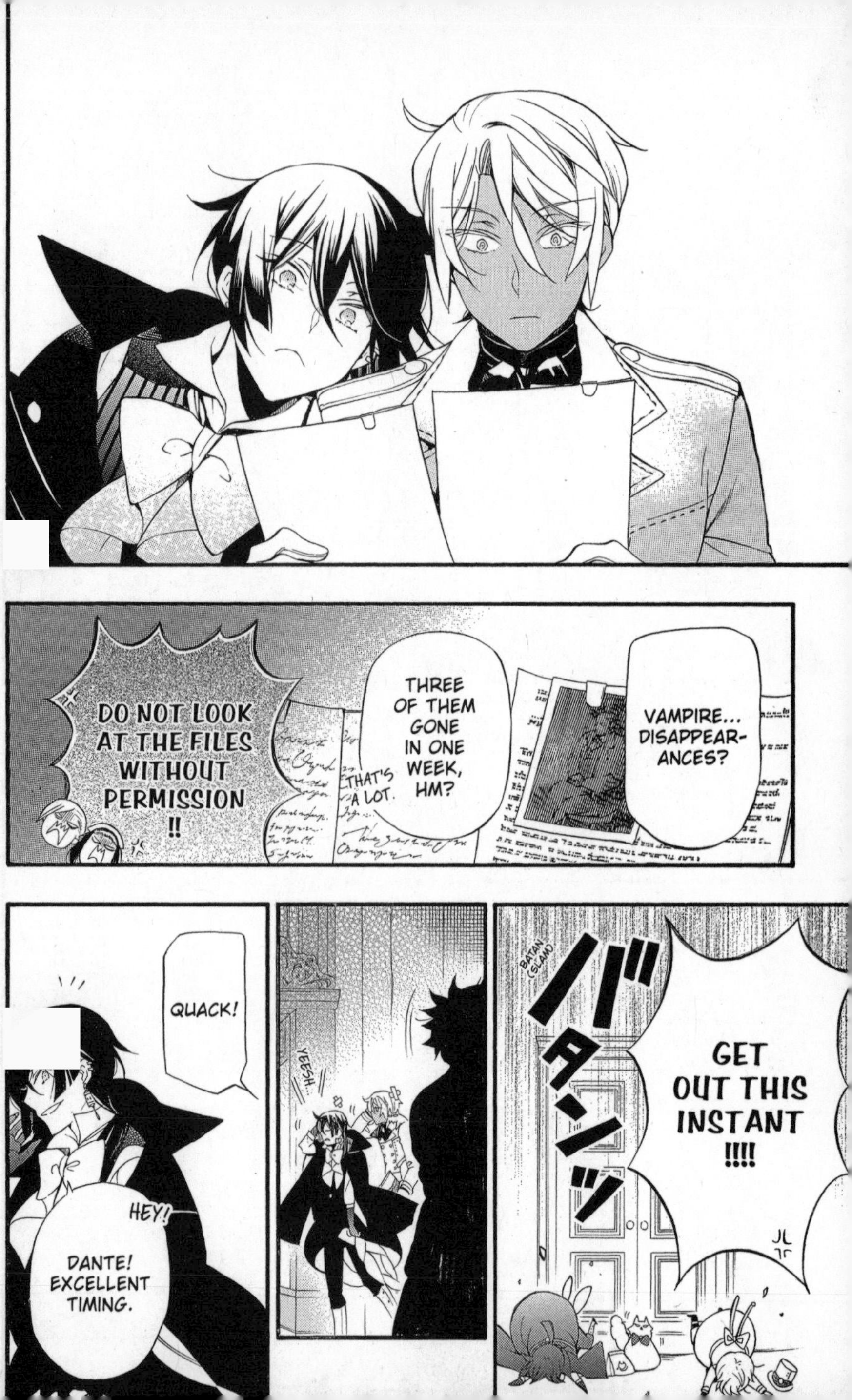
VAMPIRE... DISAPPEARANCES?
THREE OF THEM GONE IN ONE WEEK, HM?
THAT'S A LOT.
DO NOT LOOK AT THE FILES WITHOUT PERMISSION !!
バタンッ
BATAN (SLAM)
GET OUT THIS INSTANT !!!!
YEESH...
QUACK!
HEY!
DANTE! EXCELLENT TIMING.

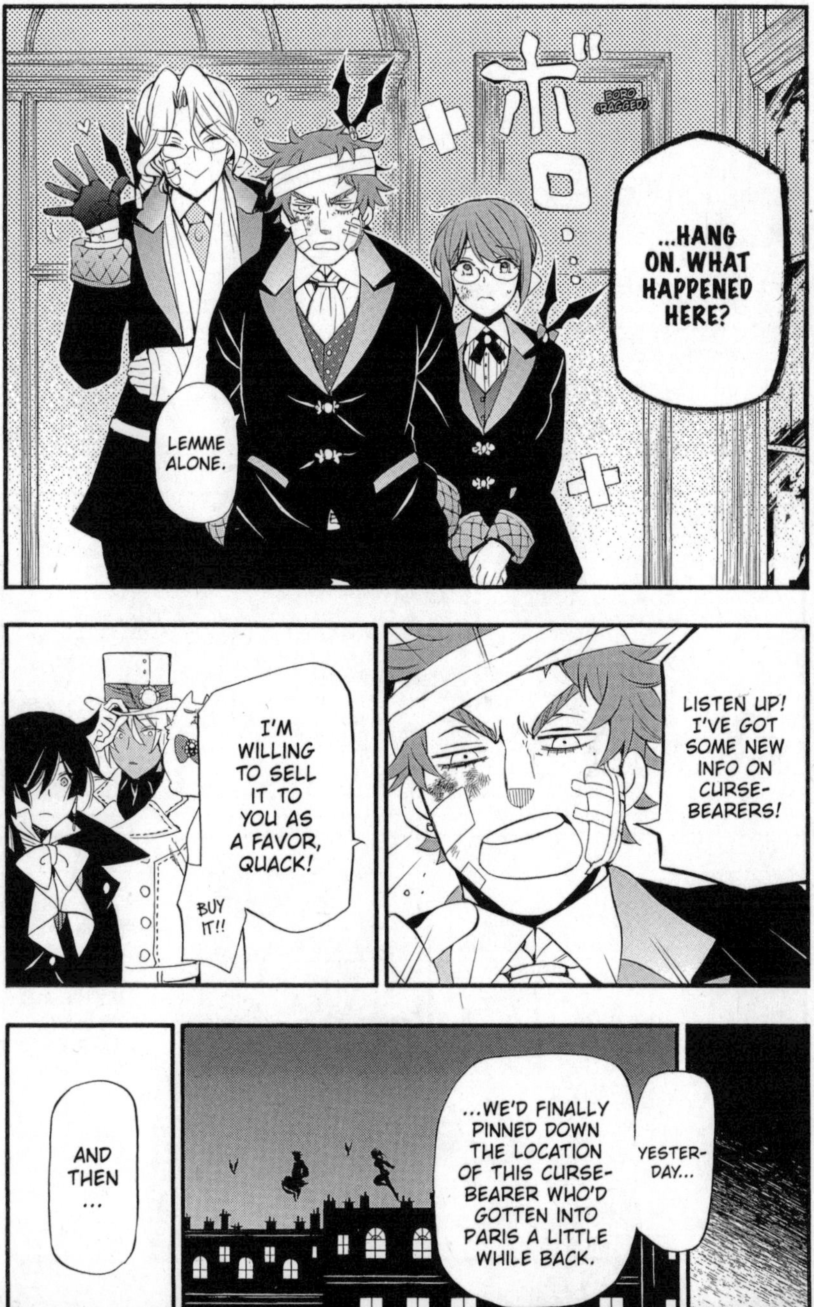
ボロ
BORO (RAGGED)
...HANG ON. WHAT HAPPENED HERE?
LEMME ALONE.
LISTEN UP! I'VE GOT SOME NEW INFO ON CURSE-BEARERS!
I'M WILLING TO SELL IT TO YOU AS A FAVOR, QUACK!
BUY IT!!
YESTER-DAY...
...WE'D FINALLY PINNED DOWN THE LOCATION OF THIS CURSE-BEARER WHO'D GOTTEN INTO PARIS A LITTLE WHILE BACK.
AND THEN ...

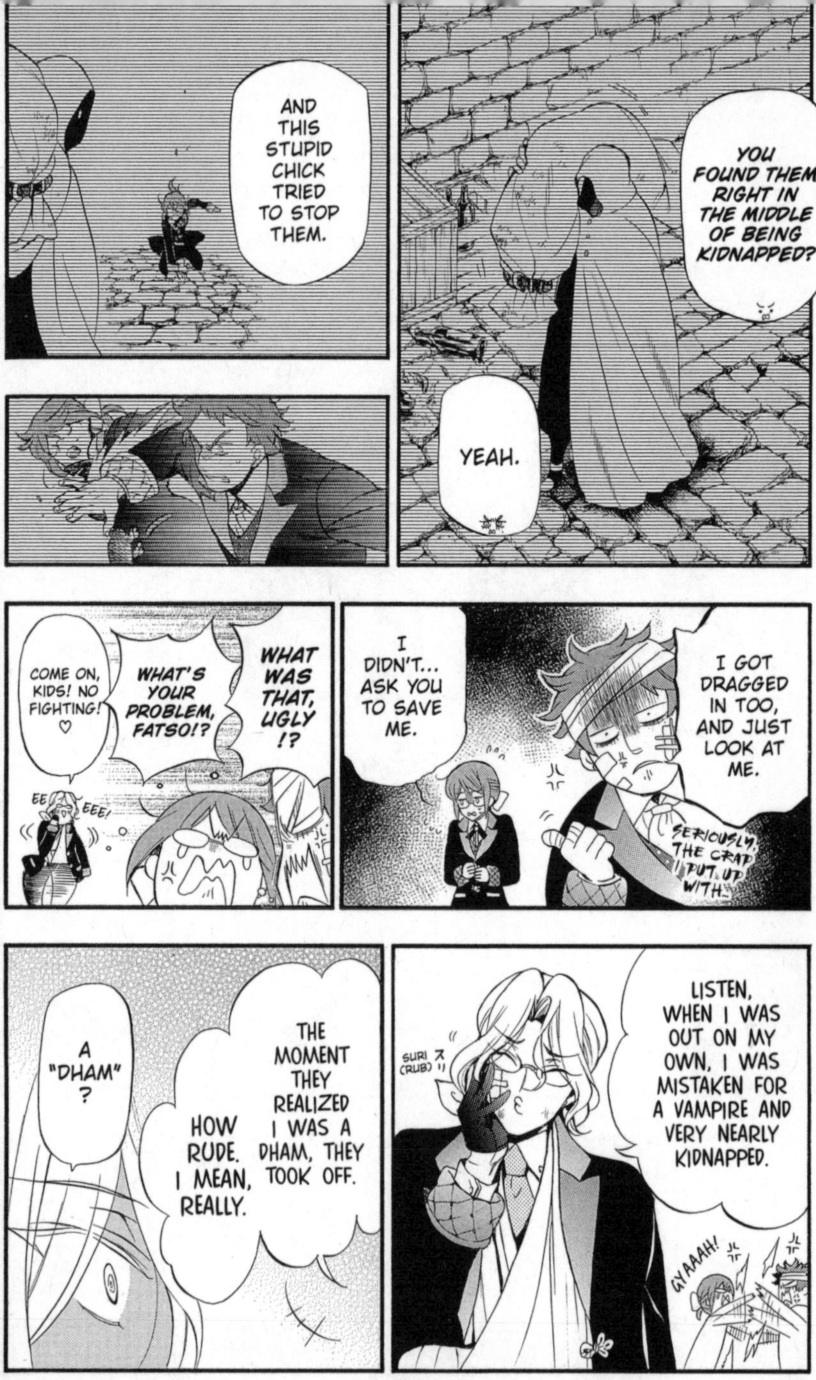
YOU FOUND THEM RIGHT IN THE MIDDLE OF BEING KIDNAPPED?
YEAH.
AND THIS STUPID CHICK TRIED TO STOP THEM.
I GOT DRAGGED IN TOO, AND JUST LOOK AT ME.
SERIOUSLY, THE CRAP I PUT UP WITH...
I DIDN'T... ASK YOU TO SAVE ME.
WHAT WAS THAT, UGLY!?
WHAT'S YOUR PROBLEM, FATSO!?
COME ON, KIDS! NO FIGHTING! ♡
EEEEE!
LISTEN, WHEN I WAS OUT ON MY OWN, I WAS MISTAKEN FOR A VAMPIRE AND VERY NEARLY KIDNAPPED.
SURI (RUB)
GYAAAH!
THE MOMENT THEY REALIZED I WAS A DHAM, THEY TOOK OFF.
HOW RUDE. I MEAN, REALLY.
A "DHAM"?

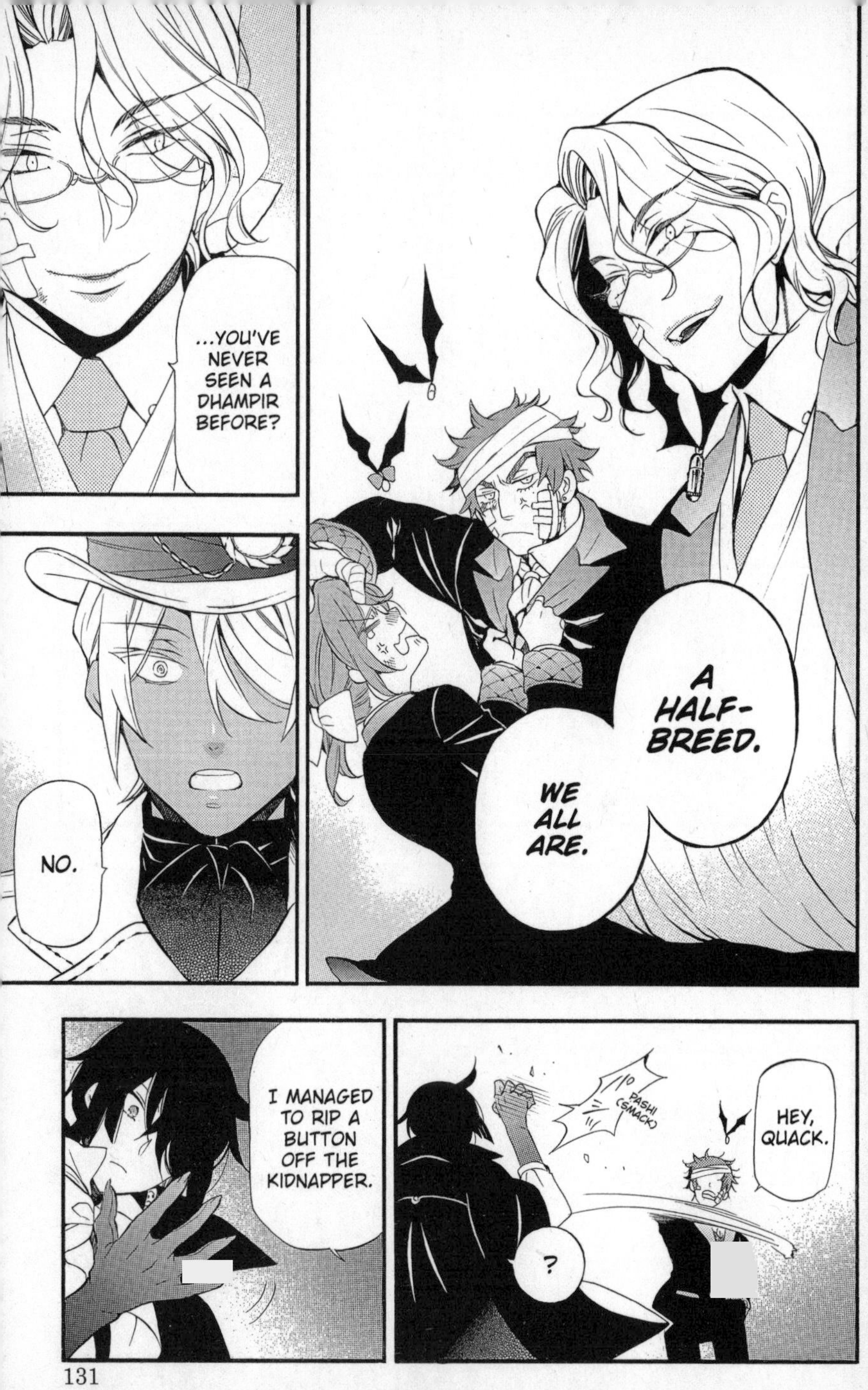
A HALF-BREED.
WE ALL ARE.
...YOU'VE NEVER SEEN A DHAMPIR BEFORE?
NO.
HEY, QUACK.
PASHI (SMACK)
?
I MANAGED TO RIP A BUTTON OFF THE KIDNAPPER.

A SWORD AND SIX WINGS ...?

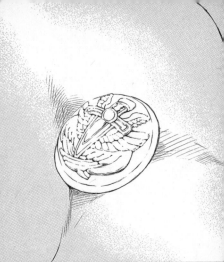

VANI...

THE ONES OLD ORLOK'S AFTER, THE CULPRITS IN THE VAMPIRE DISAPPEARANCES ...

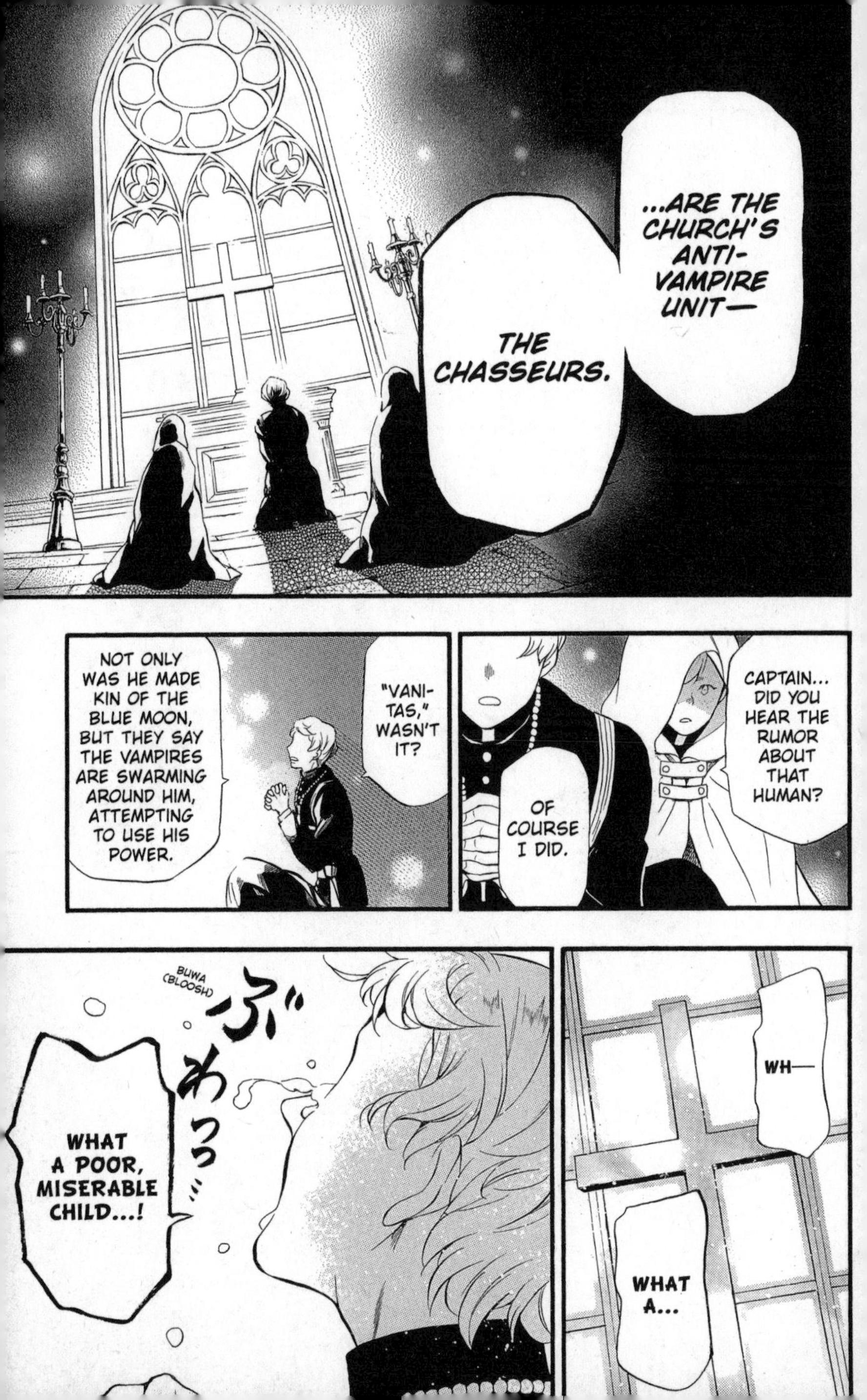
...ARE THE CHURCH'S ANTI-VAMPIRE UNIT—
THE CHASSEURS.
CAPTAIN... DID YOU HEAR THE RUMOR ABOUT THAT HUMAN?
OF COURSE I DID.
"VANITAS," WASN'T IT?
NOT ONLY WAS HE MADE KIN OF THE BLUE MOON, BUT THEY SAY THE VAMPIRES ARE SWARMING AROUND HIM, ATTEMPTING TO USE HIS POWER.
WH—
WHAT A...
ぶわっっ
BUWA (BLOOSH)
WHAT A POOR, MISERABLE CHILD...!

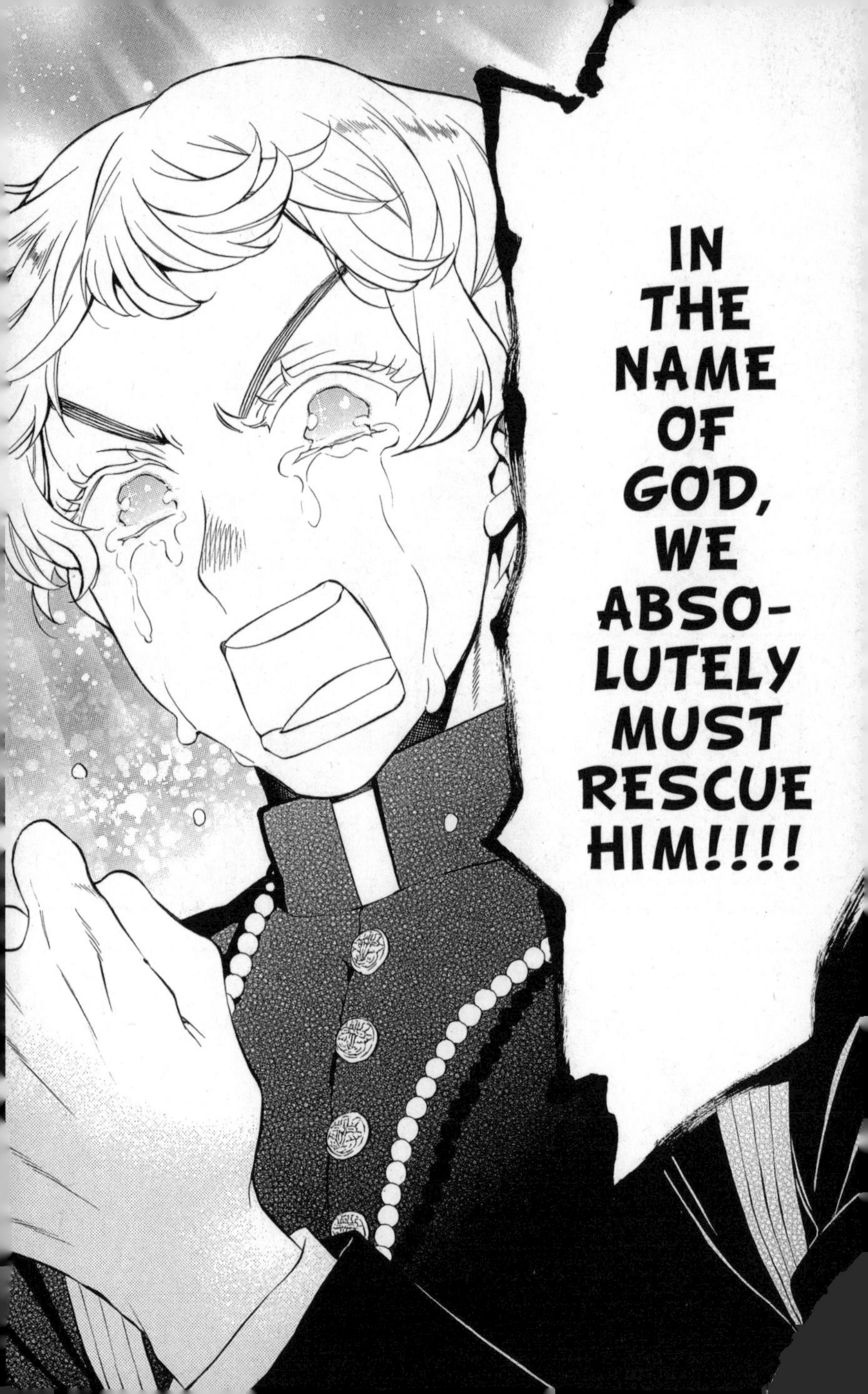
IN THE NAME OF GOD, WE ABSO-LUTELY MUST RESCUE HIM!!!!

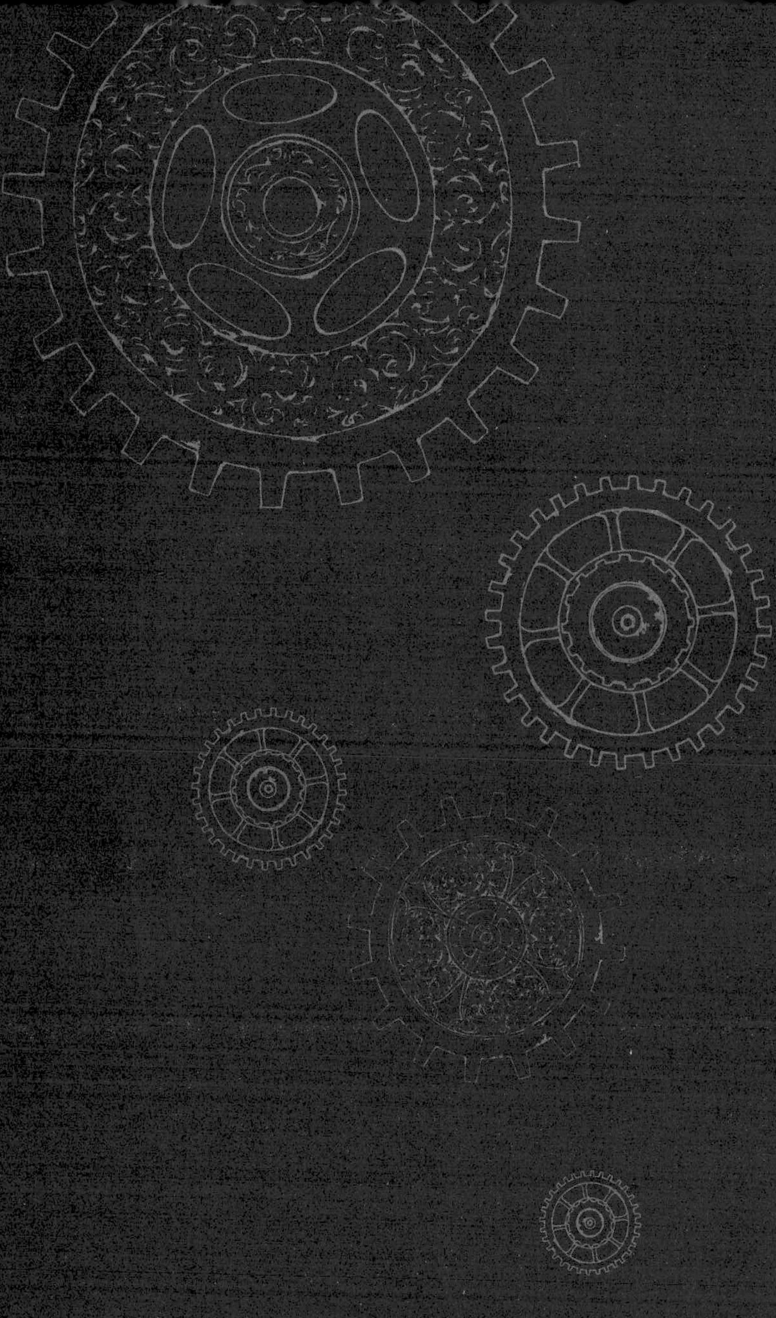

Mémoire 13 Glissando GLISSANDO

Les Mémoires de Vanitas

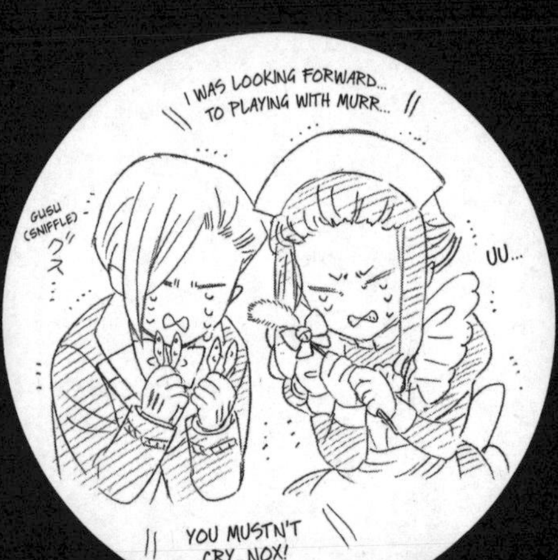

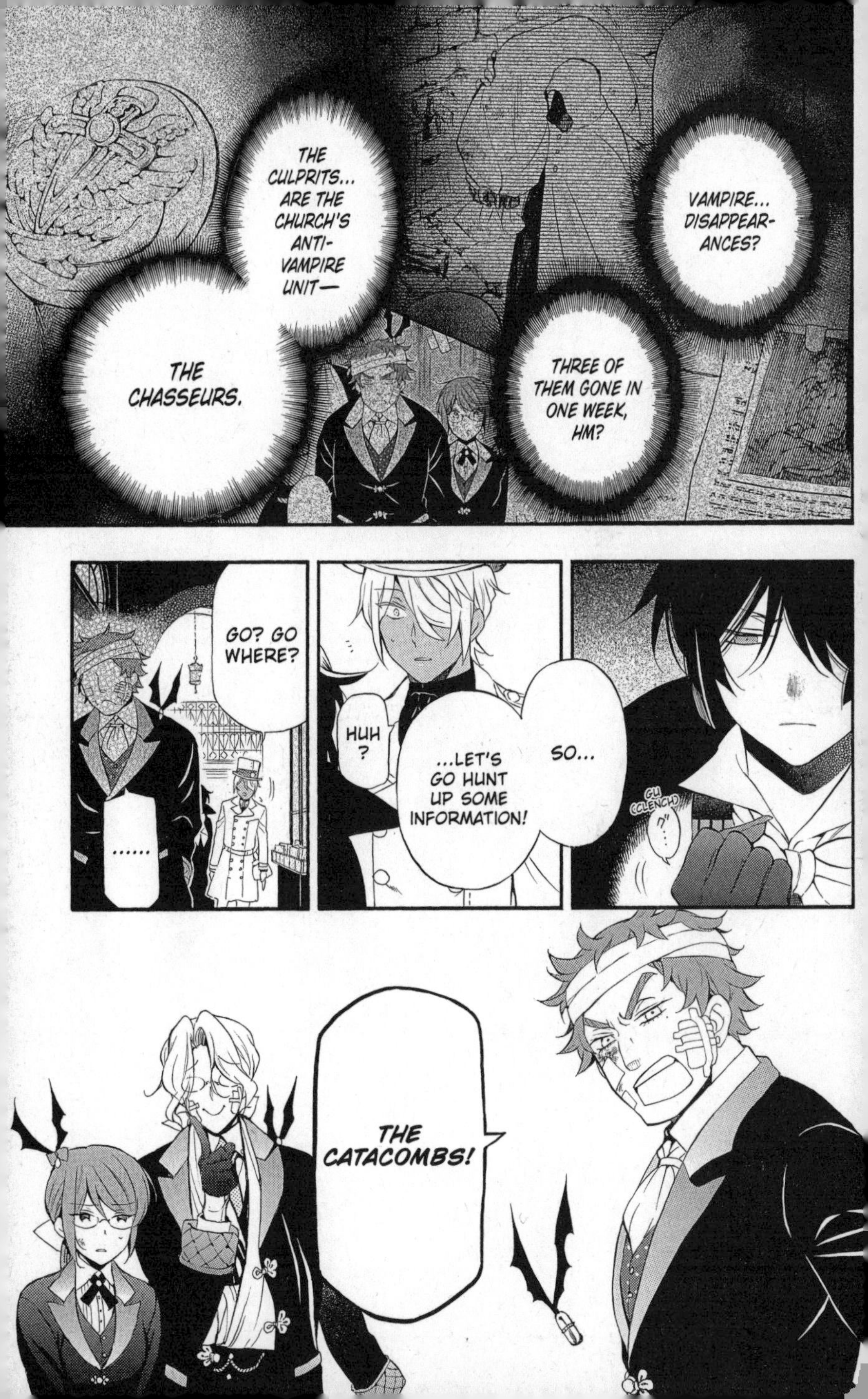
VAMPIRE... DISAPPEAR-ANCES?
THREE OF THEM GONE IN ONE WEEK, HM?
THE CULPRITS... ARE THE CHURCH'S ANTI-VAMPIRE UNIT—
THE CHASSEURS.
GU (CLENCH)
SO...
...LET'S GO HUNT UP SOME INFORMATION!
HUH?
GO? GO WHERE?
......
THE CATACOMBS!

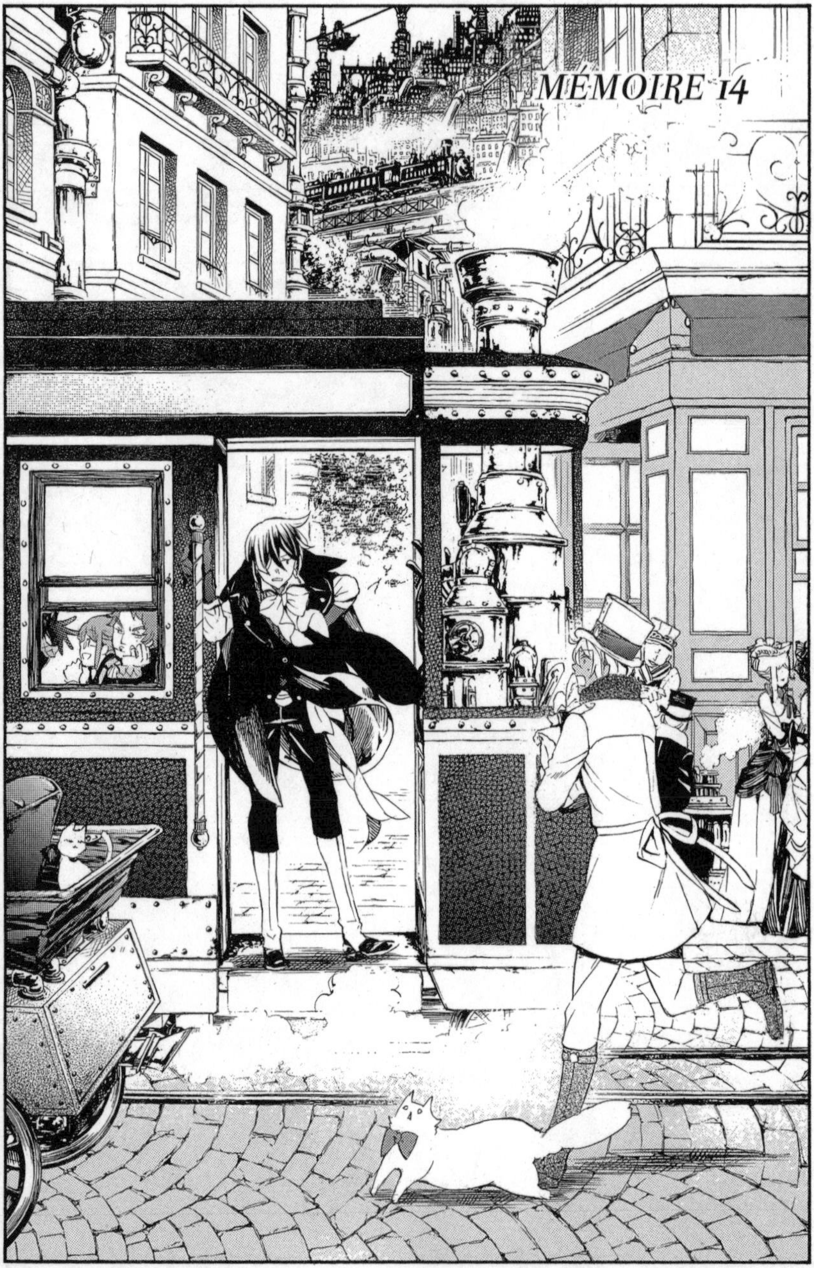
MÉMOIRE 14

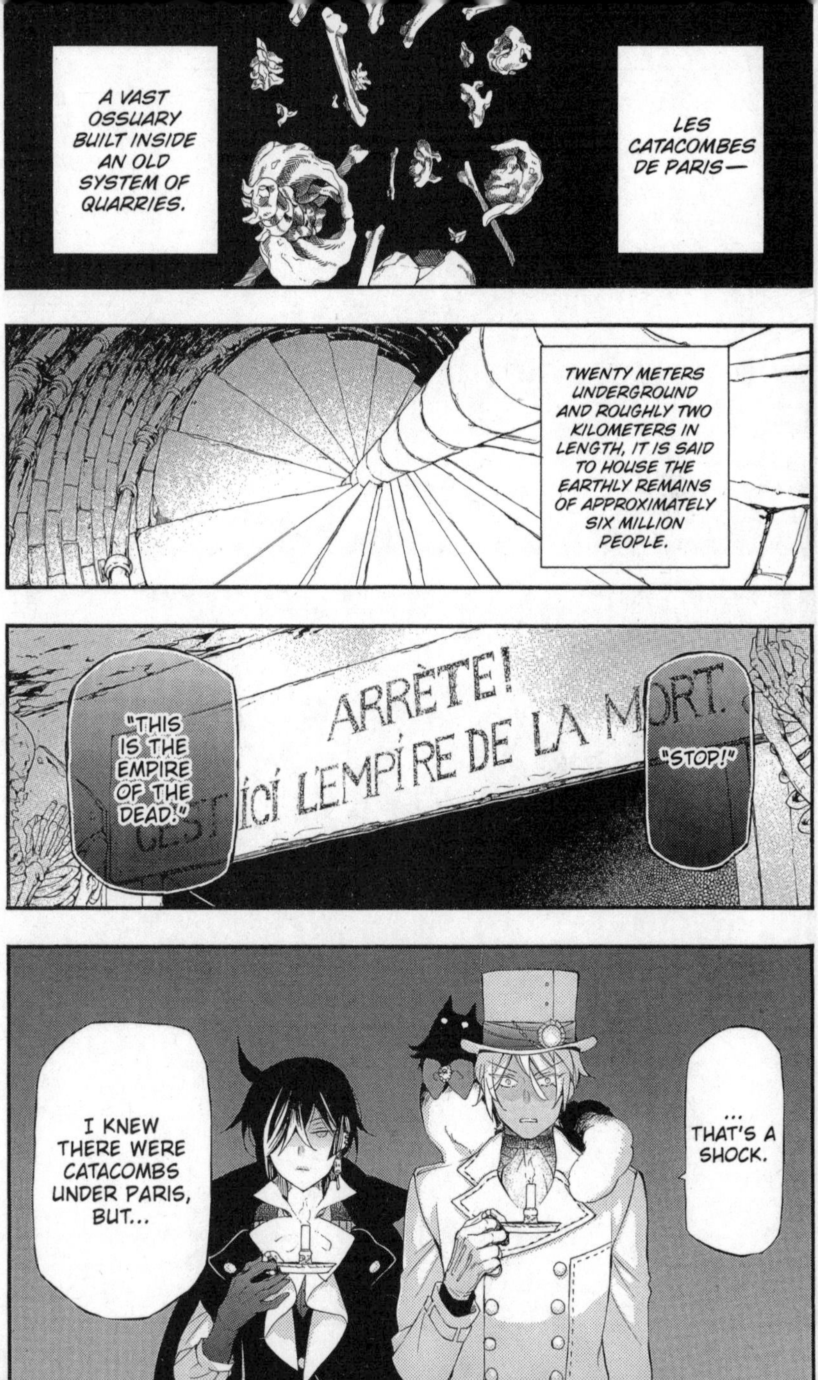
LES CATACOMBES DE PARIS—
A VAST OSSUARY BUILT INSIDE AN OLD SYSTEM OF QUARRIES.
TWENTY METERS UNDERGROUND AND ROUGHLY TWO KILOMETERS IN LENGTH, IT IS SAID TO HOUSE THE EARTHLY REMAINS OF APPROXIMATELY SIX MILLION PEOPLE.
ARRÈTE!
ÍCI L'EMPÍRE DE LA MORT.
"STOP!"
"THIS IS THE EMPIRE OF THE DEAD."
I KNEW THERE WERE CATACOMBS UNDER PARIS, BUT...
...THAT'S A SHOCK.

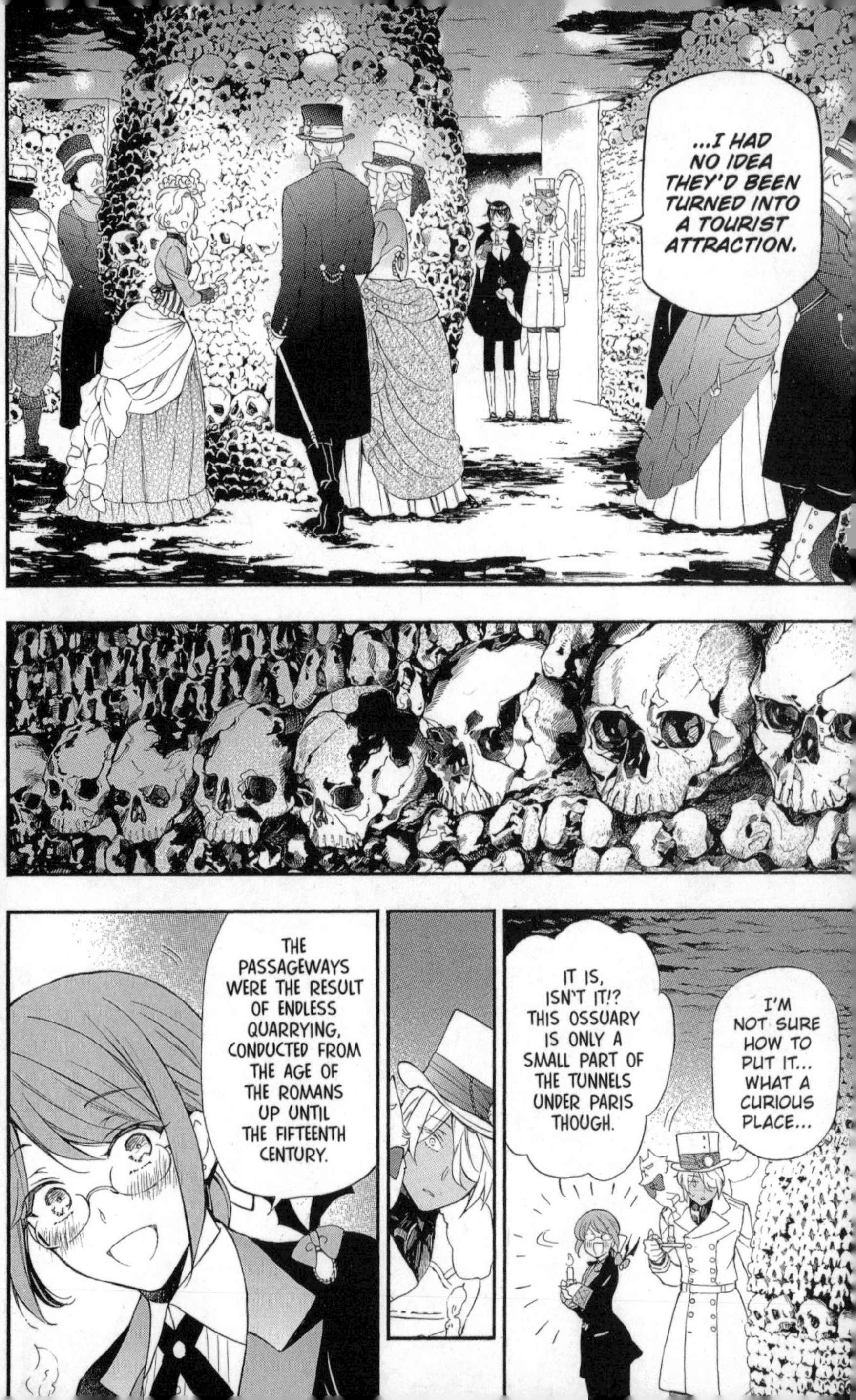
...I HAD NO IDEA THEY'D BEEN TURNED INTO A TOURIST ATTRACTION.
I'M NOT SURE HOW TO PUT IT... WHAT A CURIOUS PLACE...
IT IS, ISN'T IT!? THIS OSSUARY IS ONLY A SMALL PART OF THE TUNNELS UNDER PARIS THOUGH.
THE PASSAGEWAYS WERE THE RESULT OF ENDLESS QUARRYING, CONDUCTED FROM THE AGE OF THE ROMANS UP UNTIL THE FIFTEENTH CENTURY.

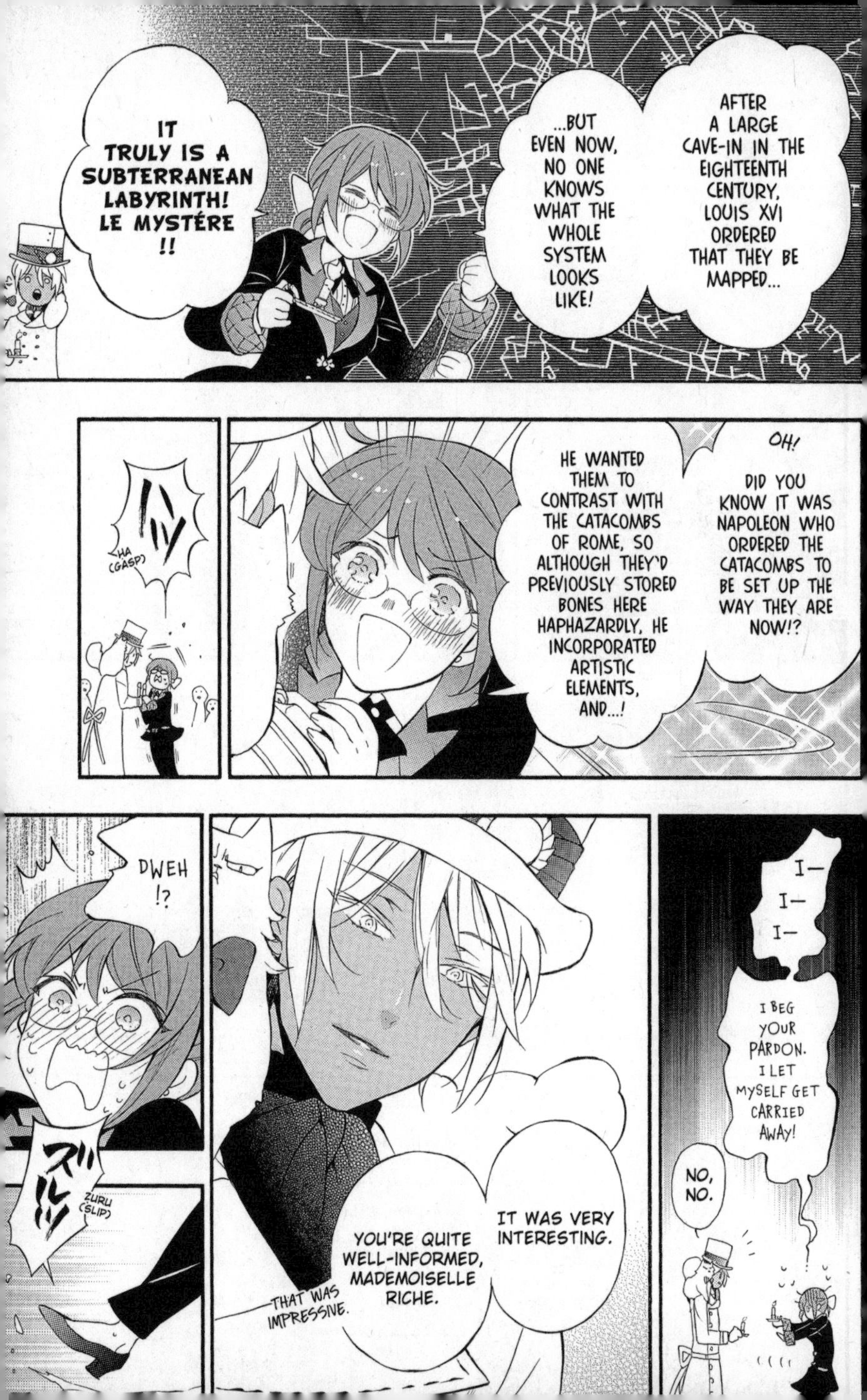
AFTER A LARGE CAVE-IN IN THE EIGHTEENTH CENTURY, LOUIS XVI ORDERED THAT THEY BE MAPPED...
...BUT EVEN NOW, NO ONE KNOWS WHAT THE WHOLE SYSTEM LOOKS LIKE!
IT TRULY IS A SUBTERRANEAN LABYRINTH! LE MYSTÉRE !!
OH!
DID YOU KNOW IT WAS NAPOLEON WHO ORDERED THE CATACOMBS TO BE SET UP THE WAY THEY ARE NOW!?
HE WANTED THEM TO CONTRAST WITH THE CATACOMBS OF ROME, SO ALTHOUGH THEY'D PREVIOUSLY STORED BONES HERE HAPHAZARDLY, HE INCORPORATED ARTISTIC ELEMENTS, AND...!
HA (GASP)
I— I— I—
I BEG YOUR PARDON. I LET MYSELF GET CARRIED AWAY!
NO, NO.
IT WAS VERY INTERESTING.
YOU'RE QUITE WELL-INFORMED, MADEMOISELLE RICHE.
THAT WAS IMPRESSIVE.
DWEH !?
ZURU (SLIP)

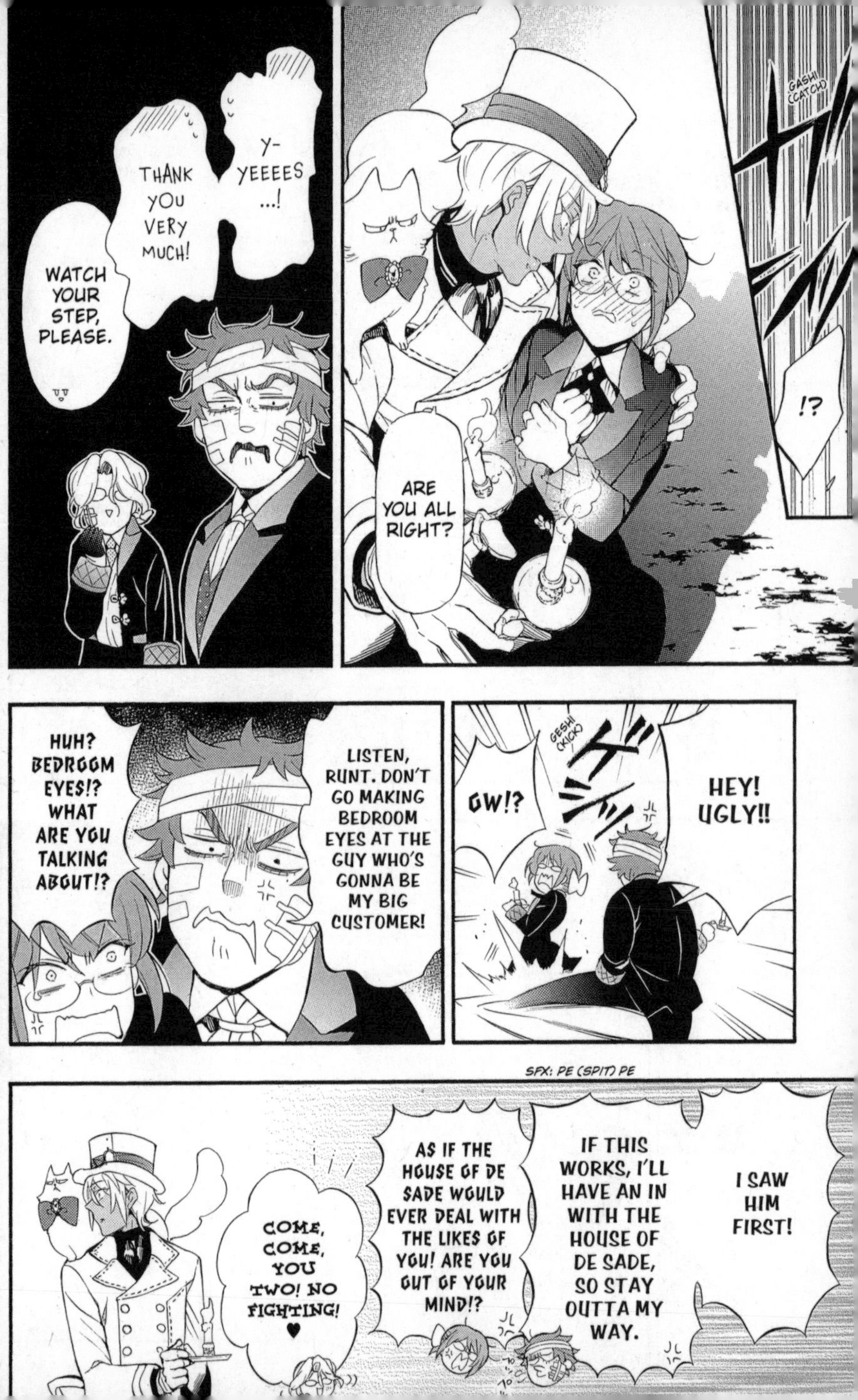
GASHI (CATCH)
!?
ARE YOU ALL RIGHT?
Y-YEEEES ...!
THANK YOU VERY MUCH!
WATCH YOUR STEP, PLEASE.
HEY! UGLY!!
GESHI (KICK)
OW!?
LISTEN, RUNT. DON'T GO MAKING BEDROOM EYES AT THE GUY WHO'S GONNA BE MY BIG CUSTOMER!
HUH? BEDROOM EYES!? WHAT ARE YOU TALKING ABOUT!?
SFX: PE (SPIT) PE
I SAW HIM FIRST!
IF THIS WORKS, I'LL HAVE AN IN WITH THE HOUSE OF DE SADE, SO STAY OUTTA MY WAY.
AS IF THE HOUSE OF DE SADE WOULD EVER DEAL WITH THE LIKES OF YOU! ARE YOU OUT OF YOUR MIND!?
COME, COME, YOU TWO! NO FIGHTING! ♥

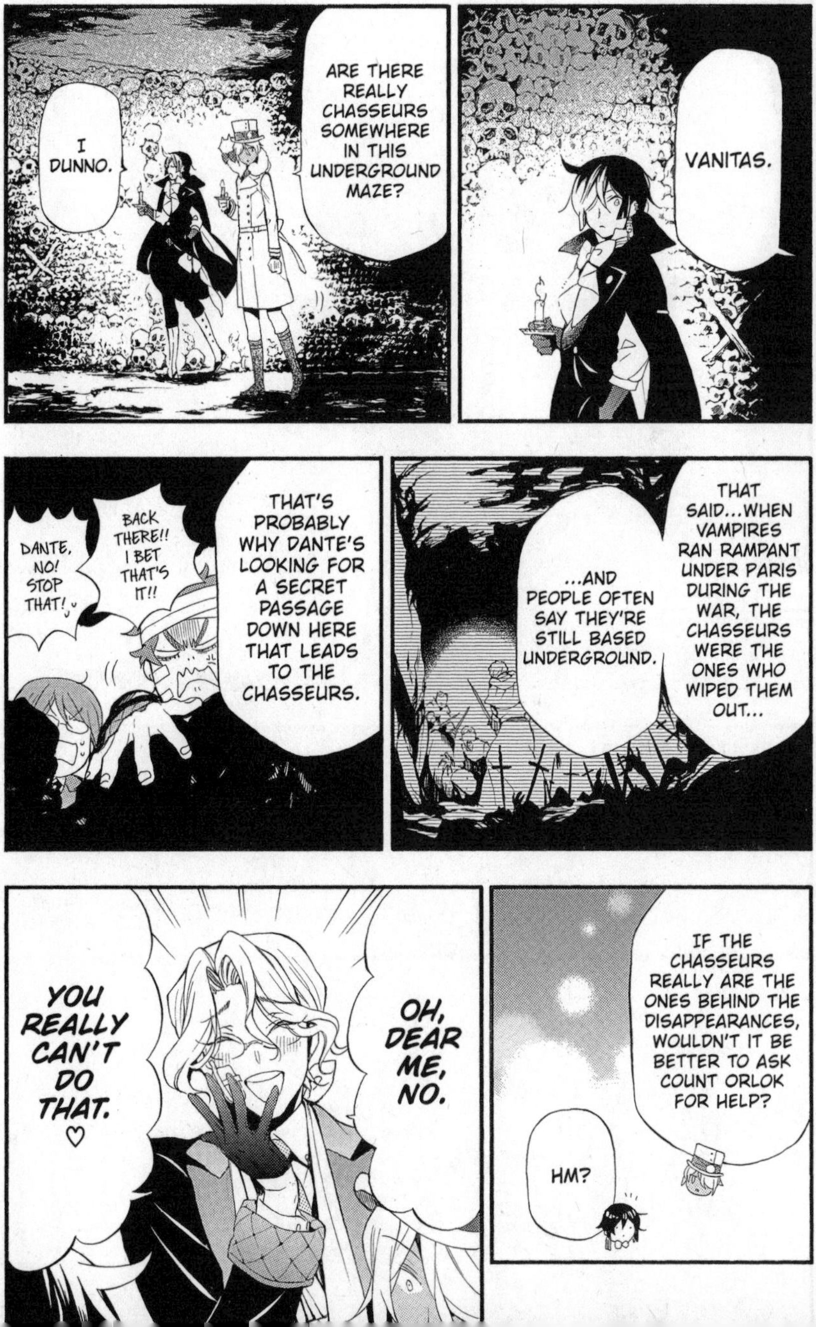
VANITAS.
ARE THERE REALLY CHASSEURS SOMEWHERE IN THIS UNDERGROUND MAZE?
I DUNNO.
THAT SAID...WHEN VAMPIRES RAN RAMPANT UNDER PARIS DURING THE WAR, THE CHASSEURS WERE THE ONES WHO WIPED THEM OUT...
...AND PEOPLE OFTEN SAY THEY'RE STILL BASED UNDERGROUND.
THAT'S PROBABLY WHY DANTE'S LOOKING FOR A SECRET PASSAGE DOWN HERE THAT LEADS TO THE CHASSEURS.
BACK THERE!! I BET THAT'S IT!!
DANTE, NO! STOP THAT!
IF THE CHASSEURS REALLY ARE THE ONES BEHIND THE DISAPPEARANCES, WOULDN'T IT BE BETTER TO ASK COUNT ORLOK FOR HELP?
HM?
OH, DEAR ME, NO.
YOU REALLY CAN'T DO THAT. ♡

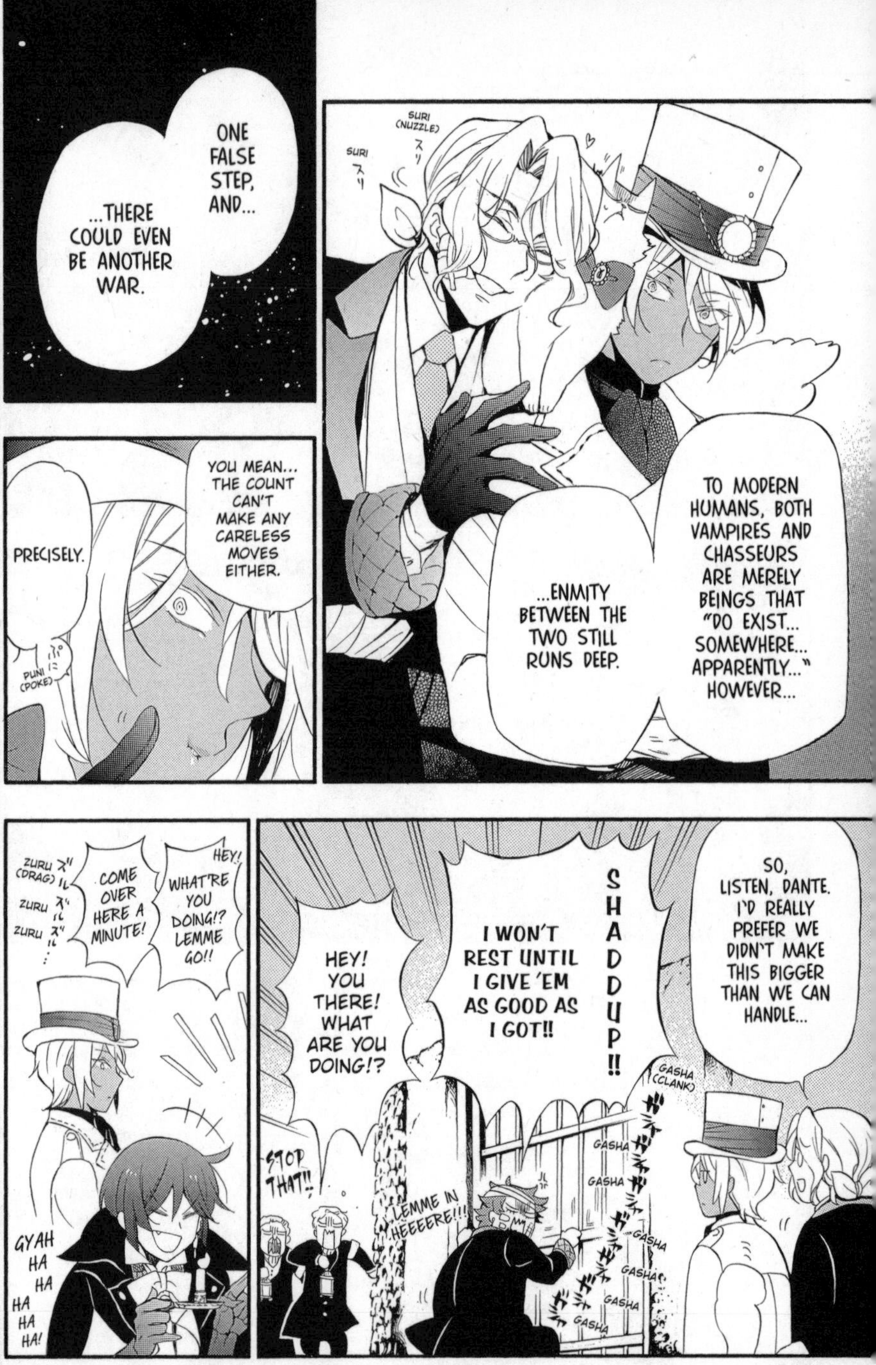
SURI (NUZZLE)
SURI
TO MODERN HUMANS, BOTH VAMPIRES AND CHASSEURS ARE MERELY BEINGS THAT "DO EXIST... SOMEWHERE... APPARENTLY..." HOWEVER...
...ENMITY BETWEEN THE TWO STILL RUNS DEEP.
ONE FALSE STEP, AND...
...THERE COULD EVEN BE ANOTHER WAR.
YOU MEAN... THE COUNT... CAN'T MAKE ANY CARELESS MOVES EITHER.
PRECISELY.
PUNI (POKE)
SO, LISTEN, DANTE. I'D REALLY PREFER WE DIDN'T MAKE THIS BIGGER THAN WE CAN HANDLE...
SHADDUP!!
I WON'T REST UNTIL I GIVE 'EM AS GOOD AS I GOT!!
HEY! YOU THERE! WHAT ARE YOU DOING!?
GASHA (CLANK)
GASHA
GASHA
GASHA
GASHA
GASHA
GASHA
STOP THAT!!
LEMME IN HEEEERE!!!
HEY! WHAT'RE YOU DOING!? LEMME GO!!
COME OVER HERE A MINUTE!
ZURU (DRAG)
ZURU
ZURU
GYAH HA HA HA HA HA HA!

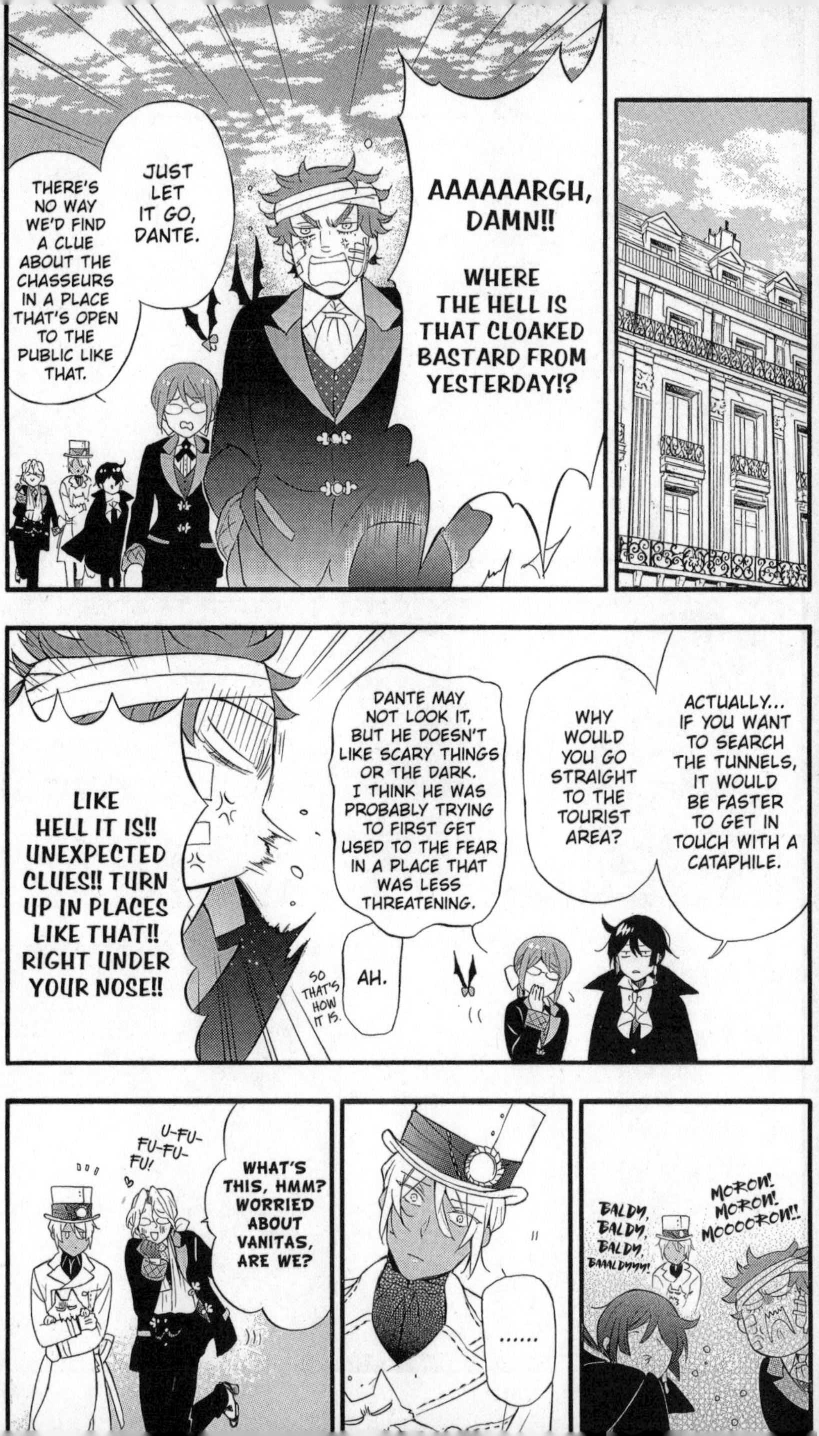
AAAAAARGH, DAMN!!
WHERE THE HELL IS THAT CLOAKED BASTARD FROM YESTERDAY!?
JUST LET IT GO, DANTE.
THERE'S NO WAY WE'D FIND A CLUE ABOUT THE CHASSEURS IN A PLACE THAT'S OPEN TO THE PUBLIC LIKE THAT.
ACTUALLY... IF YOU WANT TO SEARCH THE TUNNELS, IT WOULD BE FASTER TO GET IN TOUCH WITH A CATAPHILE.
WHY WOULD YOU GO STRAIGHT TO THE TOURIST AREA?
DANTE MAY NOT LOOK IT, BUT HE DOESN'T LIKE SCARY THINGS OR THE DARK. I THINK HE WAS PROBABLY TRYING TO FIRST GET USED TO THE FEAR IN A PLACE THAT WAS LESS THREATENING.
AH.
SO THAT'S HOW IT IS.
LIKE HELL IT IS!! UNEXPECTED CLUES!! TURN UP IN PLACES LIKE THAT!! RIGHT UNDER YOUR NOSE!!
MORON! MORON! MOOOORON!!
BALDY, BALDY, BALDY, BAAALDYYY!
......
WHAT'S THIS, HMM? WORRIED ABOUT VANITAS, ARE WE?
U-FU-FU-FU-FU!

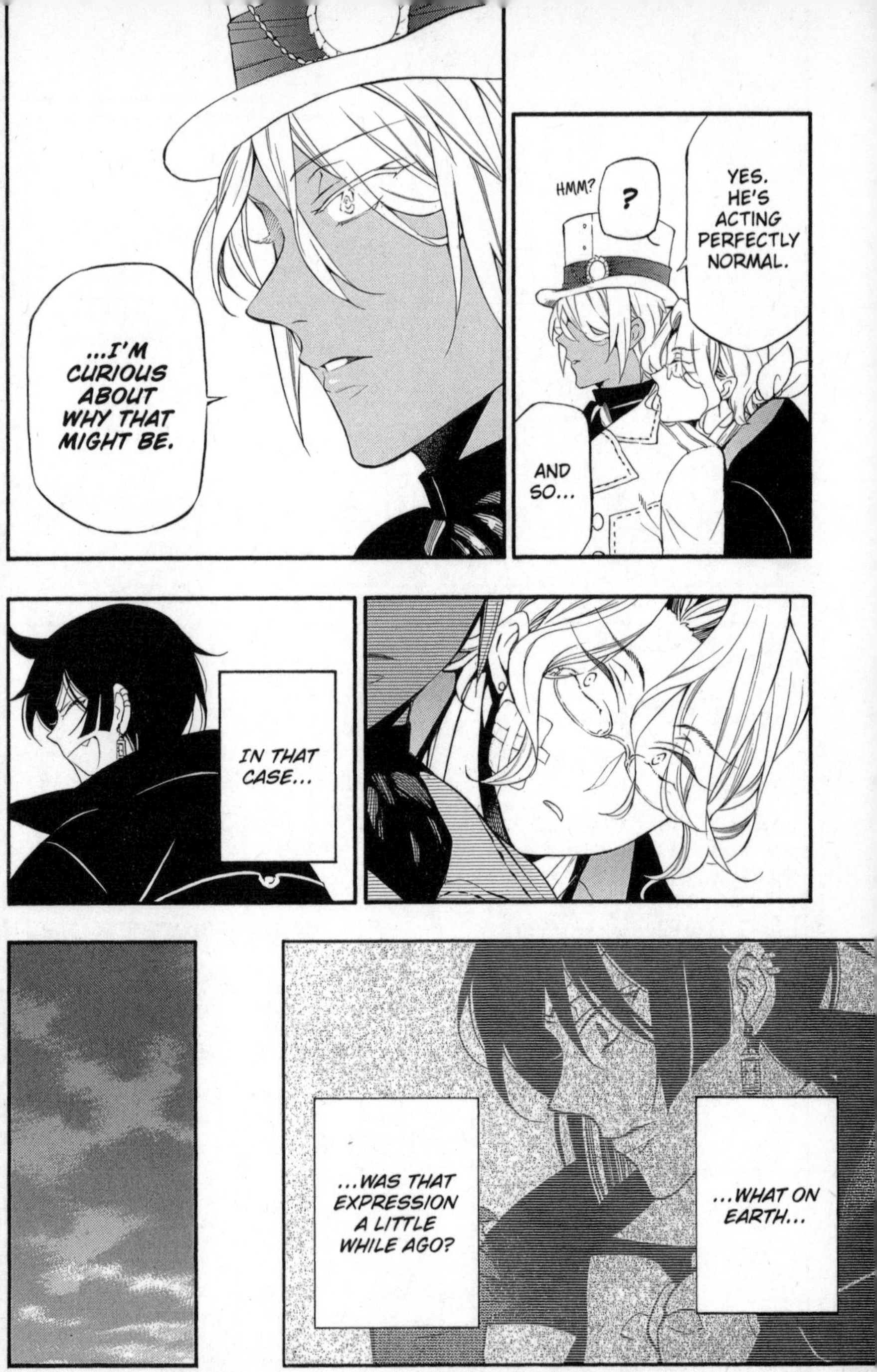
YES. HE'S ACTING PERFECTLY NORMAL.
HMM?
?
AND SO...
...I'M CURIOUS ABOUT WHY THAT MIGHT BE.
IN THAT CASE...
...WHAT ON EARTH...
...WAS THAT EXPRESSION A LITTLE WHILE AGO?

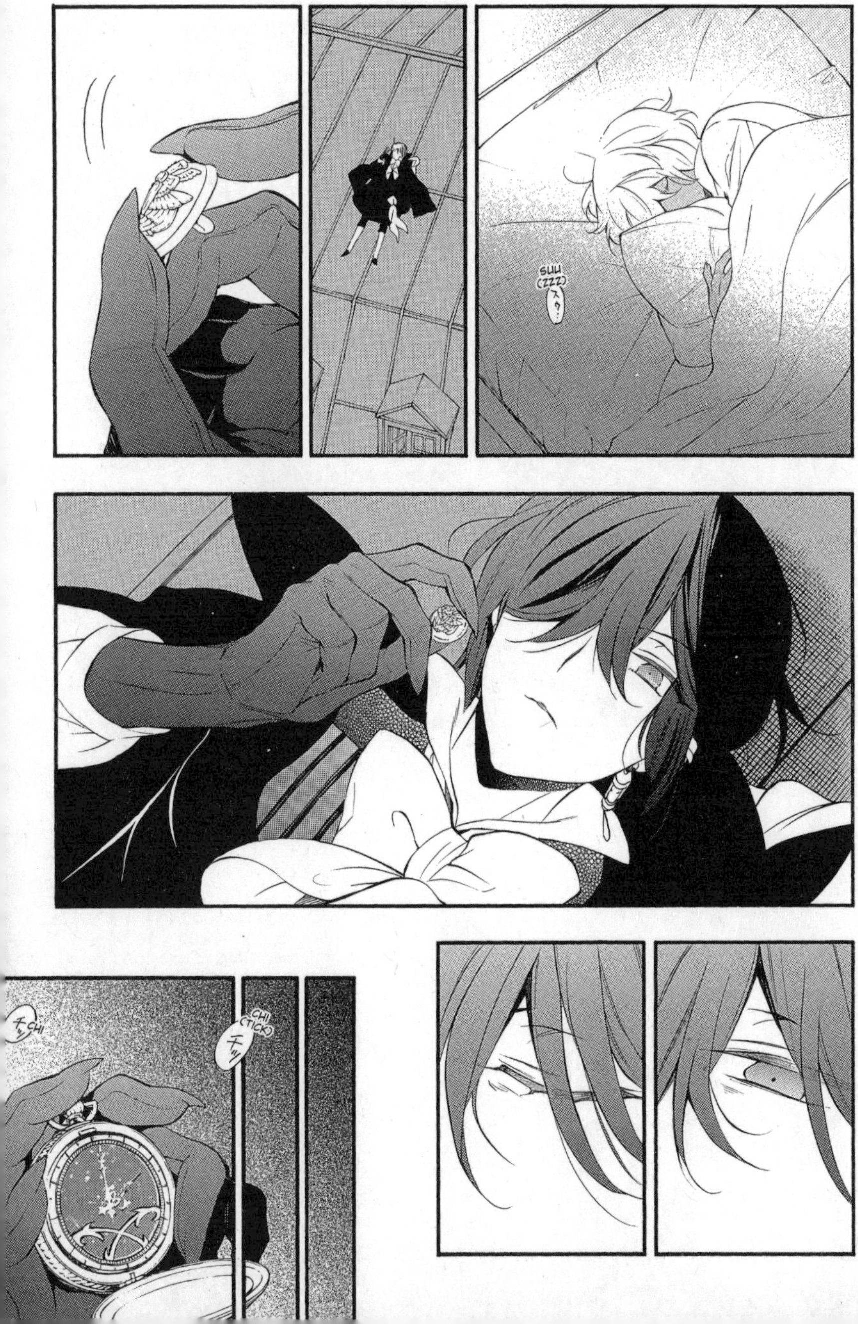
SUU (ZZZ)
スゥ…
CHI (TICK)
チッ
チッ
CHI

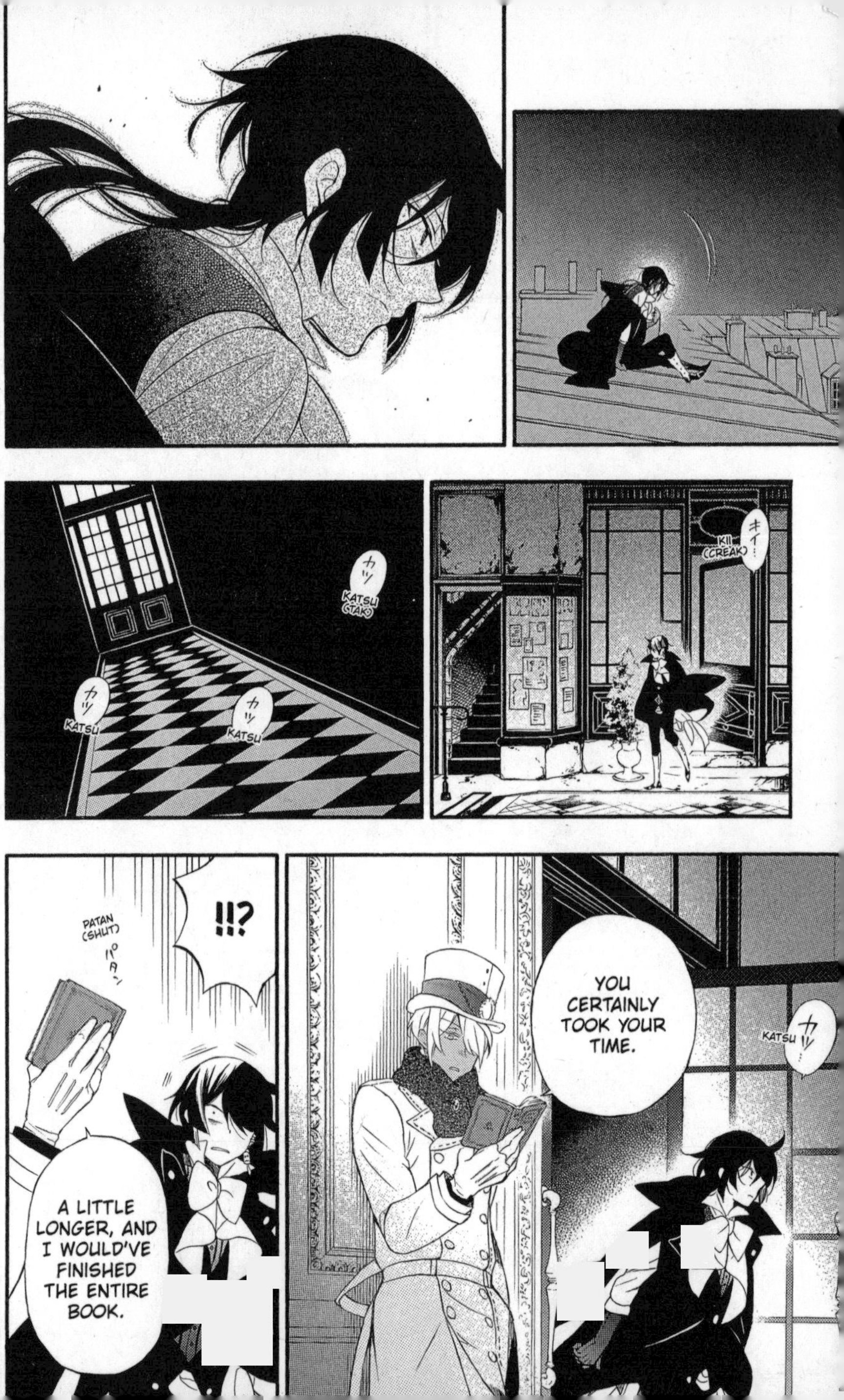
キイ…
KII (CREAK)
カッ
KATSU (TAK)
カッ
KATSU
カッ
KATSU
カッ…
KATSU
YOU CERTAINLY TOOK YOUR TIME.
!!?
パタン
PATAN (SHUT)
A LITTLE LONGER, AND I WOULD'VE FINISHED THE ENTIRE BOOK.

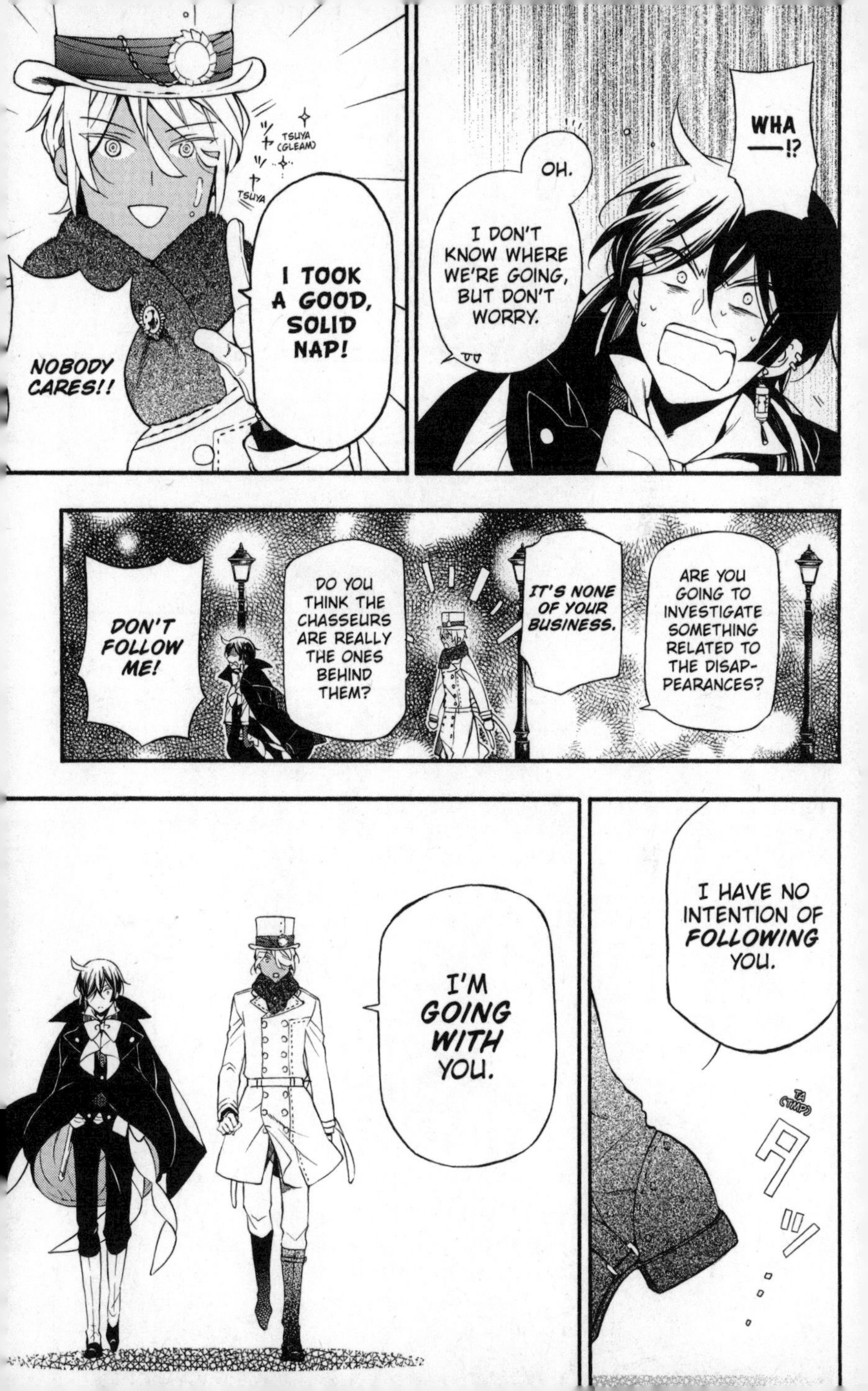
WHA—!?
OH.
I DON'T KNOW WHERE WE'RE GOING, BUT DON'T WORRY.
I TOOK A GOOD, SOLID NAP!
TSUYA (GLEAM)
TSUYA
NOBODY CARES!!
ARE YOU GOING TO INVESTIGATE SOMETHING RELATED TO THE DISAPPEARANCES?
IT'S NONE OF YOUR BUSINESS.
DO YOU THINK THE CHASSEURS ARE REALLY THE ONES BEHIND THEM?
DON'T FOLLOW ME!
I HAVE NO INTENTION OF FOLLOWING YOU.
TA (TMP)
I'M GOING WITH YOU.

I WILL, THANKS.

YES.

...DO AS YOU LIKE.

HAAH...

....
....
....

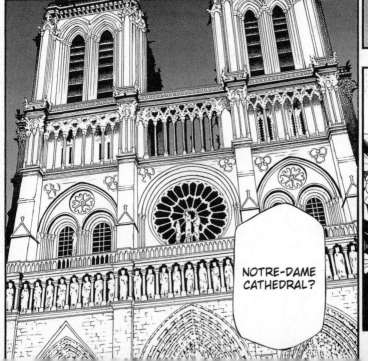

NOTRE-DAME CATHEDRAL?

ZA (ZSH)

! THIS IS...

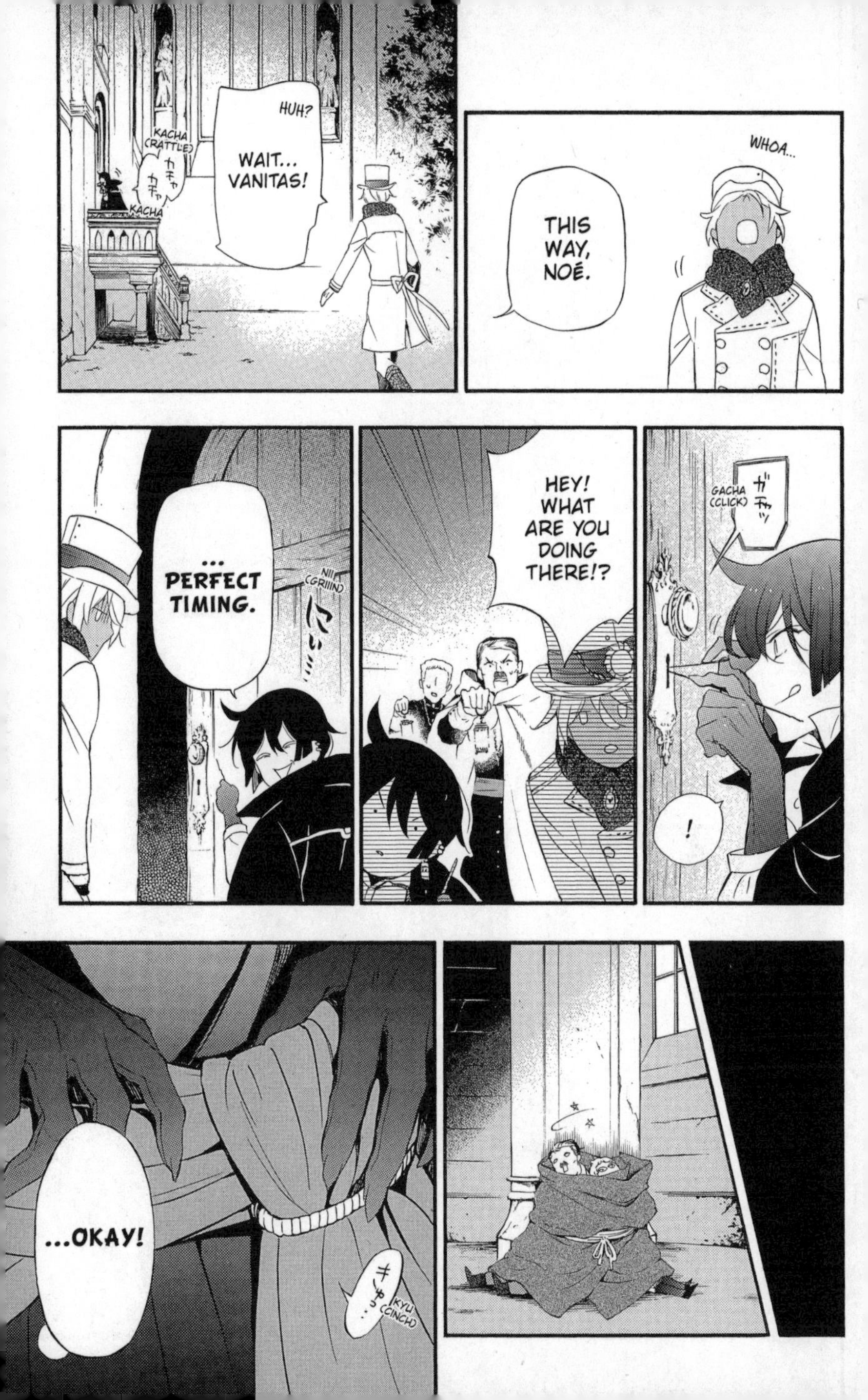
WHOA...
THIS WAY, NOÉ.
HUH?
WAIT... VANITAS!
KACHA (RATTLE)
カチャ カチャ
KACHA
GACHA (CLICK)
ガチャッ
!
HEY! WHAT ARE YOU DOING THERE!?
NII (GRIIIN)
にぃ…
...PERFECT TIMING.
...OKAY!
キュッ…
KYU (CINCH)

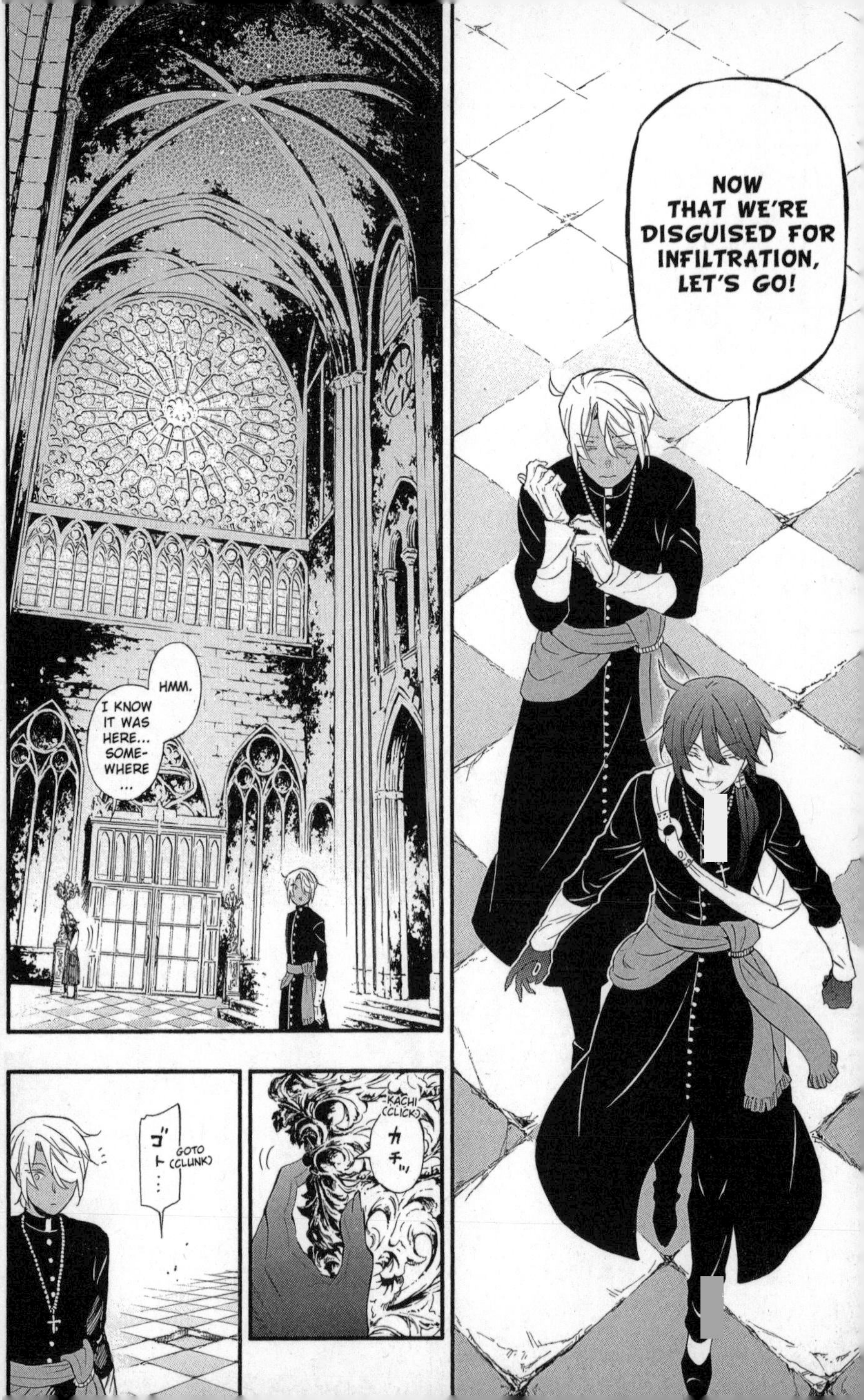
NOW THAT WE'RE DISGUISED FOR INFILTRATION, LET'S GO!
HMM.
I KNOW IT WAS HERE... SOME-WHERE ...
KACHI (CLICK)
カチッ
ゴト…
GOTO (CLUNK)

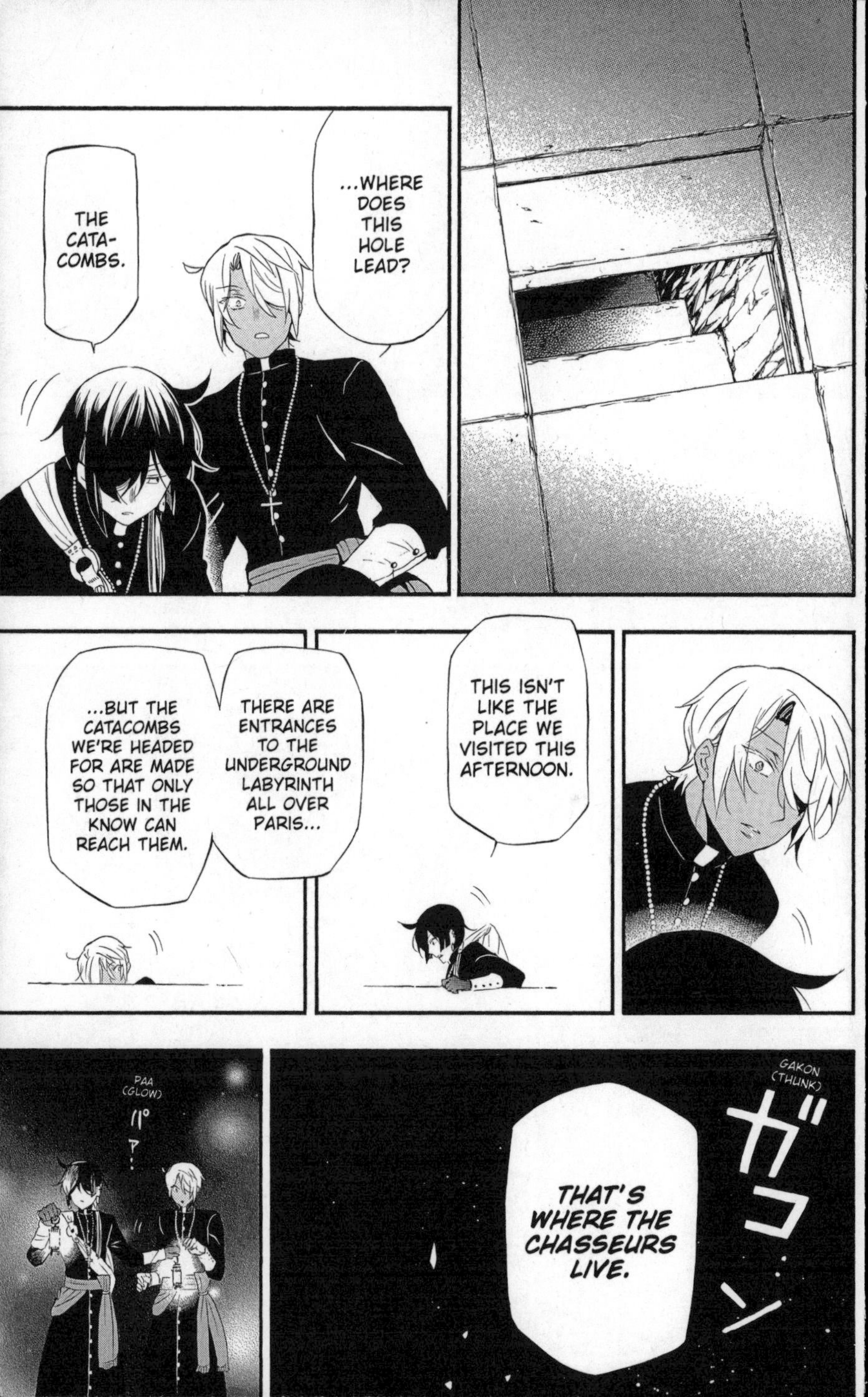
...WHERE DOES THIS HOLE LEAD?
THE CATA-COMBS.
THIS ISN'T LIKE THE PLACE WE VISITED THIS AFTERNOON.
THERE ARE ENTRANCES TO THE UNDERGROUND LABYRINTH ALL OVER PARIS...
...BUT THE CATACOMBS WE'RE HEADED FOR ARE MADE SO THAT ONLY THOSE IN THE KNOW CAN REACH THEM.
GAKON (THUNK)
ガコン
THAT'S WHERE THE CHASSEURS LIVE.
PAA (GLOW)
パァ

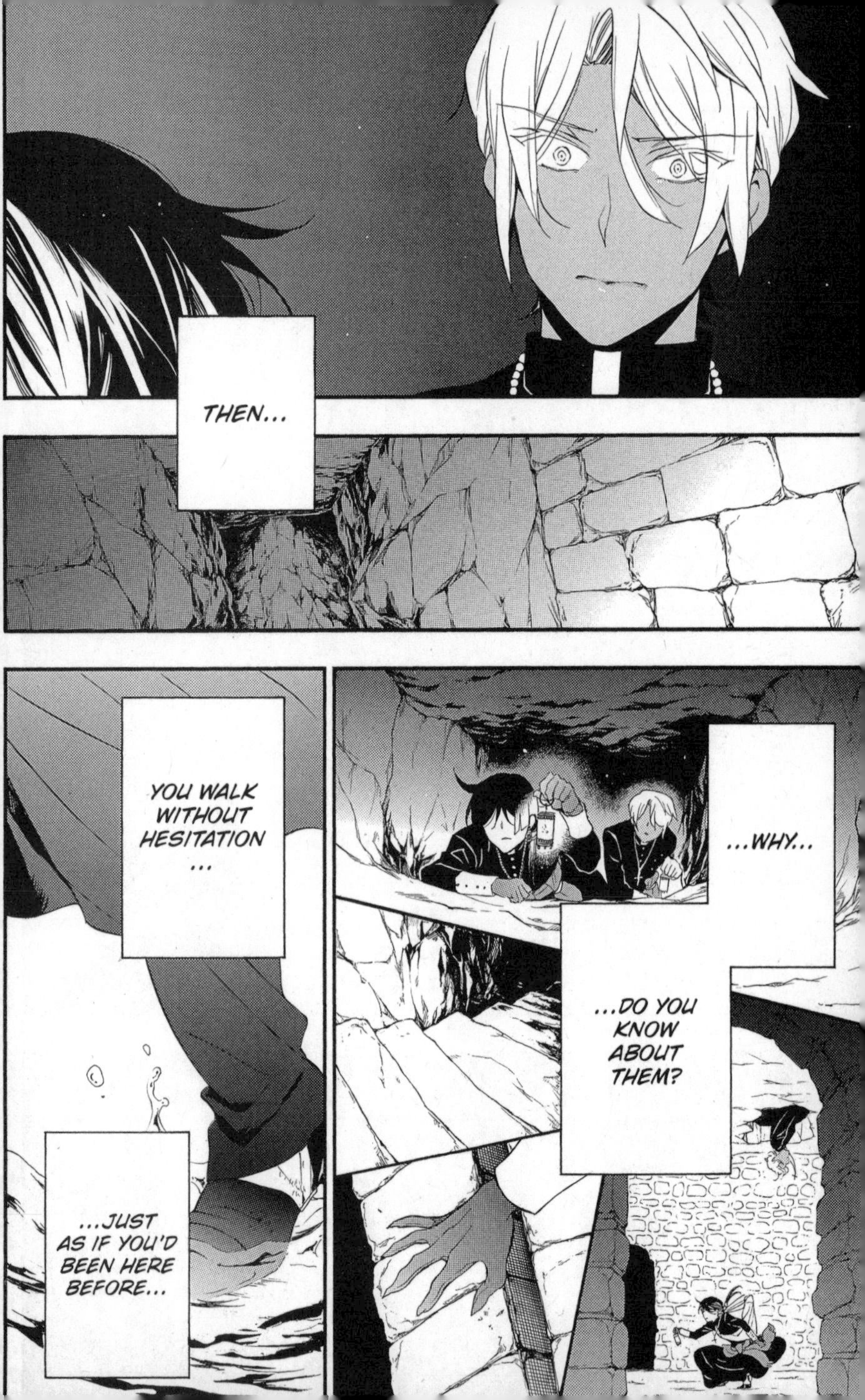
THEN...
...WHY...
...DO YOU KNOW ABOUT THEM?
YOU WALK WITHOUT HESITATION...
...JUST AS IF YOU'D BEEN HERE BEFORE...

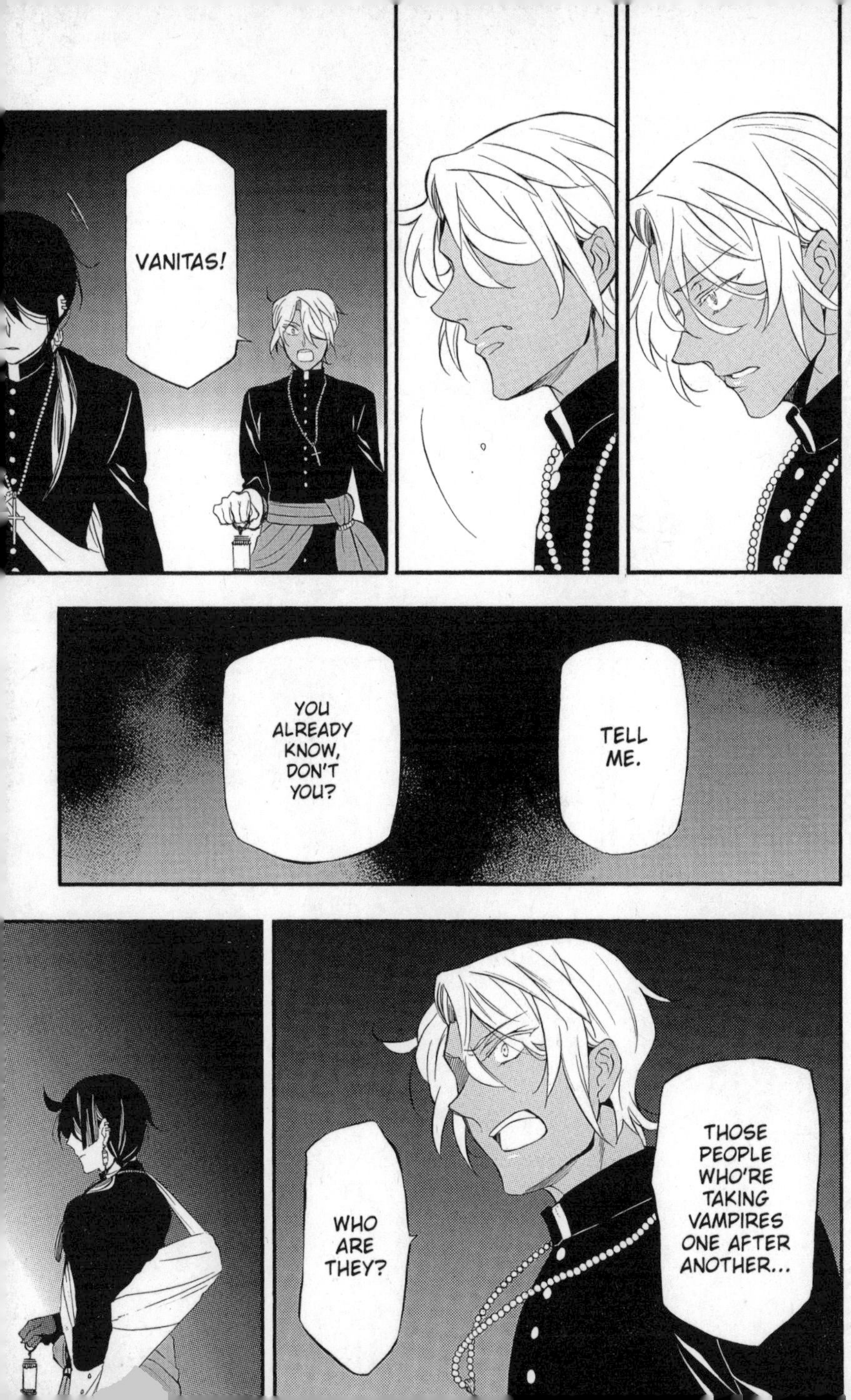
VANITAS!
TELL ME.
YOU ALREADY KNOW, DON'T YOU?
THOSE PEOPLE WHO'RE TAKING VAMPIRES ONE AFTER ANOTHER...
WHO ARE THEY?

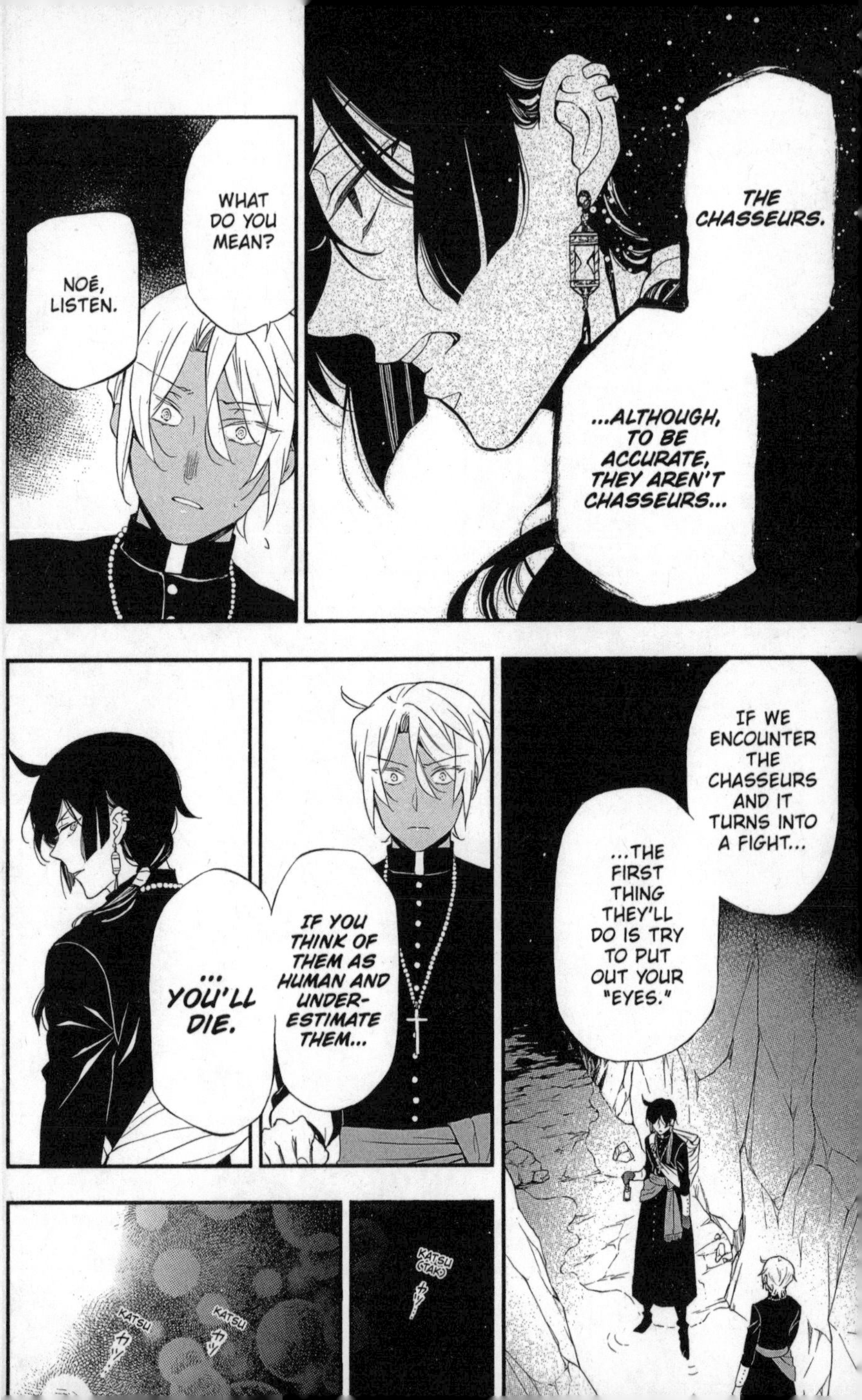
THE CHASSEURS.
...ALTHOUGH, TO BE ACCURATE, THEY AREN'T CHASSEURS...
WHAT DO YOU MEAN?
NOÉ, LISTEN.
IF WE ENCOUNTER THE CHASSEURS AND IT TURNS INTO A FIGHT...
...THE FIRST THING THEY'LL DO IS TRY TO PUT OUT YOUR "EYES."
IF YOU THINK OF THEM AS HUMAN AND UNDER-ESTIMATE THEM...
...YOU'LL DIE.
KATSU (TAK)
KATSU
KATSU

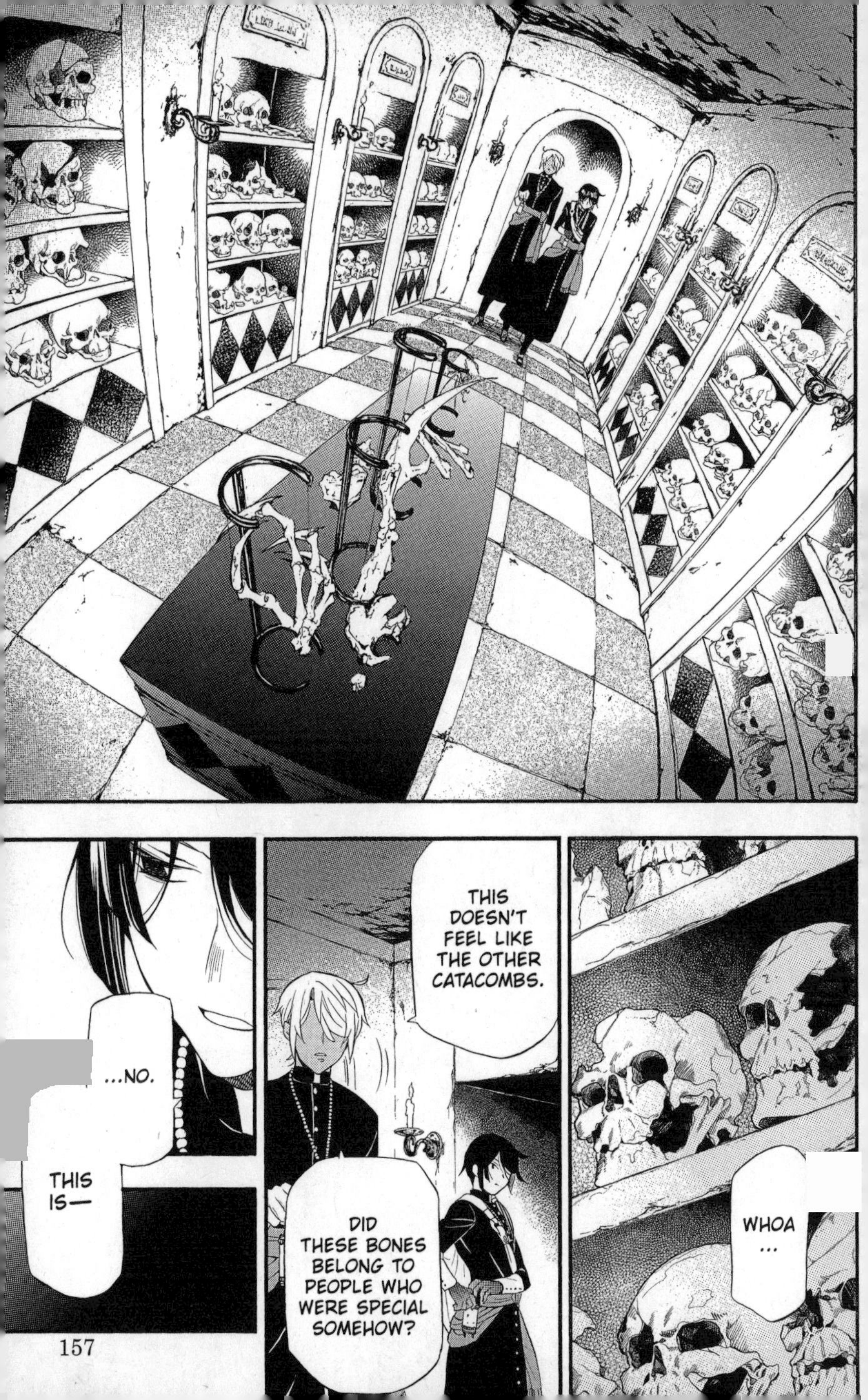
WHOA ...
THIS DOESN'T FEEL LIKE THE OTHER CATACOMBS.
DID THESE BONES BELONG TO PEOPLE WHO WERE SPECIAL SOMEHOW?
...NO.
THIS IS—

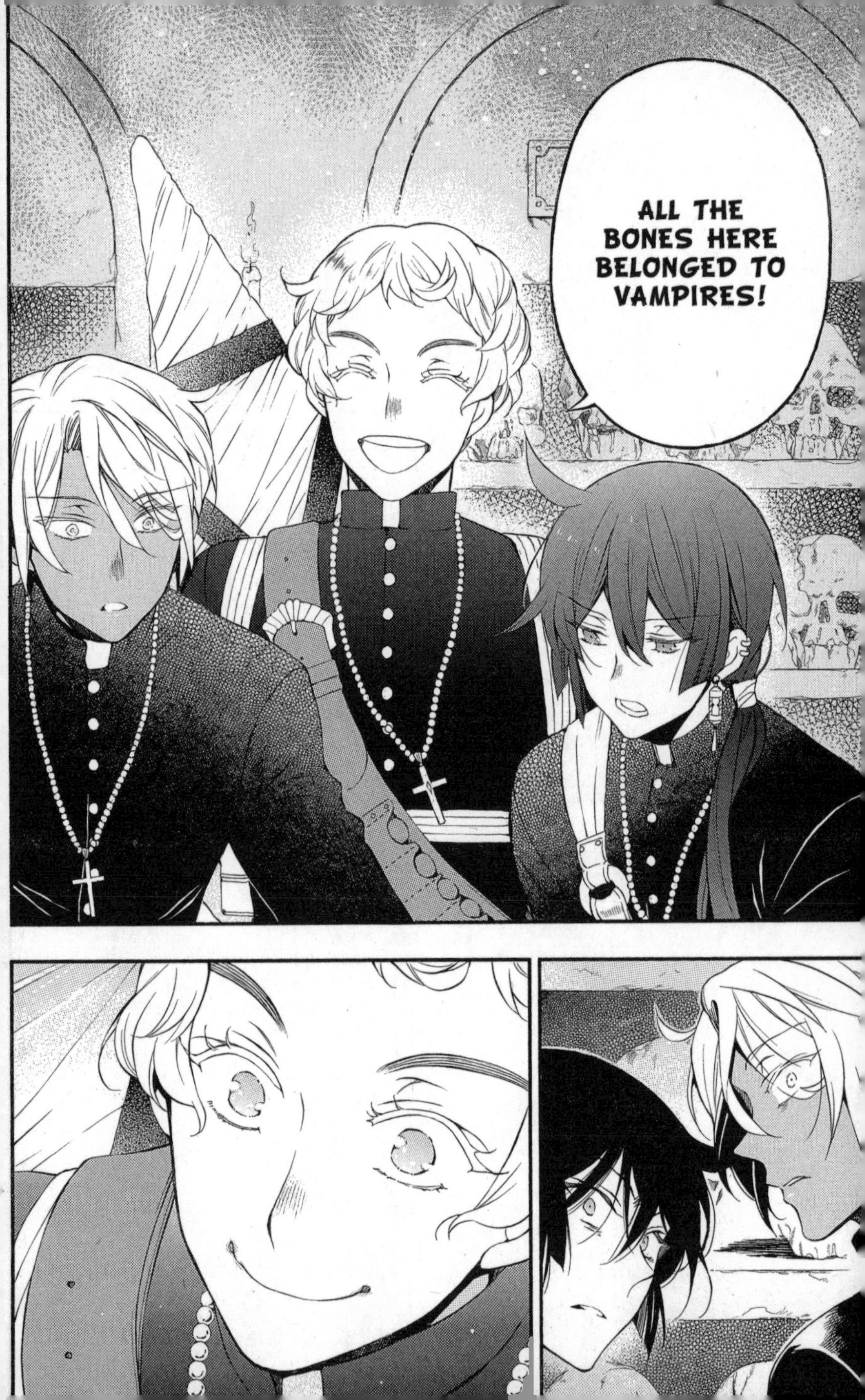
ALL THE BONES HERE BELONGED TO VAMPIRES!

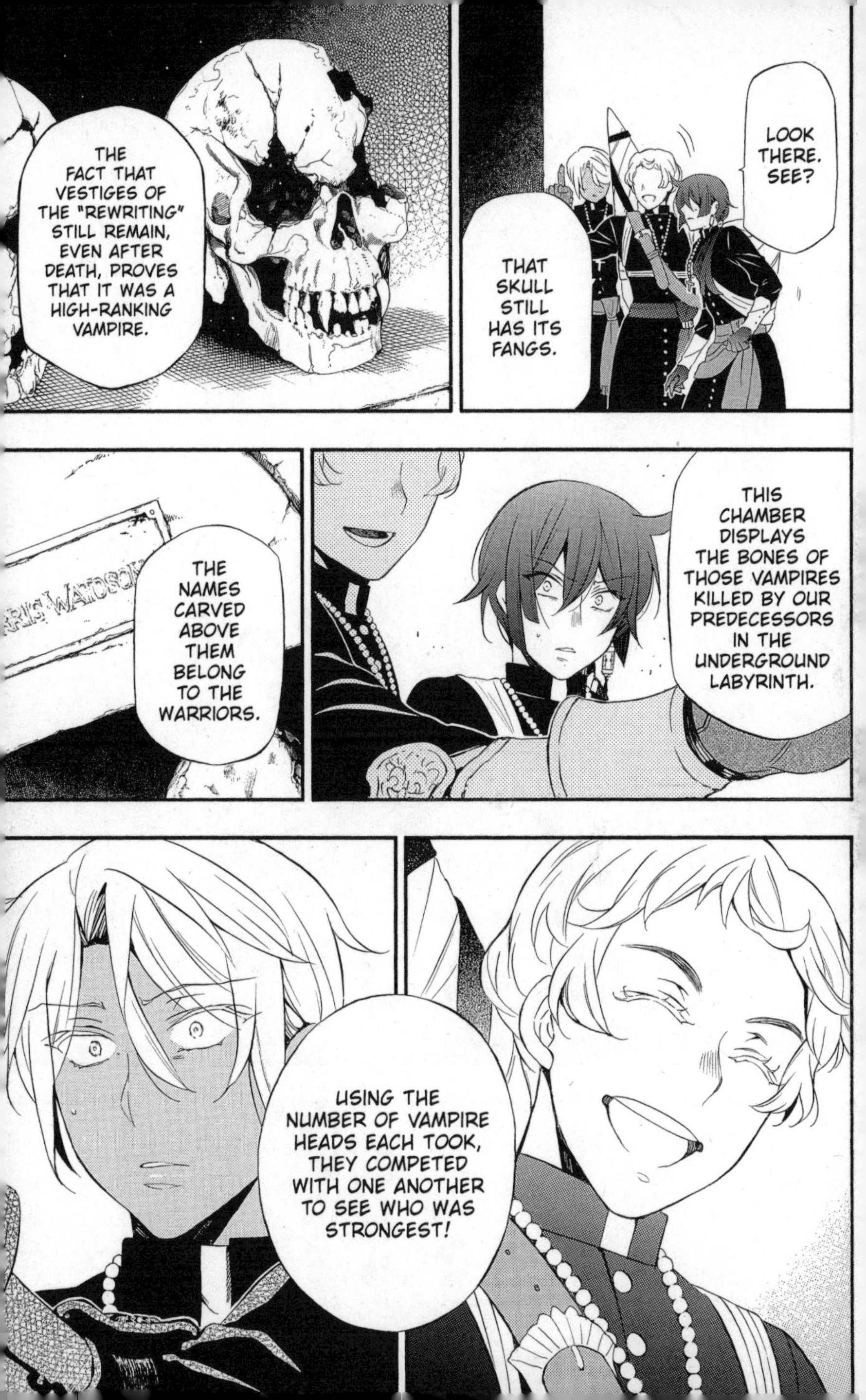
LOOK THERE. SEE?
THAT SKULL STILL HAS ITS FANGS.
THE FACT THAT VESTIGES OF THE "REWRITING" STILL REMAIN, EVEN AFTER DEATH, PROVES THAT IT WAS A HIGH-RANKING VAMPIRE.
THIS CHAMBER DISPLAYS THE BONES OF THOSE VAMPIRES KILLED BY OUR PREDECESSORS IN THE UNDERGROUND LABYRINTH.
THE NAMES CARVED ABOVE THEM BELONG TO THE WARRIORS.
USING THE NUMBER OF VAMPIRE HEADS EACH TOOK, THEY COMPETED WITH ONE ANOTHER TO SEE WHO WAS STRONGEST!

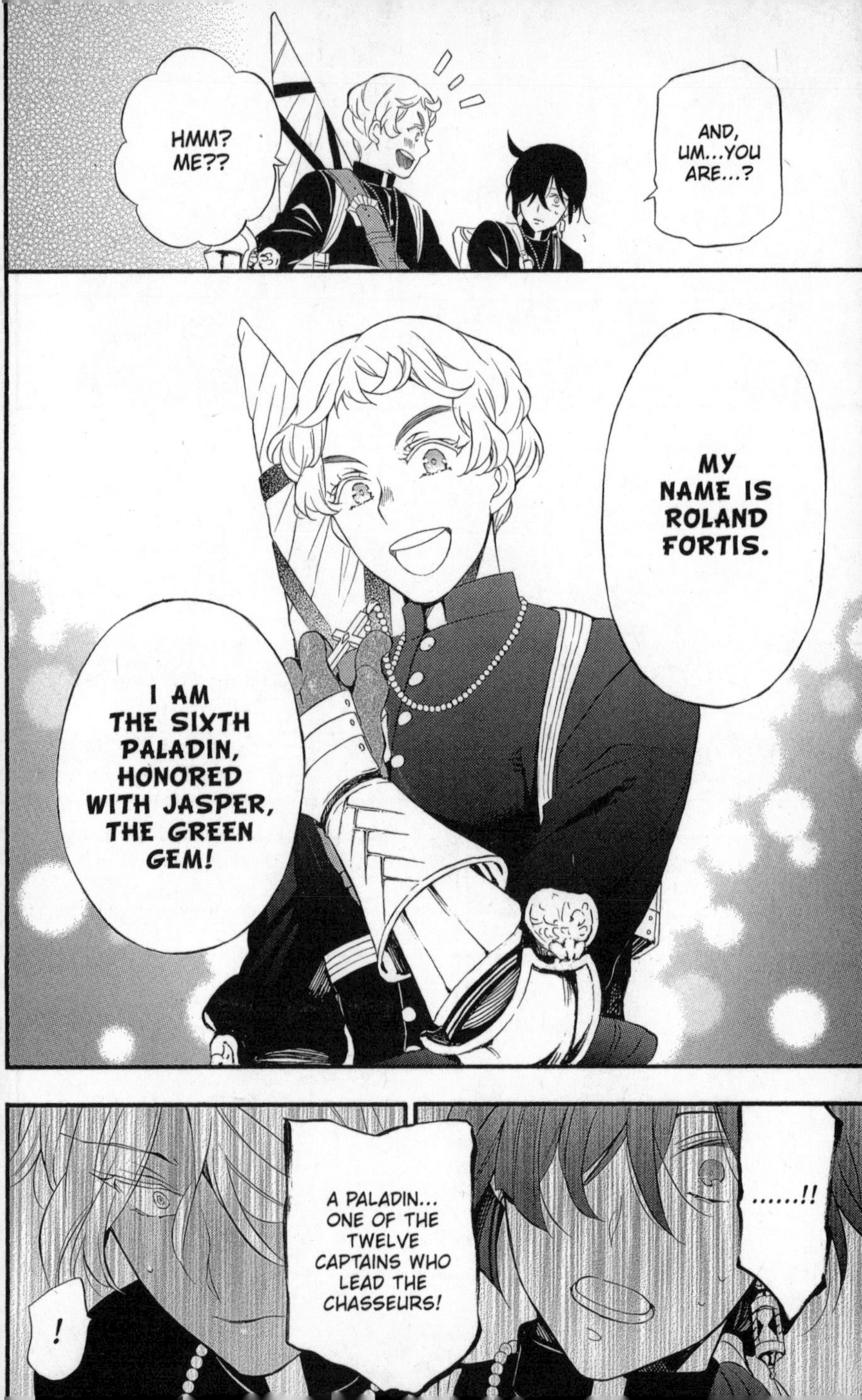
AND, UM...YOU ARE...?
HMM? ME??
MY NAME IS ROLAND FORTIS.
I AM THE SIXTH PALADIN, HONORED WITH JASPER, THE GREEN GEM!
......!!
A PALADIN... ONE OF THE TWELVE CAPTAINS WHO LEAD THE CHASSEURS!
!

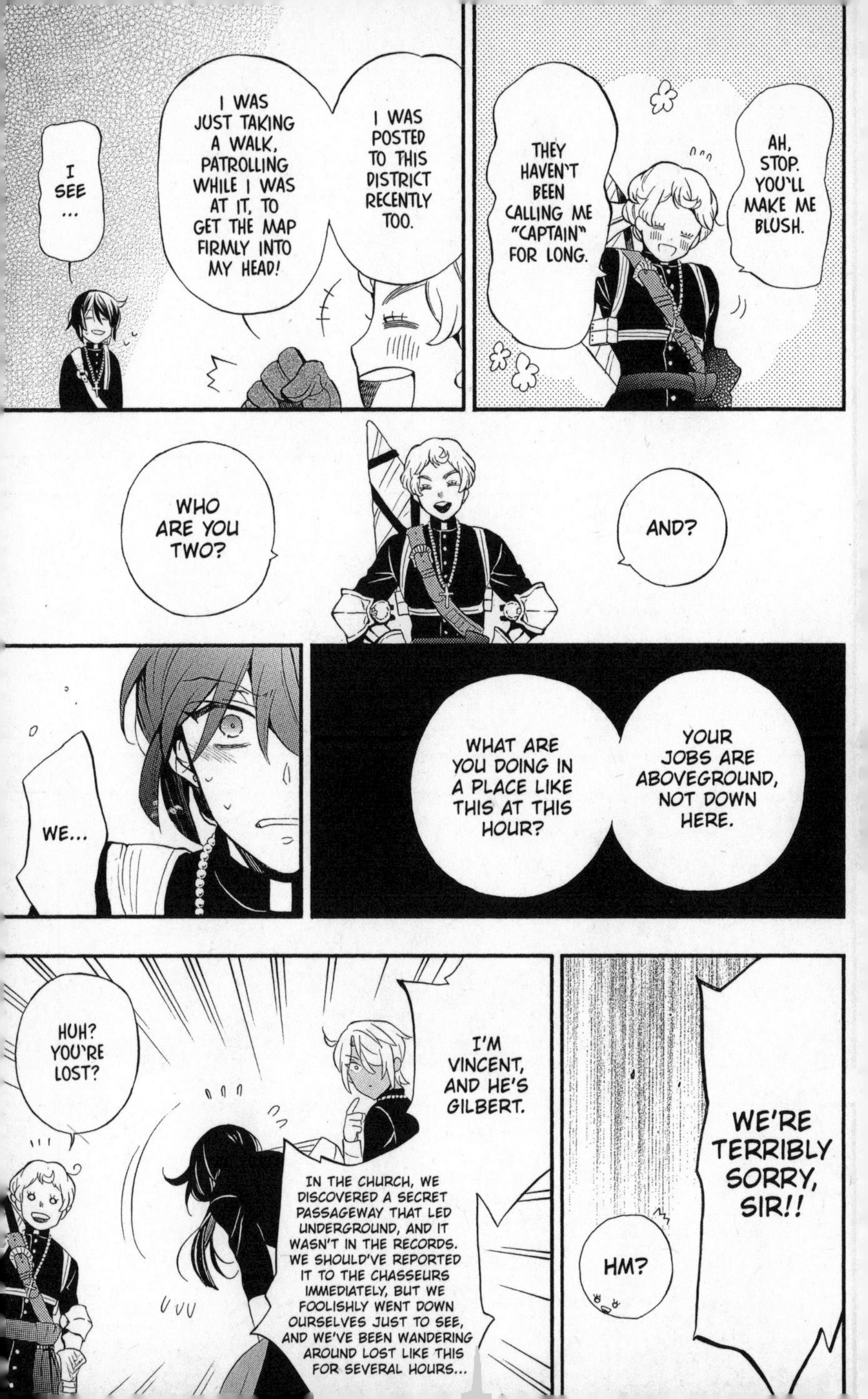
AH, STOP. YOU'LL MAKE ME BLUSH.
THEY HAVEN'T BEEN CALLING ME "CAPTAIN" FOR LONG.
I WAS POSTED TO THIS DISTRICT RECENTLY TOO.
I WAS JUST TAKING A WALK, PATROLLING WHILE I WAS AT IT, TO GET THE MAP FIRMLY INTO MY HEAD!
I SEE...
AND?
WHO ARE YOU TWO?
YOUR JOBS ARE ABOVEGROUND, NOT DOWN HERE.
WHAT ARE YOU DOING IN A PLACE LIKE THIS AT THIS HOUR?
WE...
WE'RE TERRIBLY SORRY, SIR!!
HM?
I'M VINCENT, AND HE'S GILBERT.
IN THE CHURCH, WE DISCOVERED A SECRET PASSAGEWAY THAT LED UNDERGROUND, AND IT WASN'T IN THE RECORDS. WE SHOULD'VE REPORTED IT TO THE CHASSEURS IMMEDIATELY, BUT WE FOOLISHLY WENT DOWN OURSELVES JUST TO SEE, AND WE'VE BEEN WANDERING AROUND LOST LIKE THIS FOR SEVERAL HOURS...
HUH? YOU'RE LOST?

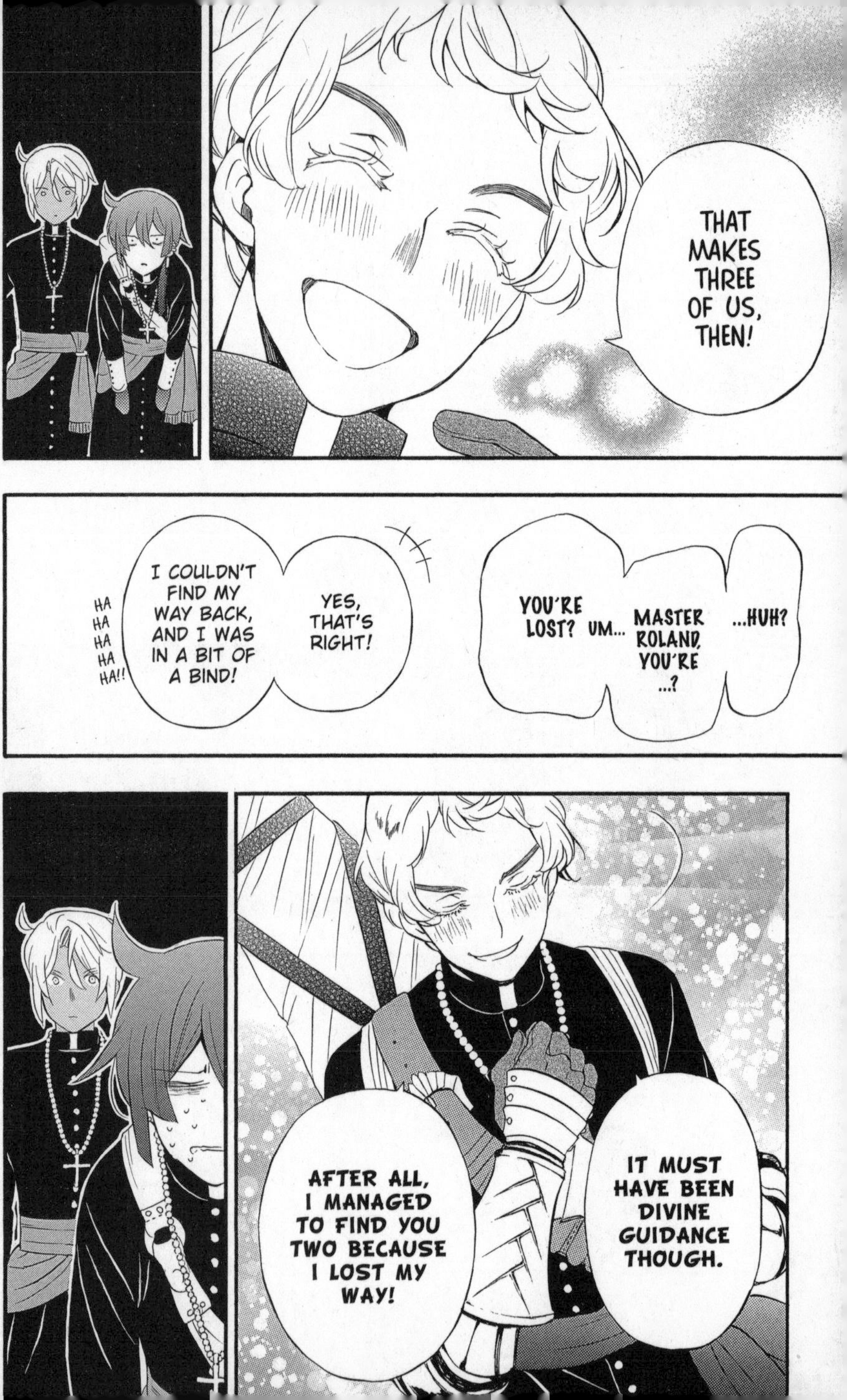
THAT MAKES THREE OF US, THEN!
...HUH?
MASTER ROLAND, YOU'RE ...?
UM...
YOU'RE LOST?
YES, THAT'S RIGHT!
I COULDN'T FIND MY WAY BACK, AND I WAS IN A BIT OF A BIND!
HA HA HA HA HA!!
IT MUST HAVE BEEN DIVINE GUIDANCE THOUGH.
AFTER ALL, I MANAGED TO FIND YOU TWO BECAUSE I LOST MY WAY!

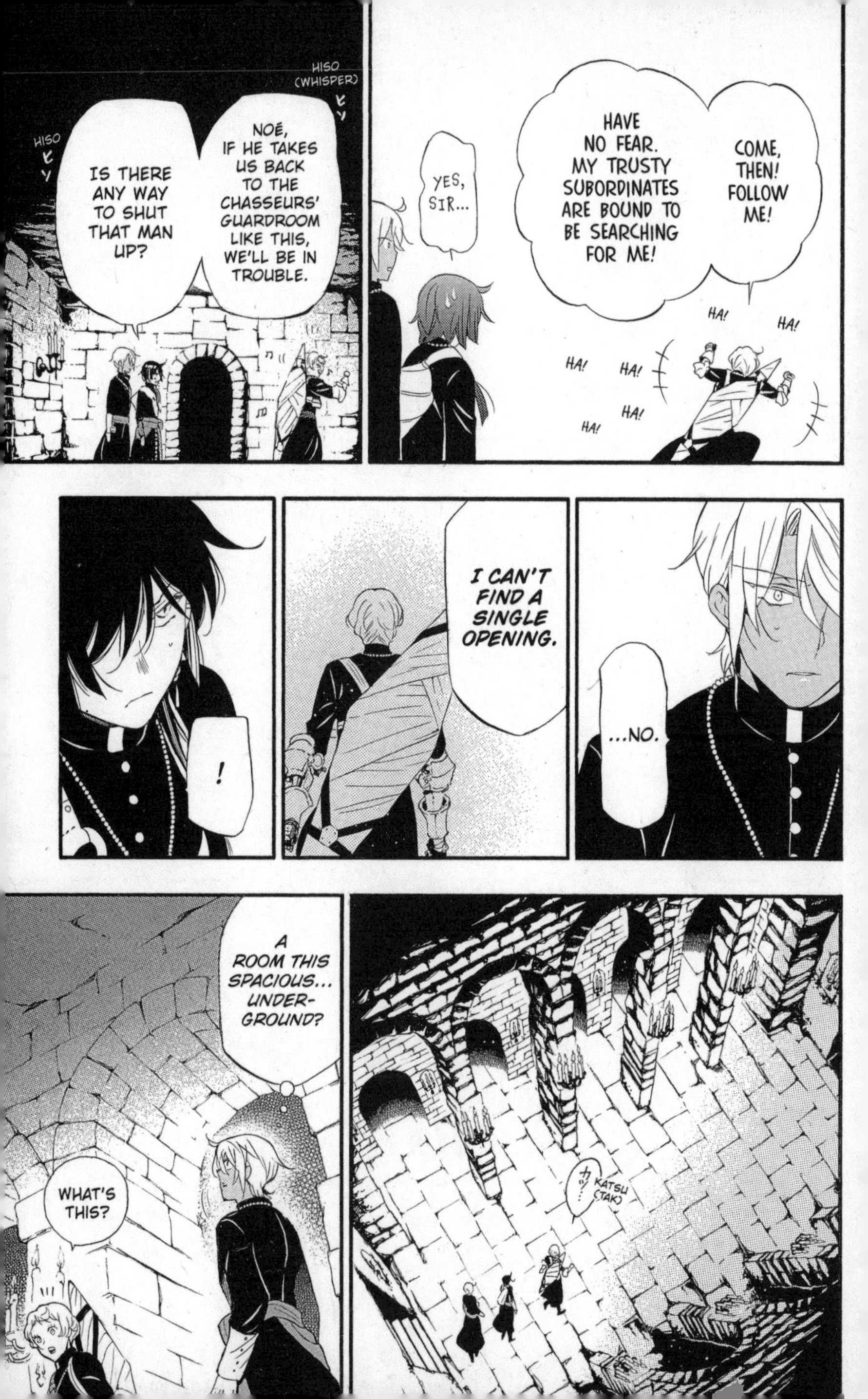
COME, THEN! FOLLOW ME!
HAVE NO FEAR. MY TRUSTY SUBORDINATES ARE BOUND TO BE SEARCHING FOR ME!
HA! HA! HA! HA! HA! HA!
YES, SIR...
HISO (WHISPER)
NOÉ, IF HE TAKES US BACK TO THE CHASSEURS' GUARDROOM LIKE THIS, WE'LL BE IN TROUBLE.
HISO
IS THERE ANY WAY TO SHUT THAT MAN UP?
...NO.
I CAN'T FIND A SINGLE OPENING.
!
KATSU (TAK)
A ROOM THIS SPACIOUS... UNDER-GROUND?
WHAT'S THIS?

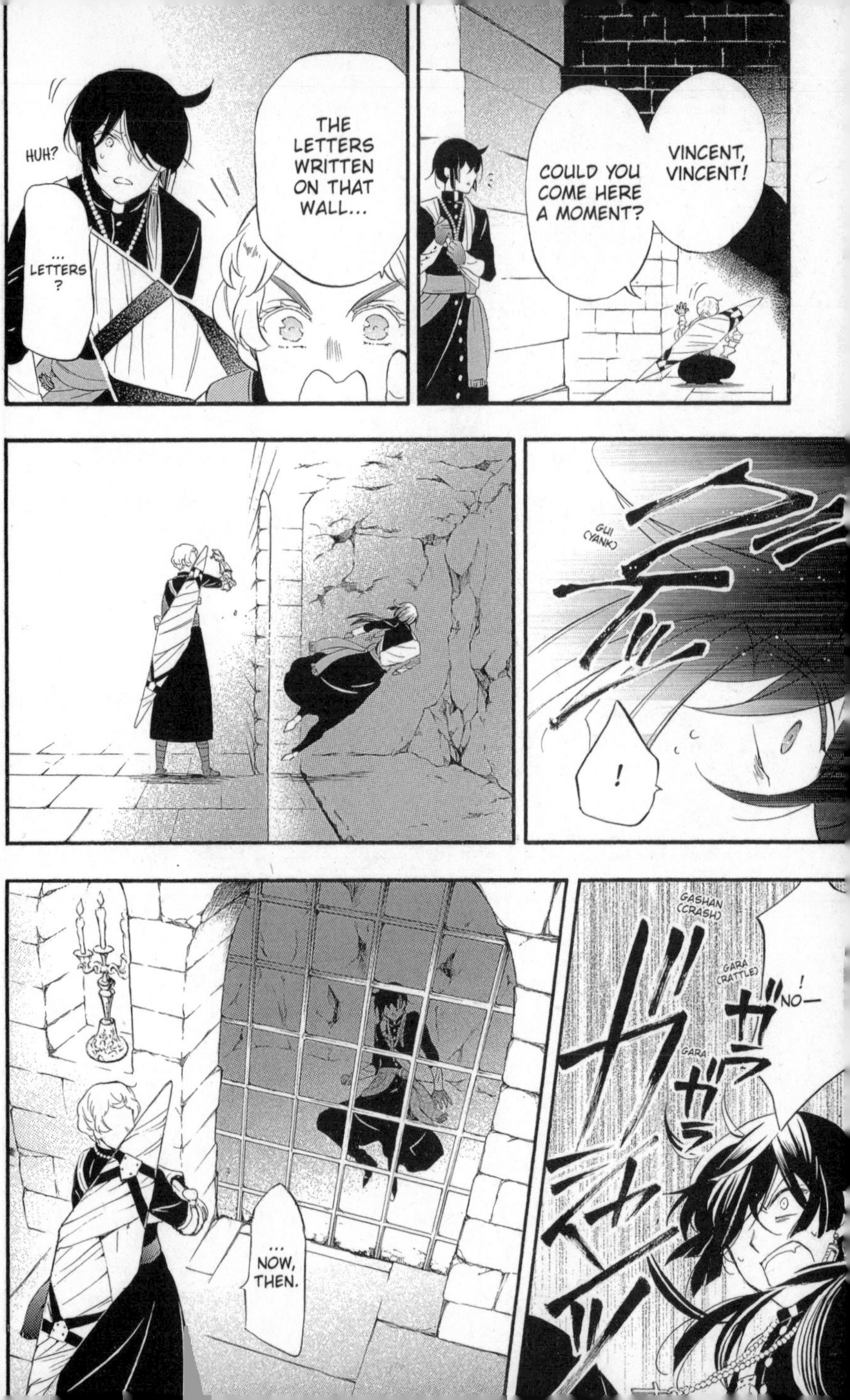
VINCENT, VINCENT!
COULD YOU COME HERE A MOMENT?
THE LETTERS WRITTEN ON THAT WALL...
HUH?
...LETTERS?
GUI (YANK)
!
GASHAN (CRASH)
GARA (RATTLE)
GARA
!
NO—
...NOW, THEN.

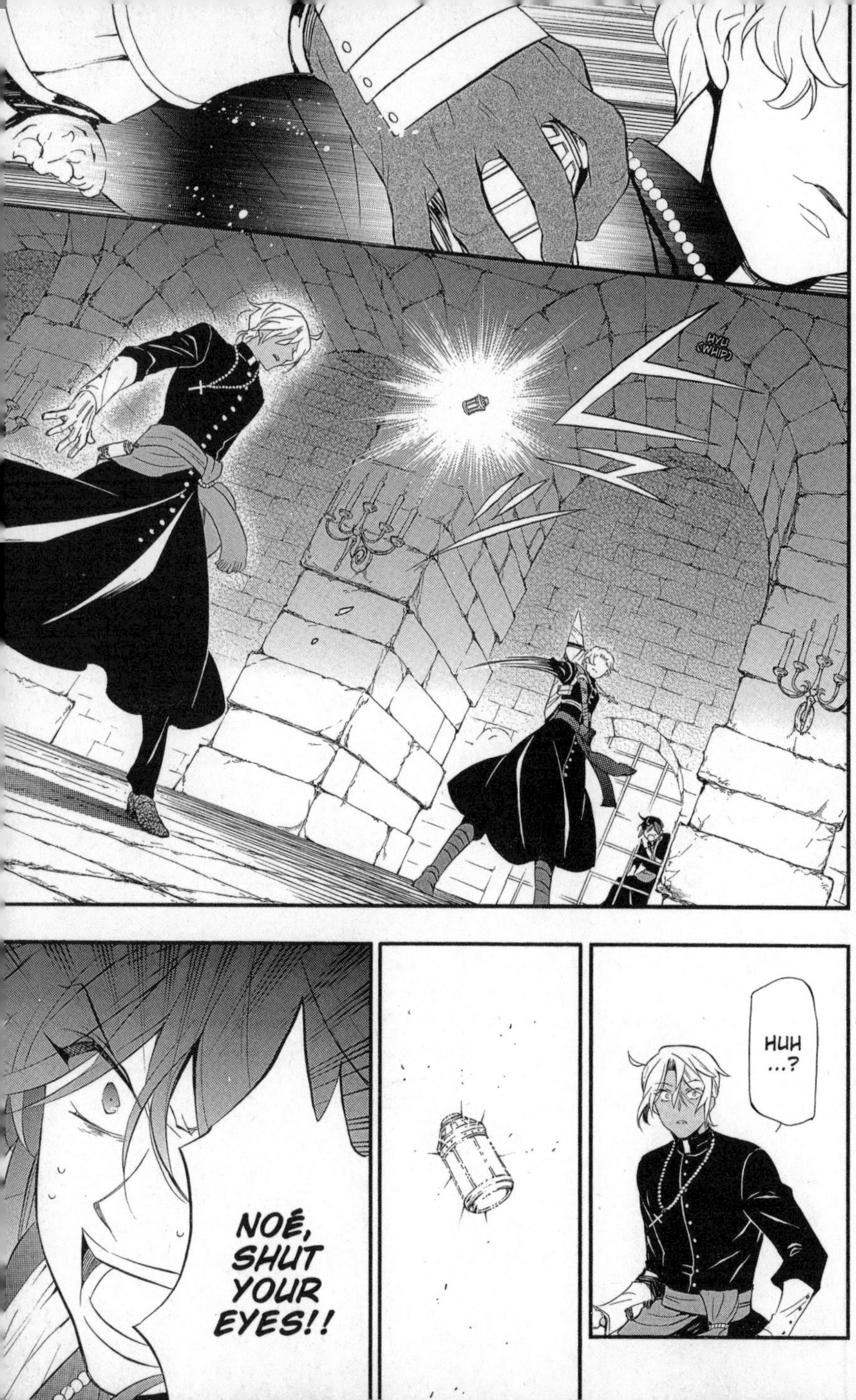
HYU (WHIP)
HUH ...?
NOÉ, SHUT YOUR EYES!!

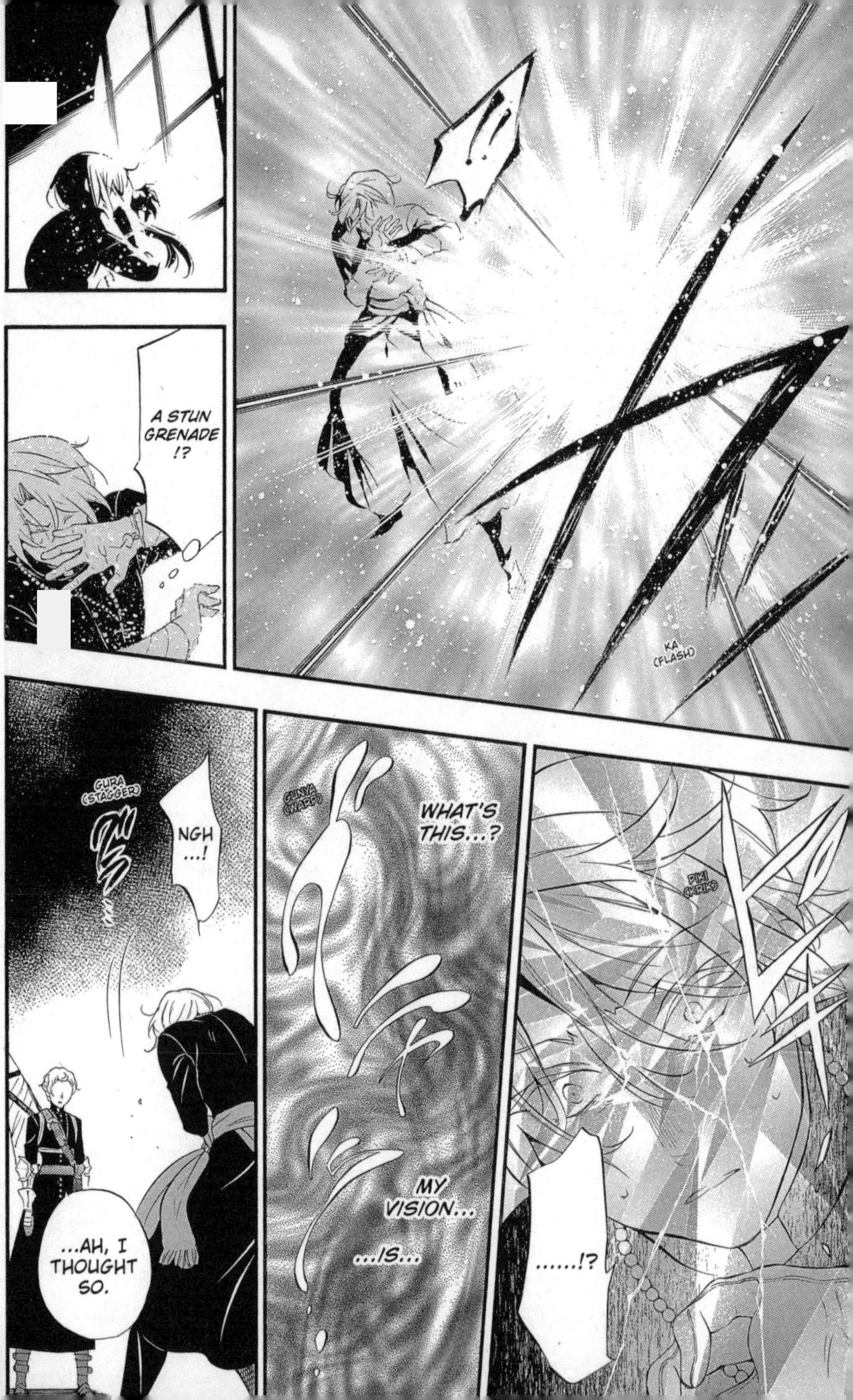
KA (FLASH)
A STUN GRENADE !?
PIKI (KRIK)
......!?
GUNYA (WARP)
WHAT'S THIS...?
MY VISION...
...IS...
GURA (STAGGER)
NGH ...!
...AH, I THOUGHT SO.

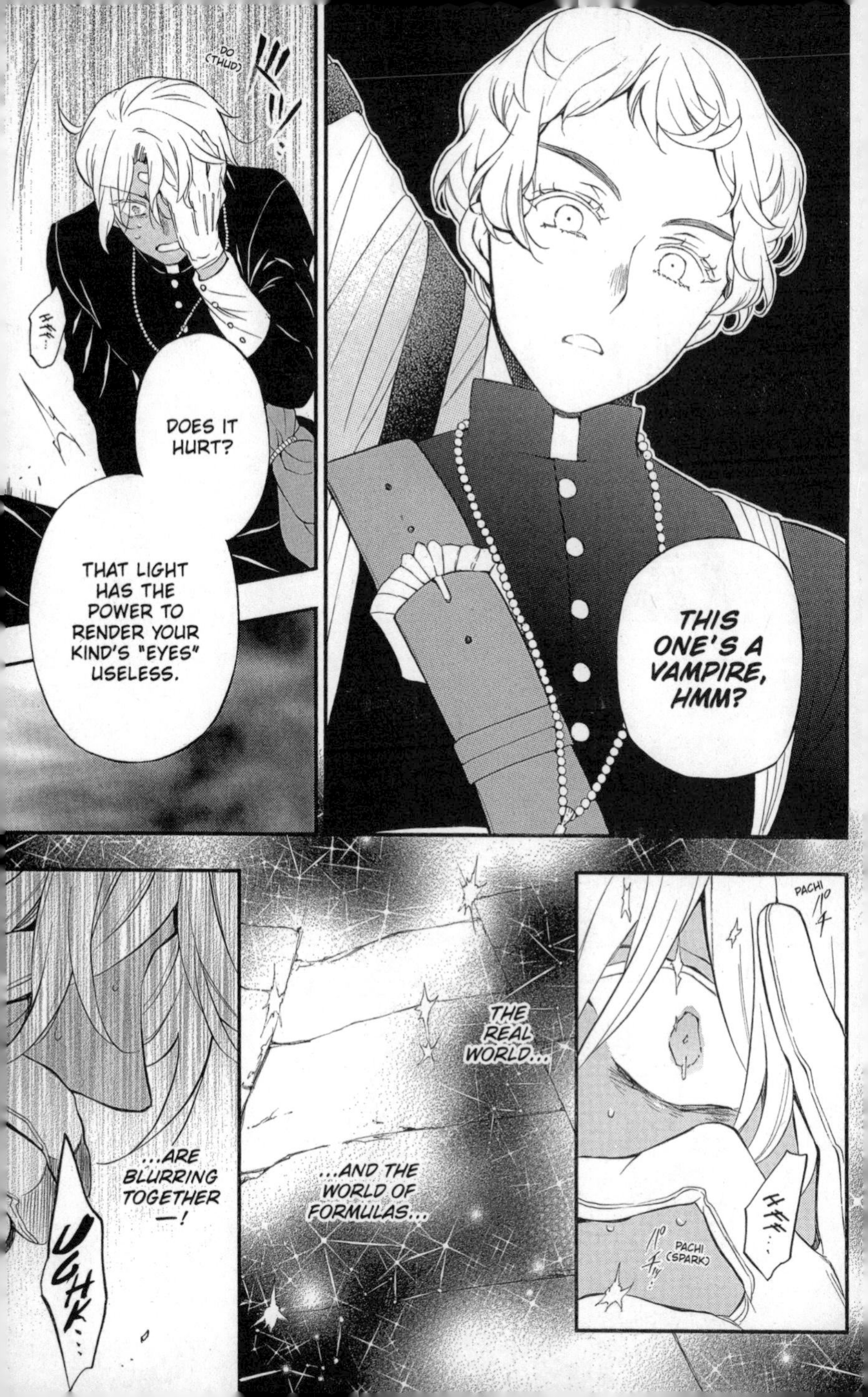
THIS ONE'S A VAMPIRE, HMM?
DO (THUD)
HFF...
DOES IT HURT?
THAT LIGHT HAS THE POWER TO RENDER YOUR KIND'S "EYES" USELESS.
PACHI
HFF...
PACHI (SPARK)
THE REAL WORLD...
...AND THE WORLD OF FORMULAS...
...ARE BLURRING TOGETHER—!
UGHK...

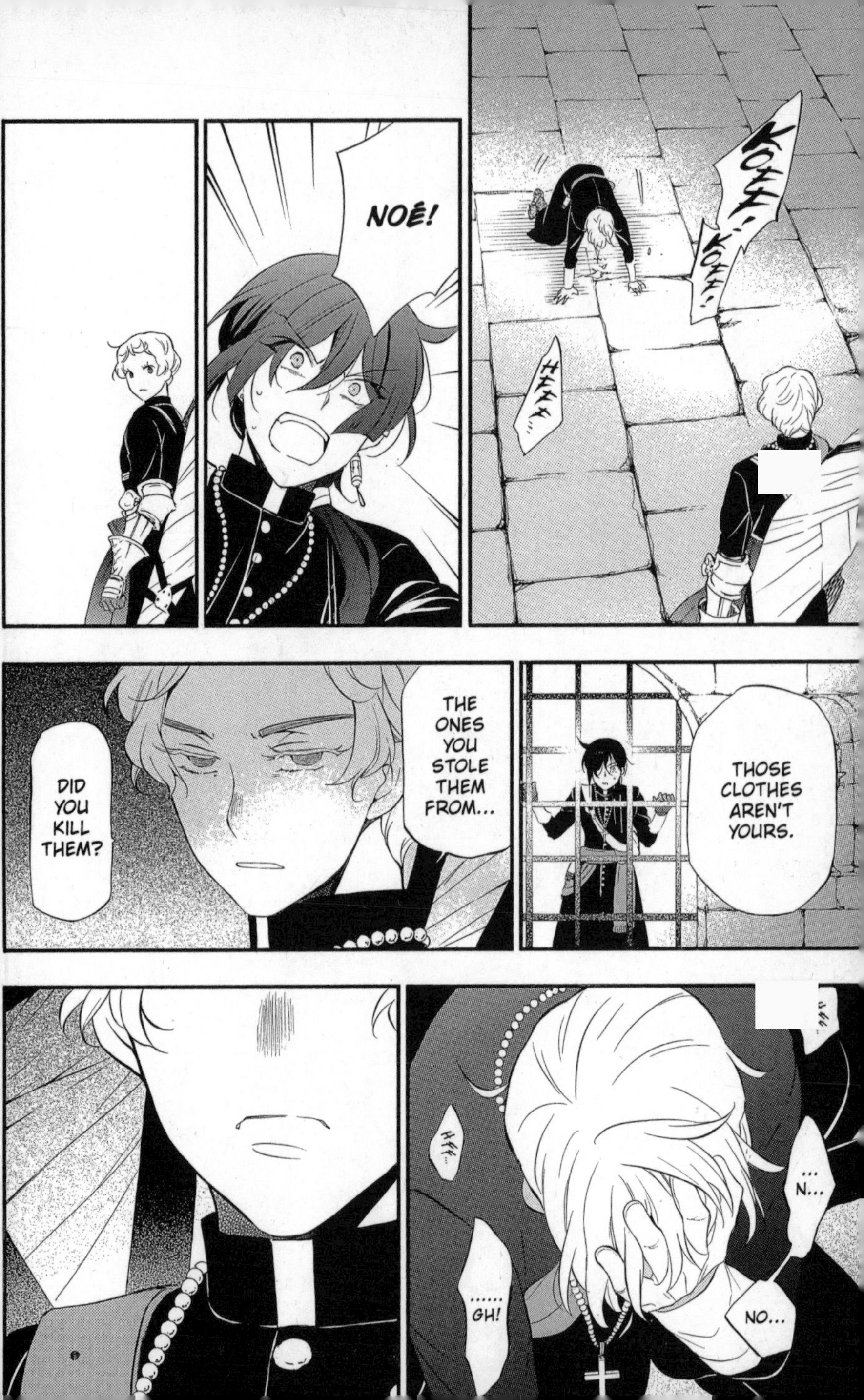
KOFF! KOFF!
HFFF...
NOÉ!
THOSE CLOTHES AREN'T YOURS.
THE ONES YOU STOLE THEM FROM...
DID YOU KILL THEM?
...N...
HFF...
NO...
......GH!

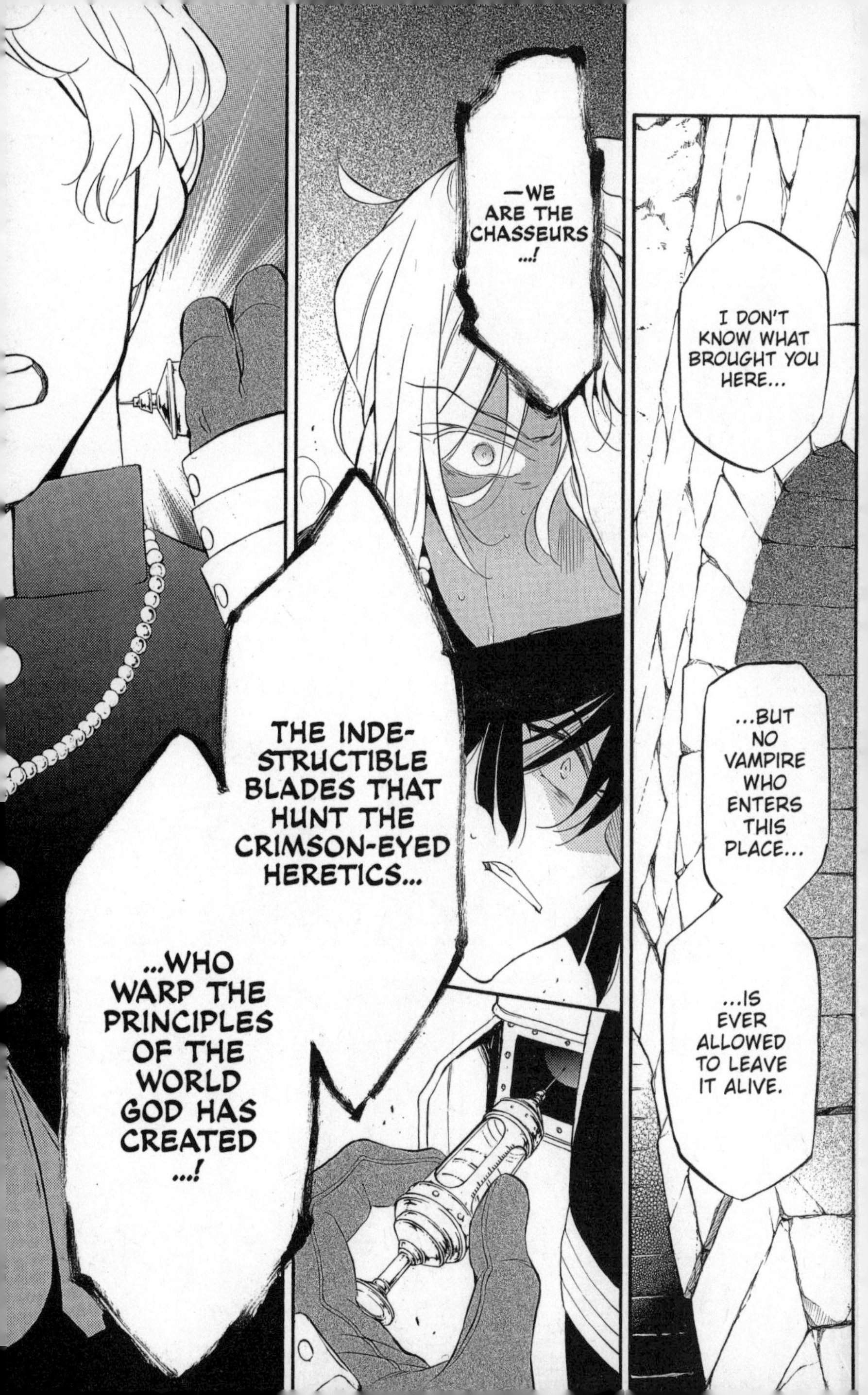
I DON'T KNOW WHAT BROUGHT YOU HERE...
...BUT NO VAMPIRE WHO ENTERS THIS PLACE...
...IS EVER ALLOWED TO LEAVE IT ALIVE.
—WE ARE THE CHASSEURS...!
THE INDESTRUCTIBLE BLADES THAT HUNT THE CRIMSON-EYED HERETICS...
...WHO WARP THE PRINCIPLES OF THE WORLD GOD HAS CREATED...!

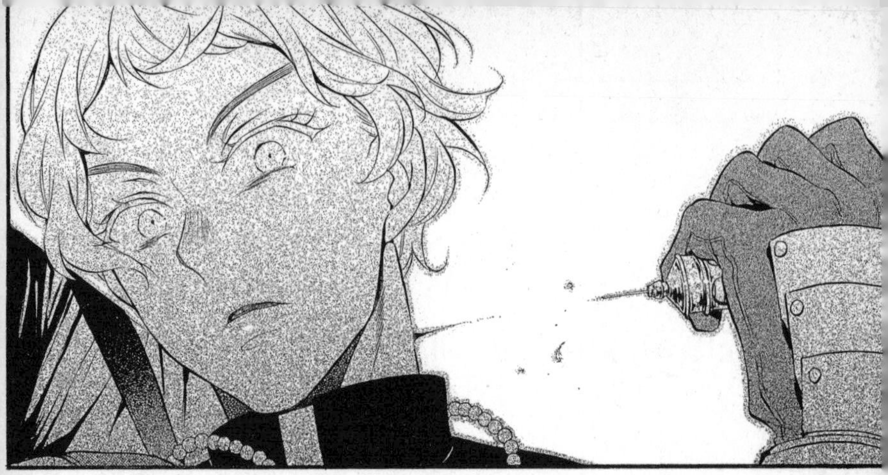

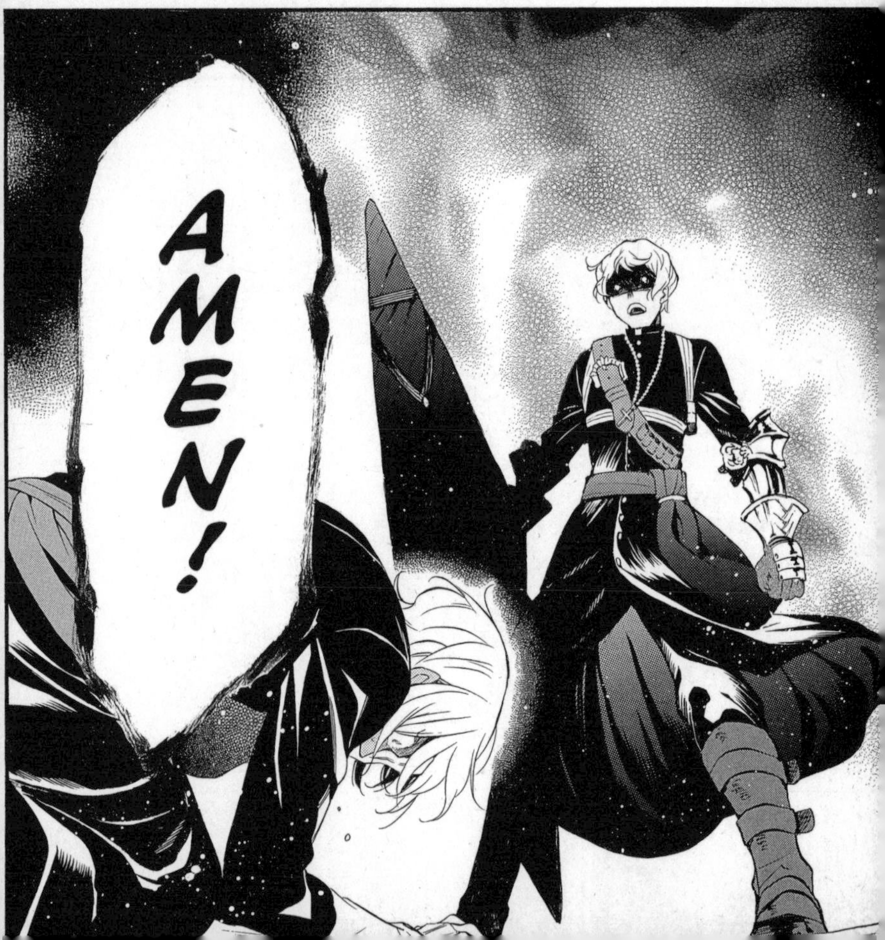
AMEN!

Mémoire 14 Catacombes WHERE THE DEAD SLEEP

CATACOMBES DE PARIS

A burial vault deep under Paris.

In earlier days, for roughly a millennium, a common burial ground had been used. However, it was eventually filled to capacity with piled-up corpses and became a breeding ground for contagious illnesses. As a result, they decided to dismantle the graveyard and move the bones to an underground quarry.

It's said that the remains of some of France's great historical figures, including Montesquieu, Pascal, and Rabelais, were among them...

Startlingly, in the 19th century, tours were put together for the general public, who went down holding candles for light.

They're still a popular Parisian tourist attraction today.

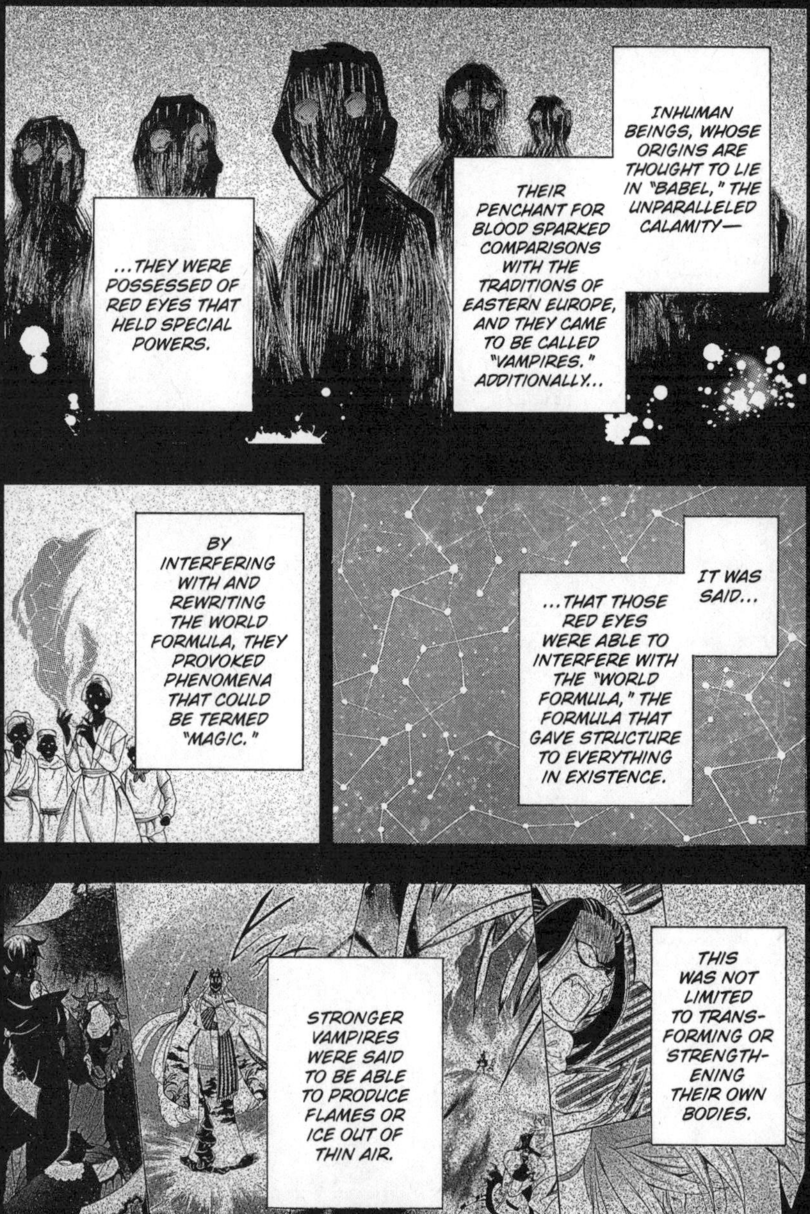
INHUMAN BEINGS, WHOSE ORIGINS ARE THOUGHT TO LIE IN "BABEL," THE UNPARALLELED CALAMITY—
THEIR PENCHANT FOR BLOOD SPARKED COMPARISONS WITH THE TRADITIONS OF EASTERN EUROPE, AND THEY CAME TO BE CALLED "VAMPIRES." ADDITIONALLY...
...THEY WERE POSSESSED OF RED EYES THAT HELD SPECIAL POWERS.
IT WAS SAID...
...THAT THOSE RED EYES WERE ABLE TO INTERFERE WITH THE "WORLD FORMULA," THE FORMULA THAT GAVE STRUCTURE TO EVERYTHING IN EXISTENCE.
BY INTERFERING WITH AND REWRITING THE WORLD FORMULA, THEY PROVOKED PHENOMENA THAT COULD BE TERMED "MAGIC."
THIS WAS NOT LIMITED TO TRANS-FORMING OR STRENGTH-ENING THEIR OWN BODIES.
STRONGER VAMPIRES WERE SAID TO BE ABLE TO PRODUCE FLAMES OR ICE OUT OF THIN AIR.

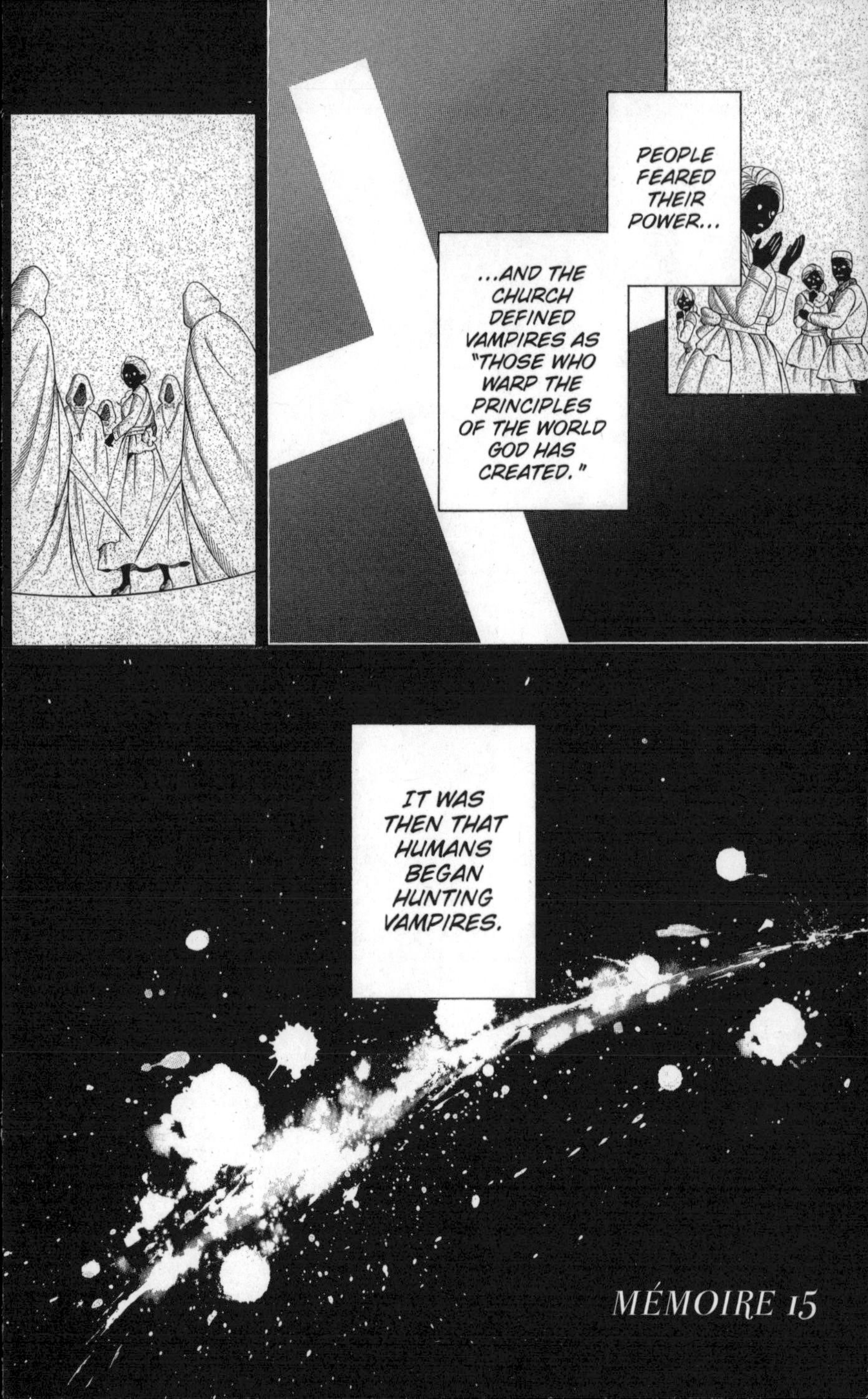
PEOPLE FEARED THEIR POWER...
...AND THE CHURCH DEFINED VAMPIRES AS "THOSE WHO WARP THE PRINCIPLES OF THE WORLD GOD HAS CREATED."
IT WAS THEN THAT HUMANS BEGAN HUNTING VAMPIRES.
MÉMOIRE 15

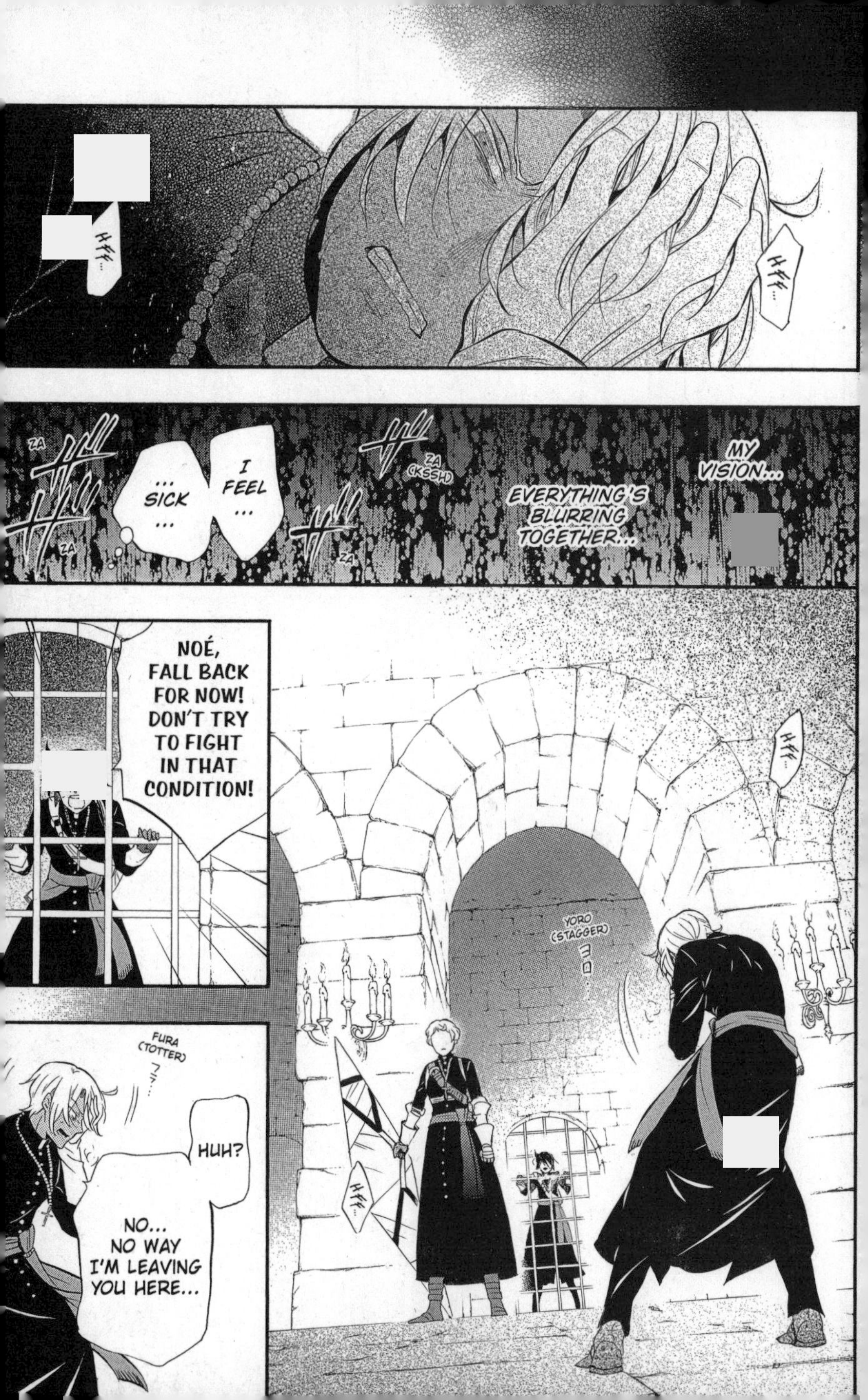
HFF...
HFF...
MY VISION...
EVERYTHING'S BLURRING TOGETHER...
ZA (KSSH)
I FEEL...
...SICK...
ZA
ZA
ZA
HFF...
YORO (STAGGER)
ヨロ…
HFF...
NOÉ, FALL BACK FOR NOW! DON'T TRY TO FIGHT IN THAT CONDITION!
FURA (TOTTER)
フラ…
HUH?
NO... NO WAY I'M LEAVING YOU HERE...

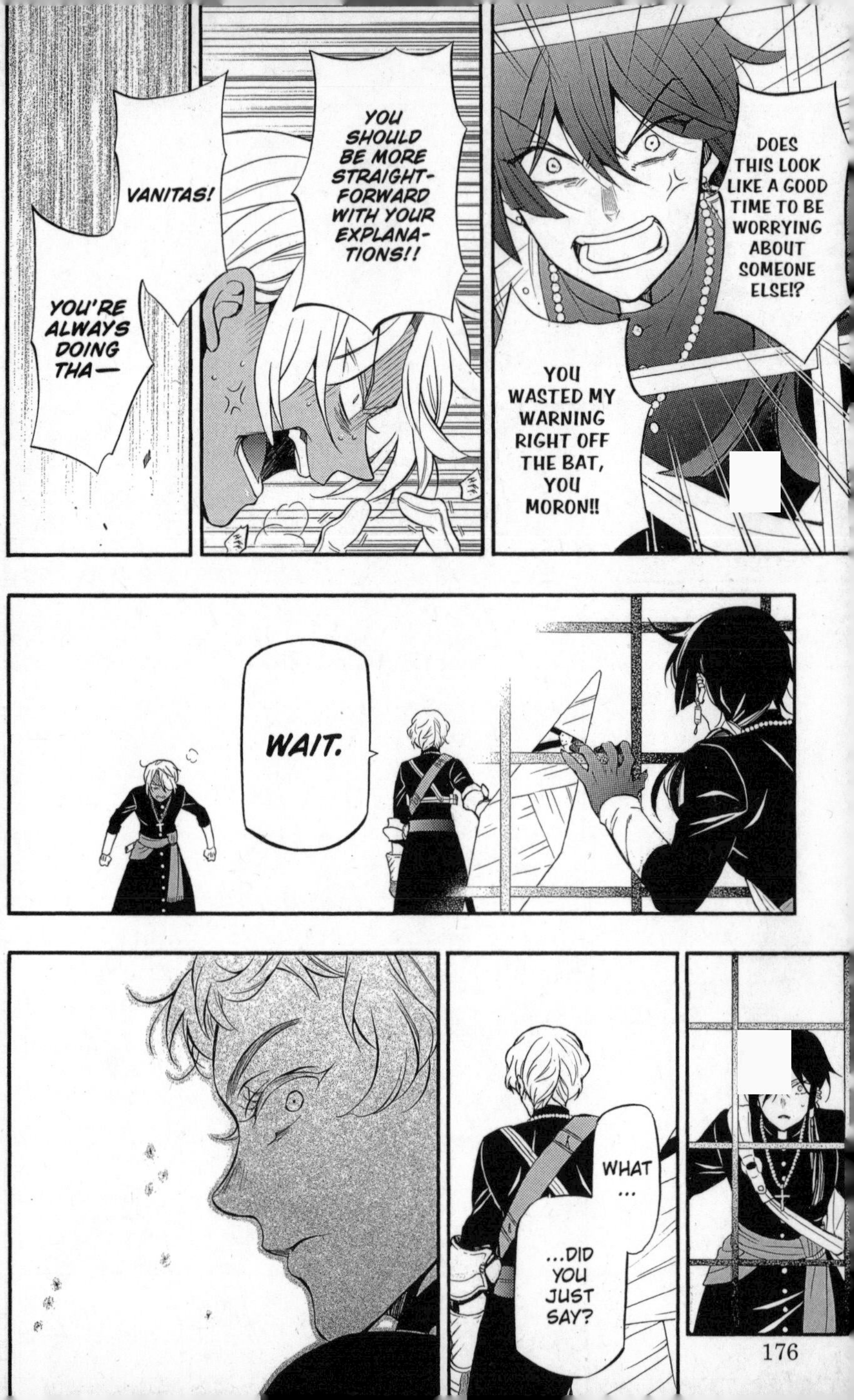
DOES THIS LOOK LIKE A GOOD TIME TO BE WORRYING ABOUT SOMEONE ELSE!?
YOU WASTED MY WARNING RIGHT OFF THE BAT, YOU MORON!!
YOU SHOULD BE MORE STRAIGHT-FORWARD WITH YOUR EXPLANA-TIONS!!
VANITAS!
YOU'RE ALWAYS DOING THA—
WAIT.
WHAT...
...DID YOU JUST SAY?

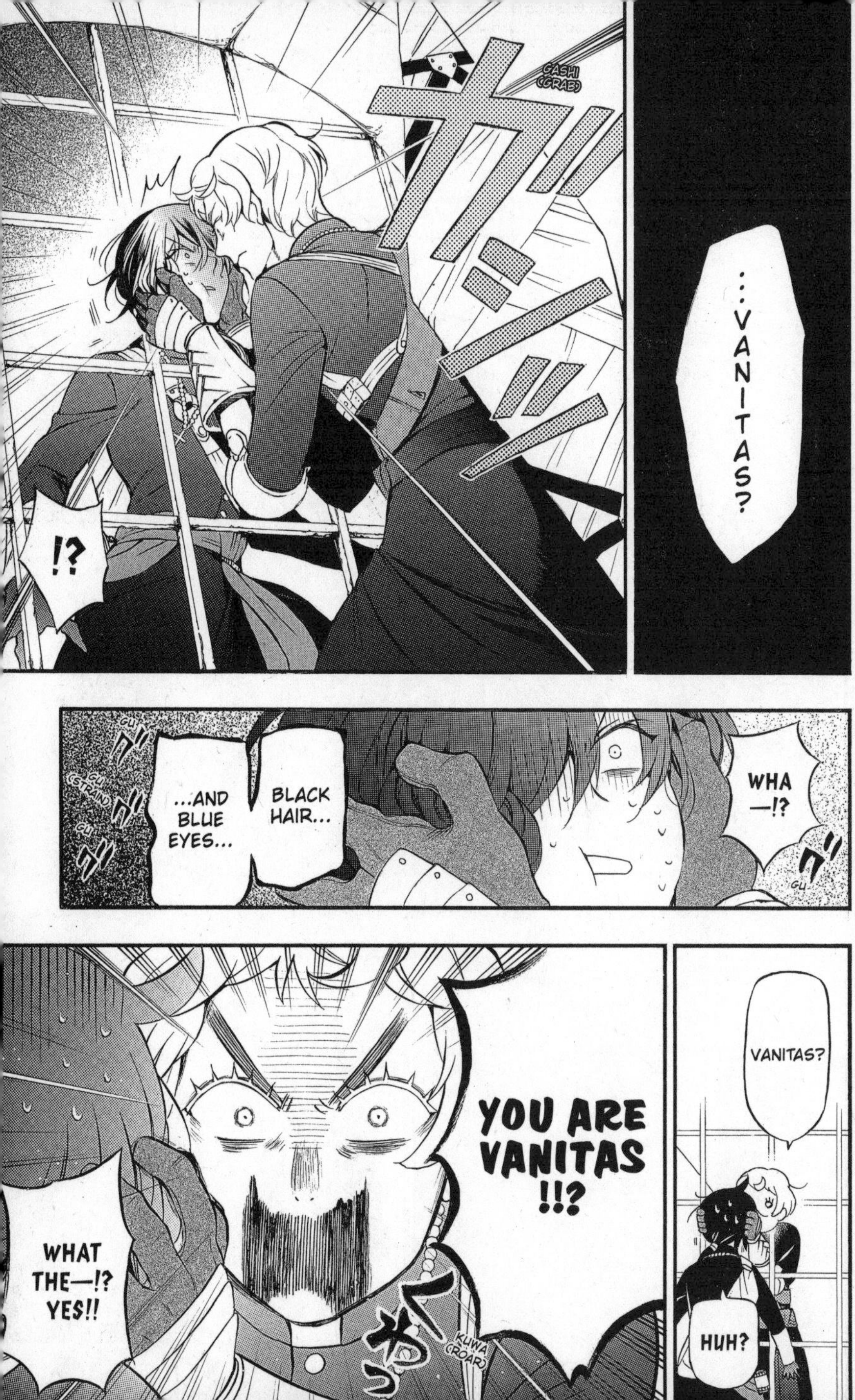
...VANITAS?
GASHI (GRAB)
!?
WHA—!?
GU
BLACK HAIR...
...AND BLUE EYES...
GU
GU (STRAIN)
GU
VANITAS?
HUH?
YOU ARE VANITAS!!?
KUWA (ROAR)
WHAT THE—!? YES!!

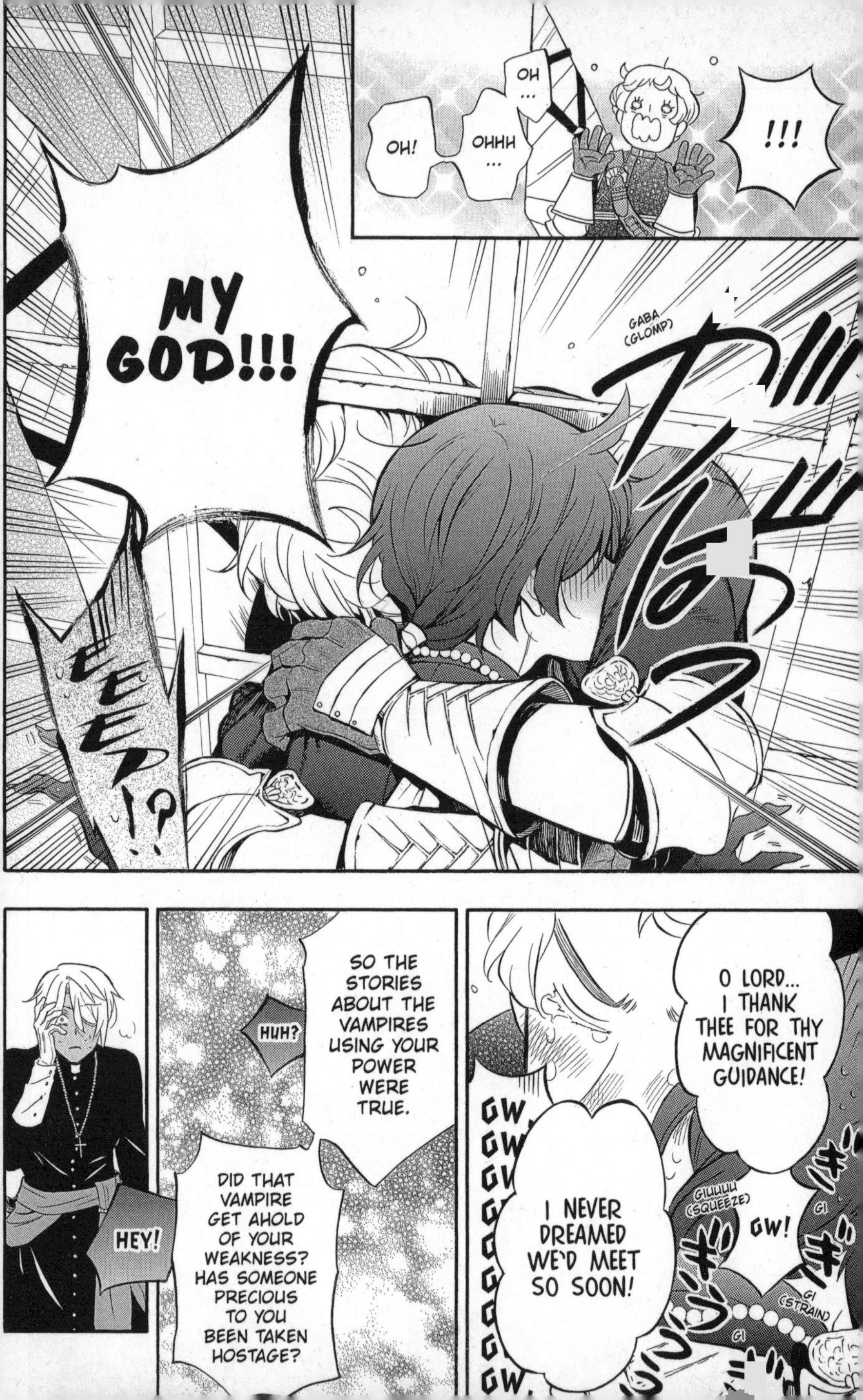
!!!
OH ...
OHHH ...
OH!
GABA (GLOMP)
MY GOD!!!
O LORD... I THANK THEE FOR THY MAGNIFICENT GUIDANCE!
GIUUUU (SQUEEZE)
GW!
GI (STRAIN)
GI
I NEVER DREAMED WE'D MEET SO SOON!
SO THE STORIES ABOUT THE VAMPIRES USING YOUR POWER WERE TRUE.
HUH?
DID THAT VAMPIRE GET AHOLD OF YOUR WEAKNESS? HAS SOMEONE PRECIOUS TO YOU BEEN TAKEN HOSTAGE?
HEY!

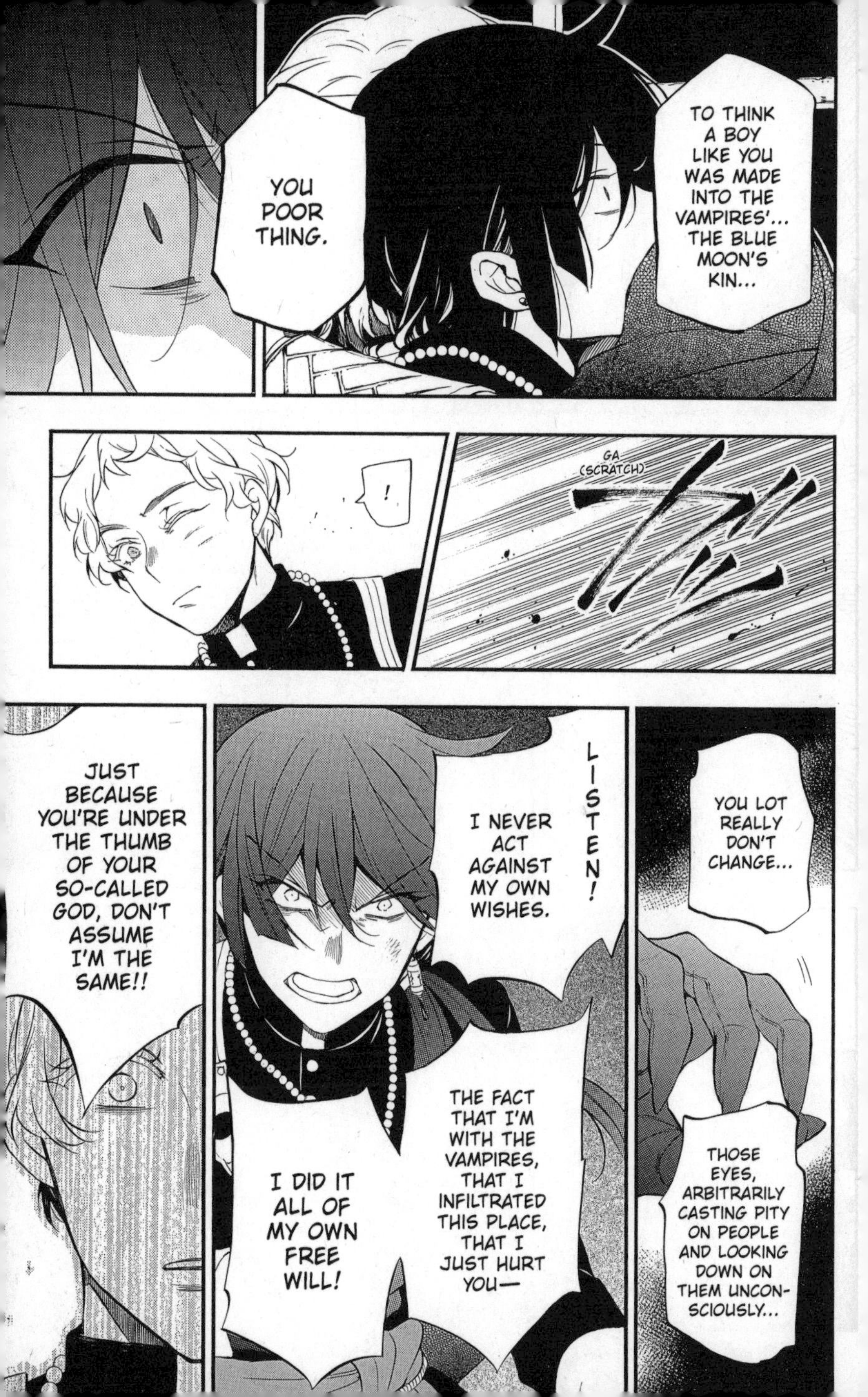
TO THINK A BOY LIKE YOU WAS MADE INTO THE VAMPIRES'... THE BLUE MOON'S KIN...
YOU POOR THING.
GA (SCRATCH)
!
YOU LOT REALLY DON'T CHANGE...
THOSE EYES, ARBITRARILY CASTING PITY ON PEOPLE AND LOOKING DOWN ON THEM UNCON-SCIOUSLY...
LISTEN!
I NEVER ACT AGAINST MY OWN WISHES.
THE FACT THAT I'M WITH THE VAMPIRES, THAT I INFILTRATED THIS PLACE, THAT I JUST HURT YOU—
I DID IT ALL OF MY OWN FREE WILL!
JUST BECAUSE YOU'RE UNDER THE THUMB OF YOUR SO-CALLED GOD, DON'T ASSUME I'M THE SAME!!

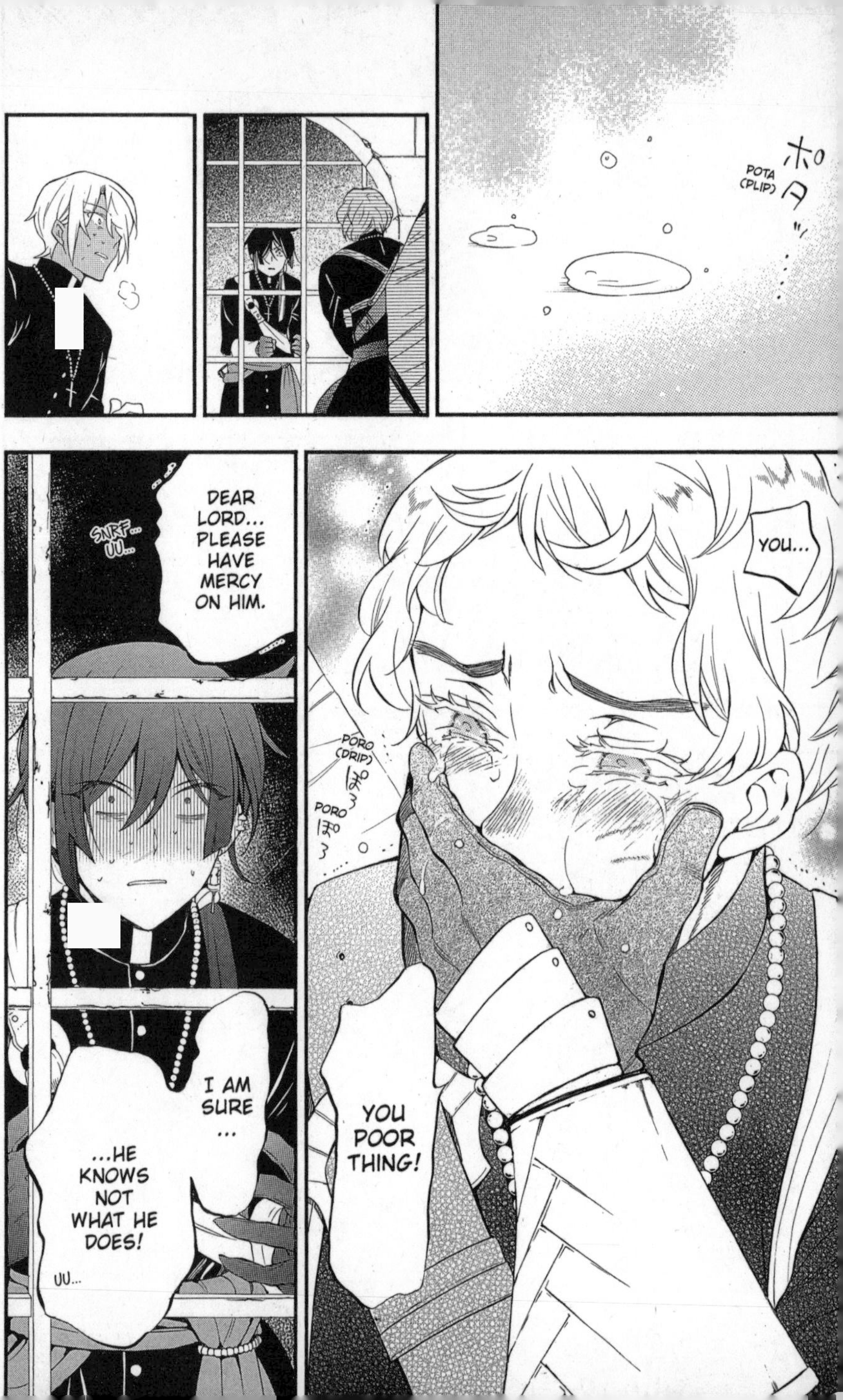
POTA (PLIP)
ポタッ
YOU...
PORO (DRIP)
ぽろ
PORO
ぽろ
YOU POOR THING!
SNRF... UU...
DEAR LORD... PLEASE HAVE MERCY ON HIM.
I AM SURE ...
...HE KNOWS NOT WHAT HE DOES!
UU...

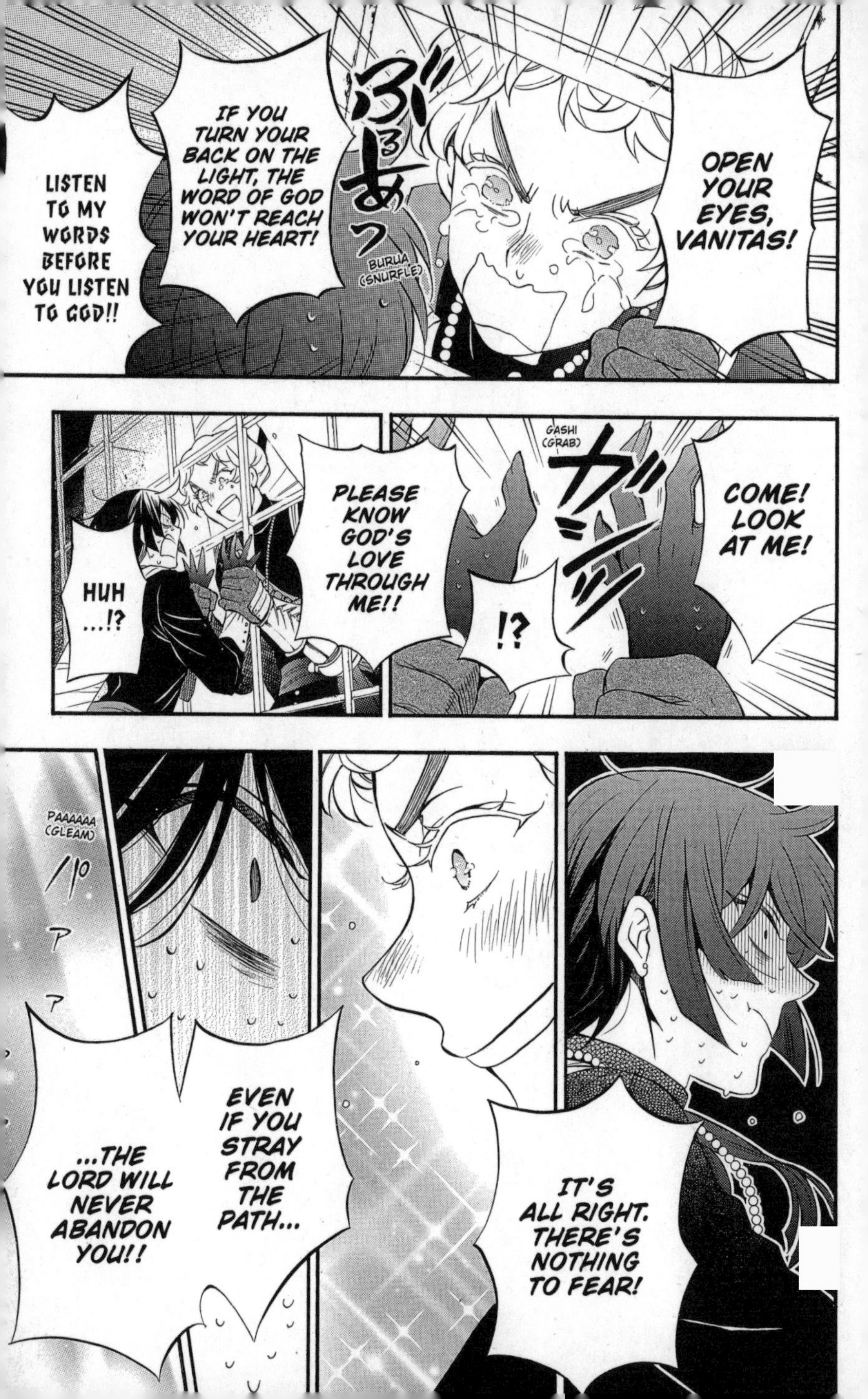
OPEN YOUR EYES, VANITAS!
ぶるあっ
BURUA (SNURFLE)
IF YOU TURN YOUR BACK ON THE LIGHT, THE WORD OF GOD WON'T REACH YOUR HEART!
LISTEN TO MY WORDS BEFORE YOU LISTEN TO GOD!!
COME! LOOK AT ME!
GASHI (GRAB)
!?
PLEASE KNOW GOD'S LOVE THROUGH ME!!
HUH ...!?
IT'S ALL RIGHT. THERE'S NOTHING TO FEAR!
EVEN IF YOU STRAY FROM THE PATH...
...THE LORD WILL NEVER ABANDON YOU!!
PAAAAAA (GLEAM)

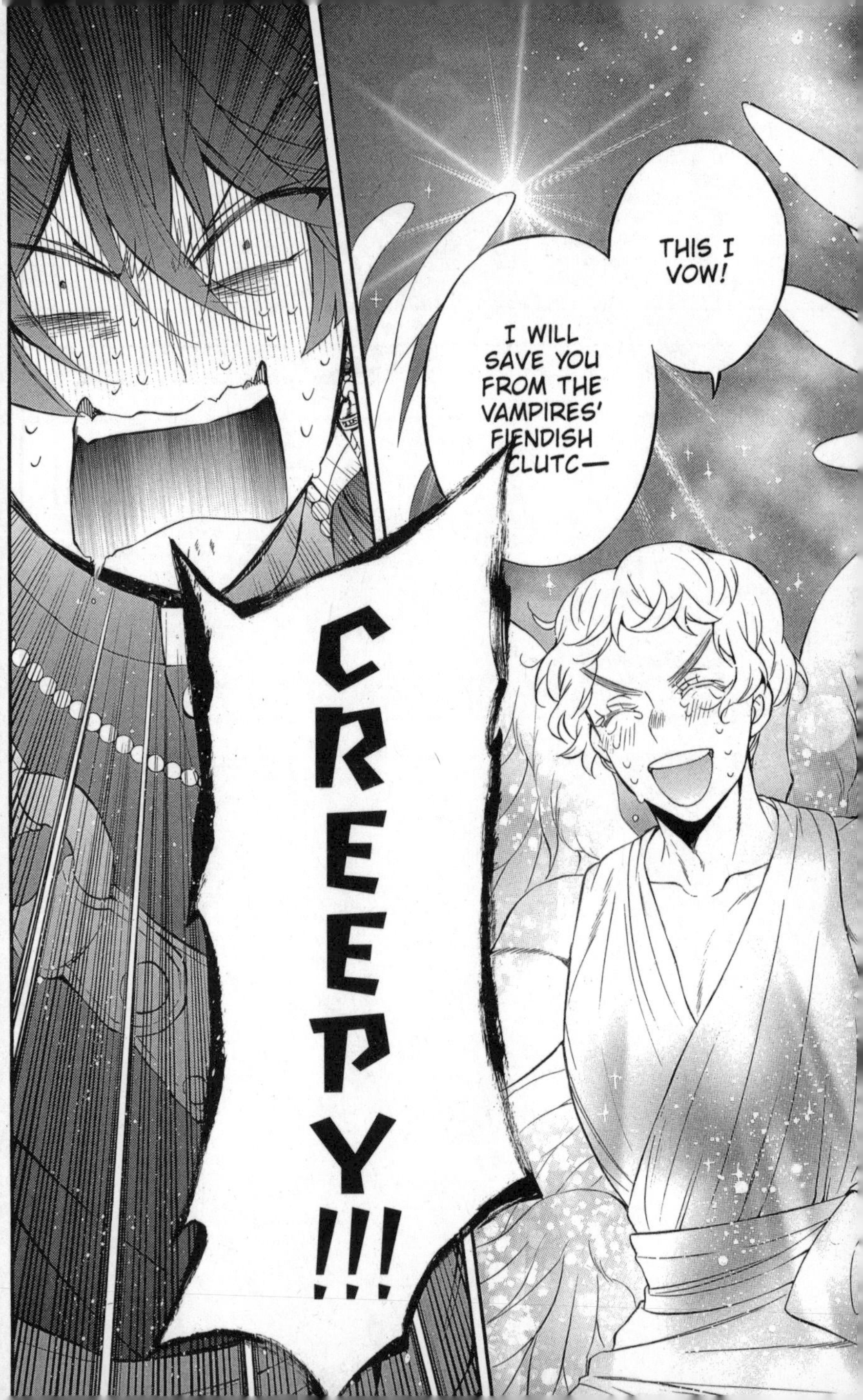
THIS I VOW!
I WILL SAVE YOU FROM THE VAMPIRES' FIENDISH CLUTC—
CREEPY!!!

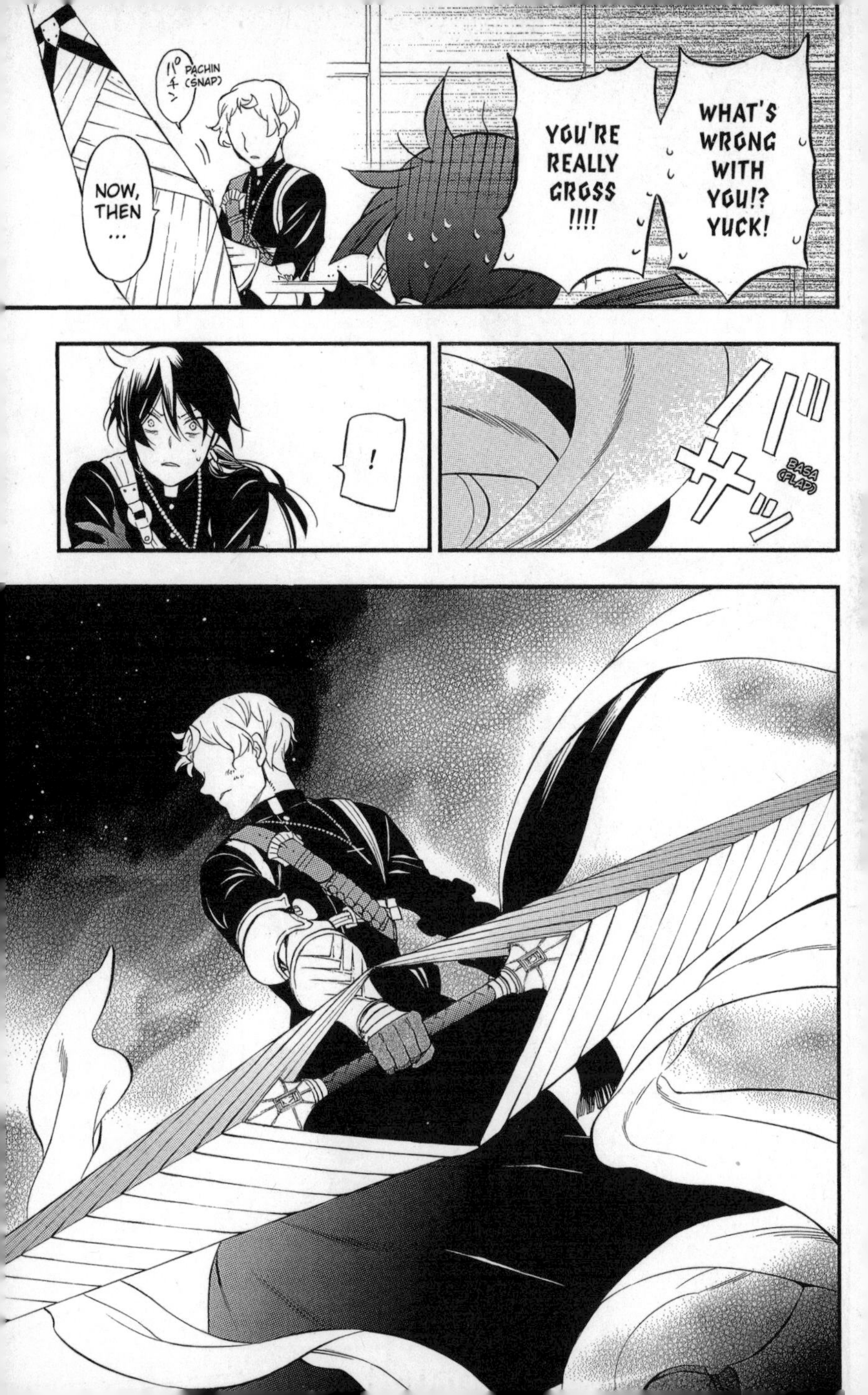
WHAT'S WRONG WITH YOU!? YUCK!
YOU'RE REALLY GROSS !!!!
パチン
PACHIN (SNAP)
NOW, THEN ...
バサッ
BASA (FLAP)
!

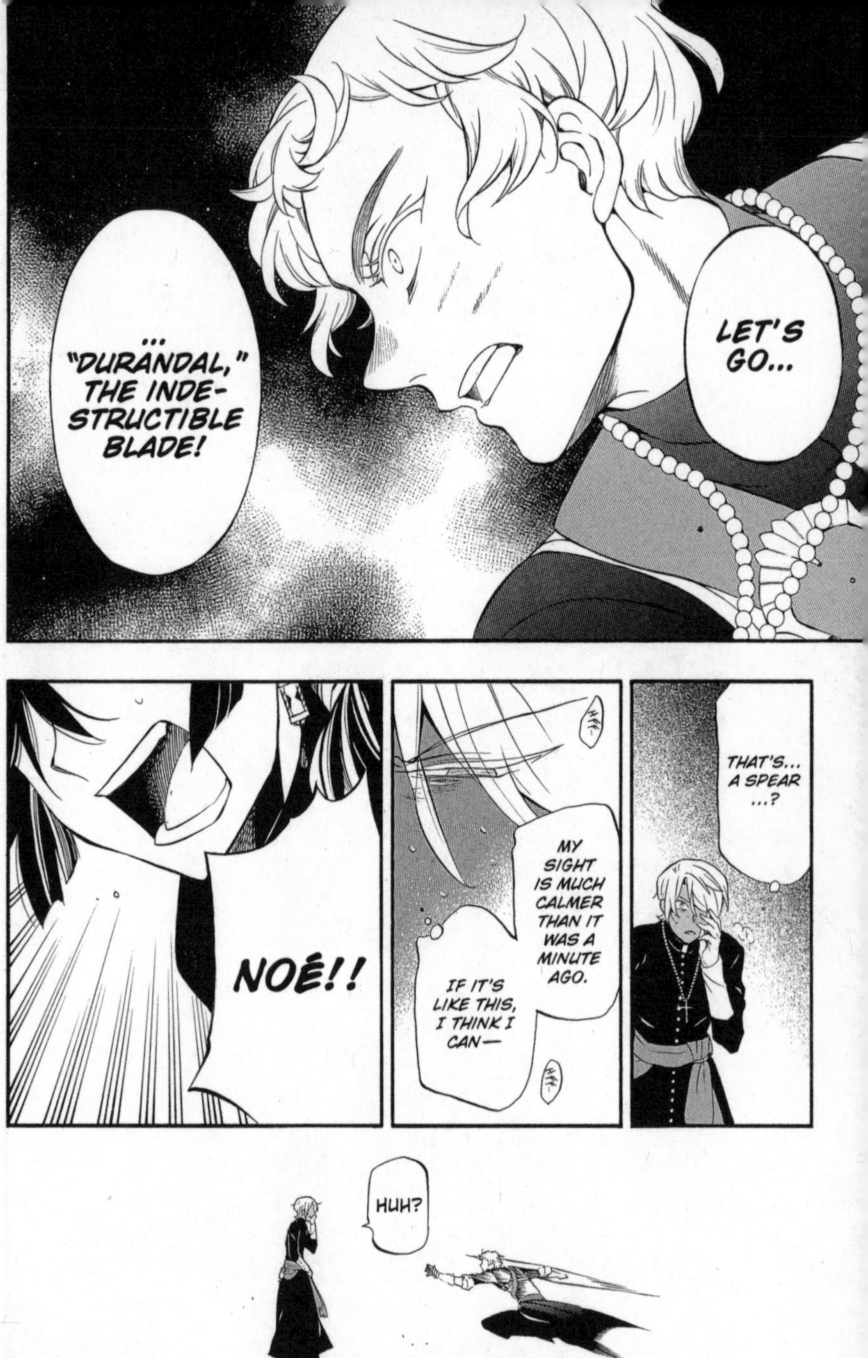
LET'S GO...
... "DURANDAL," THE INDE-STRUCTIBLE BLADE!
THAT'S... A SPEAR ...?
MY SIGHT IS MUCH CALMER THAN IT WAS A MINUTE AGO.
IF IT'S LIKE THIS, I THINK I CAN—
NOÉ!!
HUH?

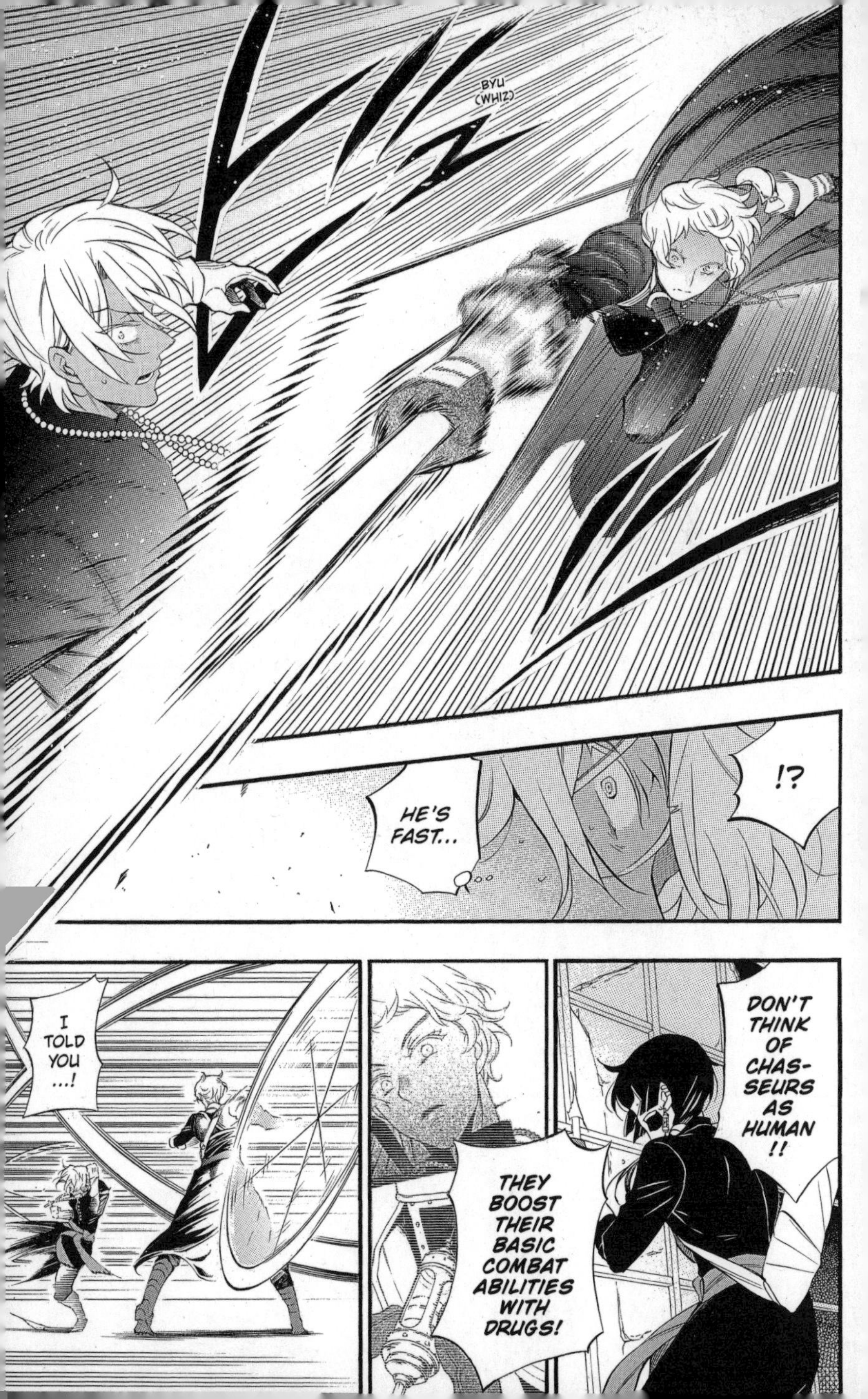
BYU
(WHIZ)
!?
HE'S FAST...
DON'T THINK OF CHAS-SEURS AS HUMAN!!
THEY BOOST THEIR BASIC COMBAT ABILITIES WITH DRUGS!
I TOLD YOU...!

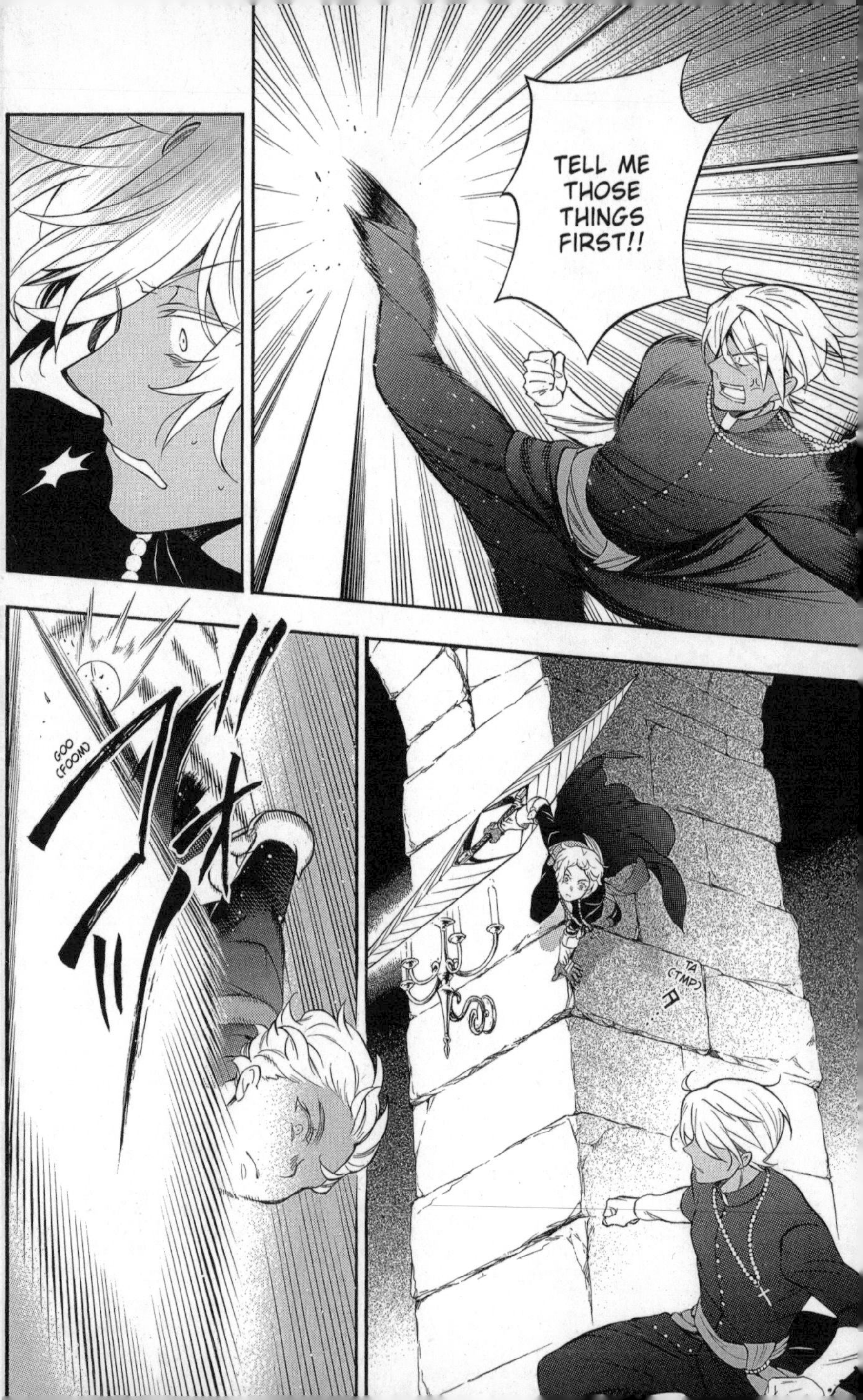
TELL ME THOSE THINGS FIRST!!
TA (TMP)
GOO (FOOM)

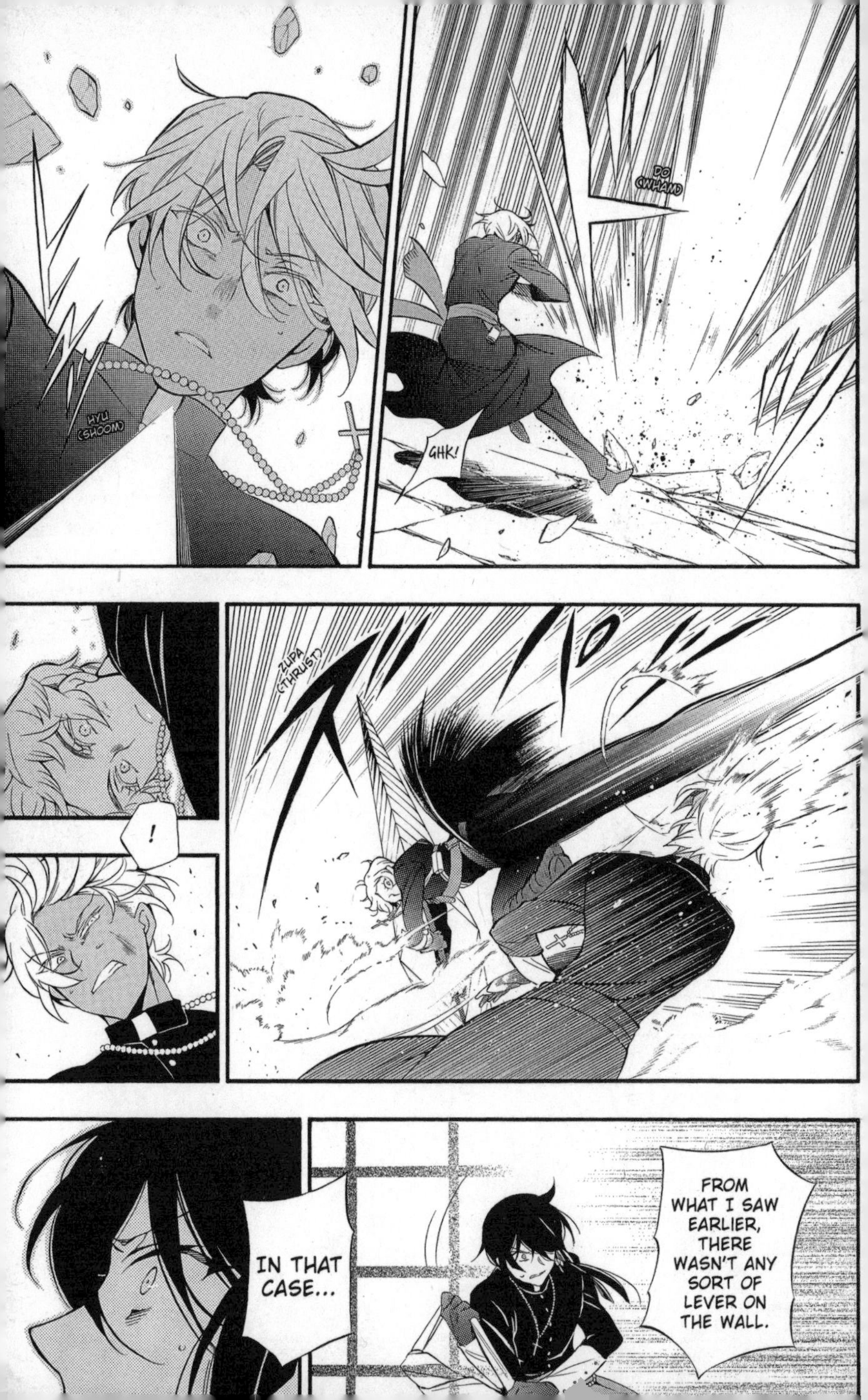
DO (WHAM)
GHK!
HYU (SHOOM)
ZUPA (THRUST)
!
FROM WHAT I SAW EARLIER, THERE WASN'T ANY SORT OF LEVER ON THE WALL.
IN THAT CASE...

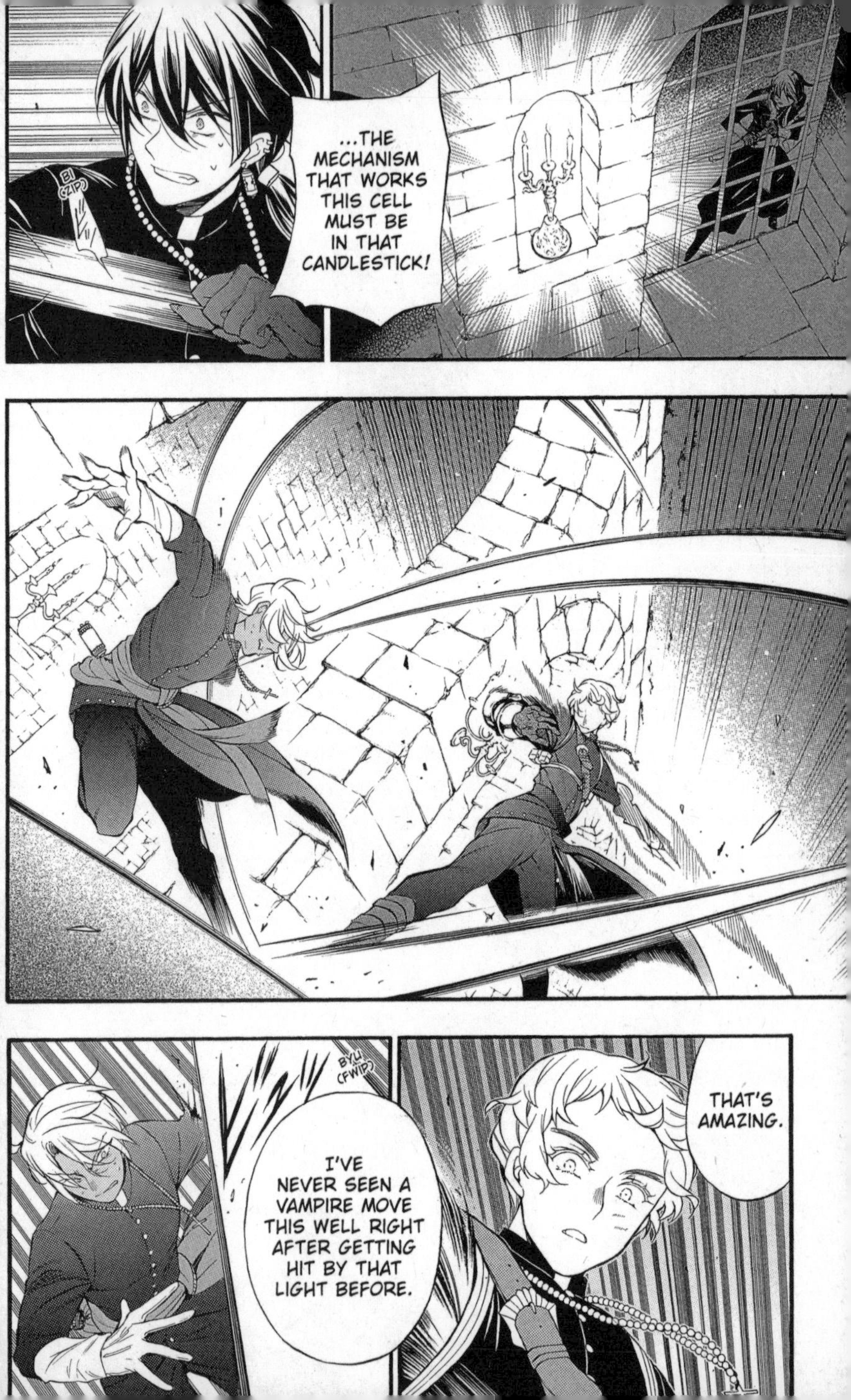
...THE MECHANISM THAT WORKS THIS CELL MUST BE IN THAT CANDLESTICK!
BI (ZIP)
THAT'S AMAZING.
I'VE NEVER SEEN A VAMPIRE MOVE THIS WELL RIGHT AFTER GETTING HIT BY THAT LIGHT BEFORE.
BYU (FWIP)

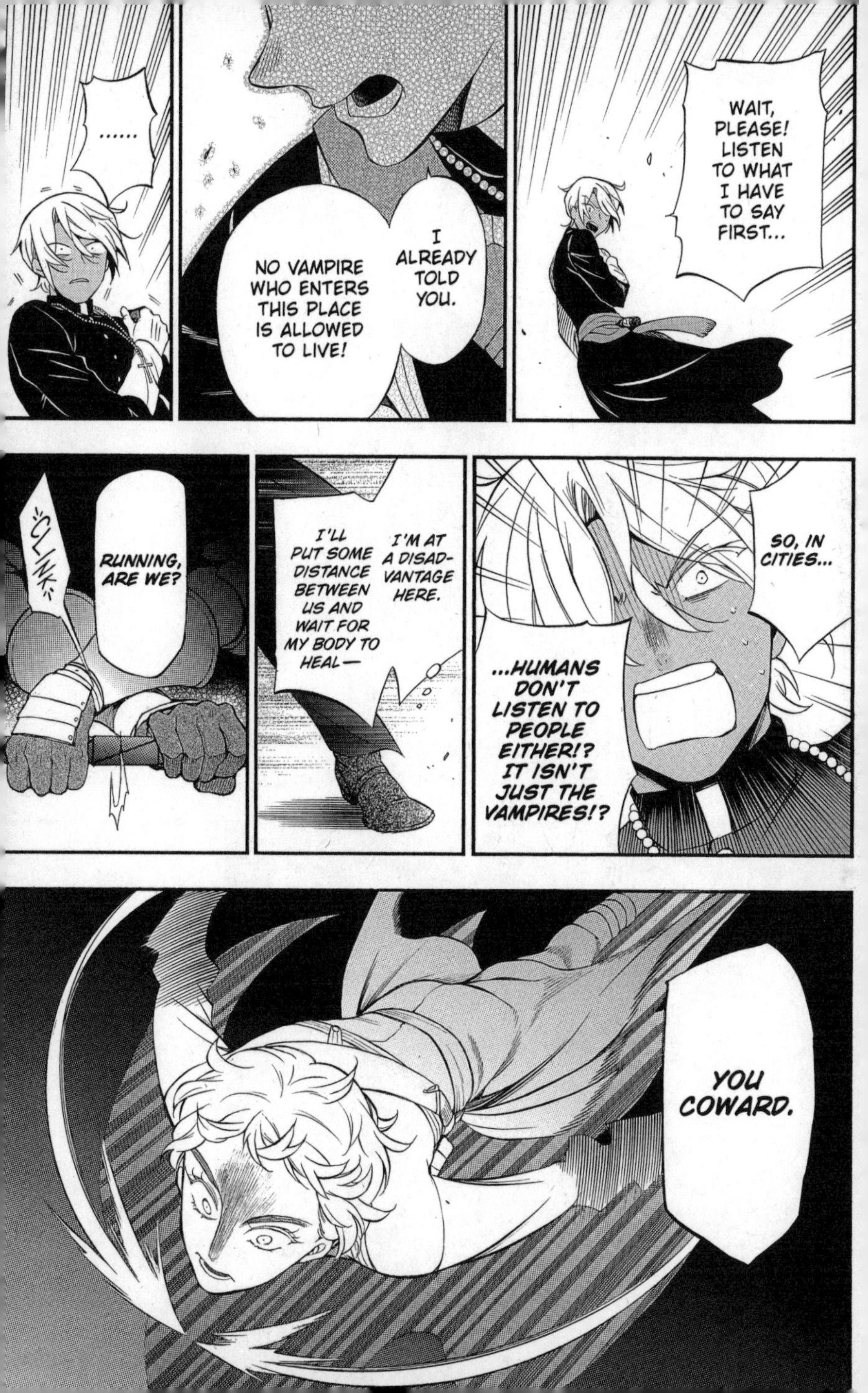
WAIT, PLEASE! LISTEN TO WHAT I HAVE TO SAY FIRST...
I ALREADY TOLD YOU.
NO VAMPIRE WHO ENTERS THIS PLACE IS ALLOWED TO LIVE!
......
SO, IN CITIES...
...HUMANS DON'T LISTEN TO PEOPLE EITHER!? IT ISN'T JUST THE VAMPIRES!?
I'M AT A DISAD-VANTAGE HERE.
I'LL PUT SOME DISTANCE BETWEEN US AND WAIT FOR MY BODY TO HEAL—
RUNNING, ARE WE?
CLINK
YOU COWARD.

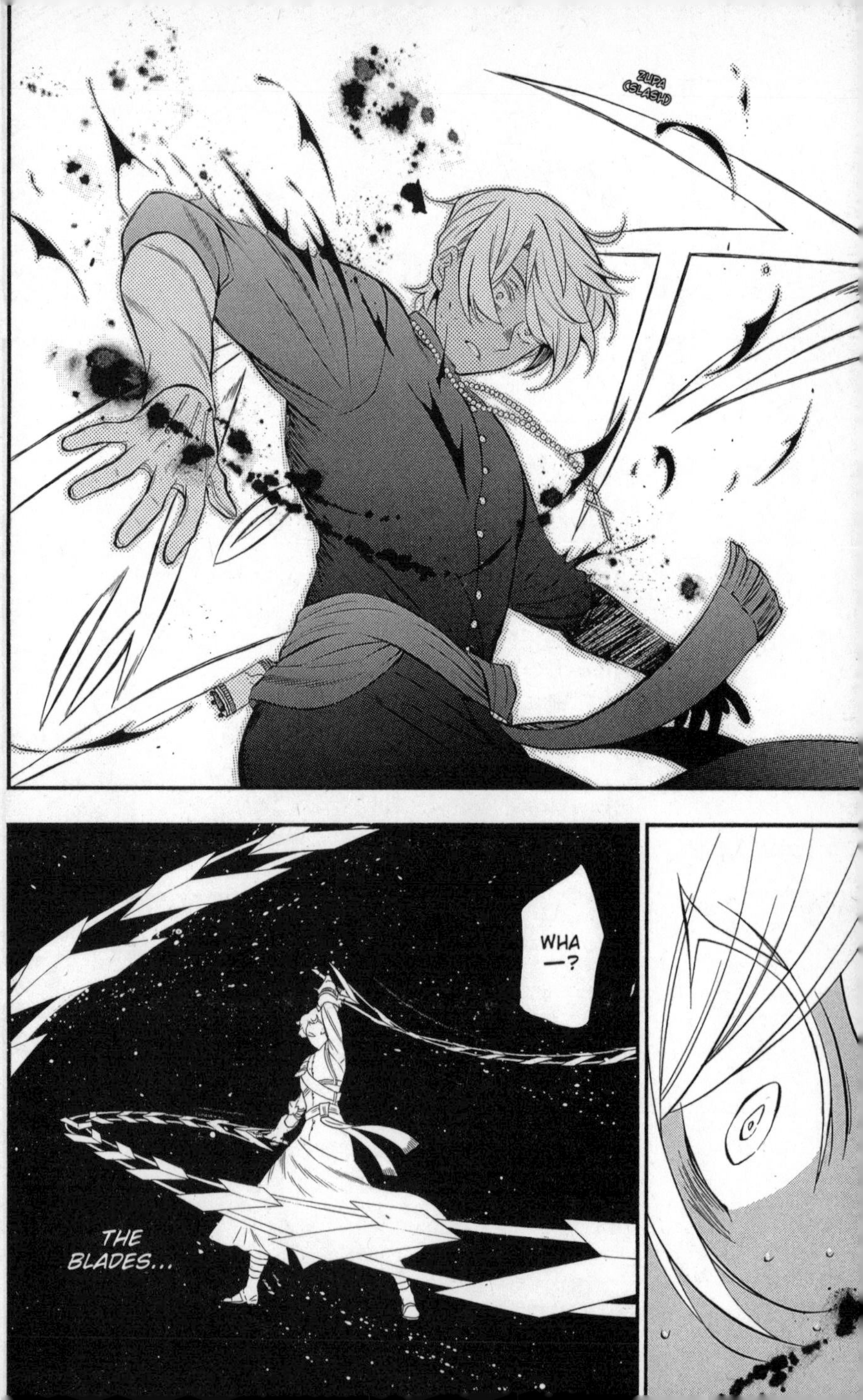
ZUPA
(SLASH)
WHA—?
THE BLADES...

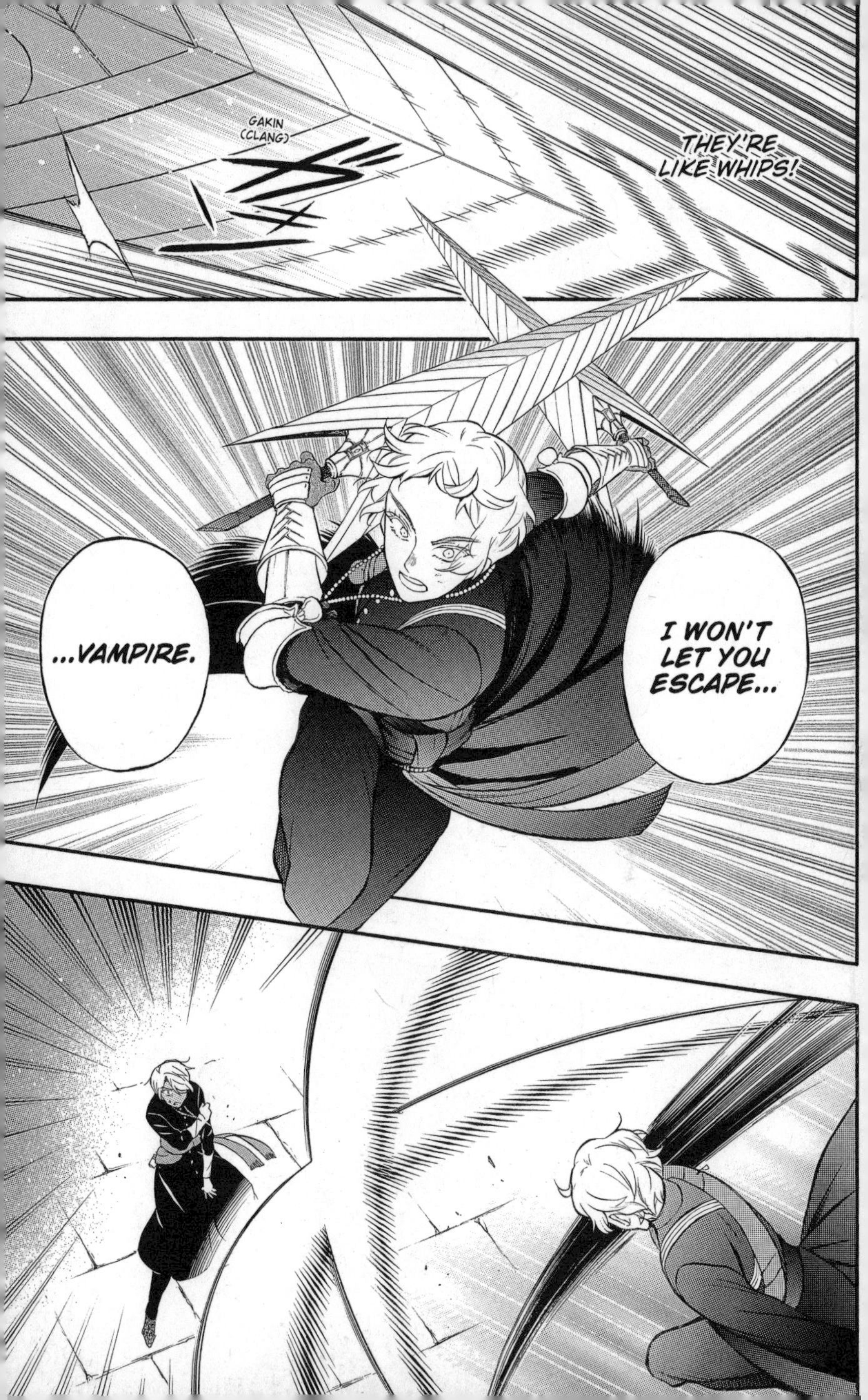
THEY'RE LIKE WHIPS!
GAKIN (CLANG)
I WON'T LET YOU ESCAPE...
...VAMPIRE.

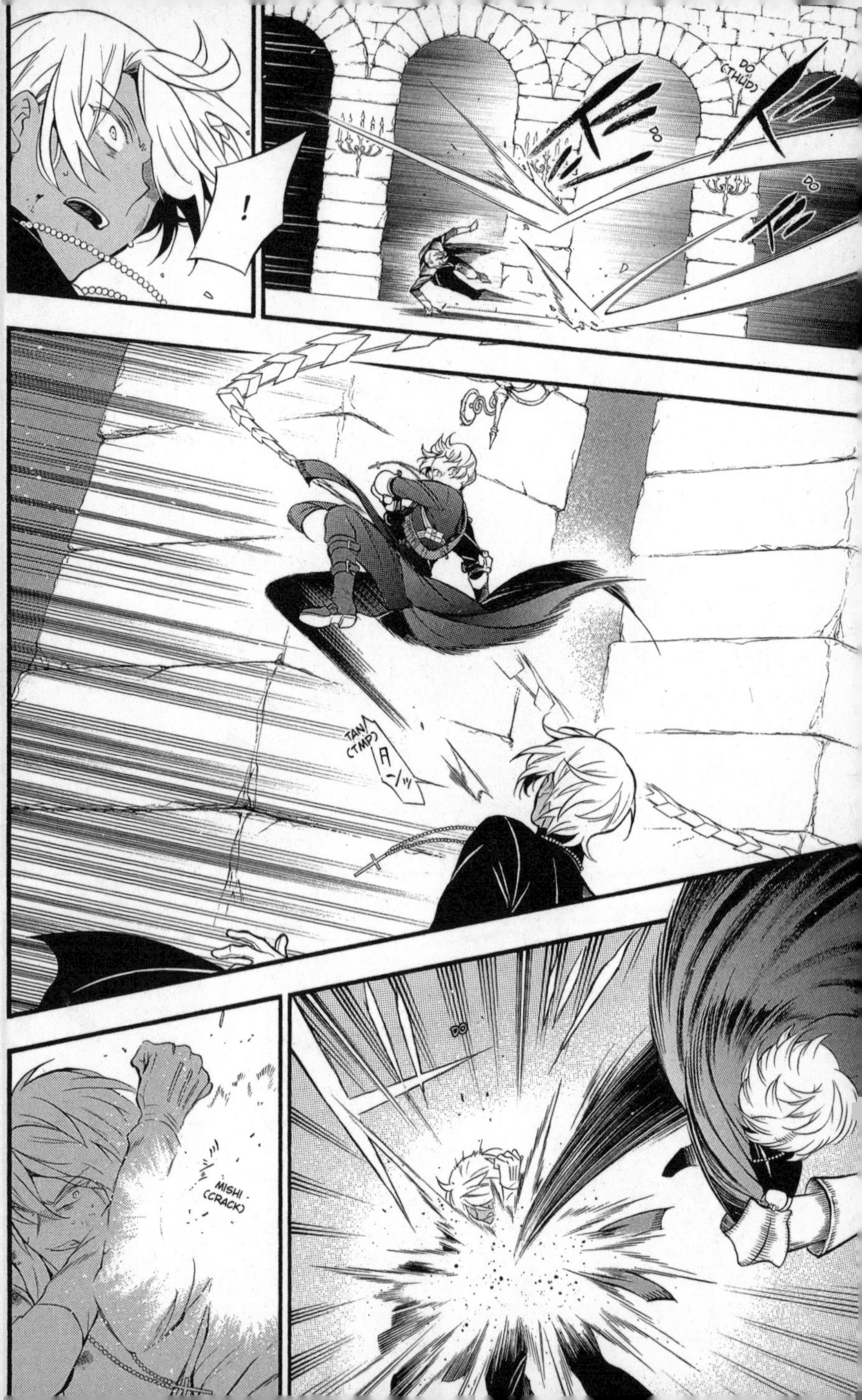
DO (THUD)
DO
DO
!
TAN (TMP)
DO
MISHI (CRACK)

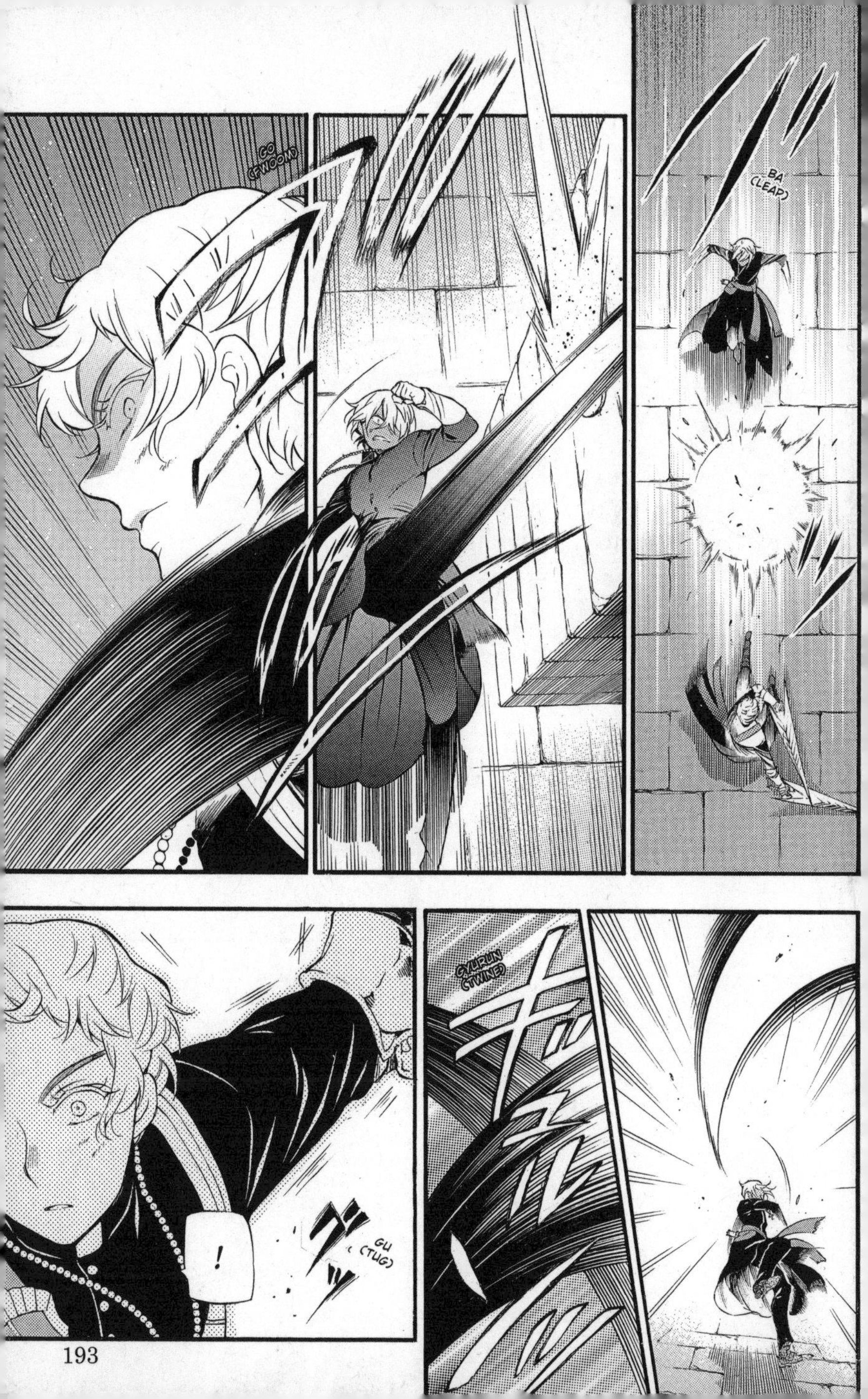
BA (LEAP)
GO (FWOON)
GYURUN (TWINE)
!
GU (TUG)

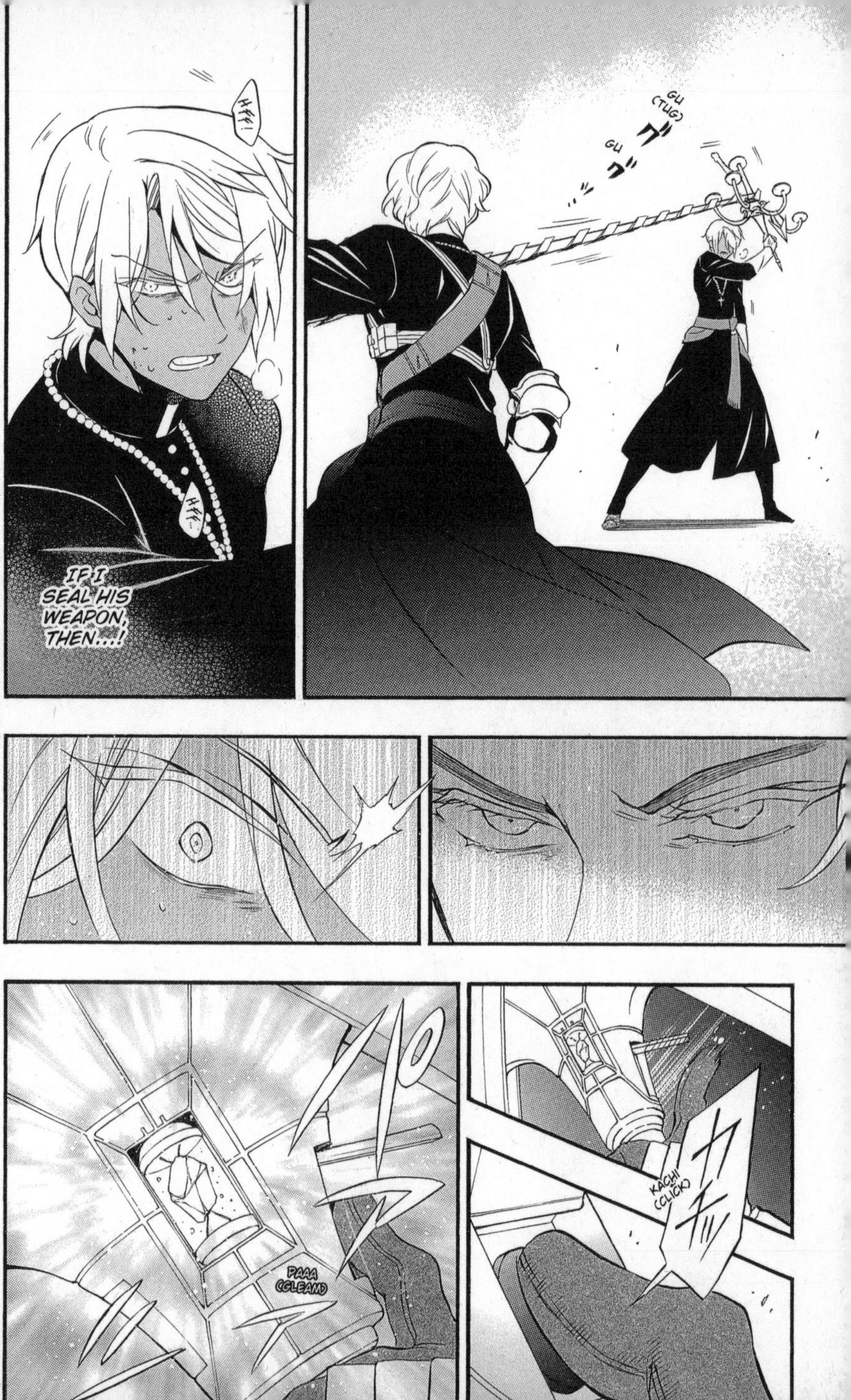
GU (TUG)
GU
HFF!
HFF...
IF I SEAL HIS WEAPON, THEN...!
KACHI (CLICK)
PAAA (GLEAM)

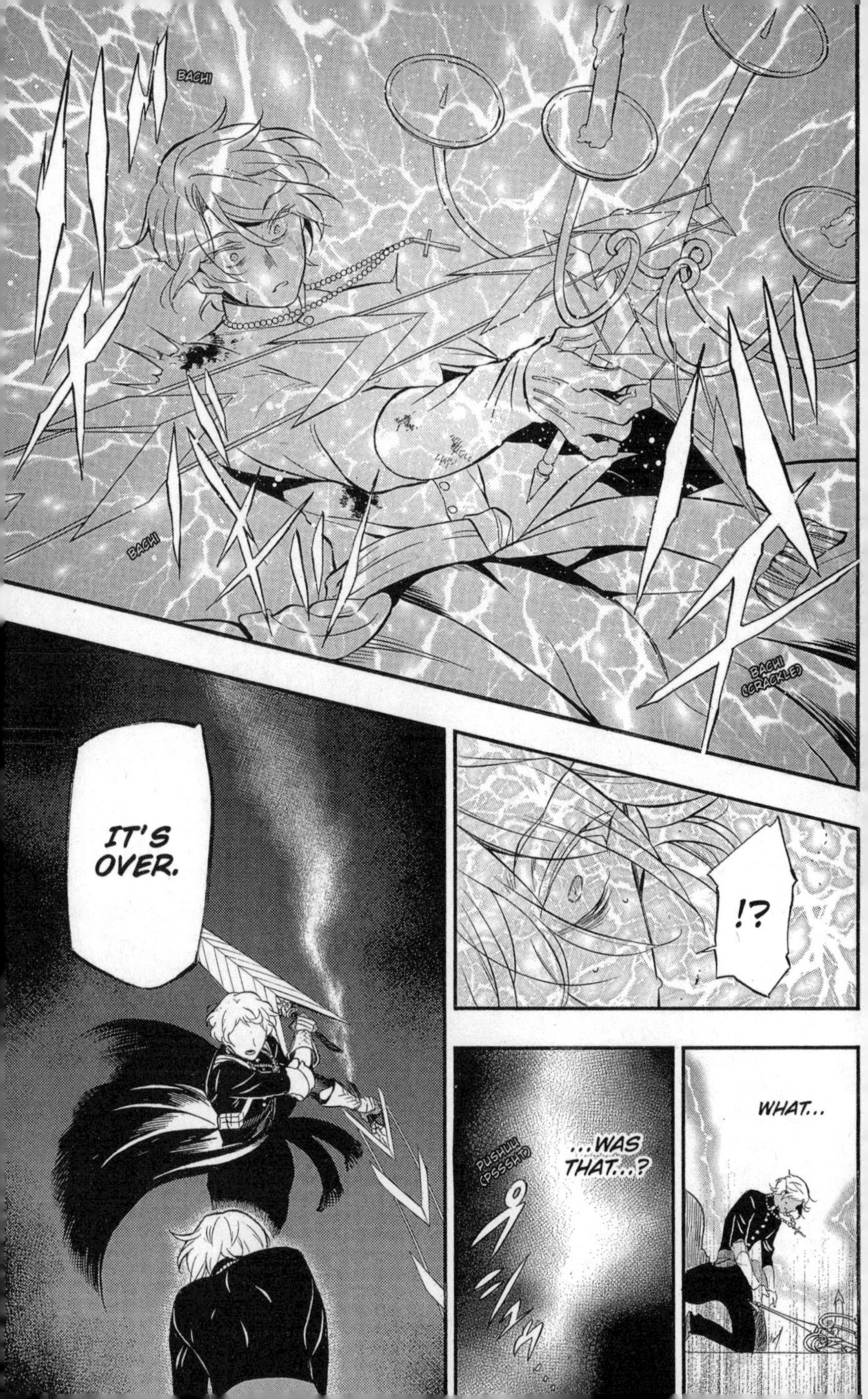
BACHI
BACHI
BACHI (CRACKLE)
!?
WHAT...
...WAS THAT...?
PUSHUU (PSSSHT)
IT'S OVER.

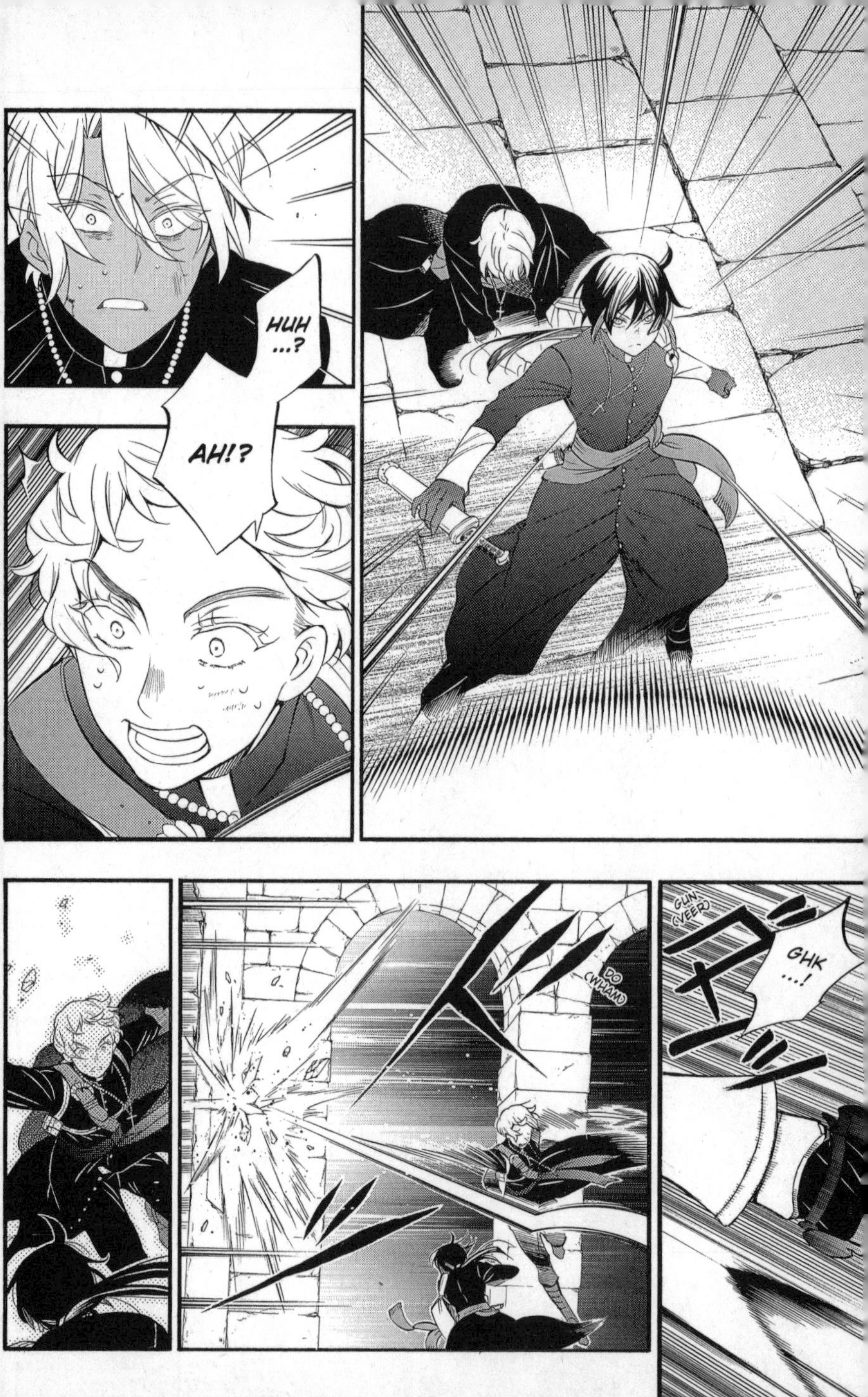
HUH ...?
AH!?
GUN (VEER)
GHK ...!
DO (WHAM)

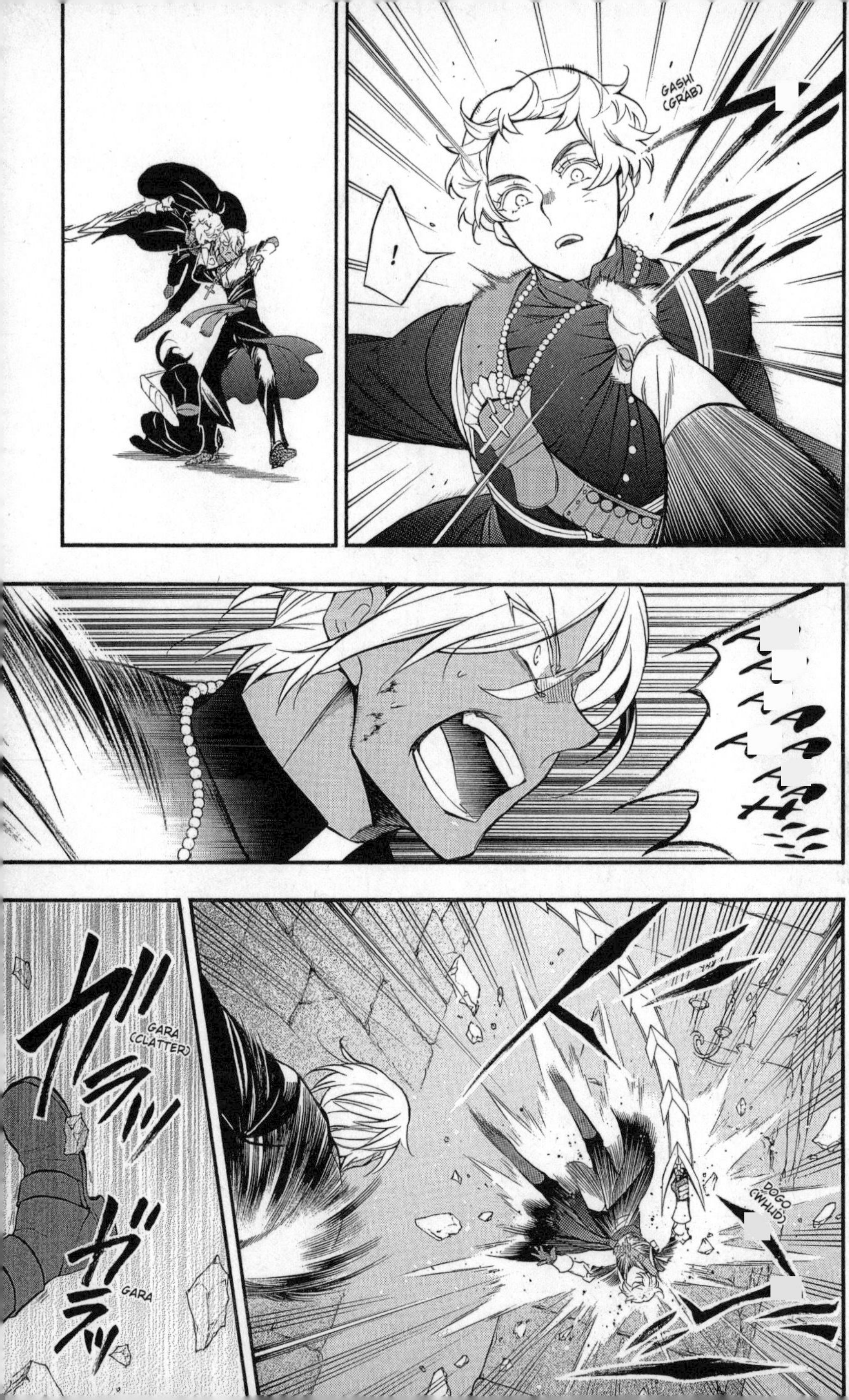
GASHI (GRAB)
!
AAAAAAAAH!!!
DOGO (WHUD)
GARA (CLATTER)
GARA

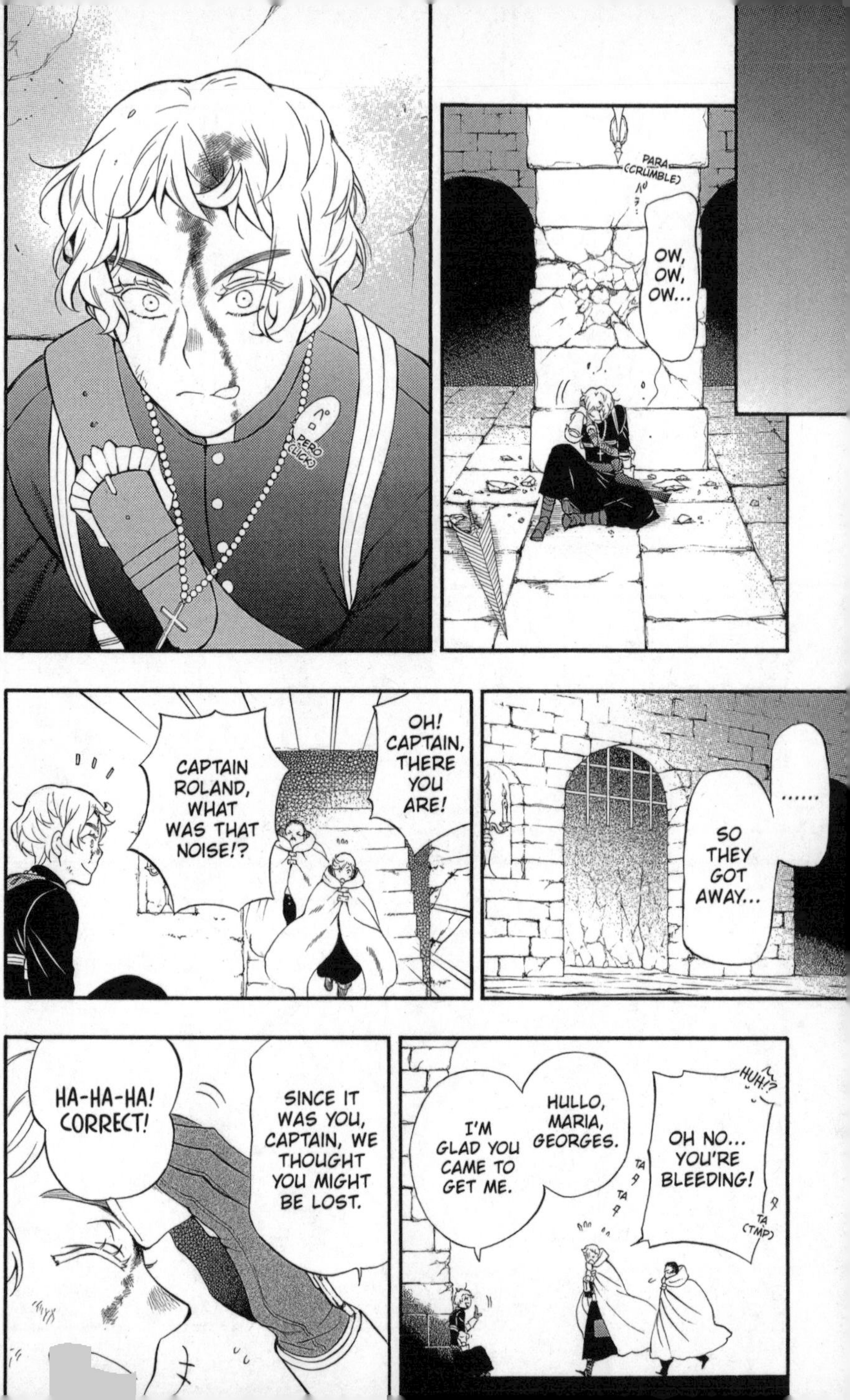
PARA (CRUMBLE)
OW, OW, OW...
PERO (LICK)
......
SO THEY GOT AWAY...
OH! CAPTAIN, THERE YOU ARE!
CAPTAIN ROLAND, WHAT WAS THAT NOISE!?
HUH!?
OH NO... YOU'RE BLEEDING!
TA TA TA (TMP)
HULLO, MARIA, GEORGES.
I'M GLAD YOU CAME TO GET ME.
SINCE IT WAS YOU, CAPTAIN, WE THOUGHT YOU MIGHT BE LOST.
HA-HA-HA! CORRECT!

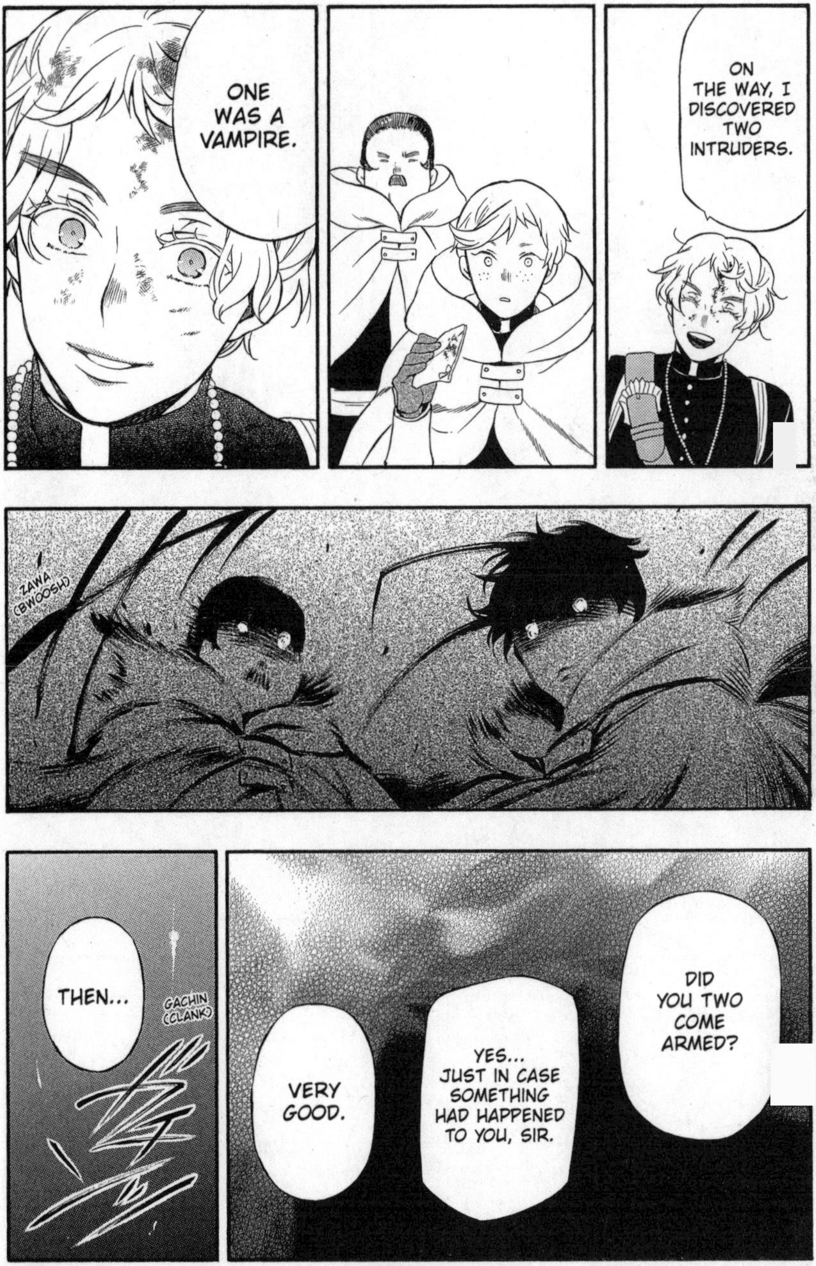
ON THE WAY, I DISCOVERED TWO INTRUDERS.
ONE WAS A VAMPIRE.
ZAWA (BWOOSH)
DID YOU TWO COME ARMED?
YES... JUST IN CASE SOMETHING HAD HAPPENED TO YOU, SIR.
VERY GOOD.
THEN...
GACHIN (CLANK)

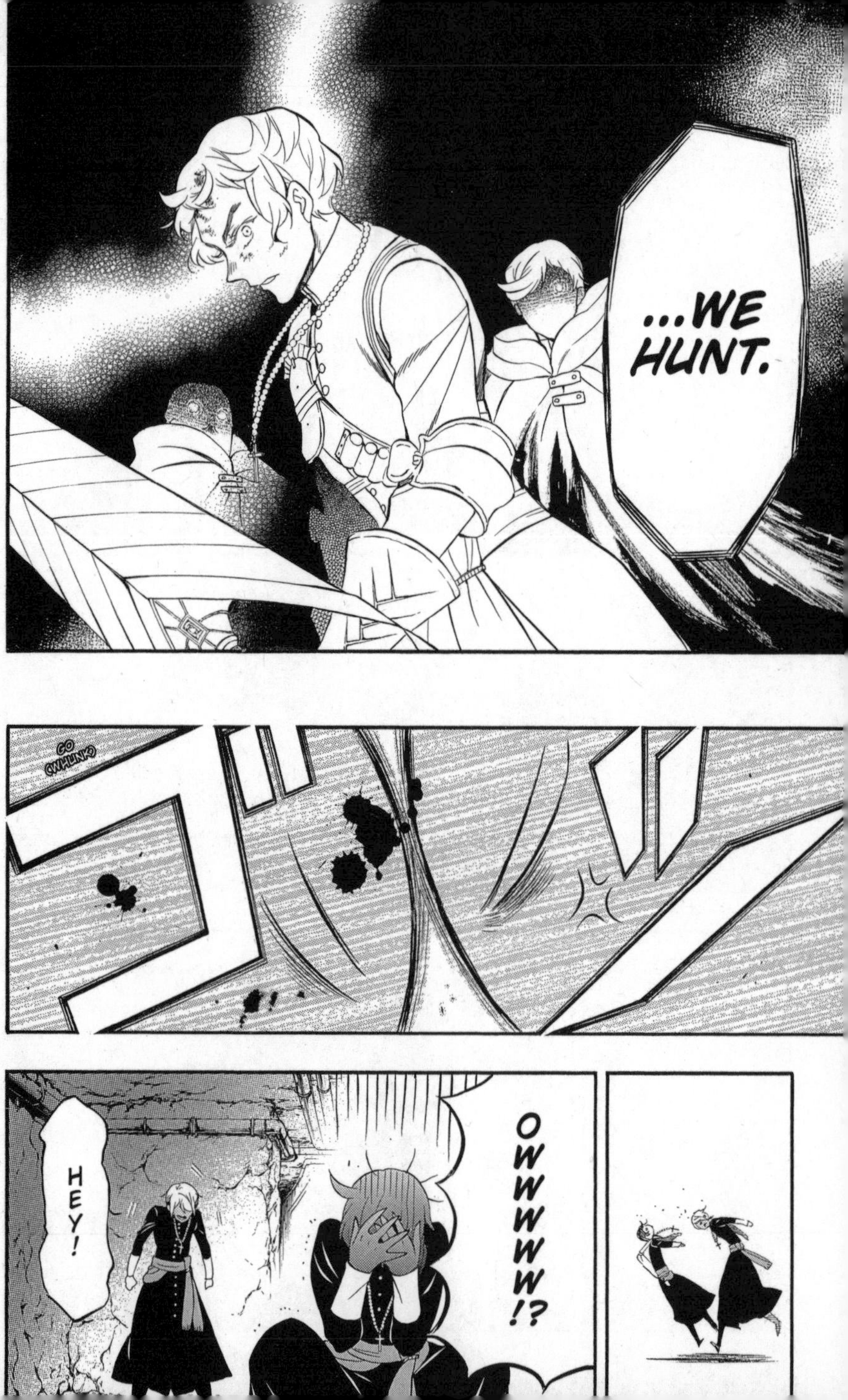
...WE HUNT.
GO (WHUNK)
OWWWWWW!?
HEY!

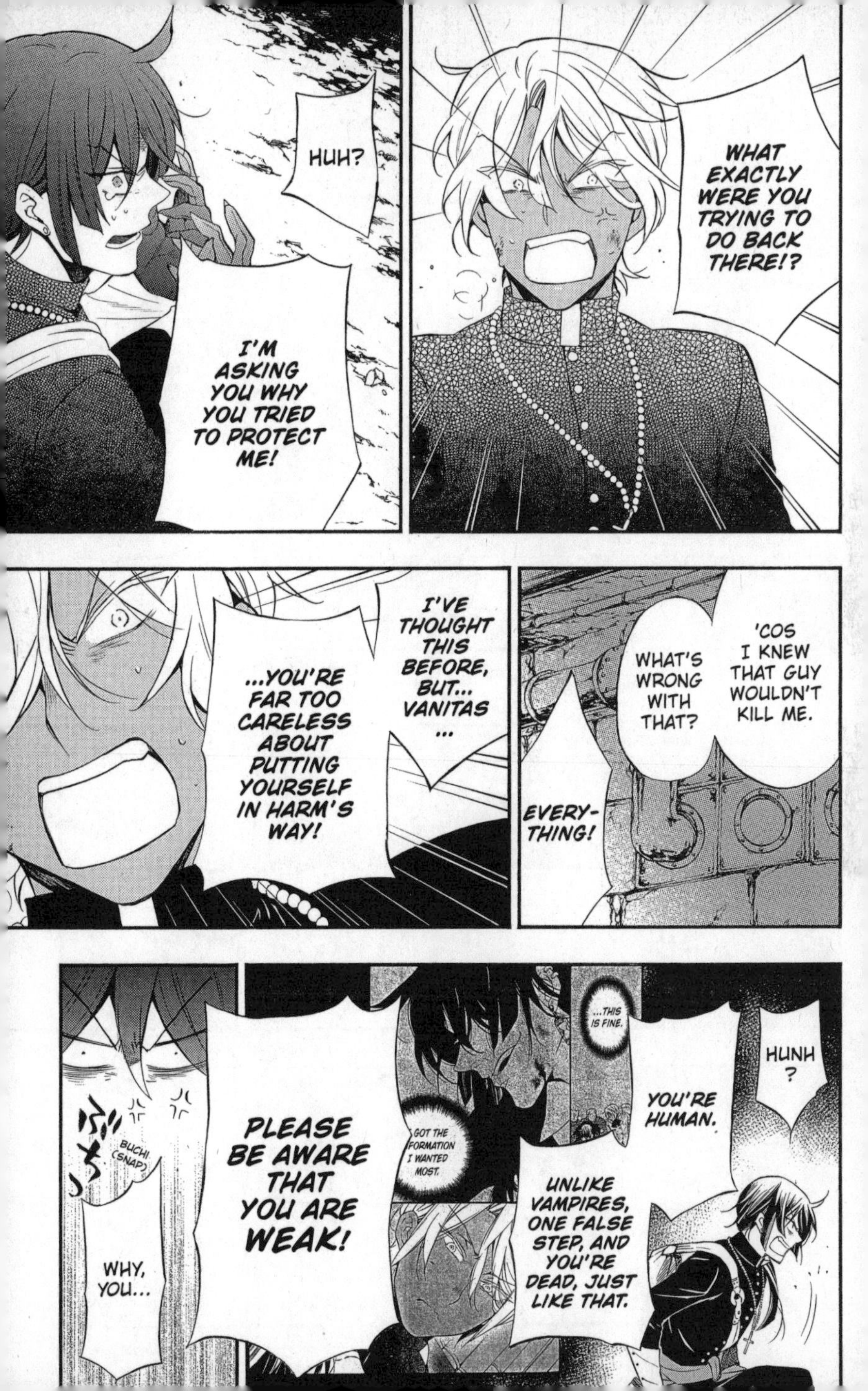
WHAT EXACTLY WERE YOU TRYING TO DO BACK THERE!?
HUH?
I'M ASKING YOU WHY YOU TRIED TO PROTECT ME!
'COS I KNEW THAT GUY WOULDN'T KILL ME.
WHAT'S WRONG WITH THAT?
EVERY-THING!
I'VE THOUGHT THIS BEFORE, BUT... VANITAS ...
...YOU'RE FAR TOO CARELESS ABOUT PUTTING YOURSELF IN HARM'S WAY!
HUNH?
YOU'RE HUMAN.
UNLIKE VAMPIRES, ONE FALSE STEP, AND YOU'RE DEAD, JUST LIKE THAT.
...THIS IS FINE.
GOT THE FORMATION I WANTED MOST.
PLEASE BE AWARE THAT YOU ARE WEAK!
ぶちっ
BUCHI (SNAP)
WHY, YOU...

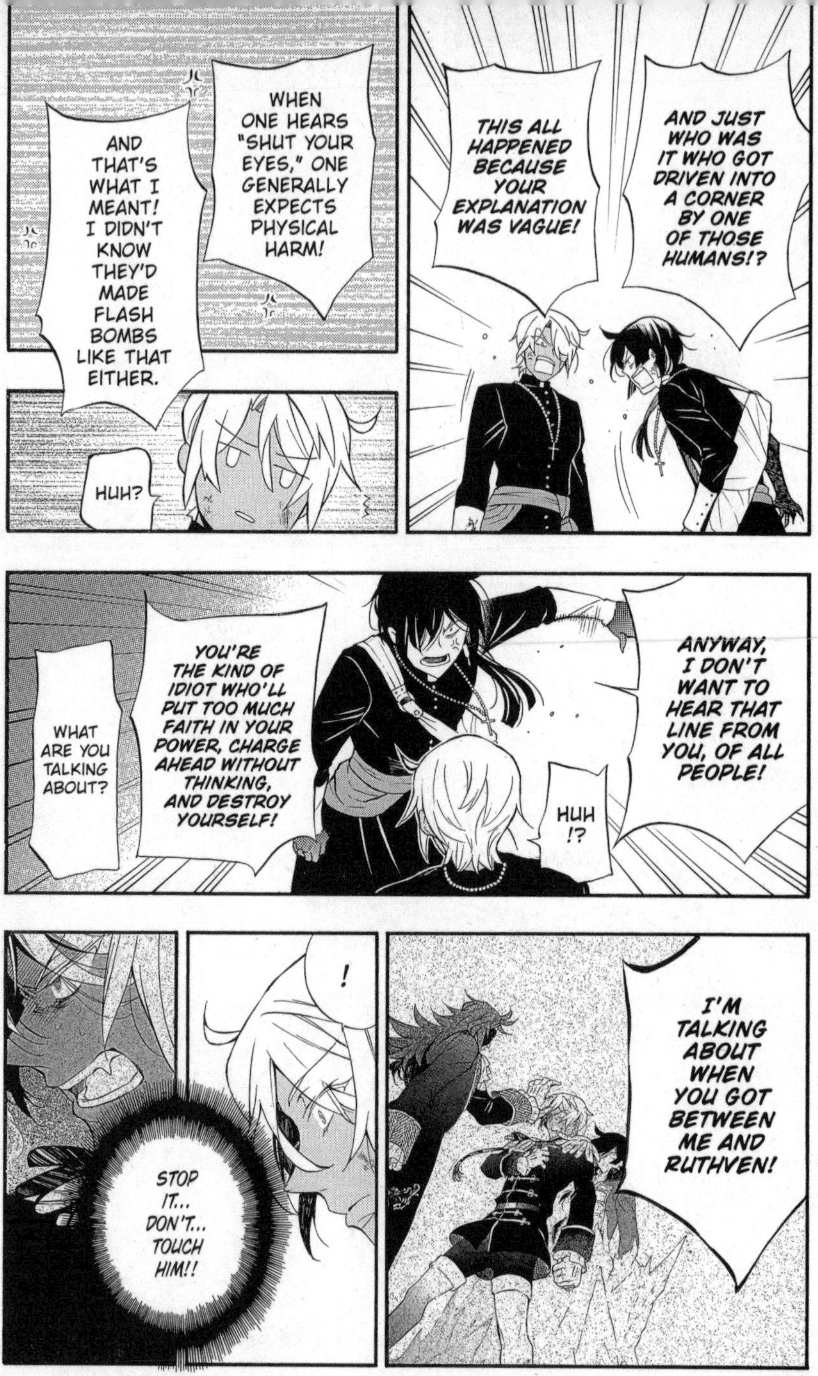
AND JUST WHO WAS IT WHO GOT DRIVEN INTO A CORNER BY ONE OF THOSE HUMANS!?
THIS ALL HAPPENED BECAUSE YOUR EXPLANATION WAS VAGUE!
WHEN ONE HEARS "SHUT YOUR EYES," ONE GENERALLY EXPECTS PHYSICAL HARM!
AND THAT'S WHAT I MEANT! I DIDN'T KNOW THEY'D MADE FLASH BOMBS LIKE THAT EITHER.
HUH?
ANYWAY, I DON'T WANT TO HEAR THAT LINE FROM YOU, OF ALL PEOPLE!
HUH !?
YOU'RE THE KIND OF IDIOT WHO'LL PUT TOO MUCH FAITH IN YOUR POWER, CHARGE AHEAD WITHOUT THINKING, AND DESTROY YOURSELF!
WHAT ARE YOU TALKING ABOUT?
I'M TALKING ABOUT WHEN YOU GOT BETWEEN ME AND RUTHVEN!
!
STOP IT... DON'T... TOUCH HIM!!

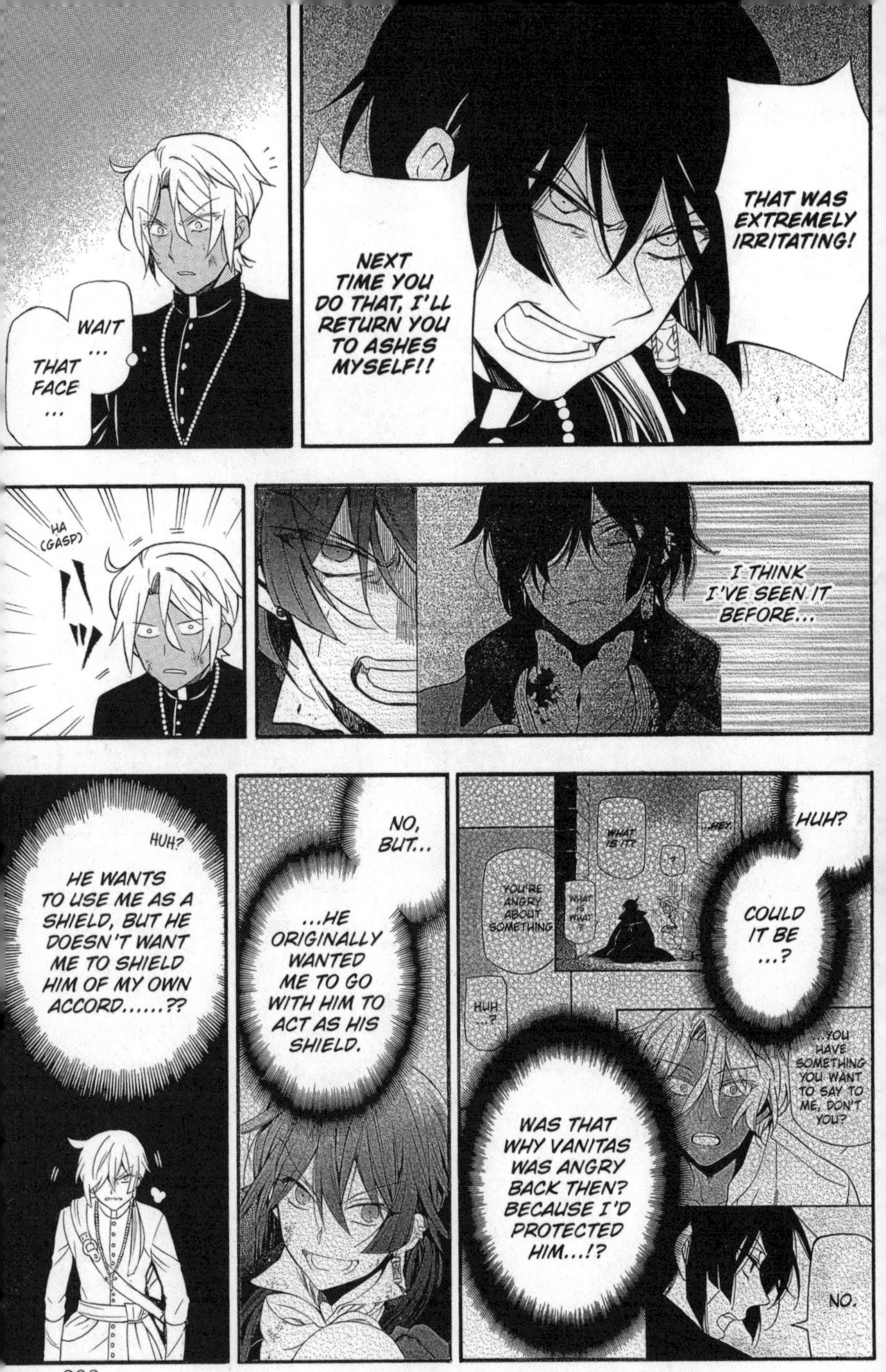
THAT WAS EXTREMELY IRRITATING!
NEXT TIME YOU DO THAT, I'LL RETURN YOU TO ASHES MYSELF!!
WAIT ... THAT FACE ...
I THINK I'VE SEEN IT BEFORE...
HA (GASP)
HUH?
COULD IT BE ...?
...HEY.
WHAT IS IT?
?
WHAT IS WHAT?
YOU'RE ANGRY ABOUT SOMETHING
HUH ...?
...YOU HAVE SOMETHING YOU WANT TO SAY TO ME, DON'T YOU?
WAS THAT WHY VANITAS WAS ANGRY BACK THEN? BECAUSE I'D PROTECTED HIM...!?
NO.
NO, BUT...
...HE ORIGINALLY WANTED ME TO GO WITH HIM TO ACT AS HIS SHIELD.
HUH?
HE WANTS TO USE ME AS A SHIELD, BUT HE DOESN'T WANT ME TO SHIELD HIM OF MY OWN ACCORD......??

WHOA...
YOU'RE AN INCREDIBLY FINICKY PERSON ...!
WHAT?!!
VANIIIITAS!
WHERE AAAARE YOOOOOU??
CAPTAIN! PLEASE DON'T SHOUT.
KATSU
KATSU (TAK)
BUT VANITAS MIGHT ANSWER ME, YOU KNOW!
HE'S NOT GOING TO ANSWER!
HE'S AN INTRUDER!!
KATSU
......
......
......
ARE THEY GONE?
... PROB-ABLY.
THE ECHOES MAKE IT HARD TO JUDGE DISTANCE, BUT...
UGH! WHAT IS WITH THAT ROLAND FELLOW ANYWAY!?
...

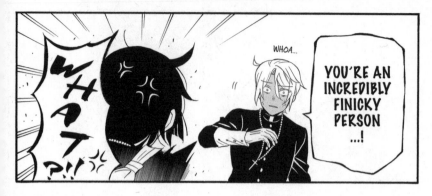

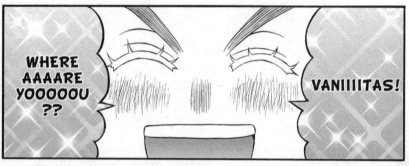

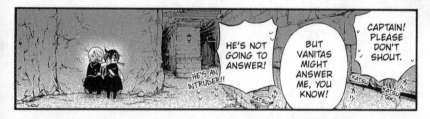

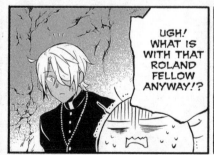

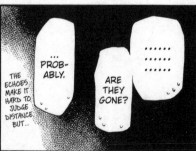

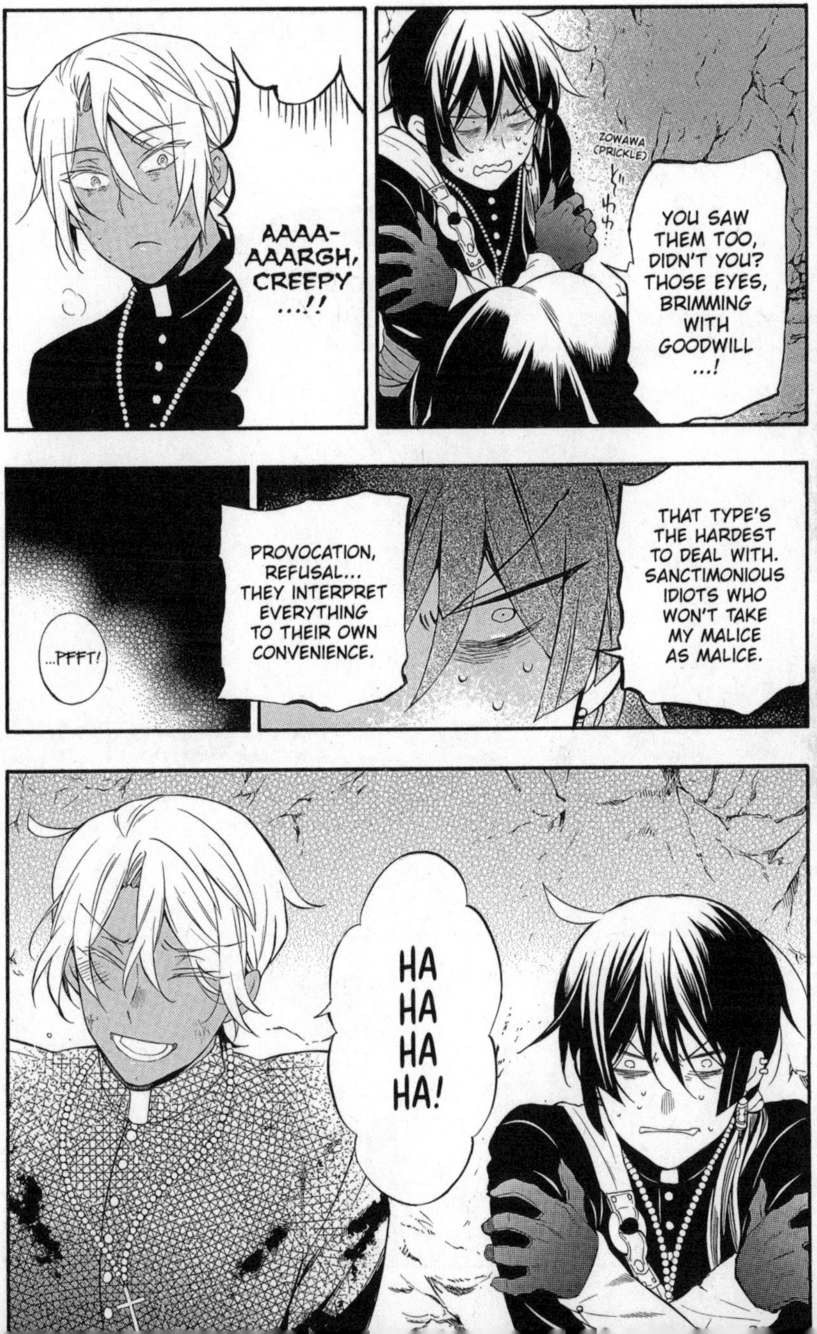
ZOWAWA (PRICKLE)
YOU SAW THEM TOO, DIDN'T YOU? THOSE EYES, BRIMMING WITH GOODWILL ...!
AAAA-AAARGH, CREEPY ...!!
THAT TYPE'S THE HARDEST TO DEAL WITH. SANCTIMONIOUS IDIOTS WHO WON'T TAKE MY MALICE AS MALICE.
PROVOCATION, REFUSAL... THEY INTERPRET EVERYTHING TO THEIR OWN CONVENIENCE.
...PFFT!
HA HA HA HA!

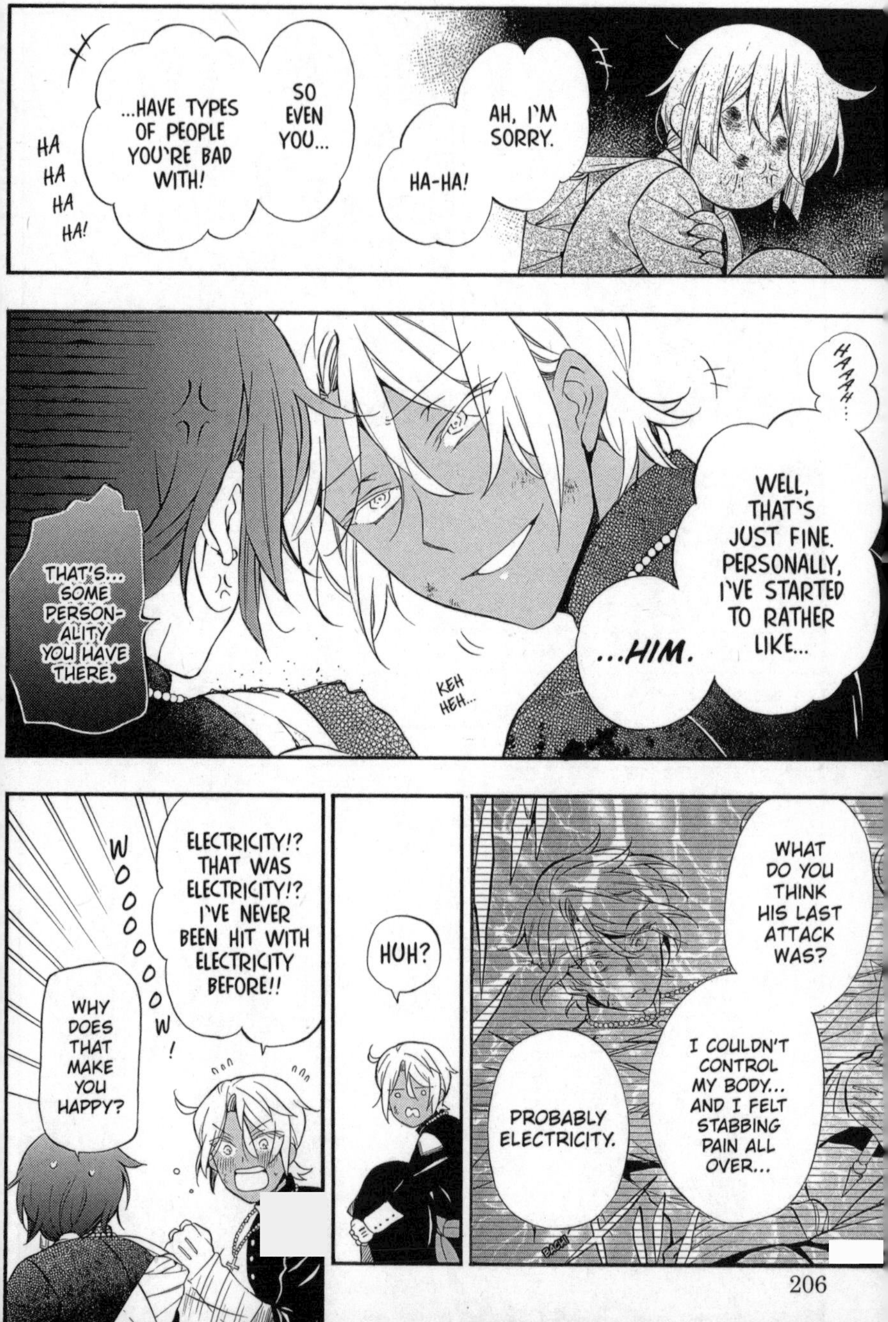
AH, I'M SORRY.
HA-HA!
SO EVEN YOU...
...HAVE TYPES OF PEOPLE YOU'RE BAD WITH!
HA HA HA HA!
HAAAH...
WELL, THAT'S JUST FINE. PERSONALLY, I'VE STARTED TO RATHER LIKE...
...HIM.
KEH HEH...
THAT'S... SOME PERSON-ALITY YOU HAVE THERE.
WHAT DO YOU THINK HIS LAST ATTACK WAS?
I COULDN'T CONTROL MY BODY... AND I FELT STABBING PAIN ALL OVER...
PROBABLY ELECTRICITY.
HUH?
ELECTRICITY!? THAT WAS ELECTRICITY!? I'VE NEVER BEEN HIT WITH ELECTRICITY BEFORE!!
WOOOOOOOW!
WHY DOES THAT MAKE YOU HAPPY?

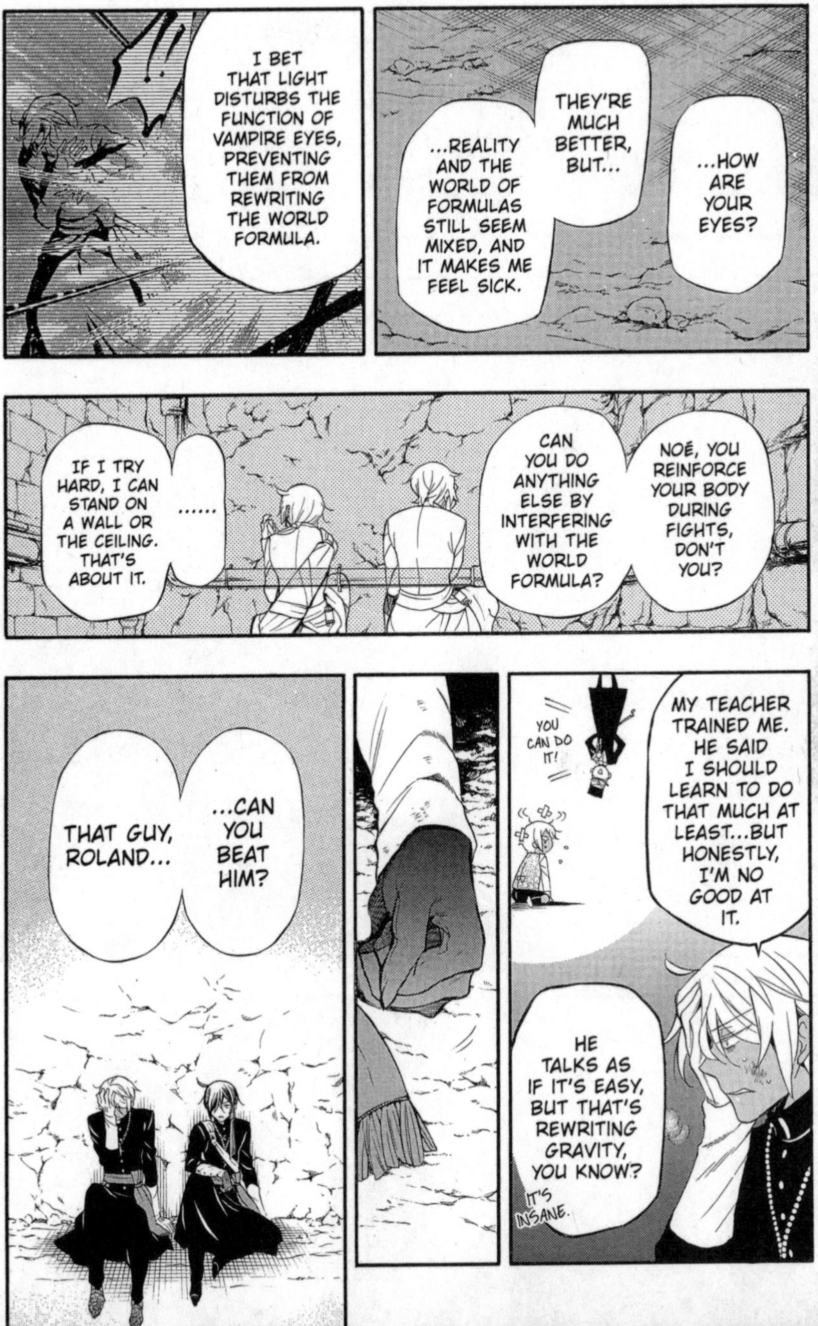
...HOW ARE YOUR EYES?
THEY'RE MUCH BETTER, BUT...
...REALITY AND THE WORLD OF FORMULAS STILL SEEM MIXED, AND IT MAKES ME FEEL SICK.
I BET THAT LIGHT DISTURBS THE FUNCTION OF VAMPIRE EYES, PREVENTING THEM FROM REWRITING THE WORLD FORMULA.
NOÉ, YOU REINFORCE YOUR BODY DURING FIGHTS, DON'T YOU?
CAN YOU DO ANYTHING ELSE BY INTERFERING WITH THE WORLD FORMULA?
......
IF I TRY HARD, I CAN STAND ON A WALL OR THE CEILING. THAT'S ABOUT IT.
MY TEACHER TRAINED ME. HE SAID I SHOULD LEARN TO DO THAT MUCH AT LEAST...BUT HONESTLY, I'M NO GOOD AT IT.
YOU CAN DO IT!
HE TALKS AS IF IT'S EASY, BUT THAT'S REWRITING GRAVITY, YOU KNOW?
IT'S INSANE.
...CAN YOU BEAT HIM?
THAT GUY, ROLAND...

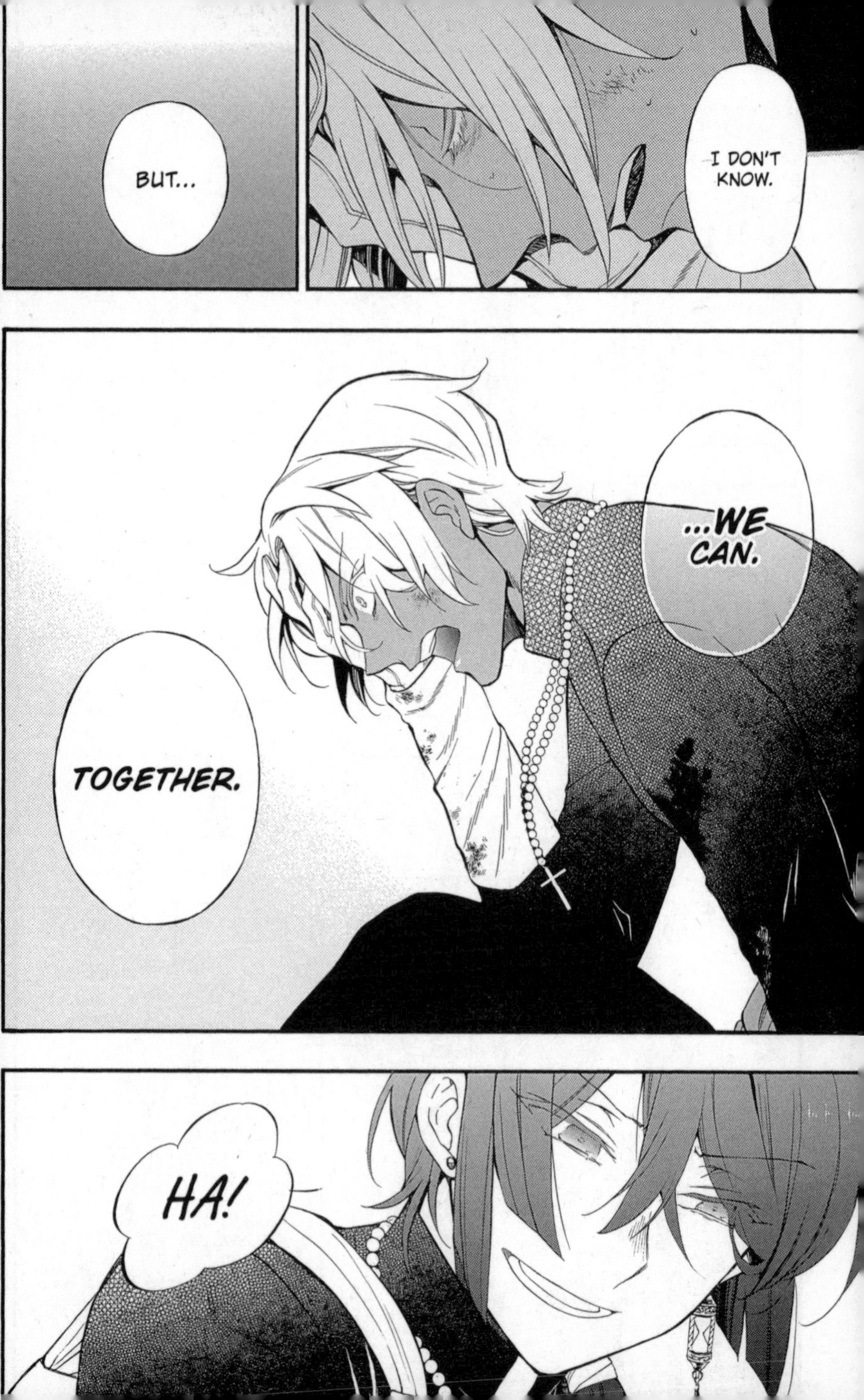
I DON'T KNOW.
BUT...
...WE CAN.
TOGETHER.
HA!

WHAT IS IT?

......?

SUKU (RISE)

...NOTH-ING.

HA (GASP)

KATAN (RATTLE)

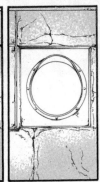

IT FELT... AS THOUGH WE WERE BEING WATCHED...

I CAME HERE...

...TO FIND A CERTAIN MAN.

NOÉ.

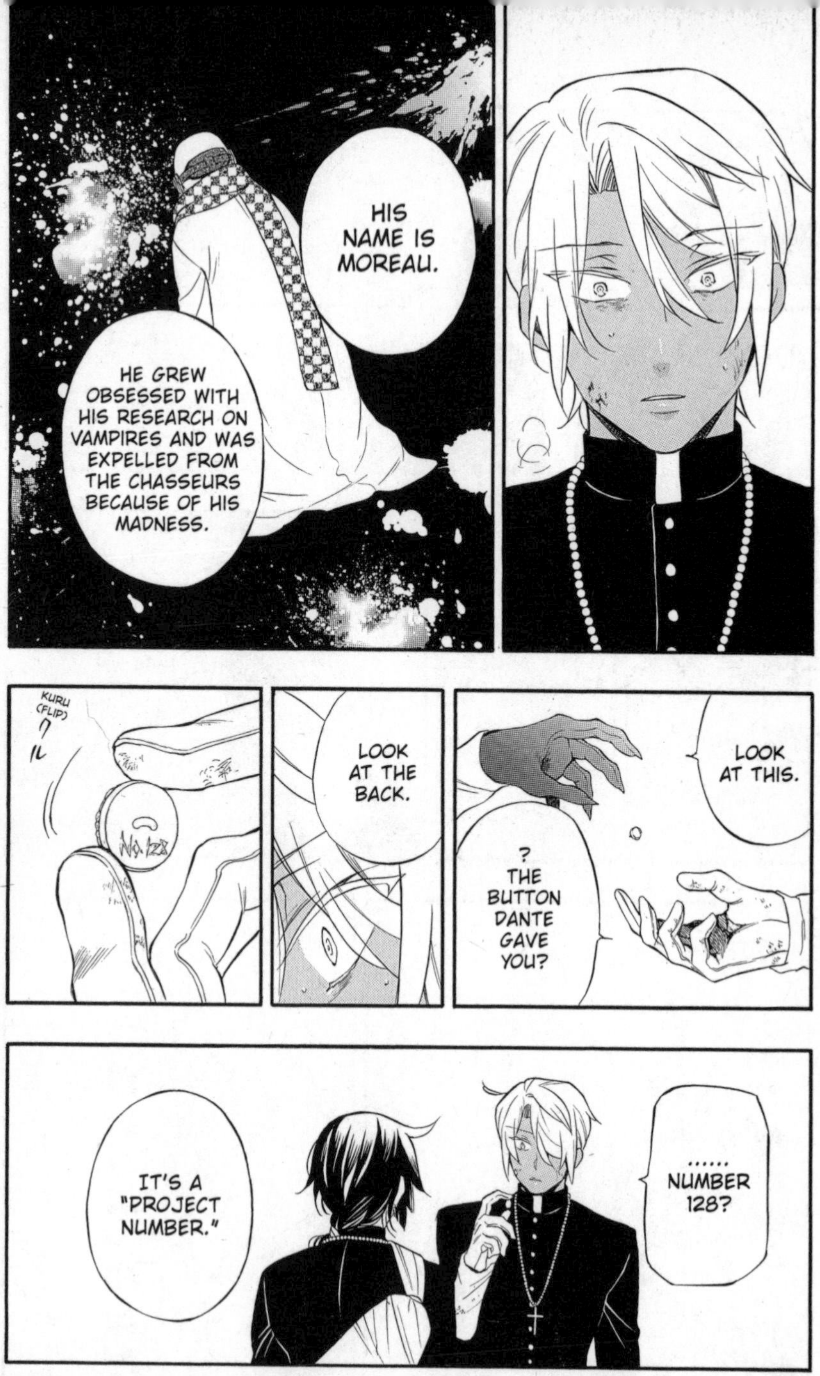
HIS NAME IS MOREAU.
HE GREW OBSESSED WITH HIS RESEARCH ON VAMPIRES AND WAS EXPELLED FROM THE CHASSEURS BECAUSE OF HIS MADNESS.
LOOK AT THIS.
? THE BUTTON DANTE GAVE YOU?
LOOK AT THE BACK.
KURU (FLIP)
クル
No.128
...... NUMBER 128?
IT'S A "PROJECT NUMBER."

THESE INCIDENTS... THE VAMPIRES WEREN'T TAKEN BY REGULAR CHASSEURS.

THEY WERE REINFORCED HUMANS MOREAU CREATED THROUGH HUMAN EXPERIMENTATION.

HIS "PROJECTS."

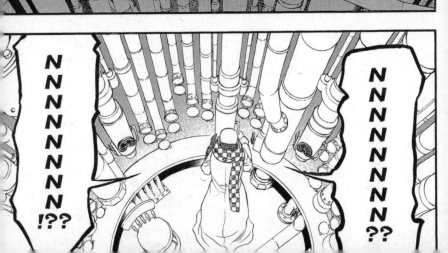

NNNNNNNN!??

NNNNNNNN??

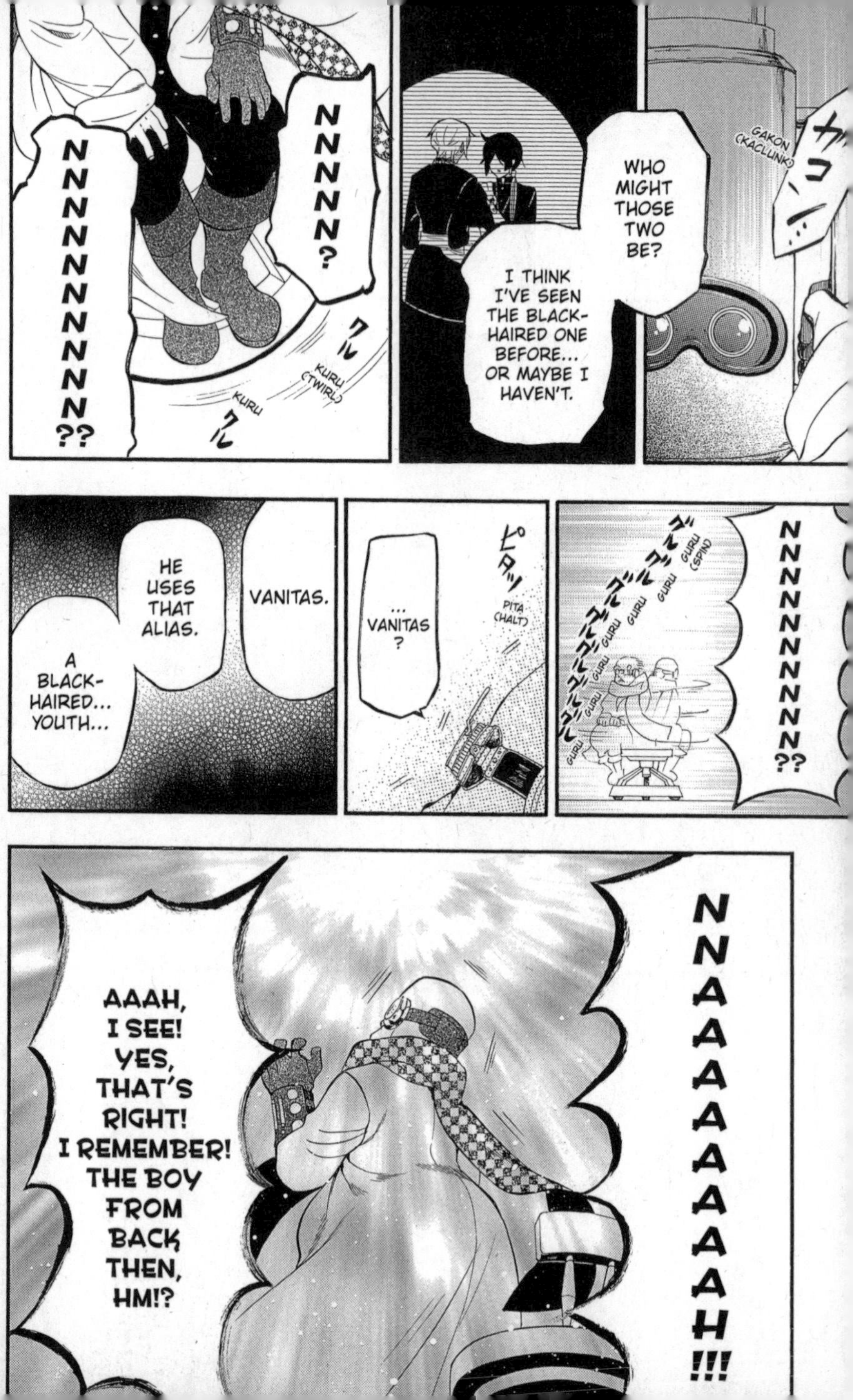
GAKON (KACLUNK)
WHO MIGHT THOSE TWO BE?
I THINK I'VE SEEN THE BLACK-HAIRED ONE BEFORE... OR MAYBE I HAVEN'T.
NNNNN?
KURU (TWIRL)
KURU
NNNNNNNNNNNN??
NNNNNNNNNN??
GURU (SPIN)
GURU GURU GURU GURU GURU GURU
PITA (HALT)
...VANITAS?
VANITAS.
HE USES THAT ALIAS.
A BLACK-HAIRED... YOUTH...
NNAAAAAAAAAAAH!!!
AAAH, I SEE! YES, THAT'S RIGHT! I REMEMBER! THE BOY FROM BACK THEN, HM!?

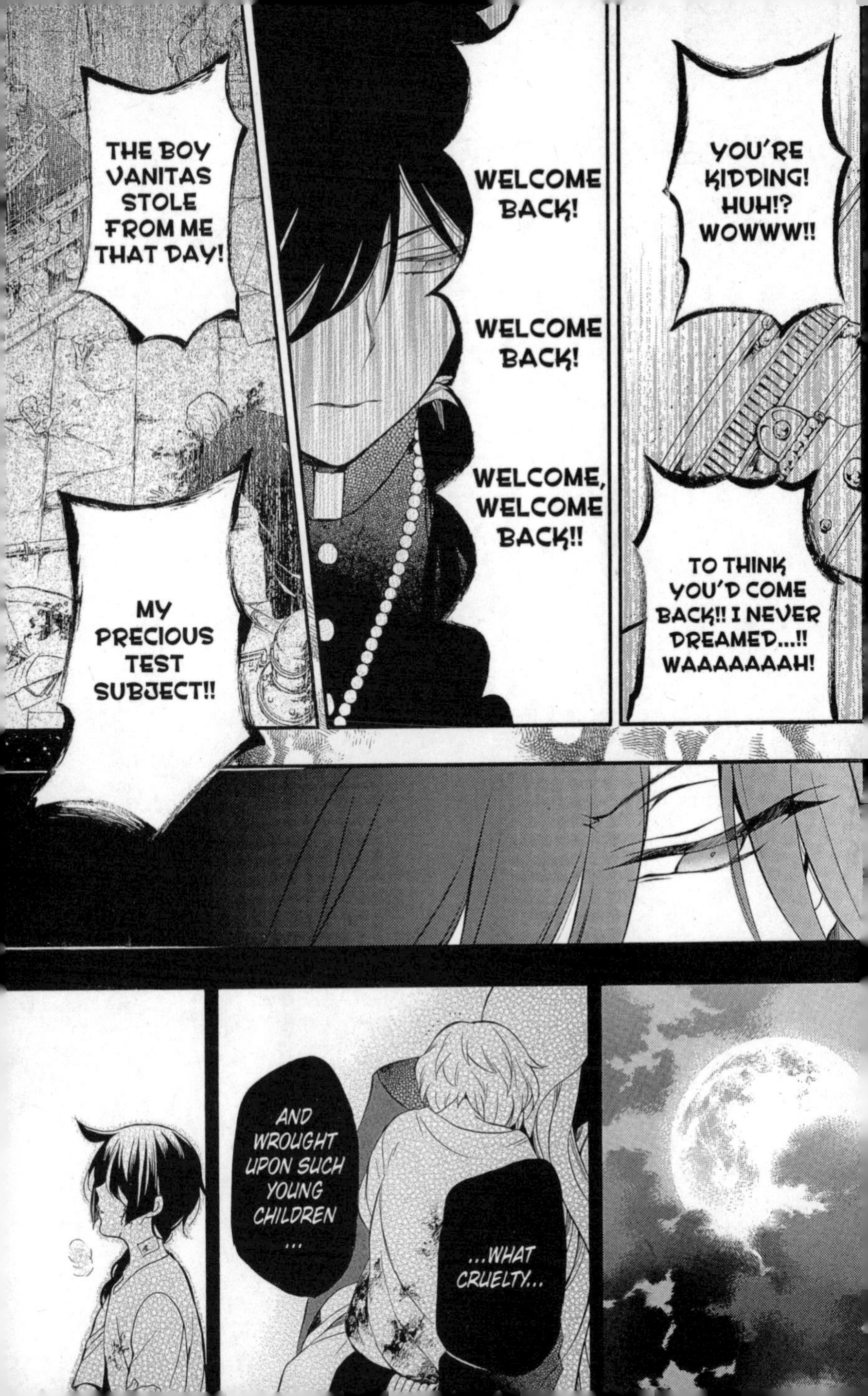
YOU'RE KIDDING! HUH!? WOWWW!!
TO THINK YOU'D COME BACK!! I NEVER DREAMED...!! WAAAAAAAH!
WELCOME BACK!
WELCOME BACK!
WELCOME, WELCOME BACK!!
THE BOY VANITAS STOLE FROM ME THAT DAY!
MY PRECIOUS TEST SUBJECT!!
AND WROUGHT UPON SUCH YOUNG CHILDREN...
...WHAT CRUELTY...

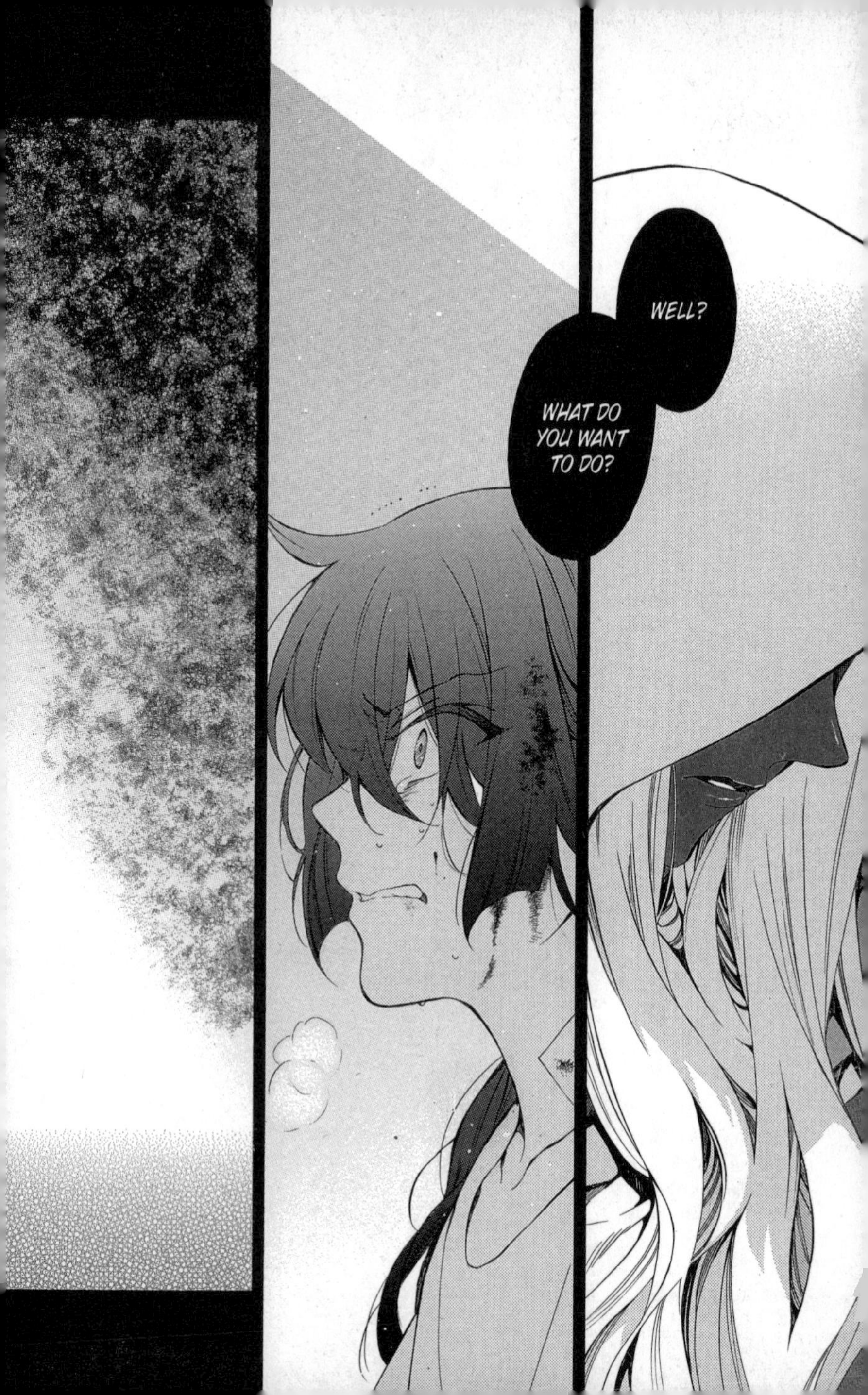
WELL?
WHAT DO YOU WANT TO DO?

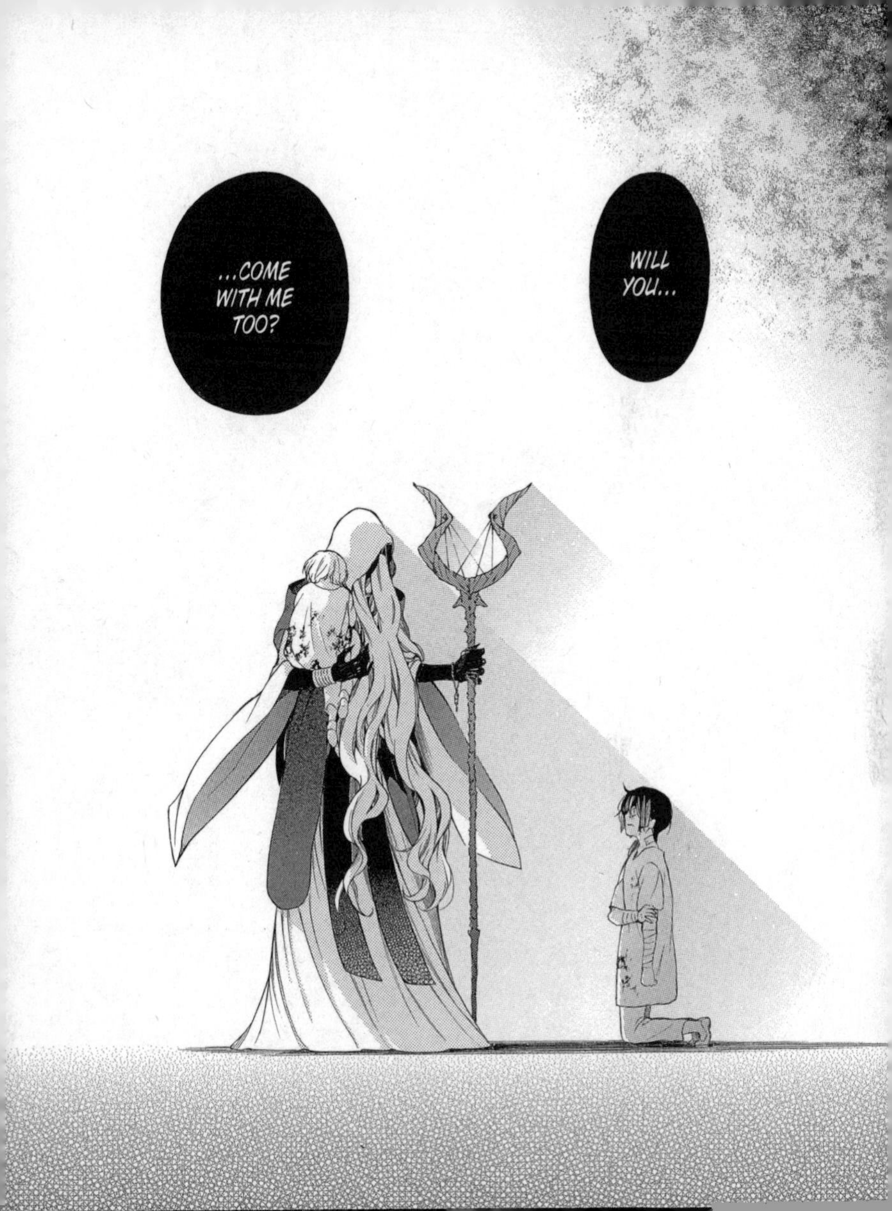
WILL YOU...
...COME WITH ME TOO?

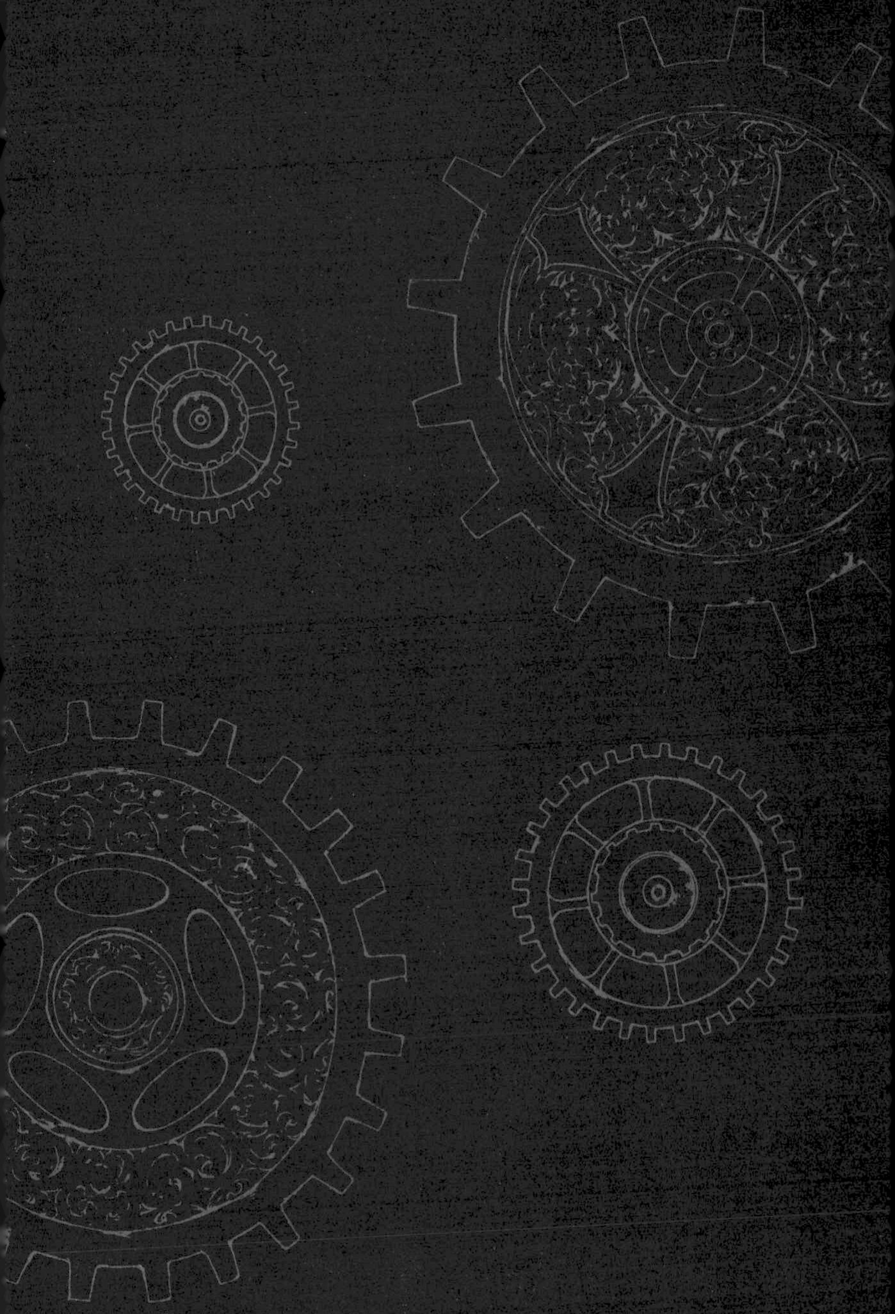

Mémoire 15 Chasseur THOSE WHO HUNT CRIMSON

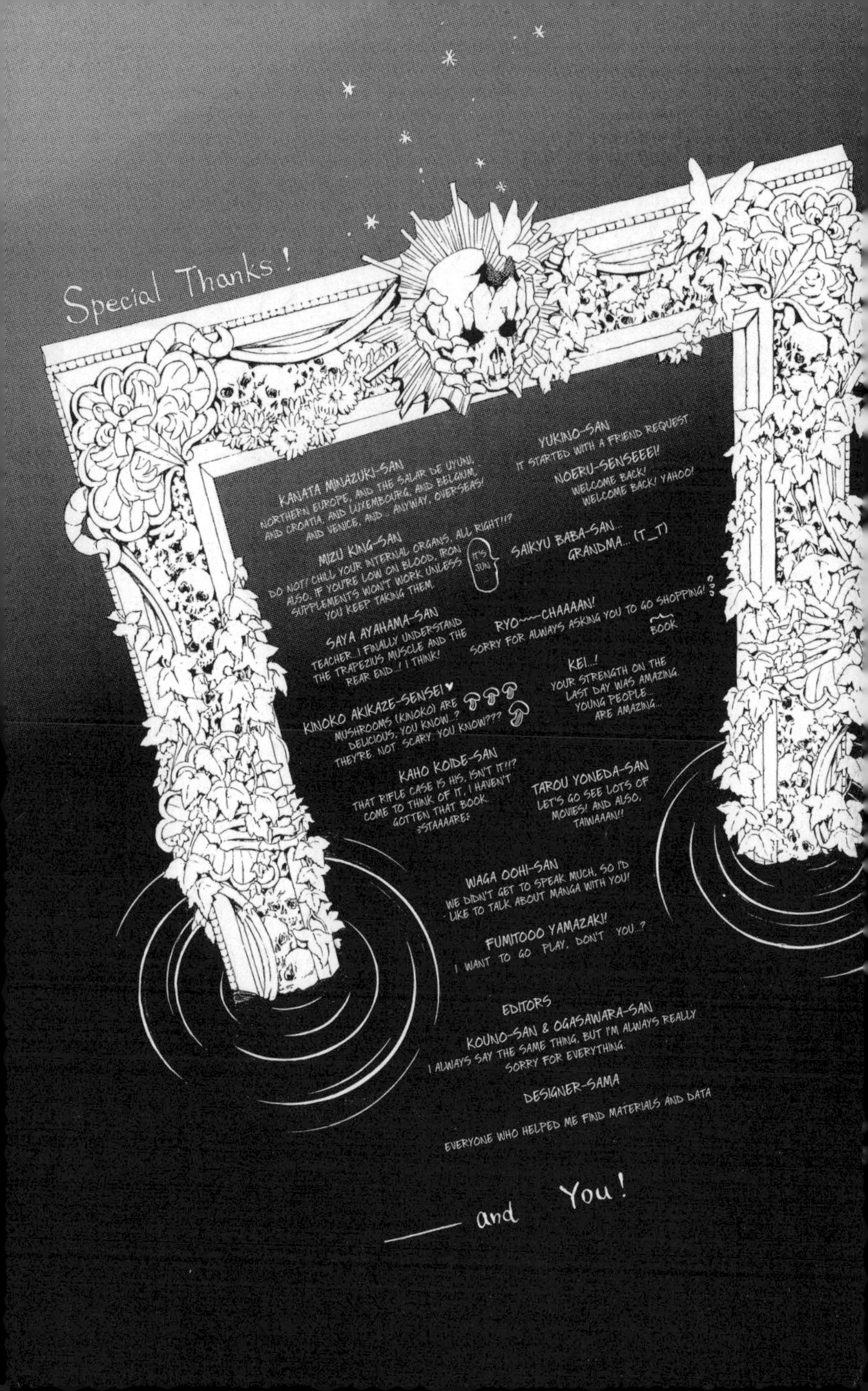

Special Thanks!
KANATA MINAZUKI-SAN
NORTHERN EUROPE, AND THE SALAR DE UYUNI, AND CROATIA, AND LUXEMBOURG, AND BELGIUM, AND VENICE, AND... ANYWAY, OVERSEAS!
YUKINO-SAN
IT STARTED WITH A FRIEND REQUEST
NOERU-SENSEEEI!
WELCOME BACK! WELCOME BACK! YAHOO!
MIZU KING-SAN
DO NOT! CHILL YOUR INTERNAL ORGANS, ALL RIGHT!!? ALSO, IF YOU'RE LOW ON BLOOD, IRON SUPPLEMENTS WON'T WORK UNLESS YOU KEEP TAKING THEM.
IT'S JUN
SAIKYU BABA-SAN...
GRANDMA... (T_T)
SAYA AYAHAMA-SAN
TEACHER...! FINALLY UNDERSTAND THE TRAPEZIUS MUSCLE AND THE REAR END...! I THINK!
RYO~~~CHAAAAN!
SORRY FOR ALWAYS ASKING YOU TO GO SHOPPING!
BOOK
KINOKO AKIKAZE-SENSEI♥
MUSHROOMS (KINOKO) ARE DELICIOUS, YOU KNOW...? THEY'RE NOT SCARY, YOU KNOW???
KEI...!
YOUR STRENGTH ON THE LAST DAY WAS AMAZING. YOUNG PEOPLE... ARE AMAZING...
KAHO KOIDE-SAN
THAT RIFLE CASE IS HIS, ISN'T IT!!? COME TO THINK OF IT, I HAVEN'T GOTTEN THAT BOOK. STAAAARE
TAROU YONEDA-SAN
LET'S GO SEE LOTS OF MOVIES! AND ALSO, TAIWAAAN!!
WAGA OOHI-SAN
WE DIDN'T GET TO SPEAK MUCH, SO I'D LIKE TO TALK ABOUT MANGA WITH YOU!
FUMITOOO YAMAZAKI!
I WANT TO GO PLAY, DON'T YOU...?
EDITORS
KOUNO-SAN & OGASAWARA-SAN
I ALWAYS SAY THE SAME THING, BUT I'M ALWAYS REALLY SORRY FOR EVERYTHING.
DESIGNER-SAMA
EVERYONE WHO HELPED ME FIND MATERIALS AND DATA
—— and You!

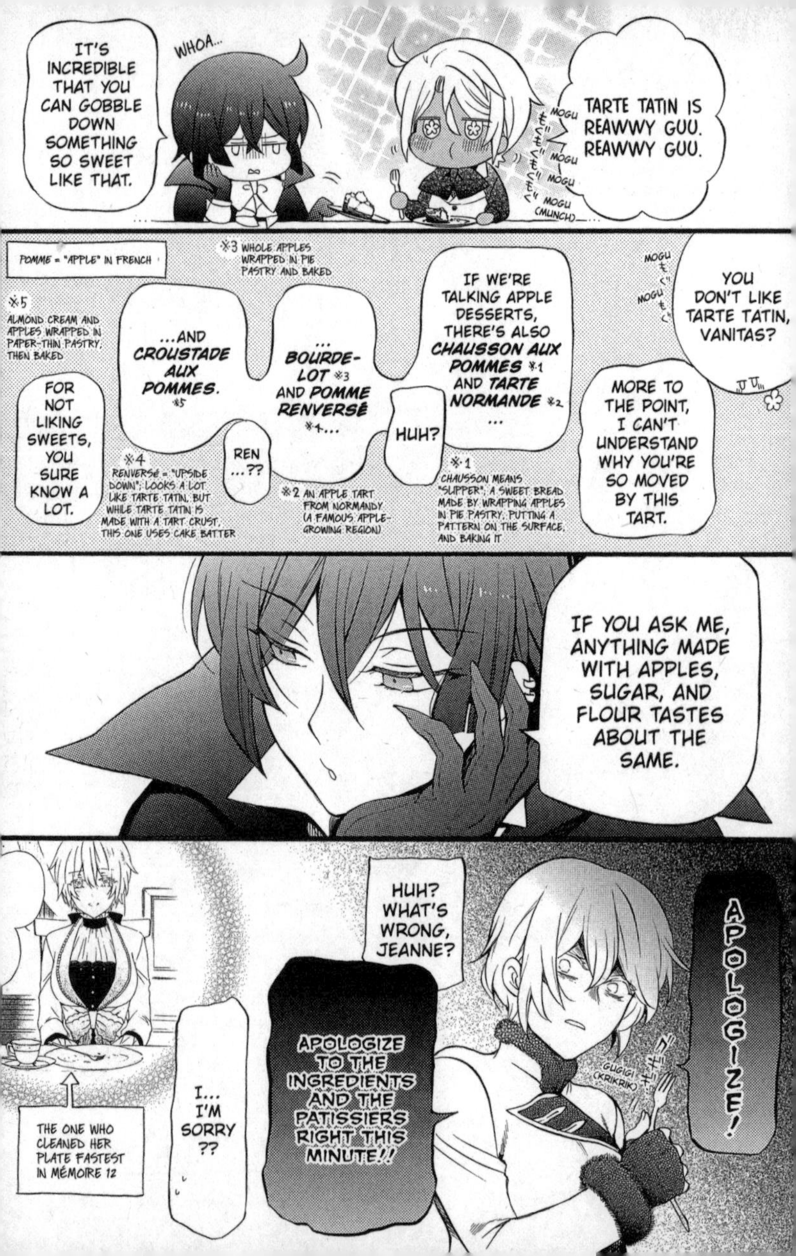
TARTE TATIN IS REAWWY GUU. REAWWY GUU.
MOGU MOGU MOGU MOGU (MUNCH)
WHOA...
IT'S INCREDIBLE THAT YOU CAN GOBBLE DOWN SOMETHING SO SWEET LIKE THAT.
YOU DON'T LIKE TARTE TATIN, VANITAS?
MOGU MOGU
MORE TO THE POINT, I CAN'T UNDERSTAND WHY YOU'RE SO MOVED BY THIS TART.
IF WE'RE TALKING APPLE DESSERTS, THERE'S ALSO CHAUSSON AUX POMMES ※1 AND TARTE NORMANDE ※2 ...
HUH?
... BOURDELOT ※3 AND POMME RENVERSÉ ※4...
REN ...??
...AND CROUSTADE AUX POMMES. ※5
FOR NOT LIKING SWEETS, YOU SURE KNOW A LOT.
POMME = "APPLE" IN FRENCH
※1 CHAUSSON MEANS "SLIPPER". A SWEET BREAD MADE BY WRAPPING APPLES IN PIE PASTRY, PUTTING A PATTERN ON THE SURFACE, AND BAKING IT
※2 AN APPLE TART FROM NORMANDY (A FAMOUS APPLE-GROWING REGION)
※3 WHOLE APPLES WRAPPED IN PIE PASTRY AND BAKED
※4 RENVERSÉ = "UPSIDE DOWN". LOOKS A LOT LIKE TARTE TATIN, BUT WHILE TARTE TATIN IS MADE WITH A TART CRUST, THIS ONE USES CAKE BATTER
※5 ALMOND CREAM AND APPLES WRAPPED IN PAPER-THIN PASTRY, THEN BAKED
IF YOU ASK ME, ANYTHING MADE WITH APPLES, SUGAR, AND FLOUR TASTES ABOUT THE SAME.
APOLOGIZE!
GUGIGI (KRIKRIK)
HUH? WHAT'S WRONG, JEANNE?
APOLOGIZE TO THE INGREDIENTS AND THE PATISSIERS RIGHT THIS MINUTE!!
I... I'M SORRY ??
THE ONE WHO CLEANED HER PLATE FASTEST IN MÉMOIRE 12

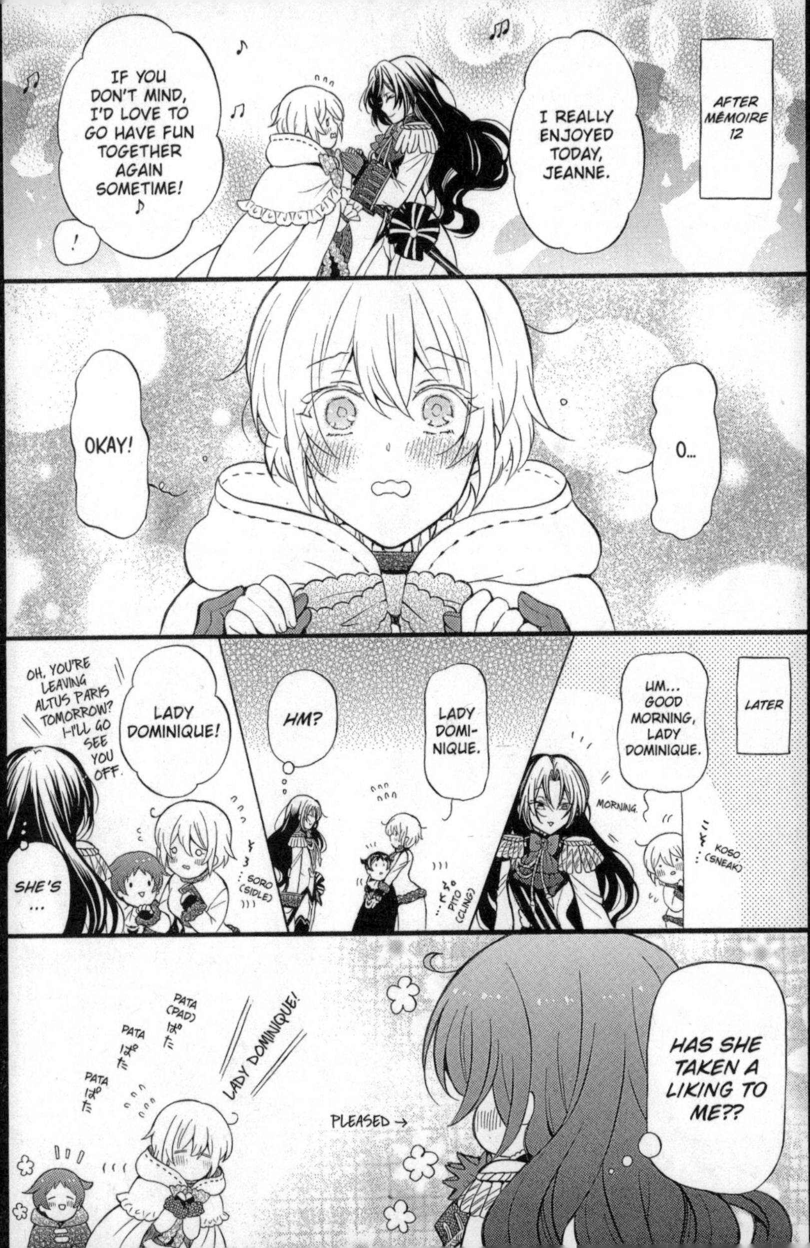
AFTER MÉMOIRE 12
I REALLY ENJOYED TODAY, JEANNE.
IF YOU DON'T MIND, I'D LOVE TO GO HAVE FUN TOGETHER AGAIN SOMETIME! ♪
!
O...
OKAY!
LATER
UM... GOOD MORNING, LADY DOMINIQUE.
MORNING.
KOSO (SNEAK)
LADY DOMI-NIQUE.
HM?
PITO (CLING)
SORO (SIDLE)
LADY DOMINIQUE!
OH, YOU'RE LEAVING ALTUS PARIS TOMORROW? I'LL GO SEE YOU OFF.
SHE'S ...
HAS SHE TAKEN A LIKING TO ME??
PLEASED →
LADY DOMINIQUE!
PATA (PAD)
PATA
PATA

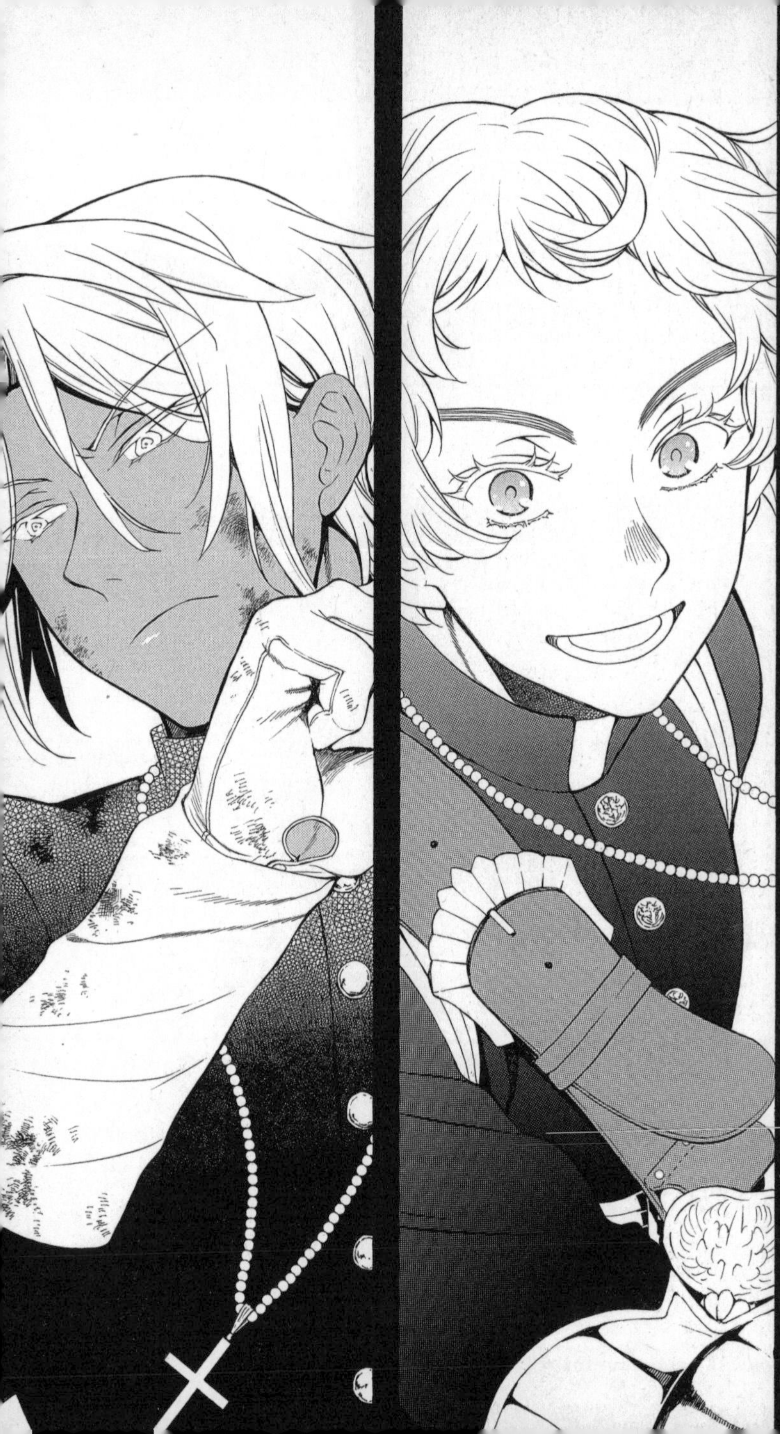

Next Volume Preview

THE MATTER
OF THE VAMPIRE
ABDUCTIONS
TAKES AN
UNEXPECTED
TURN...
WHAT
"EXPERIMENT"
IS THE MAN
WHO KNOWS
VANITAS'S PAST
PLOTTING IN
THE CATACOMBS
BENEATH
PARIS?

The Case Study of Vanitas VOLUME 4

COMING SOON!

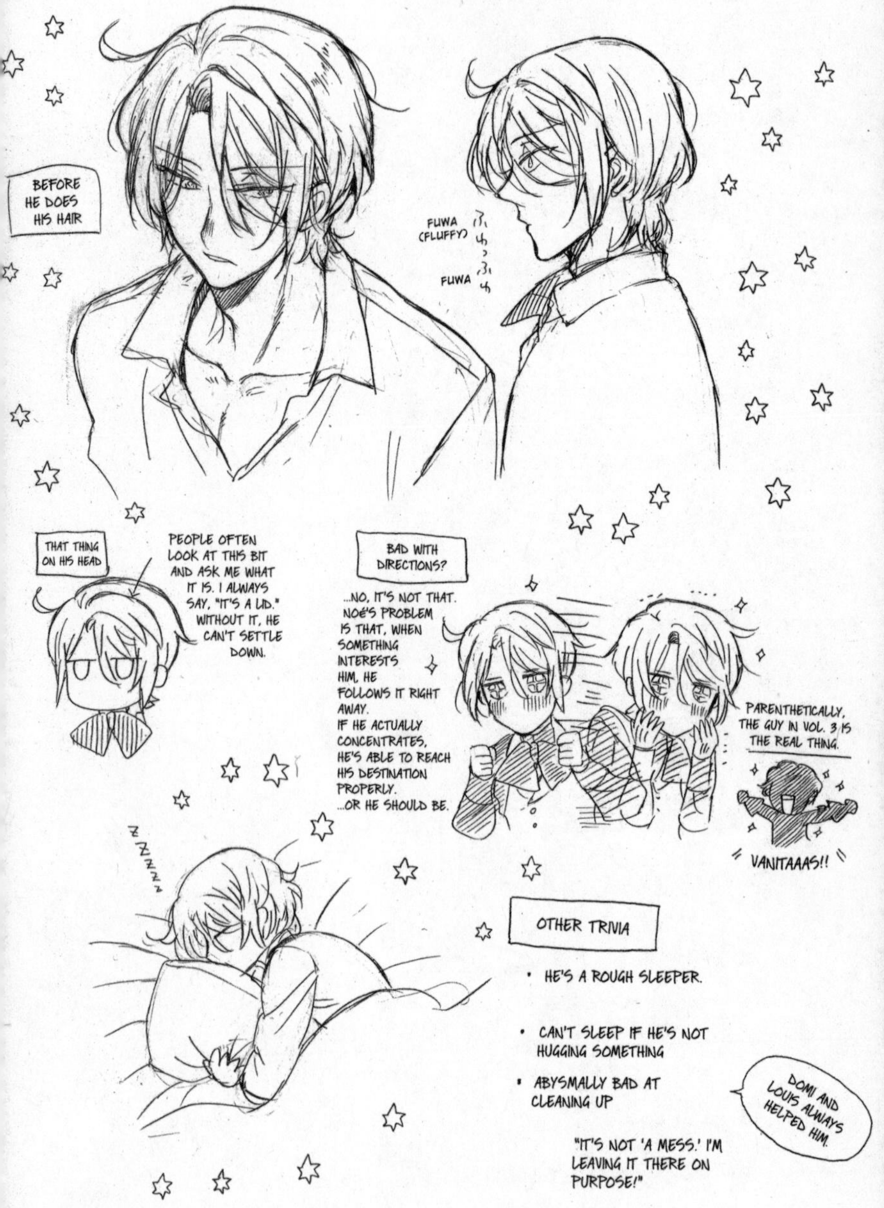
FUWA (FLUFFY) ふわっふわ FUWA
BEFORE HE DOES HIS HAIR
PARENTHETICALLY, THE GUY IN VOL. 3 IS THE REAL THING.
VANITAAAS!!
BAD WITH DIRECTIONS?
...NO, IT'S NOT THAT. NOÉ'S PROBLEM IS THAT, WHEN SOMETHING INTERESTS HIM, HE FOLLOWS IT RIGHT AWAY. IF HE ACTUALLY CONCENTRATES, HE'S ABLE TO REACH HIS DESTINATION PROPERLY. ...OR HE SHOULD BE.
THAT THING ON HIS HEAD
PEOPLE OFTEN LOOK AT THIS BIT AND ASK ME WHAT IT IS. I ALWAYS SAY, "IT'S A LID." WITHOUT IT, HE CAN'T SETTLE DOWN.
OTHER TRIVIA
• HE'S A ROUGH SLEEPER.
• CAN'T SLEEP IF HE'S NOT HUGGING SOMETHING
• ABYSMALLY BAD AT CLEANING UP
DOMI AND LOUIS ALWAYS HELPED HIM.
"IT'S NOT 'A MESS.' I'M LEAVING IT THERE ON PURPOSE!"
ZZZZZ

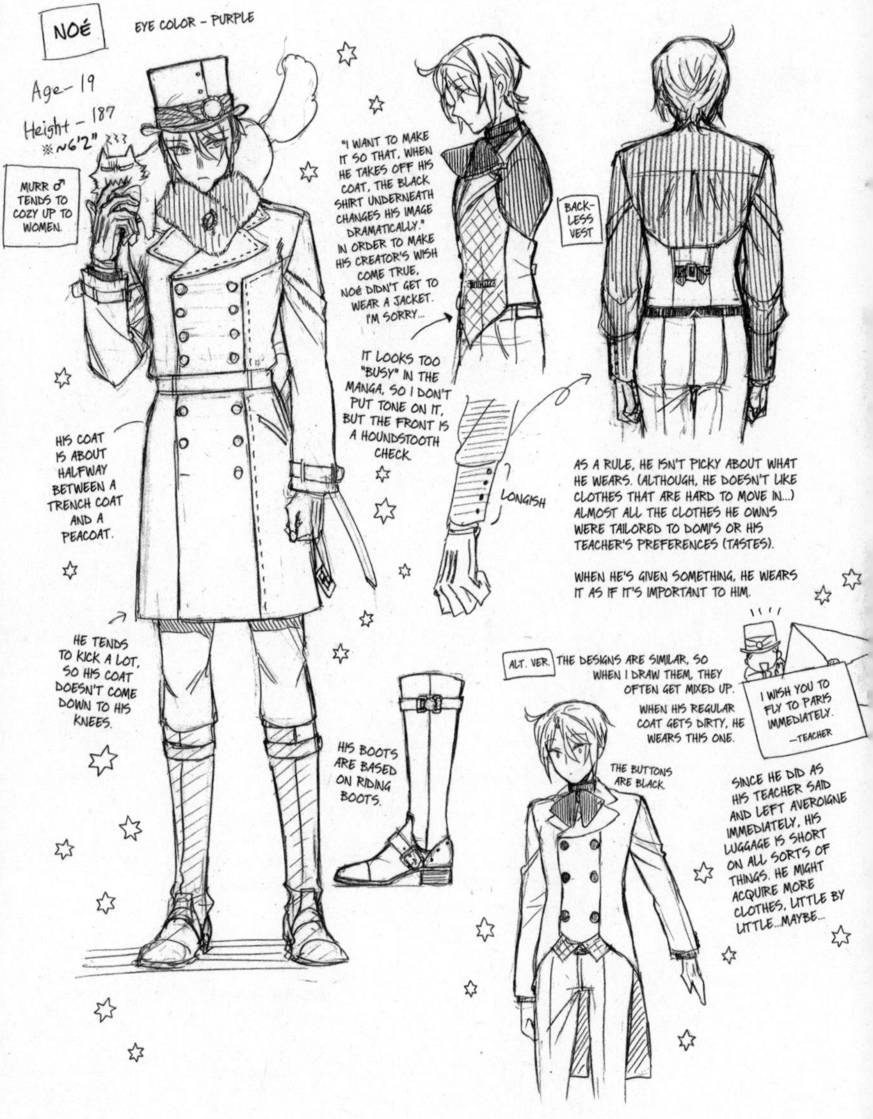
NOÉ
EYE COLOR - PURPLE
Age- 19
Height - 187
※~6'2"
MURR ♂ TENDS TO COZY UP TO WOMEN.
"I WANT TO MAKE IT SO THAT, WHEN HE TAKES OFF HIS COAT, THE BLACK SHIRT UNDERNEATH CHANGES HIS IMAGE DRAMATICALLY." IN ORDER TO MAKE HIS CREATOR'S WISH COME TRUE, NOÉ DIDN'T GET TO WEAR A JACKET. I'M SORRY...
BACK-LESS VEST
IT LOOKS TOO "BUSY" IN THE MANGA, SO I DON'T PUT TONE ON IT, BUT THE FRONT IS A HOUNDSTOOTH CHECK.
HIS COAT IS ABOUT HALFWAY BETWEEN A TRENCH COAT AND A PEACOAT.
LONGISH
AS A RULE, HE ISN'T PICKY ABOUT WHAT HE WEARS. (ALTHOUGH, HE DOESN'T LIKE CLOTHES THAT ARE HARD TO MOVE IN...) ALMOST ALL THE CLOTHES HE OWNS WERE TAILORED TO DOMI'S OR HIS TEACHER'S PREFERENCES (TASTES).
WHEN HE'S GIVEN SOMETHING, HE WEARS IT AS IF IT'S IMPORTANT TO HIM.
HE TENDS TO KICK A LOT, SO HIS COAT DOESN'T COME DOWN TO HIS KNEES.
ALT. VER.
THE DESIGNS ARE SIMILAR, SO WHEN I DRAW THEM, THEY OFTEN GET MIXED UP.
WHEN HIS REGULAR COAT GETS DIRTY, HE WEARS THIS ONE.
I WISH YOU TO FLY TO PARIS IMMEDIATELY. —TEACHER
HIS BOOTS ARE BASED ON RIDING BOOTS.
THE BUTTONS ARE BLACK.
SINCE HE DID AS HIS TEACHER SAID AND LEFT AVEROIGNE IMMEDIATELY, HIS LUGGAGE IS SHORT ON ALL SORTS OF THINGS. HE MIGHT ACQUIRE MORE CLOTHES, LITTLE BY LITTLE...MAYBE...

IF YOU GET YOUR WORK DONE IN ADVANCE, YOU CAN GO FOR AS LONG AS YOU LIKE! EDITOR ×2
I WANT TO GO... OVERSEAS...
UU... PARIS...

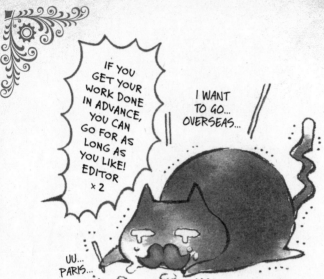

Jun Mochizuki

AUTHOR'S NOTE

I like traveling overseas.
Trying to communicate with my
broken English and gestures and
having to use all my energy just
to get through the day makes me
feel like I'm really alive.
It's loads of fun.
...And when I tell people that,
I generally get strange looks.

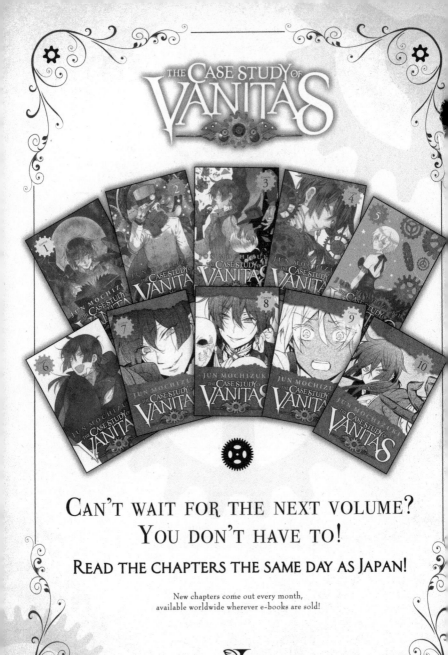

THE CASE STUDY OF VANITAS
VOLUME 3

JUN MOCHIZUKI

TRANSLATION: TAYLOR ENGEL
LETTERING: BIANCA PISTILLO

Vanitas no Carte Volume 3 ©2017 Jun Mochizuki/SQUARE ENIX CO., LTD.
First published in Japan in 2017 by SQUARE ENIX CO., LTD. English translation rights arranged with SQUARE ENIX CO., LTD. and Yen Press, LLC through Tuttle-Mori Agency, Inc., Tokyo.

English translation ©2017 by SQUARE ENIX CO., LTD.

Yen Press
1290 Avenue of the Americas
New York, NY 10104

Visit us at yenpress.com
facebook.com/yenpress
twitter.com/yenpress
yenpress.tumblr.com
instagram.com/yenpress

First Yen Press Edition: November 2017
The chapters in this volume were originally published as ebooks by Yen Press.

Yen Press is an imprint of Yen Press, LLC.
The Yen Press name and logo are trademarks of Yen Press, LLC.

The publisher is not responsible for websites (or their content) that are not owned by the publisher.

Library of Congress Control Number: 2016946115

ISBNs: 978-0-316-41284-1 (paperback)
978-0-316-41285-8 (ebook)

10 9 8 7 6 5 4 3 2 1

BVG

Printed in the United States of America